REFORMATION
TO REVIVAL

500 YEARS OF GOD'S GLORY
Sixty Revivals, Awakenings & Heaven-Sent Visitations of the Holy Spirit

MATHEW BACKHOLER

Reformation to Revival
500 Years of God's Glory
Sixty Revivals, Awakenings and
Heaven-Sent Visitations of the Holy Spirit

ISBN 978-1-907066-60-3 (paperback)
ISBN 978-1-907066-61-0 (eBook ePub)
ISBN 978-1-907066-98-6 (hardback)

British Library Cataloguing In Publication Data
A Record of this Publication is available from the British Library
Published in October 2017 by ByFaith Media
Updated in July 2021

- Jesus Christ is Lord -

Contents

The Reformation and Accounts of Revivals, Awakenings and Visitations of the Holy Spirit

Contents continued over the page

Contents

Accounts of Revivals, Awakenings and Visitations of the Holy Spirit Continued

Revivals, Awakenings and Visitations of the Holy Spirit

Preface

Peter wrote: 'We have the prophetic word confirmed, which you do well to heed as a light that shines in a dark place, until the day dawns and the morning star rises in your hearts...but holy men of God spoke as they were moved by the Holy Spirit' (2 Peter 1:19-21).

Reformation to Revival has its genesis in thought more than a decade ago when I was looking again at the life of Martin Luther and the Reformation. Then in 2007 I noted it was the 490th anniversary of this major European event, which shook the church to its core and brought about a Reformation of Christian life. With that in mind, the five hundredth anniversary was not far away, then came 2017.

The Reformation was a protest that led to Christian reform, getting back to the Bible, and brought about Protestants, and such radical change with its spiritual enlightenment to the masses, who could buy a Bible in their own language, money permitting. Even if they could not afford a Bible and many people did not have disposable income, they could hear a Christian service in their mother tongue, and not in the Latin language, which was the language of the Roman Catholic Church and the educated. The Christian truths of the Gospel were being proclaimed across civilised Europe, as was the authority of the Bible; salvation was a free gift from God (through His grace and faith in the atoning work of Jesus Christ); and there was the priesthood of all believers; that every true Christian was a priest before God and could stand in His presence without a human mediator, because Jesus Christ is the Mediator between God and man.

Reformation is not revival and revival is not Reformation, but both words and the events desire Christians to become genuine disciples of Jesus Christ, to bring them back to where they should be, focussed on Jesus Christ and His finished work and back to the core principles of the Bible, whilst being obedient to all that God wants from us and expects from us. The Reformation was a one-off event, but its repercussions are still felt today; and the events of the Reformation, and its leaders across different European cities and countries; each has its own story to tell. I have focused on Martin Luther of Germany, John Knox of Scotland and the Reformation in England under King Henry VIII and the translation of the Bible into English. The Bible declares: 'The works of the Lord are great, studied by all who have pleasure in them' (Psalm 111:2). I have studied the Reformation, British history and revivals, awakenings and Heaven-sent visitations of the Holy Spirit for more than twenty years. My collations of revivals exceeds one thousand which span across the globe and comes near to my private collection of eight hundred or so physical books on the subject, which I have been reading and studying for more than two decades.

As a revival historian, with five previously published books on the subject of revival and awakenings, I acknowledge that I have only uncovered the base of a mountain of knowledge and truth in this specialised area of study and research. My aim is to do the hard work and to write and publish these works in easily digestible formats, which glorify God, exalt Jesus Christ, explain the work of the Holy Spirit; whilst the books inform, educate, stimulate, challenge, build up in the most holy faith, and encourage us to pray for God to rend the Heavens and to pour out His Spirit on all flesh. That the Church would be revived and quickened, that Christians would come up to their full stature in Christ, surrender themselves fully to God and be His obedient servants, as they seek God for His Kingdom to come and for His will to be done on earth as it is in Heaven. The saints will be revived and sinners will be saved as they will come chasing after the Lord and embrace the cross of Calvary and the ascended Lord. Christians will go forth into all the world, spreading the Good News to those who have never heard, until every tribe, language and people group have had an opportunity to hear of God's son, Jesus Christ and what He has done for mankind, to save them from the wrath to come.

The Lord Jesus Christ was gracious enough to save me when I was just ten years old; when I was twenty-one I got *real* with God and within a few years I was called of the Holy Spirit to attend Bible College. After graduating I became a staff member for two years before joining my brother in ByFaith Media (www.byfaith.org). We both wrote for the website (and still do) and honed our craft before my first book, on the subject of Christian missions, came into print in 2006, followed in the same year by my first book on the subject of Christian revivals and awakenings. In the meantime we have had the opportunity of travelling to many countries, seeing churches and locations connected to the Reformation, its leaders, and hundreds of sites connected with revivals and awakenings in dozens of countries on four continents.

To God be the glory for the great things He has done. May He once again rend the Heavens and pour out His Spirit for His great name's sake; that the showers of blessing fall, that the thirsty are quenched, and that He comes and heals our land.

Chapter 1

Understanding Revival

Then the Lord said, "I have pardoned according to your word; but truly, as I live, all the earth shall be filled with the glory of the Lord" (Numbers 14:20-21).

What is Revival?

Revival is an incredible outpouring of the Holy Sprit that touches Christians and non-Christians. Revival is for the glory of God and the honour of His name. It is then for the Church, the body of Christ so that they can be revived and live holy and upright lives. The Holy Spirit will be given His rightful place in the Church which may cause Divine disorder as the Refiner (the Holy Spirit) comes and sifts and shakes. Out of this and during the same period of time, those who are outside the Church, non-Christians, can come under deep conviction of sin, regardless of whether they are in a church building or within the sound of a preacher or evangelist and will surrender their lives to Jesus Christ and live for Him in holiness and righteousness. During revival people have an awareness of spiritual things as never before; there is a solemn awe of God, a reverence and holy fear.

The word 'revival' comes from the Latin word 'revivere' meaning to live, to return to consciousness, to reawaken or a renewal of fervour, 'but strictly speaking, it means to bring to life again, to reanimate...' so wrote G. J. Morgan in *Cataracts Of Revival.*

The Greek word for revival is anazōrpureō, which means to stir up or rekindle a fire which is slowly dying, to keep in full flame. It is used metaphorically when the apostle Paul wrote to Timothy, '...Stir up the gift of God which is in you...' (2 Timothy 1:6).

The word 'revival' or the phrase 'Heaven-sent revival' is used to explain the amazing results of an outpouring of the Spirit of God, a visitation of the Holy Spirit, when Christians are revived and quickened, sinners are saved and communities are changed and become God-fearing. Revival also incorporates the definitions: an outpouring of the Holy Spirit, a visitation, the Holy Spirit falling, the Spirit of God descending, God coming down, God visiting His people, a Pentecost, days of Heaven on earth and the presidency of the Holy Spirit in the Church. A revival can come suddenly or gradually, accumulating in a spiritual climax and either runs its course, and gradually or suddenly ends. An awakening is a revival that is larger in its extents, often covering a country or across a people group and *generally* continues for a number of years, even a decade or more, and widely affects the moral makeup of society. Within this book a revival is recognised as a localised event, whether in a church, village, town or city; whereas an awakening refers to a move of God which has swept further afield. An awakening can be understood to move in the same way that a forest fire is swept and moved in all directions by the wind. It consumes and covers vast areas of countryside and yet can still leap across roads and ignite on the other side, and be blown as the wind chooses to the glory of God by Divine conflagration. Popular Christian terminology still records certain revivals as revivals (and not awakenings) such as the Welsh Revival (1904-1905) even though it was more characteristic of an awakening as it swept across the land and ignited fires across the globe. In these instances, I have retained the historically accepted title of such a Heaven-sent visitation of the Holy Spirit.

Dr. Martyn Lloyd-Jones preaching on Exodus 33:18-23; Moses desiring to see God's glory, said, "That's a perfect description of revival; it's the glory of God passing by. That's precisely what it is, just this glimpse of God as He passes by. The God who is there in the glory, as it were comes down, pays a visit, pours out His Spirit, descends again, and He just passes by us, and we look on and feel and know that the glory of God is in the midst and is passing by, O' it's but a touching of the hem as it were, it's but a vision of the back...a revival I say is just a kind of touch of His glory, a fleeting glimpse of something of what He is, in and of Himself...these things are possible and these things are meant for us."[1]

The dates of a revival or awakening are considered when the main 'Heaven-sent fire' fell but the 'afterglow' in some cases carries on for months or years.

Evangelism is not Revival

There is a difference between effective evangelism and revival. Evangelist, revivalist and world renowned revival historian J. Edwin Orr expressed it well when he said, "In times of evangelism, the evangelist seeks the sinner, in times of revival the sinners comes chasing after the Lord."

In evangelism the focus is on the evangelist or preacher and many who profess Christ soon fall by the wayside. But, in revival the focus is on God, and the vast majority of those who profess Christ stay true to Him as abiding fruit.

In effective evangelism, God may bless the work and people will respond to the call of repentance and give themselves to Jesus which sometimes leads to revival or an awakening, but in revival there is an overpowering presence and move of the Holy Spirit and regardless of the anointed evangelist or minister pleading and calling for people to repent and to get right with God, the people will be moved by God's Spirit to repent, often breaking down under the guilt of their sin and pouring out their hearts to the Almighty.

Revivals are Controversial

Revivals can be highly controversial. With many Christians saying, "It's from God," and some believing it's of the Devil! While others will say, "It's merely mass hysteria." In Jesus' day, there was much murmuring among the people concerning Himself. Some said, "He is good," others said, "No, on the contrary He deceives the people" (John 7:12). Even Jesus' own family members thought He was "out of His mind" (Mark 3:21). Now, if they said that about Jesus and His ministry, how much more controversial will revivals, awakenings, Heaven-sent visitations of the Holy Spirit and those that are involved appear?

In any revival there will be physical phenomena, bodily manifestations / movements as the Holy Spirit touches a person in convicting power as well as other supernatural events which affect a person bodily. The Devil will try to influence people, Christians and non-Christians as he is an infiltrator and imitator and the kingdom of darkness and the Kingdom of Light inevitably clash.

It is wrong to believe that everything you see in revival is from God, because it's not, there will always be opportunists and exhibitionists. The issue is not to focus on the excesses, but to focus on God and to give glory to Him for the great things He has done and is doing. The Pharisees looked for the negative, even when the miraculous was performed before their eyes. They watched Jesus closely to see whether He would heal on the Sabbath, just so that they might accuse Him! (Mark 3:1-6).

Since the beginning of Christianity, enemies of the cross of Christ have denounced godly people believing them to be under the influence of the evil one. John the Baptist was denounced as a glutton and a drunkard, whilst Jesus was labelled as Beezlebub (chief of demons), and later crucified. Stephen was stoned and the apostle Paul was whipped, beaten, imprisoned and stoned on several occasions. Yet, though the Devil can transform himself into an angel of light, he cannot transform someone's character to be more Christ-like and certainly does not encourage them to do so. This is the work of the Holy Spirit working with the believer who has decided to fully give of him/her self to Christ Jesus and to surrender their will to the Holy Spirit. It is also wrong to believe everything negative you are told or read about during times of revival, because even the apostle Paul was slanderously reported as saying, "Let us do evil that good may come" (Romans 3:8). Yet we all know that after his dramatic conversion he led a morally upright life and strived to keep a clear conscience before God and man.

Dr. Martyn Lloyd-Jones was inducted at Sandfields, Aberavon, South Wales, UK, in February 1927, where he saw a localised revival in 1930, though he himself was reluctant to call it revival. In that year he removed seventeen people from church membership as they 'proved themselves unworthy of membership' and saw seventy-seven converts from the world! During his eleven years at Sandfields, until May 1938, he saw over five hundred converts who joined the church. As minister of Westminster Chapel, London, England, he said, "The coming of revival has two main effects. One that it blesses all the denominations practically, irrespective of their divisions, and for the time being brings them together in a marvellous unity. There has never been anything that has so promoted spiritual unity as revival. But a revival also invariably has another effect, and that is that it creates a new and fresh division. And why does it do so? It does so for this reason, those who have experienced the blessing and the power of God are naturally one and they come together; there are others who dislike it all and who criticise it all and who condemn it all and who are outside it all and the divisions comes in."

The real judge of any revival or visitation of the Holy Spirit is this: Does it line up with Scripture? Is God being glorified? What is the fruit? Are Christians being revived and sinners being saved? Is Christ and Him crucified being preached? Is there repentance and forsaking of sins? Are Christians walking in the fruit of the Spirit and growing in the grace of God? In times of revival, the fundamental truths of Jesus' eternal Son-ship, the virgin birth, His sinless life, His death, resurrection, ascension, second coming and the judgment coupled with Heaven and Hell; alongside repentance, God's grace, the new birth, faith in Christ, His shed blood and total consecration are always preached.

The most significant thing within Jesus' ministry which demonstrated that the Kingdom of God had arrived, was when He cast out demons 'with the finger of God' (Luke 11:20). There were no instances of deliverance / exorcism (the casting out of demons / evil spirits) in the Old Testament. Jesus gave His disciples the authority to cast out demons and endued this same commission to all subsequent disciples, 'to preach the Good News, to make disciples, to heal the sick, to cast out demons and to raise the dead' (Mark 16:15-18). We should not be alarmed or concerned that people get delivered and set free from demonic powers, as well as healed or raised from the dead, during revival and outside of revival. It is fully surrendered disciples of the Lord Jesus Christ walking in the power and anointing of the Holy Spirit (Matthew 28:18-20, Mark 16:15-18, Luke 24:49, John 20:21-23 and Acts 1:8). By doing this they fulfil Jesus' last command to make disciples and to be witnesses of Him, by their actions and in demonstration of the power of the Holy Spirit (1 Corinthians 4:20 and 2 Corinthians 12:12).

J. Edwin Orr was used in many localised revivals in the mid 1930s in Eastern Europe, America, Africa and Australia and also saw revival in Brazil during 1951 and 1952. He said, "The key factor in revival is the outpouring of the Holy Spirit. The outpouring of the Holy Spirit results in the revival of the Church. That is the work of God with the response of the believers. The outpouring of the Holy Spirit also results in an awakening of the people. That is the work of God with the response of the people. The revived Church then engages in evangelising the enquirers and in teaching the disciples, that is those who wish to follow, and by many or by few, in the reforming of society."[2]

In a report, a parish minister at Barvas on the Isle of Lewis, Scotland, UK, during the Hebridean Revival (1949-1952), wrote: 'The Spirit of the Lord was resting wondrously and graciously in the different townships in the parish. You could feel His presence in the homes of the people, on meadow and moorland and even on the public road. This awareness of God to me is the supreme characteristic, the supreme feature of a God-sent revival.'[3]

Evan Roberts was the key leader in the Welsh Revival (1904-1905). In his latter years, he wrote: 'The baptism of the Holy Spirit is the essence of revival, for revival comes from knowledge of the Holy Spirit and the way of co-working with Him which enables Him to work in revival power. The primary condition of revival is therefore that believers should individually know the baptism of the Holy Ghost.'[4]

Willis Hoover founded the Methodist Pentecostal Church in Chile during the 1909 Chile Revival. He said, "I believe that the true secret of this whole thing is that we really and truly believe in the Holy Spirit – we really trust Him – we really honour Him – we really obey Him – we really give Him free rein – we really believe that the promises in Acts 1:4-5 [baptised with the Holy Spirit] and Joel 2:28-29 [I will pour out My Spirit] is for us."[5]

'And being assembled together with them, He [Jesus Christ] commanded them [the disciples] not to depart from Jerusalem, but to wait for the Promise of the Father, "which," He said, "you have heard from Me; for John truly baptised with water, but you shall be baptized with the Holy Spirit not many days from now" ' (Acts 1:4-5).[6]

Chapter 2

Revivals from the Bible

The Lord said, "If My people who are called by My name will humble themselves, and pray and seek My face, and turn from their wicked ways, then I will hear from Heaven, and will forgive their sin and heal their land" (2 Chronicles 7:14).

Biblical Principles

The Bible is full of spiritual principles and doctrines which are not as clearly laid out and defined as the Ten Commandments (Exodus 20:1-17) or the Beatitudes (Matthew 5:3-10), but are nevertheless spiritual principles. The words: trinity, rapture, missions, and soteriology (the doctrine of salvation) are all words that are not found in the Bible, though their doctrines are. The majority of the popular Bible translations do not use the word 'revival' to describe a spiritual awakening; a Heaven-sent visitation of the Holy Spirit though by direct word of inspiration, in both the Old and the New Testament, 'revivals' are recorded by inspired inference and the concepts clearly laid out in the lives and events of many individuals and groups of people.

The Holy Spirit was only poured out after the resurrection of Jesus Christ (see John 7:39) as recorded in the New Testament (Acts 1:8 and Acts 2:1-4) and throughout the book of Acts; therefore the Old Testament experiences of revival do not have examples of the Holy Spirit falling en masse, but God's glory being revealed. The Bible does record many instances of God, the Lord, Angel of the Lord (see Judges 2:1) or the glory of the Lord coming or descending upon the earth: The Lord came down upon Mount Sinai in fire (Exodus 19:18-20). Moses, Aaron and seventy-two other people saw the God of Israel on Mount Sinai and they ate and drank (Exodus 24:9-11). The pillar of cloud descended to the tabernacle door when Moses went there (Exodus 33:9-11). Moses saw the glory of God from a cleft in a rock (Exodus 33:18-23). The cloud covered the tabernacle and the glory of the Lord filled it (Exodus 40:34-38). The glory of the Lord, a cloud filled the temple during the dedication ceremony under King Solomon (1 Kings 8:10-11 and 2 Chronicles 5:13-14).

The revivals and awakenings that are documented in the Old Testament reveal mass repentance under God's conviction and the Spirit's leading as the people returned to the Lord, (or turned to the

Lord), often under the influence of a leader, a prophet or a king. Some of these moves of God are more akin to a Reformation, because the whole spiritual life of a nation was changed through the intervention and actions of one person such as King Asa of Judah, Jehoiada the priest or King Hezekiah of Judah.

Old Testament Revivals

1. From the godly line of Seth men began to call on the name of the Lord – they became conscious of their need for God and His forgiveness (Genesis 4:26). '...You will seek the Lord your God, and you will find Him if you seek Him with all your heart and with all your soul' (Deuteronomy 4:29).

2. King Asa became King of Judah and did what was right in the eyes of the Lord. He banished the male and female prostitutes from the land and removed all the idols that his father had set up. He even removed his grandmother from being queen mother because she was an idol worshiper, and cut down her obscene image to Asherah. King Asa also commanded his people to seek the Lord God of their fathers and to observe the Law and the commandments (1 Kings 15:9-15 and 2 Chronicles 14:1-15).

3. The prophet Elijah had a spiritual battle on Mount Carmel, before King Ahab and the four hundred and fifty prophets of Baal and four hundred prophets of Asherah. Once the true altar was prepared, a complete offering was given, Elijah called upon his God and the fire fell. The people fell on their faces crying out, "The Lord, He is God! The Lord He is God!" (1 Kings 18:20-40).

4. Jehoiada the priest made a covenant between the Lord, the king and the people that they should be the Lord's people. They tore down the temple of Baal and broke in pieces its altars and images. King Joash was just a child when he came to the throne and it was Jehoiada, a godly man who advised the king and in effect ruled the Kingdom of Judah (2 Kings 11:17-18, 2 Chronicles 23:16-21 and 2 Chronicles 24:2).

5. King Hezekiah of Judah reopened and repaired the house of God which had been shut up and neglected for many years. He made a covenant before God; the house of God was then cleansed and sanctified with the help of the Levites and the people brought offerings. A Passover festival was held and celebrated and all the idols, wooden images, high places and false altars were smashed, cut down and destroyed. The temple worship was reinstated and the Levites began to serve the Lord again (2 Kings 18:1-8 and 2 Chronicles chapters 29-31).

6. King Manasseh of Judah was the worst of all the kings of Judah, yet as a captive in Babylon he humbled himself. God permitted him to return to Jerusalem. He removed the idols and foreign gods and

repaired the altar of the Lord and commanded the people of Judah to serve the Lord God of Israel (2 Chronicles 33:12-16).

7. King Josiah, son of evil King Amon (who was the son of King Manasseh) brought about revival in the land when the Book of the Law was found and he acted upon it – by repenting and humbling himself before God. King Josiah called the elders of the land and made a covenant before the Lord to obey His commandments as did the people of Judah. The temple of the Lord was cleansed and all the false altars and temples etc. were destroyed, and they celebrated with a huge Passover festival (2 Kings chapters 22-23 and 2 Chronicles chapters 34-35).

8. Jonah the son of Amittai was called to preach in Nineveh to the notorious cruel Assyrians, but he fled from the call of God. Eventually the prophet Jonah preached in this large pagan city shouting, "Yet, forty days and Nineveh shall be overthrown!" The people of Nineveh believed the word of the Lord, they declared a fast and wore sackcloth as a sign of humility. The king also declared that the people should humble themselves, cry mightily to God and turn from their evil ways. God saw their humility and judgment was avoided which upset Jonah! (The book of Jonah).

The revival at Nineveh is unique in the Old Testament in that God did not come to revive His people, the Israelites, but He came to give life to those who had previously not known life who were dead in trespasses and sin. This was also seen in the Revival at Samaria under Philip the evangelist (Acts 8:5-8) and when the apostle Paul preached on Mars Hill, in the midst of the Areopagus in Athens, Greece (Acts 17:22-34).

New Testament Revivals

1. John the Baptist called the people to a baptism of repentance for the remission of sins and told them to bear fruits worthy of repentance. They came to him for baptism and confessed their sins. He told them of the One who was to come (Mark 1:4-5 and Luke 3:1-18).

2. Jesus was the promised Messiah, the Saviour of the world and the Anointed One (Luke 4:18-19). At His baptism He was filled with the Spirit and returned from his forty days in the wilderness in the power of the Spirit (Luke 4:1, 14). He preached the Kingdom of God with signs and wonders following confirming the message and thus proving He was the Promised One (Matthew 11:2-5 and Luke 8:25). The people flocked to hear His teaching (and to be healed) and many followed Him from city to city so that Jesus had periods of revival.

3. The Holy Spirit fell on the Day of Pentecost and people began to speak in tongues. Peter stood up to preach and about three

thousand people were 'cut to the heart,' under conviction of sin. They believed on the Lord Jesus Christ, repented and were baptised in the name of Jesus (Acts 2:1-41).

4. Peter and John taught the people and preached about Jesus and the resurrection from the dead, and around two thousand people were added to the Church (Acts 4:1-4). Five thousand converts in total less three thousand from Acts 2:41.

5. Through the hands of the apostles many signs and wonders were performed and they were all with one accord, in unity, and believers were increasingly added to the Lord, multitudes of men and women (Acts 5:12-14).

6. The number of disciples of Jesus Christ multiplied greatly in Jerusalem, including many of the Jewish priests who were obedient to the Christian faith, and the word of God spread (Acts 6:1-8).

7. Evangelist Philip went down to Samaria, preaching with miracles following and multitudes with one accord heeded what he said and became followers of Jesus and there was great joy in that city (Acts 8:5-8).

8. Peter visited Joppa and raised Dorcas from the dead; as this fact became known throughout Joppa, many believed on the Lord Jesus (Acts 9:36-43).

9. Peter and some brethren went to Caesarea to meet the centurion Cornelius of the Italian Regiment, Peter preached to him, his relatives and his friends and the Holy Spirit fell upon them all and they spoke in tongues (Acts 10:23-48).

10. Some of the disciples of Jesus (not the twelve) preached at Antioch to the Hellenists and a great number believed and turned to the Lord (Acts 11:19-21). When news of this revival reached the Church at Jerusalem they sent Barnabas to assist in the work and more people were added to the faith (Acts 11:22-24).

11. The apostle Paul and friends preached to the Jews in the synagogue in Antioch at Pisidia. Many of the Jews and devout proselytes (a convert from another faith) followed the teaching of Jesus Christ. The Gentiles (non-Jews) then begged that they also may hear this preaching on the following Sabbath and almost the whole town came to hear, which upset the elders of the city but nonetheless the word of the Lord spread throughout that region (Acts 13:14-50).

12. The disciples preached at Iconium in the synagogues and both Jews and Greeks believed the message. Signs and wonders were performed and the city was divided against the Jews and the apostles (Acts 14:1-4).

13. The apostle Paul preached itinerantly on his missionary journeys and a young pastor called Timothy accompanied him, as

did other Christian workers. The churches were strengthened in the faith and increased in numbers daily (Acts 16:1-5).

14. The apostle Paul and Silas went into the synagogue in Thessalonica and preached. A great multitude of devout Greeks and many of the leading women followed them, which led to a riot as people said, "These who have turned the world upside down have come here too" (Acts 17:1-9).

15. The apostle Paul and Silas were sent to Berea and they preached in the synagogue. Many believed, both Greeks and prominent women of the city, but Jews from Thessalonica stirred up the crowd and another riot began! (Acts 17:10-15).

16. Paul preached on Mars Hill, in the midst of the Areopagus in Athens to the pagans, some mocked, but others joined them and believed. This was when Paul preached his sermon, 'To The Unknown God,' and called people to repent, seek the Lord and serve the living God (Acts 17:22-34).

17. The apostle Paul, Silas and Timothy (a young pastor) travelled to Corinth and spoke at a house meeting of Justus who lived next door to the synagogue. Crispus the synagogue ruler and his entire household believed along with many of the Corinthians. They stayed there for six months, teaching the new converts (Acts 18:7-11).

18. The apostle Paul taught in the school at Tyrannus for two years and all who dwelt in Asia (Minor) heard the word of the Lord, both Jews and Greeks, but some were hardened and spoke evil of the Way (Acts 19:8-9).

19. In Ephesus, after hearing and seeing the power of God working through the apostle Paul, fear fell on the Jews and Greeks, Jesus was magnified; many who had believed on Jesus Christ publicly confessed their sins and deeds and those who had practised magical arts publicly burned their expensive occult and magic books alongside demonic paraphernalia (Acts 19:11-20).

20. The apostle Paul after being arrested and having been shipwrecked lands on the Island of Malta. Many people were healed as Paul prayed and laid his hands on them including the father of the leading citizen of the island (Acts 28:1-9). There is no recorded mention of conversions but undoubtedly there were many who would have believed his message as they thought him to be a god (verse 6) as neither shipwreck nor a snake bite could kill him.

'Isaac dug again the wells of water which they had dug in the days of Abraham his father, for the Philistines had stopped them up after the death of Abraham. He called them by the names which his father had called them' (Genesis 26:18).

Chapter 3

Martin Luther and the Reformation in Germany 1517

'Deliver those who are drawn towards death, and hold back those stumbling to slaughter. If you say, "Surely we did not know this," does not He who weighs the heart consider it? He who keeps your soul, does He not know it? And will He not render to each man according to his deeds?' (Proverbs 24:11-12).

Martin Luther

Martin Luther was born in Eisleben, Germany, on 10 November 1483, to German peasants: Hans (John) a miner, and Gretha (Margaret) Luther. Martin Luther at seven years old was sent to a school where his soprano voice gained him admission to the choir, which brought not only a musical tuition but also a meagre wage. Luther was also taught a little monkish Latin. At fourteen, Luther was sent to a harsh Franciscan School at Madgeburg to enhance his education, but he often went hungry and cold for lack of finances. To quote Luther, "I used to beg with my companions for a little food...singing from house to house." Luther attained a considerable knowledge of the divine art of song and once in the age of the Reformation led Germany to establish new customs in the revolution of church songs. Whilst singing in the choir at church one day, he caught the attention of a Mr Conrad Cotta, from a noble family who took care of his financial needs along with Mr Cotta's wife, Ursula.

In 1501, a little before Martin Luther's eighteenth birthday he enrolled at the University of Erfurt where he studied logic and philosophy followed by theology. Luther's memory was extraordinarily retentive and almost everything he had read was ready for use. "I was twenty years of age," said Luther, "before I had ever seen a Bible, and I had no notion that there existed any other Gospels or Epistles than those in church service." Luther saw his first Bible, a Latin translation in the local monastery's library which he read with great delight over the years. The years of cold and near starvation in his early years, as well as his excessive workload made Luther very ill which led to fits of deep depression.

In 1505 in his twenty-first year, Martin Luther obtained the higher degree of M.A. and Doctor of Philosophy, and began his career, teaching physics and ethics of Aristotle with other branches of philosophy. His heart was not in it, even though he was highly acclaimed at the University. Luther had a best friend and companion called Alexis who was killed in a mysterious manner. Thoughts of death and the afterlife came flooding down upon Luther's uncertain soul. In the summer he was overtaken in a terrific thunderstorm and vowed to Saint Anna that if he was rescued from the danger he would become a monk.

In Martin Luther's twenty-second year he joined a monastery hoping to find rest and peace for his soul, where he was named Brother Augustine; he went from an acclaimed scholar to a novice beggar of a monk overnight! Luther in the pursuit of salvation tried to earn it by extreme fasting and self denial. He stayed awake at night, whipping himself (self-flagellation), by performing righteous works and religious rituals and all the coenobite severities, a monk who belongs to a monastery and partakes of their duties. Sometimes, Luther would leave the monastery at daybreak and walk into the countryside to preach to the shepherds yet he was not assured of his own salvation which he desired greatly. Luther concluded after he had nearly killed himself through self denial, "I am a great sinner in the sight of God and I do not think it possible for me to propitiate Him by my own merits."

Martin Luther found a father-figure called Dr. Staupitiz who he confided in and who tried to point the despondent Luther to the cross of Calvary. By 1507, the light of glory rained in upon Luther's soul whilst in discussion with Dr. Staupitz over the issue of the forgiveness of sins, and the Apostle's Creed was prayed as a farewell, "I believe in the forgiveness of sins." Then suddenly, like a ray of light it pierced his soul; he believed in the crucified Saviour and that he was forgiven, because Jesus had paid the price. On 2 May 1507, Luther became a priest in the Roman Catholic Church but he dreaded preaching, "Oh, how I tremble when I was ascending the pulpit for the first time. I would fain have excused myself; but they made me preach. It was the regulation that the junior brethren should preach to the rest."

Dr. Staupitiz gave Martin Luther his first Bible on leaving the monastery with the words, "Let the study of Scripture be your favourite occupation." Luther came to the conclusion that, "Good works do not make a man good, but a good man does good works" and, "A Christian man is free from all things; he needs no work in order to be justified and saved, but receives these gifts in abundance from his faith alone."

The Bible (or any book) five hundred years ago was highly prized and would have cost a lot of money.

Martin Luther had been invited to work in the University of Wittenberg, as the professor of philosophy where he learnt Greek and Hebrew and was therefore able to read the Scriptures in the original languages. Luther was now twenty-five years old and worked without a wage. On 9 March 1509, Luther started studying towards a Masters of Divinity. The University book shows the following entry under his name: '...being called away to Erfurt, hath not unto this time paid his fee.' In Luther's own handwriting appears this blunt reply, 'And never will!' He later declared, "I was then poor and under the rule of monastic obedience, and had nothing to give. Let Erfurt pay!" Luther preached regularly in various chapels over the years and then the council of Wittenberg nominated him as their chaplain and was duly invited to preach in the city church. The University was wholly under the controlling power of its founder, the Elector Fredrick who did not in any way associate the University or himself with the Church of Rome, and therefore students and staff were allowed to be free thinkers.

To Rome and its Indulgences

In 1512, Martin Luther travelled to Rome, Italy, as seven convents of his order had points of controversy with their Vicar-General and so a judgment from Rome was needed to settle the issues. Luther could not believe the opulence and doubtless saw the guidebook specially prepared for visitors, *The Wonders of Rome*. This book was full of the treasures of the Papal City. One of the seven churches at Rome had powers to grant as many days of Indulgence as the number of drops of rain which could fall in three days and three nights! An Indulgence was issued by the Roman Catholic Church and was a licence to sin without Divine retribution, that had to be paid or worked for, and could be issued to the living and the dead! Luther with the zeal of a good Catholic swallowed all these idle tales and at this time still fully believed in the Pope and the Papacy. Luther was so naïve at this point that he actually regretted that his father and mother were still living, as he would have liked to have released their souls from purgatory! The relics on the Castle Church, on whose door Martin Luther later nailed his 95 thesis, were reckoned to earn a remission of 1,902,202 years and 270 days from purgatory!

From the Roman Catholic Church, any devout believer going up the staircase of Pilate on his knees was promised a thousand years Indulgence in respect to penance imposed. Luther hastened to receive this reward but while engaged in the act he thought he heard a voice crying from the bottom of his heart, as at Wittenberg and Bologna, "The just shall live by faith!" Luther rose to his feet, shuddered and felt ashamed of seeing to what a depth of superstition he had plunged and left. Luther was so disgusted that he said, "No one can imagine what sins and infamous actions are committed in Rome...if there be a Hell, Rome is built over it; it is an abyss whence issues every sin!" When Luther had cut himself off from the Church of Rome's superstitions and lies, he said, "Such a foolish saint was I, running to all the churches and sepulchres and believing all the pitiable stories that were told me."

The Papal Reform Commission and Luther's First Lecture

The Roman Catholic Church was corrupt and acknowledged it in 1536, two decades after the Reformation, when Pope Paul III (reigning from 1534-1549) ordered the 'papal reform commission.' This investigated claims of abuse, the cause of disorder within the Roman Catholic Church, what to do about it and how to make the papal bureaucracy more efficient and spiritual. The report was entitled *Advice Concerning the Reform of the Church,* which came to the conclusion that the papal office had become too secular. It gave examples of bribery in high places, simony (selling of church positions), the abuse of Indulgences, the number of prostitutes operating in Rome itself, laxity in monastic life, abuse of papal power and the evasion of church law by lay people and clergy alike. Corruption is one thing and is sadly common place, but official sanction of corruption is quite another.

The subject of Martin Luther's first lecture was an exposition from Paul's Epistle to the Romans, 'Justification by Faith.' The doctrines of good works were Rome's best friend, but Luther's and God's enemy, so the discourse was its antithesis.

In 1513, thirty-five printed publications of Luther's appeared. In the same year there were seventy-two breweries in the city. In 1516, Luther filled a vacancy for about eighteen months of the Vicar-General which meant that he travelled around his district, visiting the monasteries, enforcing discipline and educating people by the Word of God. Luther was strict, but loving and compassionate. Luther established several schools in which he ordered the Scriptures to be taught; convinced that the way of salvation could only be found in them alone. Luther's views and opinions were being slowly impressed upon the people's minds, there were signs and indications that men were openly beginning to express their views and opinions, being discontent with Rome's hypocrisy and its authority. In addition, the plague had been sweeping across Europe for years and people pondered on eternity in fear and trepidation, and needed to be sure of where they were going upon death.

The Reformation Begins, 31 October 1517

In Wittenberg, Martin Luther's work included the preparation of young theologians; six or seven were under his charge. The year 1517 has been called the 'Morning Star of the Gospel Day' as this is when the Reformation started on 31 October 1517, with Martin Luther nailing his 95 thesis (short sentences) to the Castle Church door in Wittenberg, Germany. Four hundred years later on the same date, 31 October, the Welsh Revival (1904-1905) broke out under Evan Roberts, in Loughor, South Wales, UK. Back to 1517, each thesis contained some important truth; they were divided under two headings, and generally taught, firstly, the inability and powerless of man: and, secondly, that the power and source of all good was in God. The claims of God were set forth in a way to promote discussion which was Luther's intention.

Martin Luther realised that individuals are 'justified by faith' and by faith alone, faith in the saving power of Jesus Christ. Luther now openly stood up for the Word of God over and above the established Church of Rome with their superstitions, corruptions and blatant anti-scriptural teaching. Luther had given these utterances to the unexpressed, but general convictions of thousands. Beliefs and church practice could not be justified if they were other than, outside of, or apart from the Word of God.

The Wittenberg Church is still standing, the original wooden door was burnt down centuries ago and now stands in its place from 1858 are two large commemorative bronze doors with Luther's 95 Latin statements cast into the metal. I visited Wittenberg and the related Reformation sites in the summer of 2002, with two graduates from the Bible College where I was working at in Wales, UK. To go inside the church, to see Martin Luther's statue, the different rooms he frequented, the monument in the square, and the home and haunts of Luther and his reformer friends was quite special.

The Reformation had three main principles which were:

1. God's Word as found in the Holy Bible is the final authority on matters of doctrine and dogma, therefore all doctrines and ceremonies for which there was no clear basis in Scripture is to be condemned.

2. Salvation is a free and undeserved gift given solely by Christ Jesus, being saved by grace alone and not by works (Romans 3:22-25).

3. The 'priesthood of all believers' where every believer is a priest (1 Peter 2:5-9). In the early church there was no precedent for the priest to act as a mediator and no Scriptural support for the secular power of clergy; thereby making one status before God.

Rome's Outrage

Rome was outraged by these 95 statements but at first Pope Leo X underestimated the effect they would have on the people. But attacks and opposition came from all sides, and in less than a fortnight Martin Luther stood almost alone to confront the storm that had gathered. The reputation of Wittenberg University and its attendees was tarnished. Luther challenged Rome and all who opposed him, time and time again to prove from Scripture where, and if he was wrong. A man called Wimpina who was very jealous of Luther penned two lists of antitheses; the one devoted to a defence of the doctrine of Indulgences and the other setting forth the supreme authority of the Pope. The Dominicans order of monks denounced Luther and called him such names as a madman, seducer and a demoniac.

On 7 August 1518, Martin Luther received a summons to stand before a tribunal in Rome, which he tried to have held in Germany, but to no avail. Luther had already been pre-judged and was pronounced as a heretic. Only a century before, John Huss was burnt at the stake for opposing the doctrines of transubstantiation, which Luther did not do This Is the belief that the bread and the wine during Communion literally become the body and blood of Jesus. Luther refused to go to Rome unless he was assured of his protection. On many occasions, Luther was asked to recant in front of various cardinals and religious bodies. For shrewd political reasons, St. Augustine released Luther from his obligations of his order. Luther travelled in disguise from one place to the next, he had a price on his head and was constantly in danger. Many noble people including Princes and Knights, pressed for his protection with the various authorities and invited him to their courts or castles.

A conference was held on 15 June 1520, at the Pope's villa of Malliano when the Sacred College pronounced the condemnation of all Luther's work and sanctioned the Initiatory or Preliminary Bull. This granted permission and gave orders to publicly burn all of Luther's writings, and that if Luther did not retract his writings in the space of fifty days, he would be condemned as well as his followers, as heretics. As this Bull was distributed around the Empire, many people sought to defend Luther's beliefs by assaulting the priests who distributed the Bull, much to Luther's shock; he begged his friends not to harm his adversaries, whereas in other cities the edict was duly complied to. On 7 November 1520, at the Augustine convent at Wittenberg, Luther read his public protest against his treatment from Rome. On 10 December, a great fire was kindled at the Elster Gate near the Holy Cross, where Luther and his supporters burned the Papal Law, the Bull and other anti-Scriptural teachings which the Roman Catholic Church supported.

Bible Translation and Decree of Extermination

On 6 January 1521, the Bull of Excommunication was fulminated against Martin Luther and his adherents from the Holy See, the ecclesiastical jurisdiction of the Catholic Church in Rome. On 5 May 1521, Luther was taken captive for his own safety; from his return from Worms where he had been ordered to stand before the

Emperor and Electors etc. where 206 people were present. He was asked some questions in regards to his teachings and works and then told to retract. Luther replied, "If I have spoken evil, bear witness of my evil.... Here I stand, I can do no other: God help me. Amen." Luther was carried 'captive' to Wartburg Castle where he was courteously treated by the governor, John Von Berlepsch, who supplied all his wants, "...the will of the Lord be done," said Luther! People thought that Luther was dead; he changed his appearance and took the name Junker or Squire George!

The translation of the Bible into German from Hebrew and Greek was started as early as 1517, by Martin Luther with the help of fellow scholars, so in his enforced 'retirement' he continued the work. As many as fourteen German Bibles had already been translated from the Latin and published, the first in 1462-1464, from Mentelin at Strasburg. Unauthorised translations were absolutely forbidden under the punishment of death. Luther strove to give the translation in the clearest and most intelligible form, the closest literal expression of the original text and in many cases was obliged to create new words.

English born William Tyndale published his first edition of the English New Testament in 1525-1526 and printed it at Wittenberg; he was later martyred in the Netherlands (present-day Brussels, Belgium) in 1530.

In late summer 1521, Martin Luther finished the translation of the New Testament into German, but printing did not commence until 21 September 1522, when three thousand editions in two volumes were started. By 1533, no less than fifty-eight editions had been printed; such was the demand for God's Word.

All the churches in the Imperial City of Worms were shut down and street preachers abounded preaching salvation by Jesus Christ and Him alone. Many believers were persecuted. King Henry VIII of England, wrote a book *The Captivity of Babylon* in reply to Luther's seven sacraments of the Church. The book was not actually written by Henry VIII, but by a scholar (or scholars) and his name was attached to it. Pope Leo X bestowed Henry with the title 'Defender of the Faith.' Later on Henry VIII broke away from the Church of Rome and started the Church of England, because he wanted a divorce so that he could remarry!

When Pope Leo X died, Adrian VI was crowned pontiff and issued a Decree of Extermination to Luther and his adherents, a copy of which is preserved in the British Museum as well as one of Luther's first New Testaments and many other Papal documents.

Many people in various countries no longer wanted to endure the tyranny of Rome. On 23 March 1522, the Diet of Nuremburg, representatives of the Empire and those of the Papal met to negotiate the terms of the religious Reformation. In 1523, Pope Adrian issued a Bull to declare a three year truce, in order to prevent a civil war between the Kings and Princes favouring the Reformation and those upholding the Papacy. But the Bull did not stop the persecution and the first martyr's of the Reformation were burnt at Brussels on 1 July 1523. Pope Adrian did not live long and was succeeded by Clement VII, and the persecution and imprisonment for consciences sake increased.

The Peasants' Revolt and Luther's Hymns

The peasants revolted from 1524-1525 was against all authority both ecclesiastical and civil. The Augustine monks of whom Martin Luther had been a member took his advice and all monastic vows were declared to be optional, dependant only on the individual's will and pleasure and therefore the monks and nuns were free to leave, or to remain, to marry or to stay celibate.

After a year of seclusion, Martin Luther disobeyed the Elector Fredrick's edict, who protected him, and headed for Wittenberg; followers of Luther's biblical teachings flocked to Wittenberg to be under likeminded protection even though the authorities had received authorisation to punish those who followed or commended Luther's doctrines.

Martin Luther travelled to Wittenberg to quell the trouble which had brought shame on the name of Christ. People who had been so incensed with the Roman Catholic Church took out their anger on its followers, their buildings and their possessions. Within one week of Luther's return to the pulpit he had calmed the raging storm saying such things as, "Faith is voluntary" and, "We need something more than faith and we need charity (love)."

Martin Luther's Publications

By 1523, Martin Luther had printed 183 of his writings and sermons which spread their way around civilised Europe. As Martin Luther said, "The weakest ink is stronger than the strongest memory." Luther was also a trained musician who understood and highly valued the various attainments of the various musical masters of his time, by readily availing himself of their assistance in his great reforming work. Luther clearly discerned the important value of church song, wedded to psalms and hymns, in the promotion of scriptural and vital religion. As the Reformation matured, Luther made every effort to assist in reforming the worship services. The Word of God was read aloud to the people in German and not the former Latin, and the congregation joined in the singing which was a valuable innovation, as now the people could understand in their own tongue and not the language of the clergy or the educated.

Martin Luther found very few hymns in Germany; of those that did exist, nearly all were in Latin and so he translated some and altered others that were already in use. Luther then started to compose hymns with musical settings which he initially used at his parish church in Wittenberg. The composer John Walther assisted Luther in some of these new sacred songs.

One of Martin Luther's earliest hymns dates to around 1523 and shows his rejoicing over deliverance from hard bondage (being a slave to sin), the result of conscience guilt and his entrance into pardon and liberty.

'Dear Christians, one and all, rejoice, with exultation springing,
And with united heart and voice and holy rapture singing,
    Proclaim the wonders God hath done,
    How His right arm the victory won;
Right dearly hath it cost Him!'

This particular hymn gained a large circulation and reached places where Luther's name and doctrine were little known, and by God's grace and mercy it proved itself a means of conversion to hundreds if not thousands. Luther's hymns became widespread by travelling schoolmasters who carried them through the countries they visited, reading and singing them, until his enemies declared that Luther had destroyed more souls by his hymns than by his writings! Luther said, "We should not ordain young men as preachers; unless they have been well exercised in music...the notes give life to the text." In the city of Hanover, in present-day Germany, it was said that the Reformation arrived by Luther's sacred songs and neither by the voice of a preacher nor by the reading of religious papers and documents.

In 1524, Martin Luther published his first hymn book, *Eight Songs* with music from John Walther which was but the forerunner for many other collections. Within twenty years from Luther's first publication, one hundred and seventeen collections of hymns by himself and his associates had been printed.

In 1525, Martin Luther said, "Accordingly, to make a good beginning and to encourage others who can do it better, I have myself with some others put together a few hymns in order to bring into full play the blessed Gospel; which by God's grace hath again risen, that we may know as Moses doth in his song [Exodus chapter 15] that Christ is become our praise and our song; and that whether we sing or speak, we may know anything save Christ our Saviour.... These hymns are set to music for no other reason than because of my desire that the young...might have something to take the place of world and amorous songs, and so learn something useful...."

Luther's Marriage and the Protestant Confession of Faith

Martin Luther and his friends helped rescue a small group of nuns from their monastery and one by one marriage partners were found for them, all except for Catherine Von Bora. On 13 June 1525, Luther who was now forty-two years old, secretly married Catherine who was sixteen years his junior, and they had six children. On 19 October 1525, Luther abandoned his monastic robes.

In 1529, at the Diet of Speyer, the Emperor Charles V, who was crowned Emperor of the Holy Roman Empire, attempted to curb Martin Luther's movement by force but some of the German state Princes came to his defence and stood up in 'protest.' The movement then found itself with the title 'Protestant' which had all along intended to reform Catholicism from within, separated off and became known as 'the Reformation.'

On 25 June 1530, at the Diet of Augsburg, a document called the "Confession of Faith" or "Augsburg Confession" which was signed by nearly two hundred important people of the realm was read before the Emperor Charles V, and the assembled Princes. This led Martin Luther into conflict with the Emperor as Luther believed the Gospel must be defended wherever it was attacked. The signing resulted in Christian Europe to be split into two, breaking from the Roman Catholic Church and gave rise to the churches known as Evangelical or Protestant. Three main traditions emerged: The Lutherans in Germany and Scandinavia; the Zwinglians and Calvinists in Switzerland, Holland, France and Scotland; and the Church of England.

In Martin Luther's latter years of his life he suffered greatly from physical disease and mental distress. These not infrequently were but the preludes to intense spiritual tribulation. In 1537, Luther wrote *Schmalkald Articles*, which was a doctrinal statement signed by many Lutheran theologians. Luther's final pamphlet was entitled *Against the Roman Papacy, Instituted by the Devil* which repeated his attacks on Catholicism. On his deathbed Luther was asked by a Doctor Jonas, "Reverend Father, dost thou still stand by Christ, and the doctrines thou has taught?" Luther replied firmly and clearly, "Yes." Luther passed to his Heavenly promotion on 17 February 1546. He is interred at the Lutheran church at Wittenberg, All Saints' Church; also known as the Reformation Memorial Church.[1]

'One generation shall praise Your works to another, and shall declare Your mighty acts. Men shall speak of the might of Your awesome acts...they shall utter the memory of Your great goodness, and shall sing of Your righteousness' (Psalm 145:4, 6-7).

Chapter 4

Bible Translation and the Reformation in England 1533

'All Scripture is given by inspiration of God, and is profitable for doctrine, for reproof, for correction, for instruction in righteousness' (2 Timothy 3:16).

Printing Press and Bible Translation

Johann Gutenberg invented the printing press in and around 1445, and the first book to be printed was a Latin language Bible, printed in Mainz, Germany. Born as Johann Gensfleisch (John Gooseflesh), he preferred to be known as Johann Gutenberg (John Beautiful Mountain). The invention of the movable-type printing press meant, as opposed to a scribe was that Bibles and books could be produced in large quantities in a short period of time, which was essential to the success of the Reformation.

William Caxton brought the printing press to England in 1476 and worked out of Westminster, London. In May 2017, two printed pages from *Sarum Ordinal*, dating from 1477 went on display at the University of Reading. Written in Medieval Latin the book dates from the eleventh century and was a handbook for priests, detailing feast days of English saints. Only ten pages are known to exist.

William Tyndale was the Captain of the Army of Reformers, and was their spiritual leader. He was the first person to print the New Testament in the English language. Tyndale was a true scholar and so fluent in eight languages that it was said one would think any one of them to be his native tongue.

In 1521, Martin Luther completed the translation of the New Testament into German from the 1516 Greek-Latin New Testament of Erasmus, and published it in September 1522. Luther also published a German Pentateuch in 1523 and another edition of the German New Testament in 1529. In the 1530s he would go on to publish the entire Bible in the German language.

William Tyndale wanted to use the same 1516 Erasmus text as a source to translate and print the New Testament in English. Tyndale showed up on Martin Luther's doorstep in Germany in 1525, and by the end of the year had translated the New Testament into English. Tyndale had been forced to flee England, because of the wide-spread rumour that his English New Testament project was underway, causing inquisitors and bounty-hunters to be constantly on Tyndale's trail. In 1525-1526, the Tyndale New Testament became the first printed edition of the Scriptures in the English language. These New Testaments were burned as soon as the Bishop could confiscate them in London, England, but copies trickled through and actually ended up in the bedroom of King Henry VIII. The Roman Catholic Church declared it contained thousands of errors as they burnt hundreds of New Testaments confiscated by the clergy, while in fact; they torched them because they could find no errors at all. One risked death by burning if caught in mere possession of Tyndale's New Testament!

Having God's Word available to the public in the language of the common man, English, would have meant disaster to the church at Rome. No longer would they have total control of the Scriptures. If people were able to read the Bible in their own tongue, the Roman Catholic Church's income and power would crumble. They could not possibly continue to get away with selling Indulgences (the forgiveness of sins) or selling the release of loved ones from a fictional Purgatory. People would begin to challenge the church's authority if she was exposed as a fraud and a thief. The contradictions between what God's Word said, and what the priests taught, would open the public's eyes and the truth would set them free from the grip of fear that the Roman Catholic Church held. Salvation is by God's grace through faith, not works or donations! The need for priests would vanish through the priesthood of all believers. The veneration of church-canonized Saints and idolatry of the Virgin Mary would be called into question.

William Tyndale's flight was an inspiration to freedom-loving Englishmen who drew courage from the eleven years that he was hunted. Books and Bibles flowed into England in bales of cotton and sacks of flour and landed at the docks of London. Ironically, Tyndale's biggest customer was the king's men, who would buy up every copy available to burn them and Tyndale used their money to print even more! In the end, Tyndale was caught; betrayed by Henry Phillips, an Englishman he had befriended. Tyndale was incarcerated for more than five hundred days at Vilvoorde Castle, Flanders, before he was strangled and burned at the stake on 6 October 1536. Tyndale's last words were, "Lord! Open the King of England's eyes."[1]

William Tyndale did not complete the translation of the Old Testament into English, but his work formed the basis of all subsequent English translations of the Bible, including the King James Version of 1611, also known as the Authorised Version.

In 1538, the last prayer of William Tyndale was answered when King Henry VIII gave a royal decree, of an English Bible, which was to be placed in every parish church. Printing began in Paris, France, in 1539, but soon came to England as it was deemed heretical by the French authorities! It was known as the "Great Bible" because of its size. Six editions followed, with more than nine thousand copies printed by 1541. In February 2008, I was in Egypt and visited the famous Library of Alexandria. Inside were many printing presses, some of which dated from the time of Johann Gutenberg, William Tyndale and from the eighteenth century.

In Victoria Embankment Gardens, London, next to the River Thames, where William Tyndale's New Testaments were brought into England in the late 1520s, is a bronze statue of Tyndale which was erected in May 1884. Tyndale is standing on a stone plinth dressed in academic dress, with his right hand resting on an open New Testament that is laying on an early printing press. The statue was commissioned by The British and Foreign Bible Society to commemorate its eightieth anniversary and the four hundredth anniversary of William Tyndale's birth. The inscription on a bronze plaque is as follows:

William Tyndale

First translator of the New Testament into English from the Greek. Born A.D. 1484, Died a martyr at Vilvorde in Belgium, A.D. 1536. "Thy word is a lamp to my feet, and a light to my path" – "the entrance of thy words giveth light." Psalm CXIX. 105.130. "And this is the record that God hath given to us eternal life, and this life is in his son." I. John V.II. The last words of William Tyndale were "Lord! Open the King of England's eyes." Within a year afterwards, a Bible was placed in every parish church by the King's command.

'But you must continue in the things which you have learned and been assured of, knowing from whom you have learned them, and that from childhood you have known the Holy Scriptures, which are able to make you wise for salvation through faith which is in Christ Jesus' (2 Timothy 3:14-15).

Reformation in England 1533+

Henry VIII (reigned 1509-1547) was a man who loved music and the military arts; he was also interested in building England's navy but lacked the finances for such a large undertaking. All male children born to Catherine and Henry died. Henry had no heir of his own other than Princess Mary; it was unthinkable at the time that a woman should rule England. As Henry had married his brother's widow, the solution seemed simple enough: he would have to get his marriage annulled and marry the young, Anne Boleyn. However, the king had not bargained on the obstinacy of Charles V, the most powerful monarch in Europe, the nephew of Catherine and, more importantly, the virtual keeper of the Pope.

Thomas Wolsey joined the King's council in 1509. As the king enjoyed other pursuits, he left much of the administration in Wolsey's capable hands, appointing him Lord Chancellor in 1515. The ambitious Wolsey then acquired other offices in rapid succession, including those of Archbishop of York, Cardinal and Papal Legate. Henry had been given the title 'Defender of the Faith' by Pope Leo X for his efforts to keep the forces of Protestantism at bay in England. Thomas Wolsey on two occasions tried to get himself elected Pope. Wolsey failed in getting Henry divorced and was banished from court and was eventually summoned to trial on a charge of treason. He died on his way to face the king.

The medieval church, the Roman Catholic Church was in a fossilised state, out of touch with the vast changes that had been taking place in economics, politics and social conditions. Dissenters known as the Lollards were still preaching against the Catholic bishops across England and beyond, and William Tyndale of England, who would be martyred, was busy translating the New Testament into English at Cologne. Martin Luther was in Germany, preaching against the corruption of the Church of Rome; their Indulgences etc.

King Henry VIII obtained his divorce regardless of Charles V and the Pope. He simply used the authority of the State and the so-named Reformation Parliament that was first called in 1529 and that, for the next seven years, effectively destroyed the medieval church in England. It was a process of the dissolution of the monasteries by destruction, and taking the wealth of the Roman Catholic Church in England for the needs of the Crown; such as building a navy to defend England and beyond. In 1533, Henry married the pregnant Anne Boleyn and upon the death of the Archbishop of Canterbury, appointed Thomas Cranmer to do his bidding in that office.

The official break with Rome came in April 1533, with the passing of the Act of Restraint of Appeals that decreed, "This realm of England is an empire." One month later Archbishop Cranmer declared that the King's marriage to Catherine of Aragon was null and void. Ann Boleyn was duly crowned Queen, giving birth to Elizabeth; but three months later the Pope duly excommunicated both Cranmer and Henry.

After 1534, events moved even more rapidly. The Act of Supremacy of 1534 declared that King Henry VIII was the Supreme Head of the Church of England and the Pope officially designated merely as the Bishop of Rome. There was no Catholic uprising in Britain; Henry still considered himself a staunch Catholic, retaining his title, 'Defender of the Faith.' There was no break with Rome on matters of dogma, Henry had no great desire for a complete separation, but matters came to a head with the rise to power of

Thomas Cromwell, considered by many to be the architect of the English Reformation. Cromwell carried out the policies of Henry. The dissolution of the monasteries in Britain proceeded at a rapid pace. They were an easy target to satisfy Henry's need for vast amounts of money for coastal defences and for strengthening the navy. In three years, two Acts of Dissolution brought to an end hundreds of years of monastic influence in the island of Britain. A feeble protest from Catholics in the North, known as the Pilgrimage of Grace was easily suppressed. In 1538, the same year that the last monasteries were dissolved, Henry's chief minister and architect of the Reformation in England issued injunctions stating that every parish church should have an English Bible and shrines were to be destroyed.

Many beside the king and his nobles were happy to see the monasteries disappear and the power of the Roman Catholic Church diminished. Abbots lived like princes. Piety had almost disappeared. The bishop's house at St. David's in Wales rivalled the Cathedral itself in grandeur! It has been estimated that the Roman Catholic Church had owned as much as one quarter of the arable land of the nation, plus jewels, church plates, relics and gold artefacts. Henry was determined to have it all, thus the monasteries were destroyed and their lands taken over by the Crown. Their vast land-holdings were sold off to those who could afford them. The so-called Act of Union 1542 and its corrected version of 1543 seemed inevitable. But the Statute of Rhuddlan had really achieved union with England in 1284. By the Act, 'Finally and for all time' the principality of Wales was incorporated into the Kingdom of England.

In 1544, the name The House of Lords first appeared. This was an indication of the rapid rise of the other, Lower House the House of Commons. The Reformation had been firmly established in England and the power of the Roman Catholic Church irrevocably broken. Henry was obese and gout-ridden and died in January 1547; in all he had six wives.

King Edward VI (reigned 1547-1553), his uncle, the Duke of Somerset made himself Lord Protector. He continued the late king's policy of religious changes, furthering the Protestant reforms. Cranmer's *Book of Common Prayer* (1552), was made compulsory in all churches and the Latin Mass abolished. A new Act of Uniformity was passed. The rightful heir to the throne was Mary, Henry VIII's only surviving child by Catherine of Aragon, and she was a committed Catholic. Edward declared Mary to be the heir.

Queen Mary Tudor (reigned 1553-1558) also known as 'Bloody Mary,' took her throne with high hopes of restoring England to Catholicism. By this time the Reformation had taken firm root throughout Northern Europe and in much of England. Mary set about having Parliament repeal the Act of Supremacy, reinstated heresy laws and petition for reunion with Rome. The Latin Mass was restored and Catholic bishops reinstated. The burning of 'heretics' began, such Protestant leaders and men of influence as Cranmer, Ridley, Latimer and Hooper, but also hundreds of lesser men (plus dozens of women) who refused to adopt the Catholic faith. The entire country became enraged and fearful and thousands fled abroad to Continental Europe, especially Switzerland where there were English-speaking congregations. The nation rejoiced at her death in 1558. 'When the wicked arise men hide themselves; but when they perish, the righteous increase' (Proverbs 28:28).

Queen Elizabeth I (reigned 1558-1603) needed the support of the common people to help her cut her ties with Rome, the majority of whom were overwhelmingly Protestant and anti-Rome. She did allow some of the ceremonies associated with Catholicism to remain. Mass continued for those who so wished. She chose the middle road of the Anglican Church, rather than accept the harsh doctrines of such men as John Calvin of Switzerland and John Knox of Scotland.

John Knox had arrived back in Scotland in 1544, carrying his huge two-handed sword along with his Bible. The Reformation in Scotland had taken a different path from what it was to take in England after Queen Mary, for Queen Elizabeth was no Calvinist, remaining the head of the Church of England. Her Supremacy Bill and the Uniformity Bills of 1559, made the Church of England law and substituted fines and penalties for disobedience, instead of burnings and banishment. Queen Elizabeth's reign was also the age of Shakespeare. The Welsh received the Holy Bible in their own language in 1588, by Bishop William. Any attempts to make the Counter-Reformation productive in Wales failed miserably. William Salesbury published his translation of the main texts of the *Prayer Book* into Welsh in 1551. Ireland was loyal to the Catholic Church; it was a country that resisted all attempts to impose Protestantism.[2]

'...The way into the Holiest of All was not yet made manifest while the first tabernacle was still standing. It *was* symbolic for the present time in which both gifts and sacrifices are offered which cannot make him who performed the service perfect in regard to the conscience – concerned only with foods and drinks, various washings, and fleshly ordinances imposed until the time of reformation. But Christ came *as* High Priest of the good things to come, with the greater and more perfect tabernacle not made with hands, that is, not of this creation. Not with the blood of goats and calves, but with His own blood He entered the Most Holy Place once for all, having obtained eternal redemption' (Hebrews 9:8-12).

Chapter 5

John Knox and the Reformation in Scotland 1555

'May the Lord answer you in the day of trouble; may the name of the God of Jacob defend you; may He send you help from the sanctuary, and strengthen you out of Zion' (Psalm 20:1-2).

John Knox

The life of John Knox is surrounded in controversy and some facts cannot be easily obtained or verified which include his birthplace, date of birth, where he studied; either Glasgow or St. Andrews Universities in Scotland or both, coupled with his parents social standing which was very important in the sixteenth century. Even the spelling of his name had many variations. John Knox was either born in Gifford near Haddington in East Lothian, Scotland or Giffordgate in Haddington and was born either in 1505 or 1514! When Knox was at university in Scotland in the 1530s it was illegal to teach the Scriptures in Greek; bearing in mind that the majority of the New Testament was originally written in Greek and several hundred years before Jesus was conceived by the Holy Spirit in Mary's womb, the Old Testament had been translated into the Greek Septuagint.

In April 1536, John Knox was ordained a Catholic priest by the bishop of Dunblane, and at first could not find a parish, so from 1540-1543, he became both a tutor and a chaplain to a wealthy family. On 28 March 1543, Knox wrote a document '...witnessed in faith through Christ to whom be glory' so preceding this date, Knox probably was converted to salvation by the grace of God through faith in the Saviour, Jesus Christ and in Him alone and thus became a Protestant. By this date, the notion of 'justified by faith' or 'saved by faith' as mentioned in the Holy Bible had become more popular in Scotland, as the Reformation of religion was sweeping Europe under Martin Luther in Wittenberg, Germany, and under John Calvin in Geneva, Switzerland. Europe was changing as the medieval system in which the Pope, the Holy Roman Emperor and King or Queen of a country who reigned supreme was in question and challenged. Europe was seen as a chessboard where many people were plying for power and marriages were arranged for political reasons of power, prestige and religion.

In Scotland, Protestants had been executed for their faith but some of the nobility, earls and Lairds were Protestants themselves or sympathetic to the cause and gave refuge and support for the believers. England, under King Henry VIII had broken away from Rome in 1527, over his divorce or the fact that he was refused a divorce / annulment from the Pope. England became an official Protestant country in 1534 when King Henry VIII founded the Church of England of which he naturally became the head. But in May of 1543, he passed a law stating the Bible could not be read in English which was punishable by death. In churches the Latin version was used. Cramner's *Prayer Book* also known as the *Book of Common Prayer* was to be used in church services instead, thus eliminating the need for an English Bible. Even though by this time England had become a place of refuge for fleeing Protestants from the Catholics and especially the wrath of Cardinal Beaton.

The Church of Rome was corrupt and piety was rarely shown; it was a place where even the Bishops openly flaunted their mistresses and the priesthood was seen as a good financial sound career move with plenty of perks. King Henry VIII of England had some of the Scottish nobles on his payroll who were encouraged to fight and conspire against the Roman Catholic Church and the Catholic Regent, Mary Guise and then Queen Mary.

Controversial Views

In 1544, the English army attacked Edinburgh in Scotland, and many other towns and villages, burnt and pillaged anything that got in their way. This unjust act led to John Knox's belief that if the God-given leader of a nation was ungodly they had indisposed themselves of their 'Divine' authority and standing and could be overthrown! Violence could be used as a means of advancing Reformation. John Knox was all for the dispossession of a ruler by imprisonment, capital punishment or assassination! If a ruler went outside of the will of God by disobeying His commands, then he or she forfeited all rights as God's governor and could be justifiably punished by the people. When Knox was living in Frankfurt (in Germany) and then in Geneva (in Switzerland), some of his comments and views greatly alarmed John Calvin; this controversial doctrine of John Knox was not shared by Martin Luther. John Calvin gave great emphasis on God's predestined will, that for many who followed this line of thinking to the extreme, it literally relinquished them of any responsibility for their actions. Martin Luther was anti-Semitic, he wanted all Jews to be deported to the Holy Land and their synagogues and books burned. Whilst to the day of his death he stood by the Roman Catholic doctrine of transubstantiation, that during communion the bread and the wine literally becomes the flesh and blood of Jesus Christ. Huldrych Zwingli, the German speaking Swiss reformer, authorised the killing by drowning of

Anabaptists (a Christian movement loosely organised, but who were not a cult) for those who participated in adult rebaptism. Also, Huldrych Zwingli and Martin Luther did not get along with each other, Yet all these Reformers were Christian giants in their time. As a wise man once said, "It is an ungracious and ungrateful task to dwell on a man's weaknesses. It is more profitable and more pleasant to turn to the real good that they did." And it is to this that all those Reformers are truly remembered for. None of us would doubt that they all were men of God who came into the Kingdom for such a time as theirs.

In April 2006, I visited Geneva, where there are fifteen feet (3m) tall stone statues of the Reformers along with a large stone memorial to the entire Reformation era. You can also see the site where the home of John Calvin once stood; it was demolished in 1706.

The unknown John Knox became a bodyguard to the fiery preacher and prayer warrior, George Wishart and carried a two-handed sword for their protection. Wishart was a pious man who had studied and worked in both the reformed Germany and Switzerland. Henry VIII had stumped up £1,000 for the assassination of Cardinal Beaton. Rome was allied to Catholic France who England was at war with, on and off, for many centuries and now was no exception. England and France wanted Scotland to be brought under the dominion of their control. Henry had ordered the abolition of the lavish monasteries in England to help fund the war.

The assassination attempt on Cardinal Beaton failed and George Wishart was implicated in the plot, probably due to his anti-Rome pulpit rhetoric. Wishart ordered Knox to leave him in January 1546, knowing his fate, saying "...One is sufficient for sacrifice." The Earl of Bothwell with his small army arrested Wishart and on 1 March 1546, Wishart was tied to a stake, strangled and burnt to death. Knox was broken-hearted, the Cardinal was pleased but in less than two months he too was killed.

The Protestants fought and preached against the Papal system of pardons, pilgrimages, fasts and indulgences as a means of salvation and argued straight from Scripture pointing to absolute truths which could not be denied. The sacraments under the Protestants were reduced from seven to two, baptism and communion. The Catholics believed that the church was supreme and the ultimate authority on all matters, and the church traditions were just as important and equal to the Scriptures themselves, whereas the Protestants declared that the Word of God was the exclusive foundation stone on which church doctrine and tradition must heed.

Moses declared, "You shall not add to the word which I command you, nor take from it..." (Deuteronomy 4:2).

From Chaplain to Preacher and the British Monarchy

In April 1547, John Knox reluctantly took the position of Chaplain at St. Andrews Castle in Scotland, but he was not the exclusive preacher from the parish church. Knox was summoned to attend a meeting because of his outspoken attitude against the Catholic state where he presented his inquisitors with a list of their church's heretical doctrines. In July 1547, the French captured the Castle and Knox along with others was incarcerated as a galley slave aboard a French ship. Knox along with other prisoners was released in 1549, with help from British negotiators, and was offered a job as a minister in Berwick, England, under the Lord Protector, Somerset, who was the uncle of the King to be, Edward VI. John Knox's views soon led him into trouble as he disliked traditional Anglican services as convened in Cramner's *Book of Common Prayer* and saw the Mass as idolatry and the doctrine of transubstantiations (the bread and wine literally turning into Jesus' body and blood) as heretical.

John Knox became a popular preacher and when he moved towns from Berwick to Newcastle, and then to London, England, many Scots followed him. In London, the Earl of Northumberland, the Lord Protector of England made Knox a court preacher (among many) to the young King of England, Edward VI (reigned 1547-1553) and his subjects. Edward had become King because the rightful heir, Mary was a woman and so was initially refused the position.

In 1552, the Lord Protector, for political reasons, offered John Knox the Position of Bishop of Rochester in Kent, England, which he turned down. In the same year Thomas Cranmer's *Book of Common Prayer* was made compulsory in all churches in England and the Latin Mass abolished. In 1553, Knox was offered the job of Vicar of All Hallows Church in London, which he turned down, but finally accepted a position in Amersham in April of the same year.

Four days after King Edward VI's death on 6 July 1553, Lady Jane Grey was proclaimed Queen of England from orders of the late King. However, Mary, Henry VIII's only surviving child by Catherine of Aragon, a committed Catholic, was the rightful heir to the throne according to Henry VIII's will and had the right of succession, and was gathering support in Suffolk. She and her followers rode into London nine days later and imprisoned Jane and her supporters. Mary Tudor became Queen Mary (reigned 1553-1558), later known as Bloody Mary because of the Christian 'heretics' that were martyred under her reign. She took the throne with high hopes of restoring England to Catholicism, even though she stated on 12 August 1553, 'she would not compel adherence to her faith.'

The Reformation had taken firm root throughout Northern Europe and in much of England. Queen Mary set about having Parliament repeal the Act of Supremacy, reinstate heresy laws and petition for reunion with Rome. The Latin Mass was restored and Catholic bishops were reinstated; the burning of 'heretics' began and Protestant leaders, men of influence and hundreds of lesser men alongside dozens of women who refused to adopt the Catholic faith were martyred in public displays.

John Knox who had been preaching and writing anti-Queen Mary sentiments, but wisely did not name her personally fled to Dieppe, France, and lived in a Scottish Colony. By January 1554, he travelled the one thousand kilometres to Geneva in Switzerland, arriving in September or October of the same year. Knox had fellowship with John Calvin and had a list of questions which he hoped he would be able to answer. It was here that Knox studied Hebrew for the first time.

Frankfurt in Germany had become a safe haven for European Protestants and they flocked there by their thousands. John Knox along with others was invited to be a minister to these wandering sheep and duly arrived in November where he was forced to use Cranmer's liturgy. He was able to strike a compromise until a fellow preacher arrived who outvoted him on church format. The Frankfurt church council found him guilty of treasonable offences with his anti-establishment rhetoric against Queen Mary, and referring to the Emperor as 'like Nero,' as it was the Emperor who had granted Frankfurt its safety to harbour Protestants! Knox was forbidden to preach and returned to Geneva with many of his followers in April 1555.

In 1549, the marriage of priests had become legal in Britain and in October 1555, John Knox returned to Edinburgh in Scotland, and married Majority (Elizabeth) Bowles who was twenty years his junior. Knox had corresponded with her for a long time, and was on very good terms with her mother. John Knox and Majority had two sons.

John Knox tried to reform the landowners and the minds of the nobility but to no avail, even though he had their backing when in May, he was summoned on a heresy charge which was later dropped for fear of an uprising on behalf of the Bishop and the Queen Mother, Mary of Guise, to whom Knox had even sent a letter asking her to become Protestant. Knox was then invited back to Geneva, Switzerland, which he accepted. Before he left he drew up a manifesto for Scots Protestants to follow, especially in the matter of regular Bible reading. Knox arrived in September 1556, but some Scottish nobility sent word to him to return to Scotland! He travelled back to France only to be told that perhaps now was not a good time to return and so headed back to Geneva! By December 1557, Knox had become a joint minister of an English speaking congregation from where he verbally and by pen, attacked those who had opposed him, much to the embarrassment of John Calvin. In

England, Queen Mary died; much to the jubilation of the Protestants of her realm. 'When the wicked arise men hide themselves; but when they perish, the righteous increase' (Proverbs 28:28).

In 1558, Queen Elizabeth I of England ascended the throne of England (reigned 1558-1603); she was the daughter of the late Henry VIII and Anne Boleyn. The queen needed the support of the common people to help her cut her ties with Rome, the majority of whom were overwhelmingly Protestant and anti-Rome. She did allow some of the ceremonies associated with Catholicism to remain. Later on her Protestant faith resulted in her excommunication. The communion service could be a Mass for those who wished. She chose the middle road of the Anglican Church, rather than accept the harsh doctrines of such men as John Calvin and John Knox. The Reformation in Scotland had taken a much different path than it was to take in England after Queen Mary, for Queen Elizabeth was no Calvinist, remaining the head of the Church of England. Her Supremacy Bill and the Uniformity Bills of 1559, which made the Church of England law, substituted fines and penalties for disobedience instead of burnings and banishment.

Across England there are many 'martyr memorials' commemorating those who died for their Protestant beliefs during the reign of Queen Mary (1553-1558). These stone monuments with intricate carvings, frequently topped like a crown or an obelisk are often around 15-20ft tall. Others are much smaller and plainer with metal plaques attached or engraved in stone. See *Foxe's Book of Martyrs* by John Foxe, originally published in 1563, and *Faithful Unto Death: The Martyrs of East Anglia* by Philip H. Rand (c.1980).

Spokesperson for the Scottish Reformation

John Knox returned alone to Scotland as the spokesperson of the Reformation in May 1559, and headed for Dundee, Scotland. Scotland was on the edge of a civil religious war and many preachers including him were outlawed by a proclamation in Glasgow. England under her new queen and government encouraged the Reformation as England still wanted to get Scotland under its control. The Scottish nobility were all jostling for position and swapping sides when it suited them the most while the Queen Regent, Mary of Guise, was looking to the French for help and wanted her realm to remain purely Catholic. In these days of civil and noble unrest, many treaties and truces were made and broken or conveniently forgotten.

John Knox carried on ministering the Word and stirred up the congregations when preaching on topics such as Jesus cleansing the temple and tearing down the high places. Knox even went on a secret mission to England, to try to raise more support to overthrow the 'evil regime.' By September, Knox's family returned to Scotland where his wife, Marjory, died in 1560 or 1561, and his two young children were brought up by his mother-in-law in Edinburgh. Knox sat on the council of the Kirk (the established Protestant Scottish Church as opposed to the Roman Catholic Church) which was situated in St. Andrews (which was still the Catholic headquarters) where they administered biblical justice for moral offences.

Church attendance was compulsory for those who professed to be Protestant; many priests converted and admission tokens were distributed to the believers which provided an accurate way of checking attendance. John Knox and his fellow godly revolutionaries had been preparing the Scots' Confession and the *First Book of Discipleship* which outlined how the 'new' state would run in social, civil and legal matters however the *Discipleship* book never came into affect.

On 6 July 1560, the Treaty of Edinburgh was signed between the French and the English, whereby all French troops had to leave Scotland, and the question of state religion was referred to the Scottish Parliament. The Reformation was well on its way in theory but Queen Mary would not ratify the treaty and had offered her obedience to the newly elected Pope Pius IV, and her husband King Francis was persecuting the French Protestants.

On 15 August 1560, Scotland officially became a Protestant state with the Mass outlawed and the Pope's jurisdiction denied, but the question of who financed the new church was left undone, even though the old Catholic Church could still legally demand church income. The Queen refused to endorse the policies of the Reformation Parliament but nonetheless on 20 December 1560, the first General Assembly of the new church met in Edinburgh. Mary, the eighteen year old daughter of Mary of Guise, arrived from France, and was crowned Queen Mary of Scots. It was not until 1567 that the Acts of 1560 were ratified when the Queen was forced to abdicate.

The new Catholic Queen Mary of Scots passed a law which stated the religion was to stay the same without fear of death, but legally it could be argued that either Protestant or the Catholic belief was correct as reforms had been passed without royal ratification. Five times John Knox spoke to the new Queen and on one occasion even reduced her to tears, as they had opposing views, especially concerning her marriage to be.

From 1562, the Scottish Catholics became more outspoken against the Protestant state and Jesuit priests held secret meetings with the Queen. John Knox travelled as a preacher but still held his pulpit in St. Giles, Scotland. When groups of Roman Catholics were arrested for religious offences the Queen would intervene to seek their release. The Queen had to ask the nobles permission before she married and they were encouraging her to marry a Protestant noble. In 1564, John Knox remarried, to Margaret Steward and they had three daughters.

On 29 July 1565, Queen Mary of Scots married the Catholic Henry Stuart, Lord Darnley, and assumed the role of king and his head even appeared on the coinage. Fearless John Knox preached on a few occasions while Darnley was in attendance and referred to him as Ahab and the queen as Jezebel! The Privy Council would not allow him to preach in Edinburgh when the king and queen were present.

Within the first decade of the Scottish Reformation, one thousand churches sprang into being, but due to the lack of church finances not enough ministers could be fully employed, so many lay readers filled the gap. In the last couple of years there was much starvation among the commoners and John Knox appealed to the Queen to surrender her 33% share of church income which came from the nobility's tithe. She declined and so he turned to the middle classes for voluntary contributions to help support the struggling ministers.

Overthrow of the Scottish Monarchy

In early 1566, the unstable King Henry Darnley had become jealous of Queen Mary's Italian advisor, Rizzio, and had him murdered along with a Friar called John Black. John Knox was alleged to be in on the plot so fled to England for several months before returning. Queen Mary gave birth to a son and Prince James was baptised a Catholic.

In February 1567, the King was assassinated and in late April Queen Mary was kidnapped by the married Earl Bothwell. Bothwell obtained a quick divorce and an annulment for good measures, and on 15 May they married under a Protestant ceremony. In June 1567, an army of rebels led by the nobles attacked, and called Queen Mary to renounce Bothwell, to which she refused. In the same year there was a failed assassination attempt on John Knox's life when a shot was fired through his window. Bothwell fled into exile to the Orkneys in Scotland and Mary was incarcerated in Loch Leven Castle. John Knox called for her death but she was forced to abdicate by the Lords in favour of her infant son who was crowned James VI on 29 July, and John Knox preached at the coronation. In 1604, King James VI authorised an English Bible translation, the King James Version (1611), also known as the Authorised Version.

In December 1567, the Scottish Parliament endorsed all that had been done in 1561 and all future kings were to give an oath at their coronation, to govern by the written Word of God. All officers of state were to be Protestants and all school teachers had to be approved by the church.

On 2 May 1568, Queen Mary escaped and took refuge among some nobility, the Hamiltons. On 17 May a battle took place between the Queen's forces and the infant King's Lords. The King's side won and Mary fled to England and received shelter from her cousin, Queen Elizabeth I, but both parties continued to fight on and off until on 31 July 1572, when they agreed a truce.

John Knox's Last Years & the Union of Scotland and England

John Knox had a stroke in 1571 and on 24 November 1572, he was promoted to glory. He had prophesied his own death only a week before by ordering his coffin and by purchasing a new hogshead of wine and encouraging his guest to drink freely since he would not live to finish it. In his lifetime, John Knox was known as a prophet and it was said that Queen Mary feared his prayers more than the English army. John Knox was buried in the churchyard adjoining St. Giles Cathedral, in Edinburgh, which today is a car park/parking lot for the Court of Sessions; a plaque on space twenty-three denotes the spot. Inside St. Gilles is a life-size bronze statue of John Knox. His influence in the Scottish Reformation and beyond was honoured by a monument in Geneva, Switzerland to the European Reformers. In 1586, Queen Mary of Scots conspired in the Babington plot to kill Queen Elizabeth I and was beheaded.[1]

When Queen Elizabeth died, James I from the house of Stuart in Scotland, was declared King of both England and Scotland; he reigned from 1603 to 1625. He greatly favoured a union of the two kingdoms and the new national flag, the Union flag, bore the cross of St. Andrew and St. George. But though the Estates passed an Act of Union in 1607, it wasn't until 1707 that a treaty was signed. James' attempts to impose the Five Articles on the Scots, dealing with matters of worship and religious observances, were met with strong opposition. He pushed through his reforms in 1618; they were ignored throughout Scotland. James issued a new translation of the Bible, and in 1611 the King James Bible; the Authorised Version was completed.

'We will rejoice in Your salvation, and in the name of our God we will set up our banners! May the Lord fulfil all your petitions. Now I know that the Lord saves His anointed; He will answer him from His holy Heaven with the saving strength of His right hand. Some trust in chariots, and some in horses; But we will remember the name of the Lord our God' (Psalm 20:5-7).

Chapter 6

George Fox and the Quaker Revival 1652+

"The king will mourn, the prince will be clothed with desolation, and the hands of the common people will tremble. I will do to them according to their way, and according to what they deserve I will judge them; then they shall know that I am the Lord!" (Ezekiel 7:27).

George Fox

George Fox was born in July 1624 in Drayton-in-the Clay, (now Fenney Drayton), Leicestershire, England, into a religious Puritan family. Fox's father, Christopher Fox, was a weaver by trade, and his pious ways earned him the nickname, "Righteous Christer." On his mother side, there was the heritage of Protestant martyrs and they had at least five children. By the time George Fox was eleven, he 'knew pureness and righteousness,' so he wrote in his *Journal,* having been taught by his parents and the Lord 'taught me to be faithful in all things...inwardly to God and outwardly to man.'[1]

George Fox lived through the English Civil War which broke out in 1642 and lasted for three years, ending in 1646. Some people sided with Parliament and were led by the Puritan, Oliver Cromwell (d.1658), the Royalist followed King Charles I. Cromwell beat Charles' army, and he was imprisoned on the Isle of Wight. At the time, many Christian sects were vying for converts, attention and supremacy such as: Presbyterians, Baptists, Anabaptist, Brownists (Congregationalists), Seekers, Ranters, Adamites, Soul Sleepers, Familist (Family of Love) and the Fifth Monarchy-Men who expected the millennium immediately. By 1645, Ephraim Pagit had published *Hersiography* in which he gives a description of these sects and Thomas Edwards in his book, *Gangroena* wrote of 176 sects with 'their errors, heresies and blasphemies'! By the 1660s, most of these sects had died out. In 1689, the Act of Toleration permitted relative freedom for men to worship God each in his own way.[2]

The Commons passed an ordinance establishing Presbyterianism. A purge of the moderates in Parliament, left the radical elements in the so-called 'Rump Parliament' that created a High Court of Justice to bring King Charles I to trial for high treason, where 135 judges were present. Charles did not recognise the court and so did not plead. His execution was held in public in January 1649. The Rump Parliament abolished the monarchy and proclaimed a republican form of government. First called the 'Commonwealth and Free State,' and later the 'Protectorate.'

Under the Republican Government (1649-1660), the House of Lords was abolished as was the Anglican Church in 1655, and freedom to worship was granted. In 1650, King Charles II duly arrived in Scotland to claim his Kingdom. On 12 December 1653, after he had refused an offer of the Crown, Cromwell, virtual dictator of England (1649-1658), received the title of Lord Protector. Cromwell used his office to seek reforms in the church and Parliament, which was a common aim of the Puritans. He tried to get 140 devout churchmen to run the country but it did not work, so after five months they handed power back to Cromwell. Roman Catholics were regarded as enemies of the realm.[3]

George Fox was religious, though not converted and was always different from other young men. Just after his nineteenth birthday he attended a fair with two other Christians and was more than disappointed in their drinking session. In September 1643, he left home and for four years went in search of spiritual truth. He spoke to ministers, Dissenters and others but came to no real answer – the clergy being more lost than himself and the Puritans full of self abasement, rigid and political ways, serving the law, rather than living the letter of the Spirit. After four years of seeking, Fox found the inner light in Christ (as he called it) and was converted as Christ spoke to his heart. Jesus said, "I have come as a Light into the world, that whoever believes in Me should not abide in darkness" (John 12:46). George Fox went on to confess himself as a Christian; but more importantly lived it, being Christ-like and anointed.

An Itinerate Preacher

In 1647, aged twenty-four, George Fox became an itinerant preacher and preached that people must have an individual relationship with Christ and be led of the inner light – the guidance of the Holy Spirit. Conversely, Job declared, "There are those who rebel against the light; they do not know its ways nor abide in its paths" (Job 24:13). George Fox and the Puritans were alike in some ways; simple in dress, avoidance of many recreations, disdain for music, wakes and feasts, but very different in other ways. For Fox, it was being led of the Spirit, but for the Puritans, it was the letter of the law and many barriers had been set up, hindering people from entering the Kingdom of God. Fox was very knowledgeable of the Bible. It was said of Fox that if all the world's Bibles were destroyed, he would be able to rewrite it from memory! Fox lived what he preached and expected all Quakers to do likewise. 'Friends' (what Quakers were known as based on John 15:15), that stepped out of line were brought under church discipline.

George Fox was raised up by the Lord; a John the Baptist of his day to be a shining beacon during England's dark times of confusion, bloodshed and civil war. It was the era when 24 March was the last day of the year (25 March was known as the first day of the first month) under the Julian Calendar, and execution was very common for the most minor of offences. The last "heretic" to burn in England was in 1612, but it was seriously considered in 1639 by the Privy Council and encouraged by Archbishop Laud, when a stonemason was accused of non-attendance at church, of studying the Bible at home, being opposed to the system of bishops and for being against printed prayers![4]

George Fox wrote a *Journal* which was compiled, it was believed during his last stay in prison; his Worcester imprisonments 1673-1675 and scribed by his son-in-law, Thomas Lowder, via his step-daughter. Fox's *Journal* ceased in June 1675, but the account of his life for the next sixteen years was gathered by his editor, Thomas Ellwood and others. This account which was collated shortly after Fox's death formed a continuous narrative, interspersed with letters and papers and was first published in 1694.[5]

A century later in 1789, John Gough wrote a *History of the People called Quakers* in four volumes, which was published by Robert Jackson, of Dublin, Ireland.

George Fox believed that the Church of England violated the spirit of Christianity. Fox referred to days of the week as the First Day, Second Day and Third Day etc. because of the naming of the days of the week with their pagan origin. He also wanted nothing to do with the Church's religious festivals and traditions many of which had their roots in Judaism and paganism. Fox detested priests who were paid and denounced them as hirelings (John 10:12-13), who collected the tithes of the parish; many of whom hardly turned up to teach the flock. Fox called all Christian workers "priests" regardless of their denomination. He was against compulsory tithing which was enshrined in English law, and the renting of pews (wealthy families got the best seats). He called church buildings 'steeple-houses' as the Church is the body of Christ and Quaker 'churches' were known as 'Meeting Houses.' Fox refused to swear allegiance (to make an oath) to a monarch or take up arms. He would not address people in the formal manner of the day, which looked up to the higher class and degraded others. He would not bend the knee or take off his hat as was the custom of the day, but treated all equally. The nickname Quakers, first mentioned in 1650, stuck to all Fox's fellow Christians, 'Friends' as they were known or 'Children of the Light,' followers of Jesus Christ and the apostles' teachings. George Fox used to preach, "Let Jesus be your Prophet, Priest and King."

George Fox had piercing eyes, which brought several under conviction or terror and was characterised by his leather suit, which he reputedly made himself, and his wide-brimmed hat. Some say he only had leather breeches (trousers) which were more practical rather than fashionable. For a period of time, Fox did not cut his hair, which was presumably very long as it got people's attention and he was defensive when a woman claimed to have cut a lock off. Fox was possibly partaking of a Nazirite vow, as on occasions he also refused beer and wine, see Numbers 6. Sometimes his cheeks and limbs swelled, giving him the appearance of being overweight, which was not the case and there are two generally well-known paintings of him; though one is from the nineteenth century.

On many occasions George Fox and his followers and fellow labourers were attacked, stoned, mobbed, beaten, picked up and thrown down or over a wall, threatened with death and were nearly killed on several occasions – inside and outside of a church building! Once a pistol was put to his face and fired; but it failed to go off. Yet, he could stand up and turn the other cheek to the amazement of his persecutors and tormentors; calling them to repent and to see what their priests (Christian teachers) had taught them how to live and whether or not it was Christian conduct!

George Fox was imprisoned nine times for his 'seditious ideas' and for not taking the oath; the longest term was three years and he was incarcerated in total for up to seven years, though in some Correction Houses, jails and prisons there was some measure of freedom; where people could come and visit him and meetings were held. Once he was placed in the dungeons amongst a foot of excrement and all those imprisoned had to pay the jailer for their food and accommodation! Quakers would not swear an oath in court, not even to state that property stolen was theirs, but their yea (yes) was yea and their nay (no) was nay.

George Fox's first imprisonment was in 1649 after he rebuked a minister in Derby, England, whilst he was preaching and was arrested for 'brawling in church!' These propagation tactics of denouncing falsehood and proclaiming truth within a church were the standard 'tactics' for several years until Quakerism became very well known across England, spreading from middle England, Lancaster and Yorkshire, and filtering north and south as itinerant preachers travelled. During these times it was common for the 'priest' to have to answer questions during the sermon. Though in later years, after the minister had spoken for one hour, (timed via an hour glass) the pulpit or floor of the church was generally free for anyone else to speak and often the 'priest' would flee from Fox's Scriptural arguments, much to the amusement of the parish. Sometimes Fox would preach inside a steeple-house, (sometimes by invite), but at other times he would decline and preach outside the doors, often in the graveyard or a nearby field.

In 1652, upon Pendle Hill in Lancashire, England, Fox saw a vision of a great ingathering of people, 'dressed in white raiments...coming to the Lord.' This vision of the Lune Valley and into Sedburgh, saw its fulfilment within a few weeks. Pendle Hill stands high above the surrounding area and on my visit in 2004, I could see for tens of miles, of fields upon fields reaching out in all directions. Maybe George Fox was reminded of the words of Jesus, "The fields are white unto harvest..." Anyhow, more than fifty thousand people were converted back to the pure faith in forty years; 'Bid ye tremble at the word of the Lord' was their watchword and some people used to tremble under Fox's rebukes to sinners, and those who had wronged him.

On 13 June 1652, George Fox was at Firbank Fell in Sedburgh. In the afternoon, as directed by the Lord he climbed onto a crag and waited upon the Lord for a few hours. This was within a stones throw of Sedburgh Chapel where a meeting had been held in the morning of which Fox was not a part of. More than one thousand people gathered to Fox and he preached the word of the Lord for more than three hours on what is now known as Fox's Pulpit. Fox declared of his preaching that notable day, "Directing all to the Spirit of God in themselves, that they might be turned from darkness to the light; and might be turned from the power of Satan, which they had been under, unto God; and by the Spirit of truth, be led in to all truth...that Christ might be their teacher to instruct them...and might know their bodies to be prepared, sanctified, and made fit temples for God and Christ to dwell in."

This event is widely known as the beginning of the Society for Friends, also known as Quakers, because within a short space of time, thousands were drawn into the fold of Christ, having been convinced of the truths that George Fox declared in the power of the Holy Spirit. Though in reality Fox had been preaching for nearly five years before this momentous event and Friends (that is followers of Fox's teaching) were first known in 1646. After 1652, some parish churches were virtually deserted as the people had become Quakers.

Sedburgh Chapel no longer exists; all remnants of quarried stone have been removed and in 2009 when I visited, only three gravestones remained amongst a walled patch of grass. However, a large bronze plaque, about 3ft x 1ft denotes George Fox's pulpit at Firbank Fell which is adjacent to the chapel plot and tells the story which is related from Fox's *Journal*. This plaque was put in situ in June 1952 on the four hundredth anniversary of this momentous occasion.

Quaker Principles and Practices

Quaker meetings were characterised by waiting upon the Lord in silence (even up to several hours) before someone spoke or gave a word, and sometimes the meetings were just silent, but not when Fox was there and God's presence was frequently manifested! It was quite common for Fox, after waiting on the Lord for an hour or two, to preach for three hours, so that many people were convinced of the truths he declared; surrendered to Christ and became Quakers.

George Fox was an advocate of education, better wages and welfare for the lower classes which he first propagated in 1648. Once George Fox disobeyed God and did not speak to a group of judges who were discussing the wages of servants, but decided to put if off until the next day. He woke up blind and only as he made his way to the judges was his sight restored! On another occasion he lost his sight for several weeks. Fox was also an advocate of prison reform and could speak from experience! He was a firm believer in equality for women that included women preachers and apostles. When he went to the West Indies and North America, he told slave owners to treat their slaves well, teach them Christian values and to grant them their freedom after thirty years of servitude! As time went on there was separate meetings for men and women within Quakerism and monthly, quarterly, half annually and annual meetings were set up.

Many Ranters and Seekers alongside other sects also became Quakers, though some people could not discern between Quakers and Ranters and so Fox wrote a pamphlet explaining what Friends believed. Initially, many Quakers lost trade and went hungry, as they broke the social norms of the day, no tipping of the hat, plain speech, plain clothes (no ribbons, cuffs or tassels) and being pacifists they were mistrusted. As time went on they were noted for their trusted work and it was common for people to request a weaver, cobbler or blacksmith etc. who was a Quaker. Some of the teaching of Fox can be misunderstood, which permitted much accusation of heresy and blasphemy alongside slander and seditious rumours to be levied against him and his followers, though his teaching as related via his *Journal* cannot be misunderstood. Not getting married inside church, but rather in the eyes of God, led many to believe that Quakers lived in sin. This was overcome by announcing a Quaker marriage / ceremony within a village to make it as public as possible, that there would be a union of two people for life and not merely a cohabitation.

George Fox was against compulsory sacraments, but especially sprinkling infants with water (christening / baptism) as it was then known. Both John Bunyan and Richard Baxter of Kiddeminister were against Quakerism, though the latter by his writings appears not to have known about Fox as he thought William Penn (founder of Pennsylvania in America) was the leader, even though Fox was one of the best-known men in England. Quakers believed that baptism was not in accord with the mind of Christ. They believed that no outward form of baptism need be observed, but you cannot doubt the commitment of George Fox and his followers towards the work of evangelisation during Puritan England.

George Fox and His Gifts

George Fox was a powerful man of prayer and in one house during his prayer the building literally shook! Fox was also an intercessor and as you read his *Journal* you come across his times of identification (especially in regard to Quakers in prison), travail, groanings, periods of fasting and various obediences (not cutting his hair for a period of time is alluded to, Numbers 6), as he was led of the Spirit to do God's will and moved in the power of the Spirit.

George Fox moved in many spiritual gifts, including prophecy, gifts of miracles, healings and words of knowledge. He was fearless in his denunciation of sin, was led of the Spirit and cast out demons. Fox was a prophet of his day and even told Oliver Cromwell not to take the Crown when it was offered, because of its consequences. Cromwell heeded his prophetic utterance. Fox also spoke into many other situations and people's lives and saw God's judgment fall on those who persecuted him and his followers. Some Quakers spoke in tongues and once Fox was in a trance for fourteen days. He often fasted, though on occasions it was simply by not having money for bread! Fox's *Journal* informs us that Fox frequently rejected offers of money (hospitality and food – sometimes he was forbidden by the Holy Spirit), on occasions he gave it away; or spent it at inns on accommodation and food, jail fees, helping the poor, yet he never divulged where he got his income from.

George Fox wrote six works including his *Journal* and the *Book of Miracles* which documented over 150 recorded instances of healings or plain miracles. Fox provided money and the manuscript for it to be published after his death, but it got lost; though a modern account (1948), pieced together from his *Journal* and published under the same name is available.[6]

In New Jersey, America, in 1672, one man who was bucked from his horse was picked up dead with a broken neck. George Fox got hold of his head, propped him up against a tree and forced his rag-doll head back into his socket and he came back to life, and within a few days had recovered! On another occasion, a woman who had crawled on her hands and knees for fourteen years was healed.

George Fox wrote more than 340 pamphlets, epistles and many letters, mostly whilst in prison. On one occasion, he had a woman scribe who was good at shorthand, then a secretary, and later a man whom he dictated too.

George Fox, as a prophet, mystic, seer and revivalists was very influential and had no fear of man and many notable people such as judges were convinced of the truths he freely proclaimed. Even Oliver Cromwell, Lord Protector of England came under his influence as did his daughter who was a seeker, one who is searching for Truth.

Evangelistic Advancement 1653 and Persecution

George Fox corresponded with many notable people, including members of royalty in England, Germany and Poland, and went on to become hailed as the best-known man in England. Under Fox's preaching and his Valiant Sixty, also known as the First Publishers of Truth (60 plus apostles {many former 'priests'} of whom about 11 were women), who began to spread abroad in 1654; society was beginning to change. These were joined by many women preachers (single and married) and in 1658, George Fox summoned sixty women Friends to form a group to aid Quakers who were poor, sick or in prison, and to look after widows and orphans.

George Fox visited Scotland in 1657 (though he was told to leave within seven days), Wales and Ireland in 1658; America and the West Indies in 1671-1673; and Holland and parts of Germany in 1677, and in most places he found Friends (Quakers) who had gone before him. The first meeting of Friends in London took place in 1654 in the house of two brothers, Simon and Robert Dring and within twenty-five years (1654-1679), there were 10,000 Quakers in London! Miss Ann Downer, who married twice taking the surnames Greenwell and Whitehead, about the age of thirty, was the first Quaker woman to preach in London publicly. She was also George Fox's scribe and cook when he was incarcerated in Launceston Jail.

The initial large evangelistic propagation of Fox's teaching across the country began in 1653 and continued until 1657 and literally thousands of Quakers were imprisoned for their beliefs, especially for not taking the oath and for not removing their hats; though they did remove their hats for prayer. The first public flogging of a Quaker was Elizabeth Williams and Mary Fisher due to their preaching outside Sidney College at Cambridge, England, in around the year 1654.

Waves of greater 'stiffer' persecution came because of the Quaker Act of 1662 and the Conventicle Act of 1664 and 1670; the former made all nonconformist churches illegal. In 1660, on the ascension of King Charles II, seven hundred Quakers were granted their liberty at the request of Margaret Fell, whom George Fox later married. The years 1663-1664, were known as the Great Persecution for Quakers.

Most Baptist and Presbyterians abandoned their places of worship, and met secretly, but not Quakers. Between 1661 and 1689 about twelve thousand Quakers were imprisoned and more than three hundred were executed, or died in prison, as conditions were appalling. This figure does not include those who were killed by mobs and individual acts of violence.

In Bristol, England in 1682, as most of the adult Quakers (one hundred and fifteen) were in prison, Quaker meetings were held by their children! From 1650 to 1697, the aggregate number of Quakers imprisoned in England, Scotland, Ireland and New England was more than 23,000, with the total number of those who died in jail or were executed were three hundred and eighty-eight. In 1689, the Act of Toleration was passed, granting liberty of worship to all Protestants.

E. B. Emmot in *A Short History of Quakerism* wrote: 'There were between fifty and sixty thousand Quakers in England at the end of the first forty years of the Quaker Revival' – thus making them more numerous, than Presbyterians, Baptists, Roman Catholics and Independents combined! Quakers spread abroad, often fleeing to America from persecution and 'in proportion to the population they were even more numerous in America where they had founded two colonies, and where they included more than half the inhabitants in several other important districts.'

Henry Van Etten in *George Fox and the Quakers* stated that at the end of the seventeenth century...there were at least 50,000 Quakers in England and Ireland...[but] a hundred years after Fox's death [1791], there were only 20,000 Quakers in England' because persecution and emigration had taken its toll; as the Quaker zeal and enthusiasm waned.

In 1931, the *Church Times*, reviewing *Studies in English Puritanism* by C. E. Whiting noted: 'But the unfortunate Quakers deserves much sympathy, for their gentle persistence, in face of all trials, had a great deal to do with bringing into being religious liberty as we know today.'

Quaker Missions to other Countries

The Pilgrim Fathers left for the freedom of Holland in 1608, and then sailed to the New World in 1620. Over the next six decades, thousands sailed from England's shores to the 'relative freedom' of the New World. Yet four Quakers were hanged in Boston, New England, by the bigoted Puritan professors of religion from 1659-1661, who themselves had fled there for their own religious freedoms! Quakers were also barred from entering or landing at New England. Whilst the first woman Quaker minister, Elizabeth Hooton, part of the Valiant Sixty, was stripped to the waist by order of Governor John Endecott (also spelt Endicott) and the Council of Massachusetts and mercilessly flogged through three towns in succession.[7]

Barbados in the West Indies was a Quaker missionary base to the New World; a journey of just over 1,600 miles to the pan-handle of Florida of which Jamaica was just five hundred and thirty miles away; though it was not until 1868 that the first Quaker Mission organisation was formed. However, 1658 saw the first collection for Gospel Missions in the form of a free-will offering at the Yearly meeting at Scalehouse, Yorkshire, England, for those who were going to the New World.[8]

In 1656, Mary Fisher and Anne Austin were the first Quakers to arrive in the New World with an aim to promote the Quaker doctrine. They were arrested aboard their ship, their books were publicly burnt and they were imprisoned for five weeks before being sent back to Barbados. Two years later, Mary Fisher, a Quaker, was led of the Lord to travel to Turkey to speak to the Sultan of Turkey, Mahomet IV and thus to proclaim the Gospel to him and that his religion (Islam) was false to which he agreed!"[9]

In 1652, William Caton (1636-1665) first heard George Fox preach at Swarthmoor Hall and was converted, aged just seventeen. In either 1652/3 and within a year, he began to preach in England. He soon travelled to Calais, France, the Netherlands (1656, 1659 and 1660), where he married and lived. In 1661, alongside William Ames, they went to Germany, where they spoke to a Prince at Heidelberg because of the suffering Friends within his dominion due to their conscientious objection to paying tithes. When William Caton next visited Heidelberg, he met his old preaching companion, John Stubbs, who with another Friend was on their homeward journey from Egypt![10]

Katherine Evans and Sarah Cheevers sailed from London, England to Leghorn, Italy in 1658 (Livorno is an Italian port city, traditionally known in English as Leghorn), where they preached the Gospel and distributed various books. From there they took passage to Alexandria, Egypt, but the captain put in at Malta. For three months, they were free in proclaiming the Gospel inside the English Consul where they stayed. Though frequently they were examined by the Inquisitors, who eventually arrested them through the combined affects of flattery, bribery and threats. For nearly four years they suffered terribly under Roman Catholic rule during the Inquisition until Friends in England; Gilbert Lately, Daniel Baker and George Fox had petitioned various people of high rank whilst Lord D'Aubigny, a Roman Catholic priest, mediated for their release.[11]

George Fox went to Barbados and America from 1671-1673. In his *Journal* there are at least half a dozen references to Fox holding meetings with American Indians, including various 'emperors and kings' of the Indians (chiefs), who seemed very attentive to his message. He went with a small mission team, who split up to cover the various colonies of America such as Carolina, Maryland, Virginia and as far north as Rhode Island.[12]

The colony of Pennsylvania 'The Holy Experiment' 1682-1756, was founded by William Penn, a Quaker statesman, but the years 1700-1740 was known as the Golden Age with Philadelphia being the cultural centre of the world. Whilst the land, north of Maryland was given to Penn by King Charles II of England, to pay off a £16,000 debt, Penn sent his cousin to negotiate with the Red Indians and a treaty was signed. As Voltaire noted some forty years later: 'It is the only treaty between those nations and the Christians that was never sworn to and has never been broken.... They loved these newcomers as much as they hated the other Christians who were conquering and destroying America.'[13]

George Fox wrote to many world leaders, including Kings and Queens of Europe and even to the Emperor of China, though the letter was never delivered; and Quakers did not arrive in China until more than two centuries later in 1886. The Friends Foreign Mission Association (FFMA) had been founded two decades earlier in 1866; the year in which the first Quaker missionary sailed to India, followed by a Quaker missionary to Madagascar the following year, Syria in 1869 and to Ceylon (Sri Lanka) in 1896. Thus these five fields of Quaker missionary labourer were known as the Five Mission Fields.[14]

Other Quaker Revivalists

Many of the early Quakers, both men and women were powerful ministers and a good number of them saw revival during their time of ministry, such as: William Caton (1636-1665), who when just twenty years old; would preach to 'multitudes'; Anne Audland, a revivalists in her own right. Her husband, John Audland (1630-1664), alongside John Camm preached to 'nearly four thousands persons' in a field near Bristol in England. Charles Marshall who saw 'thousands converted' and 'abundant blessings' who visited every county in England; Edward Burrough (1634-1662), 'a son of thunder and consolation' who was 'filled with power by the Spirit of the Lord' and Stephen Crisp (1628-1692), who spent six months in London in 1673 'to the rejoicing of thousands' and also preached in Holland and Germany. Other revivalists were: John Banks (1637-1710), where in Ireland the jailer thought the whole town would become Quakers; James Dickenson (1659-1741); Thomas Wilson who was reverently dubbed by one gentleman in London, England, as 'Jeremiah the Prophet.' William Edmundson (1627-1712), who saw revival in Barbados, with African slaves becoming Christians; George Whitehead (1636-1722), who ministered for sixty-eight years and William Bennet of Norfolk who was 'carried forth in meetings in more than ordinary manner, and was a blessed instrument to many, in turning them to God.'[15]

Final Two Decades

After 1666, and three years in prison, George Fox began to organise the Quakers into a denominational church, setting up various meetings, rules and ordinances. His wife, Margaret Fell, a widow, ten years his senior, greatly assisted him. She was formerly married to Judge Fell and they married in 1669; she had three grown daughters and a son. Because of Fox's imprisonments, sometimes in open-air prison, where wind, rain and snow would land on his bed, his body was greatly weakened and in his latter years, even sitting on a horse was a struggle and he had pains in his head and teeth, as well as swollen limbs.

In 1671, George Fox travelled to North America with many Friends and the West Indies where he visited most of the plantations, whilst his wife stayed in England. On his return, two years later; he was imprisoned for the last time in 1673, which brought his aged mother to the grave. Fox refused a pardon from the King of England as he was innocent!

In June 1675, George Fox went to Swarthmoor (his wife's home since the time of Judge Fell) and for the first time in thirty-two years, he was able to settle in a place called home! Fox also visited Holland and parts of Germany in 1677 and made a brief second visit to Holland in 1684. The remainder of his years were spent in and around London, England. He died in London on 13 January 1691 and more than four thousand (though some authors say more than two thousand) attended his funeral service at a Quaker burial ground near Bunhill Fields, London.[16]

George Fox's original tombstone gave the year of his death as 1690, because under the Julian Calendar, the old styled calendar, New Year's Day was on 25 March; but in 1752, Britain and America changed to the Gregorian calendar, the solar calendar, bringing us into line with the rest of Europe, thus Fox's death was in 1691, if you use the present Gregorian calendar. George Fox's headstone was replaced, sometime after WWII and reads: George Fox - Born - 7th Mo 1624 - Died 13th of the 11th Mo 1690 - Aged 66 Years. Please note that Mo = month. Whilst George Fox was the founder of Quakerism, his headstone does not denote this as within Quakerism there were no leaders and all Quaker headstones are plain and simple.

Wilfred Monroe in the preface to the French Edition of Fox's *Journal* (1935), wrote: 'It is amazing to discover what daily heroism was involved by Fox's simple, Christian attitude in matters of conduct. With the sweetness of an angel he endured the long torture of insults, slander, threats, blows, wounds, fever, hunger and cold, sickness and infirmity, being imprisoned again and again in gaols that were smoky, wet, alive with vermin or stinking with excrement. He could have adopted other tactics as he was no weakling; his powers of endurance showed that he was unusually strong, his voice could ring out above a roaring mob, and the keenness of his glance worried his adversaries and would even make them 'quake'; but he would have no other weapon than the Spirit of his Saviour, no other shield than prayer, no other banner than the cross. What supernatural capacities in the soul that is born again!'

George Whitehead (1636-1722) began preaching when just sixteen years old and became a Quaker minister at age eighteen in the year 1654. He faithfully preached the word of God, turning many to righteousness till his death in 1722 at age 87. He was the last of the early Friends; the Valiant Sixty, who had laboured near the beginning of George Fox's ministry. Whitehead lived under no less than eight sovereigns and was imprisoned nine times; which does not include his scourging till blood ran down his body or the fines he endured. John H. Barlow wrote: 'His death removed the last of that band of young earnest believers who had so valiantly spread the truth in the early days of the Society of Friends, and with him died the intense zeal that had done so much to build up the Society. For a time the Society was stationary or dwindling, but a revival of spiritual life and power was given.'[17]

It is sad to relay the fact that Quakers have so far drifted from their original mooring of Christian faith as revealed in Holy Scripture, justified by faith in Jesus Christ and enlightened by the Spirit of God; they are no longer considered a Christian sect. You can call yourself a Quaker and a Buddhist or a Quaker and a Muslim, and those of other religions can become Quakers whilst retaining their own faith in false gods and false ways! As I wrote in another book: 'Quaker, a Christian sect which used to be Christian!'

Jesus said, "A little while longer the Light is with you. Walk while you have the Light, lest darkness overtake you; he who walks in darkness does not know where he is going. While you have the Light, believe in the Light, that you may become sons of light" (John 12:35-36).

Chapter 7

A New Day Dawns

'Lord who may abide in Your tabernacle? Who may dwell in Your holy hill? He who walks uprightly and works righteousness, and speaks the truth in his heart; he who does not backbite with his tongue, nor does evil to his neighbour, nor does he take up a reproach against his friend' (Psalm 15:1-3).

Moravian Revival 1727 – Prussia

Count Nikolaus Ludwig von Zinzendorf was born in Dresden (in present-day Germany) on 26 May 1700 and grew up in a Prussian pietistic family. Pietism was a movement for the revival of piety in the Lutheran Church. Count Zinzendorf's passion was, "To live for the One who had given His life for him, and to lead others to Jesus."

The Moravians were originally from Bohemia, the native Czechs who had a Reformation in the late fourteenth century under various Bohemian preachers and in the early fifteenth century under John Huss. They were also influenced by the writings of John Wycliff of England and had suffered persecution in Bohemia and Moravia for their Christian beliefs for two centuries until they decided to move.

The revival of 1727 'was preceded and followed by most extraordinary praying,' so wrote Moravian evangelist, Rev. John Greenfield in 1927. 'The spirit of grace and supplication manifested itself in the early part of the year.' Count Zinzendorf gave spiritual instruction to a class of girls and teenagers, ranging in age from ten to thirteen. They behaved well, but Zinzendorf could not perceive any spiritual life in them, which disturbed him and brought him to his knees. A historian of that period recalls, 'In this distress of his mind he took his refuge to the Lord in prayer, most fervently entreating Him to grant to these children His grace and blessing.'[1]

In June 1722, when Count Zinzendorf was just twenty-two years old, displaced persecuted Moravian Christians (under the leadership of Christian David) began to gather on his estate, a mile outside of Berthelsdorf, Saxony, at a place called Hutberg or Watch-Hill which would later become known as Herrnhut. As the years passed, word got out that Herrnhut was a Protestant refuge and all sorts of malcontents arrived pushing their particular pet doctrines and ideas, soon there were six hundred people. After 1724, the community found it hard to live together in peace, especially when the outwardly godly, yet inwardly religious crank Krüger turned up and denounced the Lutheran Church. He called Zinzendorf "The Beast" and John Andrew Rothe (the pastor of the local church), "The False Prophet;" and even Christian David came under his spell and was led astray for a time. Up until 1727, Zinzendorf got on with his own life but he then began to try to settle the differences amongst his community. He was ordained a Lutheran minister in 1727 whilst Krüger eventually went out of his mind and was committed to an asylum in Berlin. On 12 May 1727, the community resolved to bury their disputes forever after Count Zinzendorf summoned them to the Great House on the Hutberg and taught them for three hours of the sin of schism, and stated some community rules for the benefit of all. The different followers of John Huss, Martin Luther, John Calvin, Ulrich Zwingle and Casper Schwenckfeld etc. resolved to settle their differences and gave of themselves afresh to God. Count Zinzendorf, from this time onward lived in the Herrnhut community to help teach the brethren. Soon after this meeting twelve elders were appointed as overseers of Herrnhut.

A. Bost in *History of the Moravians* wrote: 'From that time on [when the community resolved to put away their differences] there was a wonderful effusion of the Spirit on this happy church, until August the 13th when the measure of Divine grace seemed absolutely overflowing.' It was at this time that little groups of Christians, two or three persons 'met together privately, to converse on their spiritual state, to exhort, and reprove, and pray for each other.' Count Zinzendorf visited these groups which were later called 'bands.'

On 16 July 1727, Count Zinzendorf 'poured forth his soul in heart affecting prayer,' so noted a contemporary historian, 'accompanied with a flood of tears; this prayer produced such an extraordinary effect, and was the beginning of the subsequent operation of the life-giving and energetic Spirit of God.'[2]

On 22 July 1727, some brethren agreed to meet at a regular time on a hill near Herrnhut 'in order to pour out their souls to God in prayer and singing.' On this same day, Count Zinzendorf set out for Silesia, a neighbouring estate, but before his departure 'several of the brethren engaged to devote themselves to the advancement of the revival.' The first epistle of John was read and there was great blessing.

On 5 August 1727, Count Zinzendorf 'spent the whole night in watching [prayer] in company of about twelve or fourteen brethren. At midnight there was held on the Hutberg a large meeting for the purpose of prayer, at which great emotion prevailed.'

At about noon on 10 August 1727, 'while Pastor Rothe was holding the meeting at Herrnhut, he felt himself overwhelmed by a wonderful and irresistible power of the Lord and sank down in the dust before God, and with him sank down the whole assembled congregation, in an ecstasy of feeling. In this frame of mind they continued till midnight, engaged in praying and singing, weeping and supplication.'[3]

A communion service was held on the 13 August 1727 at the Bertholdsdorf's church; the whole community united as one, amidst tears and sobs they sung, 'My soul before Thee prostrates lies.' Within a few days 'a remarkable revival took place amongst the children at Herrnhut and Bertholdsdorf. On 18 August 1727, all the children of the boarding school were seized with an extraordinary impulse of the Spirit, and passed the whole night in prayer.' The work amongst the children carried on for some time.[4]

Between the 25 and 27 August 1727, the community began a 24 hour prayer meeting which lasted for one hundred years! It was based on the fact that in the temple, the fire on the altar was to perpetually burn, and that as the Church is now the temple of God, Christians ought to ascend prayers continually. These twenty-four intercessors who took an hour slot each, soon increased to seventy-seven, and even children designed a similar plan to pray amongst themselves! The intercessors met once a week, where they were told 'to consider special subjects for prayer and remembrance before the Lord.'

Count Zinzendorf, looking back on the four months of revival during the summer of 1727 said, "The whole place represented a visible tabernacle of God amongst men." Zinzendorf held meetings every day and the church at Berthelsdorf was crowded out.

Jonathan Goforth quotes Bishop Hasse who wrote: 'Was there ever in the whole of church history such an astonishing prayer meeting as that which, beginning in 1727 went on one hundred years? It is something absolutely unique. It was known as the 'Hourly Intercession,' and it meant that by relays of [24] brethren and [24] sisters, prayer without ceasing was made to God for all the works and wants of His Church. Prayer of that kind always leads to action. In this case it kindled a burning desire to make Christ's salvation known to the heathen. It led to the beginning of modern foreign missions. From that one small village community more than one hundred missionaries went out in twenty-five years....'

Moravian Missions

In January 1728, the Herrnhut church held their first missionary meeting. They studied different portions of Holy Scripture, participated in fervent prayer; 'in the midst of which the church experienced a remarkable enjoyment of the presence of the Spirit.' The Moravian Missions began in 1731; work was commenced in the West Indies in 1732. David Nitschmann, an elder had accompanied Count Zinzendorf to Denmark for the coronation of King Christian VI, where they met a converted slave of African origins called Anthony. He had a Danish master from St. Thomas Island, and told them that the West Indies needed saving. David Nitschmann and Leonard Dober were willing to sell themselves into slavery to reach the African slaves! This was because the West Indian Company's ships refused them board, which was eventually paid for by the Danish Royal family; they arrived at St. Thomas in December 1732.[5]

In 1733, two brothers, Matthew and Christian Stack followed in the footsteps of Han Egde of Norway to become missionaries to Greenland and were accompanied by Christian David to see them settled in their mission field. Han Egde had arrived with his family in the summer of 1721. This was seventy-one years before the Baptist Missionary Society was founded under William Carey and his associates! In 1733, small-pox killed between 2,000 to 3,000 Greenlanders and Egde's wife died. By 1736, Egde's had seen no fruit and by invitation of the King of Norway he returned home and used his remaining years to drum-up support for Greenland and others would see the souls that he laboured for. He died in 1758 and the mission which Egde had begun was eventually handed over to the Moravians. By the end of the nineteenth century the Greenlanders along the West coast 'had generally accepted Christianity.'[6]

German historian of Protestant Missions, Dr. Warneck wrote: 'This small church [at Herrhnut] in twenty years called into being more missions than the whole Evangelical Church had done in two centuries.' By 1757, Moravian missionaries were ministering in nearly every country in Europe and they went into Asia, South Africa, Australia and North and South America.[7]

Jesus said, "Go into all the world and preach the Gospel to every creature" (Mark 16:15). And, "Go therefore and make disciples of all the nations, baptising them in the name of the Father and of the Son and of the Holy Spirit" (Matthew 28:19).

Quotes and Citations from Count Zinzendorf's Sermons

- I am destined by the Lord to proclaim the message of the death and blood of Jesus, not with human wisdom, but with Divine power, unmindful of consequences to myself.[8]
- Christians are God's people, begotten by His Spirit, obedient to Him, enkindled by His fire; His blood is their glory.
- It is not enough to rely upon God's grace in general; we must build upon the grace of God in the blood of Jesus.
- In every degree and phase of our spiritual life and growth and service, the blood of Jesus Christ is indispensable.

- The Spirit comes to us by the way of the blood for full salvation.
- Our preaching of the wounds and blood of Jesus may not produce many sudden conversions, but they will be thorough and lasting.
- The blood of Christ is not only the sovereign remedy for sin, it is also the chief nourishment of the Christian life.[9]

The two hundredth anniversary of the Moravian Revival passed in 1927, and we are closing in on the tercentenary. Relating to the quotes and citations from Count Zinzendorf, Moravian evangelist, Rev. John Greenfield in *Power From On High* (1927) wrote: 'This was also the Gospel which the young graduate of Jena University, Peter Böhler preached in England which resulted in the conversion of many Oxford students and professors as well as ordained clergymen of the churches of England and Scotland.'[10]

Peter Böhler greatly influenced and helped John (and Charles) Wesley in their search for eternal life when John returned from America, to London, England in February 1738. John Gambold was an Oxford graduate and a friend of the Wesleys. He joined himself with the Moravians and became its first English bishop. In England the Wesleys held joint services with the Moravians from 1737, but in July 1740 they parted company over doctrinal issues. The Moravians who no longer wanted to be associated with the Methodists published this in an English newspaper which did not go down too well amongst the Methodists.

In 1747 and 1749, England passed Acts of Parliament recognising the Moravian fraternity as an ancient Protestant Episcopal Church, and granted it civil and religious privileges at home and in British colonies.

John Cennick was the greatest preacher and evangelist the Moravians ever had; he was also the best-known Moravian hymn-writer. Count Zinzendorf called him, "Paul Revived." His friend and fellow revivalist, George Whitefield of England, said of him, "He was truly a great soul, one of those 'weak things,' which God hath chosen to confound the strong. Such a hardy worker with his hands and such a hearty preacher at the same time, I have scarce known. All call him a second [John] Bunyan."[11]

On 13 August 1754, Count Zinzendorf was in England, twenty-seven years to the day when revival broke out at the communion service, where he retold some of the events, "which has made this day a generation ago to be a festival [a day to remember]...."[12]

Jesus said, "Watch and pray, lest you enter into temptation. The spirit indeed is willing, but the flesh is weak" (Mark 14:38).

Chapter 8

Blessing in Unity

'Behold, how good and how pleasant it is for brethren to dwell together in unity! It is like the precious oil upon the head, running down on the beard, the beard of Aaron, running down on the edge of his garments. It is like the dew of Hermon, descending upon the mountains of Zion; for there the Lord commanded the blessing – life forevermore' (Psalm 133).

Northampton Revival 1734-1735 – New England, America

Rev. Jonathan Edwards saw revival which had its beginnings in December 1734, in his town of Northampton, Massachusetts, New England, America. Writing in 1736, Edwards noted that he was the third minister to be settled in the town of Northampton. Mr Ebenezer Mather was the first who was ordained in July 1669. 'He was one whose heart was much in the work, and abundant in labours for the good of precious souls. He had the high esteem and great love for his people, and was blessed with no small success.' After the death of Mr Mather, Rev. Jonathan Edwards' grandfather on his mother's side, the Rev. Mr. Stoddard became minister in November, but was not ordained until 11 September 1672; he died on 11 February 1728-9, [under the Julian Calendar, New Years Day was on 25 March; but in 1752, Britain and America changed to the Gregorian calendar], and therefore ministered in Northampton for nearly sixty years. Edwards wrote: 'And as he was eminent and renowned for his gifts and grace; so he was blessed, from the beginning, with extraordinary success in his ministry, in the conversion of many souls. He had five harvests, as he called them. The first was about the year 1679; the second was about 1683; the third 1696; the fourth about the year 1712; the fifth and last about 1718. Some of these times were much more remarkable than others, and the ingathering of souls more plentiful. Those that were about 1683, and 1696, and 1712, were much greater than either the first or the last: but in each of them, I have heard my grandfather say, the greater part of the young people in the town, seemed to be mainly concerned for their eternal salvation.'[1]

Rev. Jonathan Edwards began working alongside Rev. Stoddard in 1726. He wrote: 'Just after my grandfather's death [1729], it seemed to be a time of extraordinary dullness in religion. Licentiousness for some years prevailed among the youth of the town; there were many of them very much addicted to night-walking, and frequenting the tavern, and lewd practices, wherein some, by their example, exceedingly corrupted others. It was their manner very frequently to get together, in conventions of both sexes for mirth and jollity, which they called frolics; and they would often spend the greater part of the night in them, without regard to any order in the families they belonged to: and indeed family government did too much fail in the town. It was become very customary with many of our young people to be indecent in their carriage at meeting, which doubtless would not have prevailed in such a degree, had it not been that my grandfather, through his great age (though he retained his powers surprisingly to the last), was not so able to observe them.

'There had also long prevailed in the town a spirit of contention between two parties, into which they had for many years been divided; by which they maintained a jealousy one of the other, and were prepared to oppose one another in all public affairs. But in two or three years after Mr Stoddard's death, there began to be a sensible amendment to these evils. The young people showed more of a disposition to hearken to counsel, and by degrees left off their frolics; they grew observably more decent in their attendance on the public worship, and there were more who manifested a religious concern than there used to be.'[2]

At the latter end of 1733, the young people of Northampton became more flexible in 'yielding to advice.' Often on the morning after the Sabbath, the young people used to participate in times of 'mirth and company-keeping' which was designated as a general holy day until the evening. A sermon was preached addressing this issue and urging people to reform; with an emphasis on the head of each family to govern their families correctly in the fear of God, and to keep their children at home during this time.

Rev. Jonathan Edwards wrote: 'It was also more privately moved, that they should meet together the next day, in their several neighbourhoods, to know each other's minds; which was accordingly done, and the notion complied with throughout the town. But parents found little or no occasion for the exercise of government in the case. The young people declared themselves convinced by what they had heard from the pulpit, and were willing of themselves to comply with the counsel that had been given: and it was immediately, and, I suppose, almost universally, complied with; and there was a thorough reformation of these disorders thenceforward, which has continued ever since.'[3]

The death of several people in the town of Northampton affected many, especially in April 1734, when a young man became ill and died within two days; this was a shock to many. Then followed the death of a married woman 'who had been considerably exercised in mind, about the salvation of her soul, before she was ill, and was in great distress...but seemed to have satisfying evidence of God's saving mercy to her, before her death, so that she died very full of comfort, in a most earnest and moving manner, warning and counselling others.'

In the autumn of 1734, Rev. Jonathan Edwards proposed 'to the young people, that they should agree among themselves to spend the evenings after lectures in social religion.' They divided 'into several companies [groups] to meet in various parts of the town...and those meetings have been since continued, and the example imitated by elder people. This was followed with the death of an elderly person, which was attended with many unusual circumstances, by which many were much moved and affected.'

Rev. Jonathan Edwards continued: 'About this time many who looked on themselves as in a Christless condition, seemed to be awakened by it, with fear that God was about to withdraw from the land, and that we should be given up to heterodoxy and corrupt principles; and that then their opportunity for obtaining salvation would be past. Many who were brought a little to doubt about the truth of the doctrines they had hitherto been taught, seemed to have a kind of trembling fear with their doubts, lest they should be led into bypaths, to their eternal undoing; and they seemed, with much concern and engagedness of mind, to inquire what was indeed the way in which they must come to be accepted with God. There were some things said publicly on that occasion, concerning justification by faith alone.'[4]

These were the precursors of the revival which began in Northampton in 1734. It started when five or six people got wonderfully converted and a young lady started telling everyone about how she met the Saviour, who had given her a new heart; it had been truly broken and she was now truly sanctified. Rev. Jonathan Edwards said, "The spirit of those that have been in distress for the souls of others, so far as I can discern, seems not to be different from that of the apostles who travailed for souls."

On the evening of the day preceding the outbreak of revival, some Christians met and spent the whole night in prayer. The whole town was affected. Rev. Jonathan Edwards wrote: 'The work of conversion was carried on in a most astonishing manner, and increased more and more; souls did as it were come by flocks to Jesus Christ.' But Jonas Oramel Peck in *The Revival and the Pastor* (1894) noted that 'for years Dr. Edwards and his saintly wife had been besieging the throne of grace, praying day and night, "O Lord, revive Thy work!" [Habakkuk 3:2].'

Within six months around three hundred people were saved, including children, adults and the elderly. Later on, 620 people, amongst 220 families were entitled to take communion at Rev. Jonathan Edwards' church, including almost all the adults of the town. Some people came under such conviction that they were unable to sleep at night knowing the damnation that awaited them in Hell.

The work of God was so great that by the second year Rev. Jonathan Edwards wrote: 'The town seemed to be full of the presence of God; it was never so full of love, nor of joy, and yet so full of distress, as it was then. There were remarkable tokens of God's presence in almost every house.... The goings of God were seen in His sanctuary, God's day was a delight, and His tabernacles were amicable.' At the height of the revival at least four souls were saved each day, an average of thirty each week for five or six weeks during March and April 1735.[5]

A Narrative of Surprising Conversions by Jonathan Edwards (1736) is about the revival in Edwards' town of Northampton in Massachusetts, New England and is an eyewitness account, coupled with references to other revivals in nearby towns, all within 30 miles.

American Great Awakening 1735-1760

The American Great Awakening began in 1735, which was largely a continuation of Jonathan Edwards' ministry in Northampton, New England, though it affected many other congregations, towns and districts. It continued for about twenty-five years and was powerful in many of the American States (still under the British flag) on the east coast. The leaders were mainly Rev. Jonathan Edwards, the Tennents (three brothers, John, William and Gilbert), James Davenport, and George Whitefield (also spelt Whitfield), though there were many other ministers of the Gospel who were used by God during this time of Divine visitation. When Count Zinzendorf visited America in 1741, the Tennents wrote tracts opposing him, alongside some other preachers. Yet they were all ministers of God, preached the pure Gospel and all saw revival! This is what can happen when people put *their* non-essential doctrines before their devotion to God and the fellowship of unity in Christ.

From Northampton the revival spread to South Hadley, Suffield, Sunderland, Green River, West Springfield, Long Meadow, Enfield and Northfield. From these towns as the epicentre, it spread throughout New England and the Middle States. But J. Edwin Orr speaking in 1981, stated that the revival began about 1727 (eight years previous to the generally widely accepted date) in New Jersey, through the preaching of a Dutch Reformed minister named Frelinghuysen. It then spread to the Scotch-Irish Presbyterians under Tennent, then to the Baptists of Virginia and through

Jonathan Edwards to the Congregationalists of New England and the preaching of George Whitefield stirred the whole country.[6]

In 1858, William Conant wrote: 'It cannot be doubted that at least 50,000 souls were added to the churches of New England, (those who could prove a confession of faith) out of a population of 250,000. A fact sufficient, as indeed it did [to change], the religious and moral character, and to determine the destiny of the country. Not less than 150 new Congregational churches were established in twenty years. The increase of Baptist churches in the last half of the century was still more wonderful, rising from nine to upwards of four hundred in number, with a total of thirty thousand members.' There was similar growth in the Presbyterian and other churches.

In this revival many people were stirred to share the Good News with their neighbours, 'warning every man and exhorting them to turn to the Lord. There was a deep conviction of the evil of sin, and of peril of a rebellious state. The earnest appeals of those involved made the stout hearted tremble, awed many a reprobate into silence, and wrung tears from daring and hardened offenders...some of the most powerful preachers immigrated to other States and wherever they went, the floods of blessing poured over the land.'[7]

In 1743, in the midst of the American Great Awakening (1735-1760), Rev. Jonathan Edwards published the *Treatise Concerning the Religious Affections* as he identified a lot of froth without the fruit – stirred emotions, but not changed lives and it was this minority that brought the work of God into disrepute, as some people always focus on the negative. During the awakening, 'many...exaggerated the intensity of their emotions and the heat of their zeal. When others saw that their intense emotions came to nothing, they reacted and went from one extreme to another' and 'the error of discarding all religious affection as having nothing solid or substantial about them.'

Rev. Jonathan Edwards' *Religious Affections,* can be summarised as 'true faith is manifested by fruits of the repentant sinner's gratefulness to a merciful God.'[8] Edwards rightly noted that 'although the Scripture is full of rules, both how we should judge our own state and also how we should conduct ourselves before others, there are no rules by which to judge emotions.'[9]

Rev. Jonathan Edwards' *Treatise Concerning the Religious Affections* (1743), chapter two, concerns false signs of true religious affections. He noted: That enthusiasm can quickly end, just like the Israelites deliverance through the Red Sea, who habitually complained in the wilderness. People have been enlightened as in Hebrews 6:4-5, but are unacquainted with the better things that 'accompany salvation' (verse 9). A counterfeit love of which the apostle Paul alludes to in Ephesians 6:24, 'grace be with all those that love our Lord Jesus Christ in sincerity. Amen.'

Godly sorrow without a change of character, such as: Pharaoh and the ten plagues, "I have sinned," yet carried on defying God (Exodus 9:27). King Saul who wept before David whom he tried to kill at least three times (1 Samuel 24:16-17, 26:21). King Ahab humbled himself (1 Kings 21:27) but carried on in sin and the dogs licked up his blood (1 Kings 22:37-38). The children of Israel in the wilderness who tested God ten times and still doubted Him (Numbers 14, especially verse 22).

Rev. Jonathan Edwards and his congregation at Northampton in America were so fearful of losing the blessing of the Holy Spirit through division that they made a community resolution, a covenant which is dated 16 March 1742.

- In all our conversations, concerns and dealings with our neighbours we will be honest, just and upright.
- If we wrong others in any way, we will not rest until we have made restitution.
- We promise that we will not permit ourselves to indulge in any kind of backbiting.
- We will be careful not to do anything to others out of a spirit of revenge.
- When there is a difference of opinion concerning another's rights, we will not allow private interests to influence us.
- We will not tolerate the exercise of enmity or ill will or revenge in our hearts.
- If we find that we have a secret grudge against another we will not gratify it, but root it out.
- We will not allow over-familiarity in our talk with others, or anything that might stir up licentious behaviour.
- We resolve to examine ourselves on a regular basis, knowing that the heart is very deceitful.
- We will run with perseverance the race that is set before us, working out our salvation with fear and trembling.

Howell Harris (1714-1773), Wales

In 1735 there arose an Elijah of his day amongst the Welsh valleys and mountains, Howell Harris (the son of a farmer), began to traverse the country of Wales, UK; the year of his conversion. To his assistance came Daniel Rowland, 'the thunderer' as he was called.[10] If you go to Llangeitho, Cardiganshire, Wales, you can see a white stone statue of Rowland which in recent years has undergone restoration.

Howell Harris was a young praying man and was baptised in the Holy Spirit early on from his conversion and instantly began to do the work of an evangelist, telling his former companions of the saving work of grace. He went from house to house and then into other villages and multitudes came to Christ. As a lay preacher (he was four times refused ordination!), he preached for hours at a time, even six hours! Howell Harris was a good organiser and formed Societies where his converts met for fellowship. This led to the beginning of the Welsh Calvinistic Methodism; George Whitefield states that by 1739 there were thirty such Societies.[11]

Howell Harris met George Whitefield in 1739 and they preached together in their respective languages. Howell Harris visited John Wesley in Bristol, England, on 18 June of the same year. Initially, Harris had been quite reluctant to meet the father of Methodism due to the many evil reports that had been given to him, but said after hearing him preach, "As soon as I heard you preach, I quickly found what spirit you were of. And before you were done, I was so over powered with joy and love that I had much ado [trouble] to walk home."[12]

John Wesley visited Wales in October 1739, and in his *Journal* wrote: 'I preached in the morning at Newport...to the most insensible ill-behaved people I have ever seen in Wales. One ancient man, during a great part of the sermon, cursed and swore almost incessantly; and, towards the conclusion, took up a great stone, which he many times attempted to throw. But that he could not do.' Wesley continued, writing on another day: 'Most of the inhabitants are ripe for the Gospel, they are earnestly desirous of being instructed in it; and as utterly ignorant of it they are, as any Creek or Cherikee Indian. I do not mean they are ignorant of the name Christ. Many of them can both say the Lord's Prayer and the Belief, nay, and some all the Catechism; but take them out of the road of what they have learned by rote, and they know no more (nine in ten of those with whom I conversed) either of Gospel salvation, or of that faith whereby alone can we be saved, than Chicali or Tomo Chachi [Creek Native Americans whom John Wesley had met in Georgia]. Now what spirit is he of, who had rather these poor creatures should perish for lack of knowledge, than that they should be saved, even by exhortations of Howell Harris, or an itinerant preacher?'[13]

In 1752 Howell Harris turned his New House In Trevecca, North Wales, into a centre for revivalist activity. He later became associated with the Countess of Huntington, who after 1768 sent her own students for the ministry to Trevecca for training.[14]

Jesus said to His disciples, "The harvest truly is great, but the labourers are few; therefore pray the Lord of the harvest to send out labourers into His harvest" (Luke 10:2).

Chapter 9

The Birth of Methodism

'Lord who may abide in Your tabernacle? Who may dwell in Your holy hill? He who walks uprightly and works righteousness, and speaks the truth in his heart; he who does not backbite with his tongue, nor does evil to his neighbour, nor does he take up a reproach against his friend' (Psalm 15:1-3).

British Great Awakening 1739-1791

The British Great Awakening is also known as the Evangelical Revival, the Methodist Revival or the Wesleyan Revival. During this time a quarter of the population, approximately 1.25 million people were converted to the Lord Jesus Christ. Over a period of time, many places, villages and towns were completely transformed, so much so that the whole character of the nation was changed. Many historians believe that it was because of this move of God that Britain did not have a revolution, a blood-bath, such as the French Revolution of 1789.

Prior to the time of the Great Awakening in Great Britain, the nation was in a desperate state, and the Church was just as bad. As Edward Miller in his book, *John Wesley The Hero of the Second Reformation* (1906) wrote: 'When the Church fails in her mission, the whole of society becomes corrupt.'

Across Britain, before the Great Awakening, there was a rise in deism, a decline of Christian observances, a massive rise in gin consumption and other alcoholic beverages which led to poverty and abuses within families. Every sixth house in London was a grogshop (where spirits were sold, gin and rum etc.), and you could get drunk for a penny or dead drunk for two pence and straw would be provided in the cellar to aid recovery from your carouse. In 1714, two million gallons of spirits was distilled; by 1742, it was seven million gallons and by 1750, it was more than eleven million. Vast sways of the Church were corrupt and the historian Montesquieu, stated that only four or five members of Parliament were regular attendants at church. The population had doubled (just under five million) since the settlement of the Church under Queen Elizabeth I, towns and cities had expanded greatly, but no endeavour had been made for any adequate religious instruction for these great masses.

This was the land and age of highwaymen in the countryside, burglars in the cities, profanity, bear-baiting, bull-baiting, prizefighting, cock-fighting – the amusements of all classes were calculated to create a cruel disposition. It was the age of mobs and riots and the state of the criminal law was cruel in the extremes. There were no fewer than one hundred and sixty crimes for which a man, woman or child could be hanged! In the remote regions of England, such as Cornwall in the west, Yorkshire and Northumberland in the north, and especially in the midlands, Staffordshire, the manners were wild and savage, passing all conception and description.[1]

Parliamentary life was rotten through and through. Walpole, the great leader, laughed aloud at appeals to the loftier motives of action. There was a great and growing neglect of Sunday observance among the ruling elite. Cabinet dinners and even cabinet councils were constantly held on that day. Sunday concerts and card-parties were common. Drunkenness was almost universal, and the drunkards walked unashamed.

In the higher ranks the young "Bloods" (nobility) often banded themselves together and paraded the streets in search of victims for what they were pleased to call their wit. As the Scriptures declare: 'To do evil is like sport to a fool...' (Proverbs 10:23). Many a man, and many a woman died in their hands, in consequence of their ferocious treatment.[2]

In 1728, at Oxford University, Charles Wesley (a future hymn writer and preacher) was called a "Methodist" because of his methodical study habits. Charles founded the Holy Club, but it was his elder brother John who would quickly become its leader.

In October 1735, John and Charles Wesley sailed for the colony of Georgia, America, and settled in different areas. On the trip, the Wesley brothers were greatly impressed and influenced by the Moravians aboard. So much so that John Wesley began to learn German so that he could converse more freely with them. During a storm when it seemed likely that all would be lost at sea, the Moravian were singing praises to God, regardless of the elements and had joy in their souls.

In America, John and Charles Wesley, both ministers of the Anglican Church upset a lot of people with their strict and rigid forms of Christianity. Charles was sent back to England in August 1736, whilst John Wesley fled from Georgia, America, in December 1737, back to England. Neither of the Wesley brothers ever returned to America.

On the morning of Wednesday, 24 May 1738, at about 5am, John Wesley opened his Bible and read, "There are given unto us exceeding great and precious promises, even that ye should partakers of the divine nature" (2 Peter 1:4). In the afternoon John Wesley was asked to go to St. Paul's Church, London. He noted in his *Journal:* 'The anthem was, "Out of the deep have I called unto Thee, O Lord: Lord, hear my voice. Oh, let Thine ears consider well the voice of my complaint. If Thou, Lord, wilt be extreme to mark what is done amiss, O Lord, who may abide it? For there is mercy with Thee; therefore shalt Thou be feared. O Israel, trust in the Lord: for with the Lord there is mercy, and with Him is plenteous redemption. And He shall redeem Israel from all his sins" ' (Psalm 130). In the evening he went 'very unwillingly to a society in Aldersgate Street,' London. In his *Journal,* John Wesley wrote: '[Some]one was reading [Martin] Luther's preface to the Epistle to the Romans. About a quarter before nine, while he was describing the change which God works in the heart through faith in Christ, I felt my heart strangely warmed. I felt I did trust in Christ, Christ alone for salvation; and an assurance was given me that He had taken away my sins, even mine, and saved me from the law of sin and death."

The Methodist movement was born in the power of the Holy Spirit. Wesley in his *Journal* for 1 January 1739 wrote: 'Mr Hall, Kinchin, Ingham, Whitefield, Hutchins, and my brother Charles, were present at our love-feast in Fetter Lane [in London, England, at a Moravian Society], with about sixty of our brethren. About three in the morning, as we were continuing instant in prayer, the power of God came mightily upon us, insomuch that many cried out for exceeding joy, and many fell to the ground. As soon as we were recovered a little from that awe and amazement, at the presence of His Majesty, we broke out with one voice, "We praise thee, O God, we acknowledge thee to be the Lord."' Of this love feast George Whitefield said, "It was a Pentecostal season indeed, sometimes whole nights were spent in prayer. Often we have been filled as with new wine, and often I have seen them overwhelmed with the Divine Presence, and cry out, 'Will God, indeed, dwell with men on earth? How dreadful is this place! This is none other than the house of God, and the gate of Heaven!' "

The British Great Awakening began on 17 February 1739, when George Whitefield preached to the colliers at Kingswood near Bristol, England, in the open-air, as there was no church or school in this area. One author wrote: 'Here lived a godless, ferocious race, men living beyond the pale of religion or even the law...they were a people apart, a byword for vice and crime.'[3] Two hundred people attended. Whitefield wrote: 'I thought I might be doing the service of my Master.' The second time he preached there were two thousand! Thousands of people heard him and were deeply moved by his preaching. Soon ten or twenty thousand flocked to hear him. A gentleman lent him a large bowling green in the centre of Bristol, and for six weeks he preached to vast congregations. Whitefield encouraged John Wesley to take charge of the work in Bristol and Kingswood, whilst he visited other places. Wesley was preaching in London and finally relented and came to Bristol, even though he was preaching to hundreds in crowded churches and in the fields after service at St. Katherine's, Islington, and other places.

In London, John Wesley preached at Blackheath, in mid-June 1739 (George Whitefield was present) where twelve or fourteen thousand people had assembled. At 7am on a Sunday, John Wesley preached in Upper Moorefield, to six or seven thousand people, Charles Wesley says, "Above ten thousand as were supposed" and at 5pm to fifteen thousand at Kennington Common. The next Sunday Charles began field preaching, having been driven from his curacy at Islington, by the action of his churchwardens.[4]

George Whitefield crossed the Atlantic thirteen times, was a major player in the American Great Awakening and preached a total of 18,000 sermons in his lifetime. He travelled extensively around the British Isles and was involved in the Cambuslang Revival (1742) in Scotland, where 30,000 people turned up for a communion weekend in Rev. William McCulloch's parish of nine hundred! Wherever he went thousands gathered to hear the word of the Lord. He lived constantly with a clear realisation of the reality of eternity: of Heaven and Hell, and that the eternity of souls was in the balance. George Whitefield once said, "It is not for me to tell how often I use secret prayer; if I did not use it, nay, if in one sense, I did not pray without ceasing, it would be difficult for me to keep that frame of soul, which by Divine blessing, I daily enjoy."

John Wesley began preaching Methodism at Bristol, England, in April 1739, and the first Methodist Conference was held in 1744. Wesley was banned from many Church of England pulpits (after he had preached at least once in the parish) for his fiery sermons, preaching "justification by faith" and rode around the country preaching; revivals broke out everywhere. He rode annually between four and five thousand miles and would preach at 5am to crowds in excess of twenty thousand! In England, John Wesley established more than one hundred preaching circuits and enlisted three hundred ministers and thousands of local lay preachers were making Jesus known. John Wesley had three main bases, Bristol, London and Newcastle, and from these he pushed year after year, into remote and inaccessible corners of the kingdom, visiting the Channel Islands, crossing also into Ireland and penetrating far into Scotland. He also visited Holland twice.

Methodism took root in North America where ideas of political independence from Britain were to merge with ideas of religious independence from the Church of England.

John Wesley on his return from Georgia, America, in 1738 until his death in 1791, preached 42,400 sermons, which was an average of fifteen per week for fifty-three consecutive years. 'Cheaper, shorter, plainer books' was his motto and he kept up a constant supply of tracts, pamphlets and sermons. Wesley was probably the most widely read person of his day and felt it his duty after reading a book to make comment on it and the author. His final, often repeated sentence was, "The best of all is, God is with us – farewell."

By 1791, there were seventy-nine thousand Methodists in England; in America, fifty thousand. In the various English preaching circuits there were three hundred preachers. And as one man once said, "The world has yet to see what God can do with one man who is wholly consecrated to Him."

Other notable persons who were used in the awakening were: Lady Huntington, who was a financial backer for the spread of the Gospel; in Wales the main characters were Howell Harris, Daniel Rowland and Christmas Evans; in English parishes there were John Berridge, William Romaine, Roland Hill, William Grimshaw and Henry Venn whilst in Cornwall, England, there was Samuel Walker of Truro, and at Cambridge, England, Isaac Milner resided, and does not include social reformers, other notable ministers, laymen and hymn writers of the day.

A visual account of this revival can be found on the DVD *Great Christian Revivals* by ByFaith Media.

The Moravians in Britain
In 1728, Moravians came to Britain to tell of the revival that they were seeing in Herrnhut, whilst Count Zinzendorf wrote letters to Oxford University, the chaplain of King George I, the lady in waiting to the Queen, and to the Society for Promoting Christian Knowledge. In the spring of 1735, ten Moravian missionaries bound for Georgia, America, docked in London, England. These were the Moravians and their families that John and Charles Wesley met aboard ship and were greatly influenced by their Christian witness, and the lives of the Moravians that they met from 1735-1739. Peter Böhler was one of the Moravians who had good talks with John Wesley about his salvation over a few months and often challenged him, as well as Charles Wesley. They had their first meeting in London, England, on 7 February 1738, when they met at a Dutch merchant's house where Böhler was lodging. 'A day much to be remembered,' so wrote John Wesley in his *Journal*. John helped procure lodgings for Böhler and his two friends and set out with Böhler on 17 February for Oxford. On the following day John wrote: 'All this time I conversed much with Peter Böhler, but I understood him not; and least of all when he said, "My brother, my brother, that philosophy of

yours must be purged away." Böhler met both Charles and John Wesley on a number of occasions over the next two months. On 4 April, John Wesley wrote: 'Peter Böhler left London in order to embark for Carolina. Oh, what a work hath God begun since his coming into England! Such a one as shall never come to an end till Heaven and earth pass away.'

The most notable areas across Britain for the Moravians were Yorkshire and Wiltshire in north and south England, respectively, and in Ireland. A. Skevington Wood in *The Inextinguishable Blaze* wrote: 'It must not be supposed that the remainder of Britain was untouched. There was scarcely a county which did not feel the impact.' South Wales was missioned by John Gambold, a former member of the Holy Club in Oxford. John Caldwell reached as far as Lerwick in the Shetland Isles, Scotland. 'The south country is associated with the names of Heatley; Bedfordshire with Jacob Rogers and Francis Okely; Oxford with Abraham Louis Brandt; Northamptonshire with William Hunt, the Midlands with Ockerhausen, Brockshaw and Simpson, with Ockbrook as the centre; and Lancashire and Cheshire with David Taylor.'[5]

Theological Issues and Disputes

The main blight on the history of the British Great Awakening was the doctrines of 'Election' (Calvinism) as preached by George Whitefield, versus 'Free Grace' (Arminianism) as preached by John and Charles Wesley. This led to two camps being birthed within Methodism. The ironic thing is that these men of God were striving for the same goal, to preach Christ and to see men turn back to God, and regardless of their theology, God brought about revival wherever they went.

At the end of March 1741, John Wesley went to hear George Whitefield preach, having heard much of his unkind behaviour since his return from Georgia, New England, though this debate had been going on in private between them; Charles, the Moravians and their close associates for over a year. Wesley in his *Journal* wrote: 'He told me, he and I preach two different Gospels; and, therefore, he not only would not join with, or give me the right hand of fellowship, but was resolved to publicly preach against me and my brother, wheresoever he preached at all.'

George Whitefield then wrote a letter to John Wesley, which had been printed, without either party consenting and was distributed in great numbers. The Methodists foolishly decided to embrace one and denounce the other, so the Societies were divided. Whitefield then decided to print a letter that he had written in answer to Wesley's *Sermon on Free Grace*. Wesley in his *Journal* wrote: 'It was quite imprudent to publish it at all, being only the putting of weapons into their hands who loved neither the one nor the other.' Wesley also stated that if he wanted to write anything then he should not have called his name into question. Wesley continued, 'He has said enough of what wholly foreign to the question, to make an open (and probable, irreparable) breach between him and me; seeing "for a treacherous wound, and for the bewraying [betraying] of secrets, every friend will depart." ' Though they both met again in May 1742, when they were summoned before the Archbishop of Canterbury and the Bishop of London.[6]

In August 1743, John Wesley tried to arrange a conference, where he and his brother would be present along with George Whitefield and the Moravians. He was even prepared to make concessions for the sake of the peace; but as neither Whitefield nor the Moravians would take part in the conference, the whole matter fell through.[7]

Within a decade, their friendship had been healed. John Wesley in his *Journal,* on 28 January 1750 wrote: 'I read prayers, and Mr Whitefield preached. How wise is God in giving different talents to different preachers.'[8] George Whitefield died on 30 September 1770 in America. John Wesley was informed on 10 November and preached a memorial sermon in London on 18 November by the request of the executors of Whitefield's will.[9]

Physical Phenomena – Bodily Manifestations

Under the revivalists' preaching there were physical phenomena (bodily manifestations) as there have been in all revivals. Charles Wesley wrote: 'Many, no doubt, were, at our first preaching struck down, both soul and body, into the depth of distress. Their outward affections were to be easily imitated.'

Some of these manifestations were of the flesh (to which John Wesley rebuked), the majority were of God, when those under deep conviction of sin cried out, in screams and deep anguish of soul, some slumped to the ground, while others convulsed, shook, or trembled. Some of the manifestations were clearly demonic and the people concerned were delivered from the oppression of the Devil when they cried out to God.

The first occurrence of these physical phenomena was on 21 January 1739, when a well-dressed middle-aged woman cried out as in the agonies of death, which continued for some time. The doctors and clergy prior to this had thought she was mad, but the next day she told John Wesley that she had been under conviction of sin for three years but under Wesley's preaching had found hope.

Often in meetings, John Wesley would have to stop preaching because of the cries and groans of those under conviction of sin. Sometimes violent trembling seized its hearers and they sank to the ground. A Quaker who was greatly displeased at these sights dropped down in a moment. His agony was terrible to witness. Prayer was made and he soon cried out, "Now I know thou art a prophet of the Lord." Similar convulsions seized some of John Wesley's hearers in Newcastle and London.

A physician who suspected that fraud had much to do with these manifestations was present at a meeting in Bristol. One woman whom he knew broke out 'into strong cries and tears.' He stood close to her observing every symptom, till great drops of perspiration ran down her face, and all her bones shook. He was puzzled because he saw that this was neither fraud nor any natural disorder. But when both body and soul were healed in a moment the doctor acknowledged the finger of God.[10]

John Wesley noted in his *Journal* on 15 June 1739, that whilst he was preaching at a society at Wapping, and 'earnestly exhorting sinners to "enter into the holiest" by this "new and living way" [Hebrews 10:19], many of those that heard began to call upon God with strong cries and tears. Some sunk down, and there remained no strength in them; others exceedingly trembled and quaked; some were torn with a kind of convulsive motion in every part of their bodies, and that so violently, that often four or five persons could not hold one of them. I have seen many epileptic fits, but none of them were like these in many respect. I immediately prayed that God would not suffer those who were weak [in the faith] to be offended. But one woman was greatly offended; being sure they might help if they would – no one should persuade her to the contrary; and was got three or four yards, when she also dropped down in as violent agony as the rest. Twenty-six of those who had been thus affected (most of whom, during the prayers which were made for them, were in a moment filled with peace and joy), promised to call on me the next day. But only eighteen came; by talking closely with whom, I found reason to believe that some of them had gone home to their house justified.'[11]

John Wesley on 7 July 1739, had to talk to George Whitefield 'of those outward signs which had so often accompanied the inward work of God.' Wesley continued in his *Journal:* 'I found his objections were chiefly grounded on gross misrepresentations of matter of fact. But the next day he had opportunity of informing himself better: for no sooner had he begun (in the application of his sermon) to invite all sinners to believe in Christ, than four persons sunk down close to him, almost in the same moment. One of them lay without sense or motion. A second trembled exceedingly. The third had strong convulsions all over his body, but made no noise, unless by groans. The fourth equally convulsed, called upon God, with strong cries and tears. From this time on I trust, we shall all suffer God to carry on His work in the way that pleaseth Him.'[12]

Wesley records in his *Journal* many instances of people being tormented and delivered from demons. On one occasion in November 1739, Wesley preached at a Society in Bristol, England. Five people were severely tormented and were ordered to be removed to the door as their cries were drowning out the preaching and interrupting the attention of the congregation. After the sermon, Wesley and his companions prayed with them from evening till nine the next morning! Wesley wrote: 'Three of them sang praises to God; and the others were eased, though not set at liberty.'[13]

One lady who was about twenty, was being held down by three people, her face was deadly pale and into which was seen her anguish and horror. Wesley stated 'that it was a terrible sight...the thousand distortions of her whole body showed how the dogs of Hell were gnawing her heart. The shrieks intermixed were scarce to be endured. She screamed... "I am damned, damned; lost forever...I am the Devil's now. I have given myself to him. His I am. Him I must serve. With him I must go to Hell." She then began praying to the Devil.' Wesley stated that he and his companions prayed and called upon God, whilst another lady in the room began to roar out as loud as she could – demonically manifesting. Five hours later, 'God in a moment spoke peace into the soul, first of the tormented, and then of the other.'[14]

John Haydon, a weaver and a godly churchman regular in all his life and habits heard of these 'strange fits' and came to investigate. After the meeting he tried to persuade his friends that it was all a delusion of the wicked one. The day after the meeting he was at home reading a sermon, *Salvation by Faith* and as he read the last page, he changed colour, fell from his chair and began screaming terribly and beating himself against the ground. The neighbours flocked to see what was happening. Mrs Haydon tried to keep the people outside, but Mr Haydon said, "No; let them all come; let the world see the judgment of God." John Wesley was called for and saw Mr Haydon, on the floor being restrained by three men. Stretching out his hand John Haydon cried, "Ay this is he who, I said was a deceiver of the people. But God has overtaken me. I said it was all a delusion; but this is no delusion. He then roared out, "O thou Devil! Thou cursed Devil! Yea thou legions of devils! Thou canst stay. Christ will cast thee out. I know His work is begun." He then began to beat himself on the ground and perspired greatly as his chest heaved. Wesley and his friends prayed for him until he was set free.[15]

"The glory of this latter temple shall be greater than the former, says the Lord of Hosts. 'And in this place I will give peace,' says the Lord of Hosts" (Haggai 2:9).

Chapter 10

Re-Digging the Wells

'And Isaac dug again the wells of water which they had dug in the days of Abraham his father, for the Philistines had stopped them up after the death of Abraham. He called them by the names which his father had called them' (Genesis 26:18).

Bethelsdorp Revival 1813 – South Africa

In 1798, Theodosius Vander (also spelt Van der) Kemp of Holland, one of four early missionaries of the non-denominational London Missionary Society (LMS) set sail for ministry in Southern Africa and arrived the following year. In 1803, Kemp founded the Betheldorp Mission near Aloga Bay which is situated 10km inland from Port Elizabeth, which was founded in 1820. Within seven years of the commencement of the mission they saw a thousand Hottentots converts. Theodosius Vander Kemp passed into glory in 1811.[1]

Revival broke out at Betheldorp in 1813. Revival historian, J. Edwin Orr, sourcing from the Transactions of the London Missionary Society Volume IV wrote: 'In 1813 and 1814, awakenings were reported from many of the stations of the London Mission. Many Hottentots repented of their sins and turned to God at Bethelsdorp.... The movement was marked by strong conviction of sin and by tears and it arose through strong preaching.'[2]

In July 2008, I visited the Bethelsdorp Mission which the local authorities recognise as an important site of historical interest. The site stands at the centre of a hill which is now a residential suburb. To the north, are two large rolling hills that split like a small valley through which a nature reserve is now located. The first Bethelsdorp mud and reed church collapsed in 1809. On the site of the present cross shaped recently white washed Vander Kemp Memorial Church (rebuilt in 1902), once stood two or three other church buildings, so the present minister informed me, but was unsure whether the one standing was the third or fourth.

In the nature reserve is the botanical garden which Vander Kemp planted around two hundred years ago. The local council had recently tried to bring it back to its former glory, but by moving boundary stones and altering the layout of the garden, thus not keeping to the original plan, they have ruined it, so I was informed by a member of the council. The Betheldorp Mission (1803-1926) was taken over by the Congregationalist in 1926 and a row of five small alms houses, built in 1822 are still inhabited.

Student Revival 1816-1819 – Geneva, Switzerland

In 1816, Robert Haldane was strongly moved to visit the Continent of Europe. The journey was meant to take six weeks, but took three years! At the end of the year, he set out accompanied by his wife, both of whom longed to see Europe revived, where once much light had shone during the Reformation of the sixteenth century.

In Paris, France, Robert Haldane sensed a spiritual gloom that could be felt and after diligent search he could not find a single copy of the Scriptures. In vain he sought for an opening for the Gospel, but with none, he headed onto Geneva, Switzerland. As he passed through its ancient gates he fervently prayed for Divine leadings as he knew not one person within it. Robert was on the point of departure when an old pastor, due to sickness was unable to go with Robert on a short excursion beyond the walls and so in his place he sent a young student of Divinity. Robert, ever eager to share the Gospel did so, and the student returned to his lodging where they continued in discussion till late at night.

The city of Geneva had long since disregarded the faith of her fathers and a deep darkness shrouded the once 'Fount of Evangelical Truth.' Geneva's noble school of theology had long since lost is nobility and had rapidly declined since the days of John Calvin, the great Reformer of Geneva. It was corrupted by Unitarianism, thus denying Jesus Christ's deity and magnified the goodness of man. The Bible was entirely set aside as a textbook; Plato and Seneca taking the place of Christ and Paul. During the four-year theology course, the only time the Bible was used was for the teaching of Hebrew, when a few Psalms and chapters were read!

On the following day, the Divinity student appeared with a friend. So astonished were these two by what they had heard that they told their fellows. The students were intrigued by a man of one book, and this book the Bible, was indeed a great book, well worth the perusal of Divinity students! The students stated, "He knew the Bible like Calvin!" and was "a living concordance." They were amazed to find that the problems which had vexed them for so long were easily solved as Robert turned to various passages of Scripture.

Soon Robert Haldane was besieged with enquirers, so many students sought out his knowledge that he started his famous Home Bible College. About thirty attended, three times a week for two hours of evening Bible study. The home (and college) was located at 19 Promenade St. Antoine – a suite of apartments. The students were seated around a long table where copies of the Bible in French, German, English, Greek, Hebrew and other languages were placed.

The students fired off many questions, to which the Scriptures were turned to, he spent no time in argument, but pointed to the relevant text and said, "Look here – how readest thou? What thinketh thou?" Soon the students after having their concerns answered from the truth of God's Word were prepared for the essential truths of salvation.

Robert Haldane commenced a systematic study of the epistle to the Romans, where the students were told of man's depravity and their need for a Divine Saviour. Soon intellectual knowledge burst forth into deep spiritual concern. One by one they surrendered their lives to Jesus Christ – and this became known as the Student Revival, where the theological class, became a class of anxious enquirers. Robert knew that by winning one student of Divinity to Christ it could lead to a chain of grace that could affect thousands who would later come under their influence. Bitter persecution soon followed from professors and clergy alike as a living Church arose and this work of God became known as 'Geneva's Second Reformation.' No doubt, Robert Haldane and his students would have been inspired by many of the Reformation characters and because of the smallness of Geneva, which is like a bowl surrounded by mountains, their presence must have made quite an impact on the community.

When Robert Haldane left to preach the Gospel at Montauban, God sent another teacher to continue the work, Henry Drummond, a talented and wealthy Englishman, who was devoted to Jesus Christ. He was on a voyage to the Holy Land, when a storm compelled his ship to seek refuge in Genoa, Italy, about 280 miles from Geneva. Here he heard of the Student Revival, changed his plans and came to Geneva, arriving just two days before Robert's departure, the Lord's timing is always perfect!

The persecution eventually encouraged the students to scatter across Europe; many in time were to become in themselves famous for their work for the Lord. Just as Robert Haldane had foreseen as a spiritual strategist, they influenced thousands for Christ Jesus, as preachers, authors and missionaries across Europe and beyond.[3]

Two of these pupils were Madame Feller and Pastor Louis Roussy; they went to French Canada and began a work in a log cabin near St. John's, Quebec Province. They founded the Grande Ligne Mission and its school, the Feller Institute which was 'born in prayer, continued in prayer, and has grown by prayer.' As they began evangelising their province, the school grew. Roussy died in 1880, a dozen years after the saintly Madame Feller had passed into glory, and was succeeded by Rev. Alphonose de L. Therrin, a former Mission student whose ministry was marked by many blessed revivals.[4]

Twelveheads Revival c.1824 – Cornwall, England

In June 1794, William 'Billy' Bray was born in Twelveheads, in the parish of Kea, Cornwall, England, UK. The village is seven miles from the city of Truro, and at the end of the eighteenth century consisted of a few thatched cottages inhabited by tinners (those who worked in tin or mined it) and a humble Methodist Chapel, which had been built with the assistance of Billy's grandfather. Billy's 'pious father' as his biographer F. W. Bourne called him, died when he was young and with his brother, two sisters and mother, they moved in with their grandfather who had been converted under John Wesley when he first came to Cornwall in the 1740s.

In 1811, when Billy Bray was seventeen he moved to Devonshire and soon came under bad influences and often got drunk. As a drunkard, he got into fights, spent his wages on alcohol and on one occasion stole a hat and narrowly escaped being sent to jail. For a time, Billy lived in a beer shop which did not help his situation. His oaths and blaspheming were so foul 'and smelt of sulphur' that his companions, many of whom were fellow miners, thought they came from the very 'pit of Hell.' He was a natural liar and used to tell stories to amuse his companions and was full of wit and sarcasm. After seven years, Billy Bray the drunkard returned to his native county and in July 1821, he married Johanna, a backslidden Christian whom he affectionately called Joey.

It was not until November 1823, that Billy Bray had a strong desire to be a better man; he read John Bunyan's *Visions of Heaven and Hell,* and within a week, after seeking God in prayer was converted. Instantly he stopped drinking, though his pipe smoking was harder to give up and he soon came under conviction for compromising – by chewing tobacco, 'sqid' as it was known. He became a 'Bible Christian,' formerly known as 'Bryanites' (which was very similar to the Primitive Methodist Connection) and had many Quaker friends. Within a year in 1824, he was on the plan (list) of circuit preachers and on occasions walked twenty miles to preach!

Billy Bray was very obedient to the voice of the Lord, and at the age of twenty-nine, he began to fast once a week from Saturday evening to late Sunday afternoon. Billy was a man of prayer and great faith and saw some notable healings, including a man who could not speak for two years and two lame persons healed. As an itinerant preacher and former drunkard, he always mentioned teetotalism, honoured the Sabbath and condemned intoxicating drink, smoking, taking snuff and outward excesses, e.g. wearing: feathers, artificial flowers in the hair, ribbons and those who spent more time in 'oiling their cobs' or 'twirling their whiskers' (moustaches) than in prayer or reading of the Bible. Preachers were not above his rebukes, such as pipe smoking.

Billy Bray was a poor man, yet the 'son of the King;' a man of boundless joy. He would sing God's praises; shout "Glory" or "Hallelujah" and dance or skip anywhere; at church, in a stranger's house, round the dinner table, at a market or on the public highway. He was so full of joy that on many occasions he would pick up the preacher (or another) and carry him around the pulpit or church much to the amusement of the congregation! This happened to Rev. William Haslam in 1851, three months after he got converted under his own preaching which led to the Baldhu Church Revival (1851-1854). As Billy was a small man, he sometimes had to drag the preacher whilst shouting and jumping! Billy Bray is buried in Baldhu Churchyard which is less than two miles from Twelveheads and a monument has been erected in his memory after the success of his biography, and by public subscription.

Billy Bray built three chapels with his own hands, using his own wages and asking for subscriptions, praying in materials, whilst still working a three-shift rotation down the mines. He was always a poor man and often had to pray in his clothes and often gave away his last shilling to those who were worse off than himself. On one occasion, whilst he had four children he found two young abandoned siblings by the river and took them in and brought them up as his own. But it is reported that they may have been his brother's children; his biographer did not mention this as it would have brought shame on the family.

In around late 1824, one year after his conversion, Billy Bray worked on a level of the mine which filled with water every twelve hours which had to be drawn to the surface. One Sunday, he was at Hicks Mill Chapel, Bissoe, Truro, less than two miles from Twelveheads when it was his turn to draw up the water. The Lord spoke to him, "Stay here and worship Me this day." "I will Lord," was his reply in the firm belief that the water would find its way to the bottom of the shaft without any harm. On Monday, he arrived at the mine at 6am to sort the water out. Captain Hosken (the foreman) was very annoyed with Billy and told him that men in the mine had to work on Sunday. Billy point-blank refused and was sacked. But then the Captain relented and gave him the job of barrow and ash-heap (labourer) which left him free each evening and on Sundays.

At around the same time, in late 1824, there was a revival in the Twelveheads Chapel – Billy Bray's home village and his services were much in demand at this Methodist chapel. Billy, believing it was the Lord's will, left his barrow and the ash-heap and went to the chapel. He said, "I was much wanted for the old professors were very dead at the time; they would come into the chapel with their hats under their arms, and look very black at us. But the Lord was with us, and soon tore a hole in Satan's kingdom. We had, I think nearly a hundred converts in one week, the first week I ever worked all the time for the Lord in His house."

On the Friday of that blessed week, it was 'taking-on' day, as workers did not have contracts and were employed only when they were needed and told to go home when they were not. Captain Hosken then sent two men to get Billy Bray for the mine's services. He was paid £5 a month or more, whereas his last job only paid £2 per month! Billy said, "I did not lose by serving the Lord, but got £3 per month more than I got before; and did the will of the Lord which is better than all the money in the world."

Billy Bray was also used in the Cross Lanes Revival c.1830, the Baldhu Church Revival (1851-1854) when Billy began assisting Rev. William Haslam in 1852, the Crantock Revival c.1867, near Newquay, Cornwall, and saw at least five additional localised revivals.[5]

When Billy Bray's wife Johanna (Joey) was promoted to glory in 1864, somebody met him and said, "Well, William, I hear your wife's dead." But Billy replied in his thick Cornish accent, "Naw she edd'n; [no she aint] she's gone away to live! We shall never die, because Christ died for 's [us]. May Christ maaek us aol rech! [make us all rich]."[6]

Johanna (Joey) Bray is interred at Baldhu Church graveyard, although the exact location is not known. Baldhu Church is the former Church of St. Michael and All Angels, which at the time of my visit in August 2007 was being converted into residential accommodation. Billy Bray died in May 1868 and possibly lay beside his wife, or his casket was buried above her coffin – though the monument later erected to the memory of Billy Bray does not mention her.

In 1875, a letter appeared in *The Royal Cornwall Gazette* (17 April), written to the editor, complaining that Billy Bray had an unmarked grave, and asking, why had no monument been erected? Others who also wanted to honour Billy Bray shared the writer's sentiments. A monument was officially proposed in 1878 (the year of the 15th edition of *The King's Son*, F. W. Bourne's life of Billy Bray), and was built in 1880 from some of its profits and by subscription as a sign of gratitude of the Bible Christian Society, an offshoot of the Methodist denomination.

The large granite obelisk etched in capital letters reads: In memory of William better known as Billy Bray who died at Twelveheads May 25th 1878, aged seventy-three years. On the left hand side of the obelisk it reads: By his sanctified wit, Christian simplicity, fervid faith and many self-denying labours he commended himself to a wide circle of friends whilst living and the published record since his death of his memorial sayings and doings has made his name familiar as a household word in our own and other lands. On the right hand side of the obelisk it reads: He was a local preacher with the Bible Christians [for] forty-three years.

Blaenau Ffestiniog Revival 1830s – Wales

In the early 1830s, in a Welsh mining town in North Wales, UK; revival broke out which affected the slate mining community. At the time, Blaenau Ffestiniog was noted for its iniquity, cheating, gambling, blasphemy, prostitution and crime.

On the precincts of the town, about four miles away is a place called Ffestiniog, where at 6pm one Sunday evening, a visiting minister at the small local Methodist chapel asked if one of the members would like to open in prayer. A man rose to his feet, who for some time had been concerned about the community and exercised in his soul. He began to pray for the slate mining community that the Holy Spirit would sweep through the town and the usual opening prayer which would generally take about two minutes lasted twenty, as the Holy Spirit came upon the man in intercessory prayer. As he sat down, another rose to his feet and began to pray as the spirit of intercessory prayer came on the congregation, and then another and another – this continued for some time.

Nine hours later at 3am, it was decided that the prayer meeting should come to an end as many of those present had to start work at 6am in the slate quarries. They left the chapel and at a set of crossroads, they bid each other farewell and split into four distinct groups. They had only got about forty metres when they fell down on their knees and continued to pray in their four respective groups. After a short while, they decided to go back to the chapel and continue in prayer. By 5am some of the slate mining men, departed the prayer meeting and headed for work. As they entered the slate mining quarry their colleagues fell on their knees under deep conviction of sin, crying out to God for mercy. The Methodist's went amongst them and prayed them through into the Kingdom of God. Work was stopped and this scene continued for the entire day. The owners of the quarry also came under conviction of sin and it affected everyone in the community for about twenty or thirty miles in every direction.[7]

In June 2006, I visited Blaenau Ffestiniog and Ffestiniog, where, I saw what remains of the Methodist chapel, whilst St. Michael's Church gate was locked, with a notice stating 'locked due to vandalism.'

'For the earth shall be filled with the knowledge of the glory of the Lord, as the waters cover the sea' (Habakkuk 2:14).

Chapter 11

Days of Pentecost

'Unto You I lift up my eyes, O You who dwell in the Heavens. Behold, as the eyes of servants look to the hand of their masters, as the eyes of a maid to the hand of her mistress, so our eyes look to the Lord our God until He has mercy on us' (Psalm 123:1-2).

Revivals at Kilsyth 1839 and Dundee 1839-1841 – Scotland

During 1839-1840, revival was quite general across parts of Scotland under William Chalmer Burns, Andrew Bonar, Robert Murray McCheyne and Alexander Somerville. In 1843, revival also broke out in Collace when 400 ministers separated from the Established Church during the Disruption as they were opposed to the pretensions of the civil courts.

William C. Burns was born in April 1815; as an adult he: 'Prayed for hours daily as he began his public ministry at the age of twenty,' so wrote James A. Stewart, a twentieth century Scottish-born evangelist and revivalist. 'One morning, when his mother came to his bedroom to call him to breakfast, she found him lying on the floor where he had been detained by the Spirit all night in mighty pleadings. He greeted her with the words, "Mother, God has given me Scotland today!" In a short while the whole of Scotland was shaken by a mighty spiritual upheaval without any organised effort.'[1]

Rev. William C. Burns, a missionary in waiting, preached for a time in the church of Mr Robert Murray McCheyne, at St. Peter's, Dundee, Scotland. McCheyne was born on 21 May 1813 in Edinburgh, Scotland; it was the city where he went to university and he studied theology under Dr. Chalmers. He was licensed to preach by the Presbytery of Annan in 1835 and ordained at St. Peter's Church, Dundee, on 24 November 1836. In April 1837, McCheyne due to his strenuous workload had a breakdown, and developed heart trouble and so went to Edinburgh to recuperate. In late March 1839, he travelled to the Holy Land with Andrew Bonar to promote mission works amongst the Jews and their story is told in a *Mission Inquiry to the Jews* (1842).

Whilst away from his flock Rev. William C. Burns did not cease to pray for them in agony of soul and travail. It was one day whilst he was on the brink of eternity in Bouja [near İzmir in Turkey] that the great showers of blessing began to fall in Dundee, though they heard about the revival on their return journey when at Hamburg.[2]

Prior to the outpouring in Dundee, Rev. William C. Burns went to the communion at Kilsyth, a quiet country village, where on 23 July 1839, the Lord began to employ him in a way so remarkable for the awakening of sinners. As he preached in the marketplace a large assembly gathered, but as the rain came they entered the church which was soon filled to overflowing, even the porch was blocked with eager listeners. Solemn prayer was offered and Rev. Burns read from Acts chapter two, the Day of Pentecost and proceeded to preach from Psalm 110:3, 'Your people shall be willing in the day of Thy power.' As he spoke hearts were melted and tears began to flow. At the close of the meeting he retold the story of the Shotts Revival (1630); how John Livingston a native of Kilsyth, in preparation for an after-communion service, spent a whole night in prayer and that the following day five hundred people were converted after hearing him preach.

As Rev. William C. Burns was speaking he could see that the Spirit was moving and felt compelled to urge his hearers to accept Christ there and then and closed with the words, "No cross, no crown." Suddenly the whole audience broke down and cries of mercy went up before God. Some remained under conviction for days and the church was open daily for services for many months. In the marketplace and in the churchyard crowds of up to four thousand would gather to hear the word of the Lord. The whole town was changed as the vice of drinking took a fatal blow and loom shops became a place of prayer.[3]

On returning to Dundee, a large manufacturing town, amidst such a revival, Rev. William C. Burns decided to defer his missionary call, but not relinquish and to remain where he was, to fulfil the work which God was laying upon him with His mighty hand. On 10 August 1839, at a weekday prayer meeting, he spoke of the wonder that he had witnessed at Kilsyth and challenged those present to stay behind 'who felt the need of an outpouring of the Spirit to convert them.' About one hundred waited behind and the Spirit came as Rev. Burns spoke and the entire congregation was bathed in tears. This work of God carried on for four months, the church became packed night after night and the whole city was moved. A great spirit of reverence came upon the community and sin was greatly restrained.[4]

A member of St. Peter's wrote: 'Scarcely had Mr Burns entered the work at St. Peter's here, when his power as a preacher began to be felt. Gifted with solid and vigorous understanding, possessed of a voice of vast compass and power, and withal fired with an ardour so intense and an energy so exhaustless that nothing could damp or resist it. Mr Burns wielded an influence over the masses which was almost without parallel since the days of Wesley and Whitefield.

Crowds flocked to St. Peter's from all the country round; and the strength of the preacher seemed to grow with the incessant demands made upon it. He was frequently at Kilsyth, labouring in connection with a remarkable religious awakening which was going on there. The word of the Lord mightily grew and prevailed. Mr Burns was full of prayer; his preaching was sensible, clear, orthodox, unobjectionable; and in that he never altered, for in the midst of all the excitement there was never any eccentricity or extravagance. He never expected conversion by any means, but the plainly-stated Gospel, and the power of the Divine Spirit to accompany it.'[5]

Andrew Bonar in his *Memoirs* of Robert Murray McCheyne wrote: 'For some time before, Mr Burns had seen the symptoms of deeper attention than usual, and real anxiety in some that had hitherto been careless. But it was after his return that the people began to melt before the Lord.' McCheyne returned from the Holy Land in late November 1839, when Rev. William [C.] Burns' connection with St. Peter's ceased, but the revival continued until around 1841.

In Dundee the scenes at Kilsyth were repeated. Mr Bonar wrote: 'The crowded and deeply attentive assembled in the church from night to night, for months together; the eager throngs of enquirers, sometimes so numerous as to be really themselves a congregation; the varied and weighty instructions of ministers, followed generally by more special counsels and prayers for those whose overmastering anxiety constrained them to remain behind; the numberless prayer meetings [one author puts the prayer meetings at thirty-nine, which were held weekly in connection with the church, five of these were carried on wholly by children![6]] of old and young, in private rooms, in workshops, in retired gardens, in open fields; the nightly journey of thirsty souls from far distances in the outskirts of the city, and in the rural parishes around; the general sensation and spirit of inquiry were here as none who lived through it, and entered in any measure into the feeling of it can never have forgotten.'[7]

The church of Robert Murray McCheyne (from 1836-1843), St. Peter's Free Church in Perth road, Dundee, which first saw revival under W. C. Burns and then R. M. McCheyne during 1839-1841 was unused for a number of years and was returned to the Free Church in 1988. R. M. McCheyne was promoted to glory on 25 March 1843; he died from typhus fever after strenuous evangelists work.

In 1847, Rev. William C. Burns sailed for China as its first missionary under China Mission – the Presbyterian Church of England, residing first at Hong Kong. He ministered in 'the areas of Canton (Guangzhou), Amoy (Xiamen), Shanghai, Swatow (Shantou) and Foochow (Fuzhou) before any results became apparent.' Rev. Burns laboured patiently for seven years before he saw his first convert which was soon followed by the Peh-Chuia Awakening (c.1854); also spelt Pehchuia (Baichuan) in south Fukien (Fujian) which reminded him of the work at Kilsyth.[8]

In 1855 Rev. William C. Burns met J. Hudson Taylor and they worked together for some time in the interior of China, preaching where no-one had ever preached the Good News before. Taylor was influenced by Rev. Burns' prayer life, whilst Rev. Burns was influenced by Taylor's native Chinese dress and appearance with his hair died black, the traditional long pigtail and Chinese skullcap, so as to be able to better identify with the Chinese in the proclamation of the Good News. As a foreigner it was common to be called a "White Devil!" or a "Foreign Devil!" and native dress and look helped alleviate this. Rev. Burns also worked in Peking (Beijing) and Newchang (Yingkou) from where he was promoted to glory in April 1868 after a short illness.

J. Hudson Taylor said, "Man's extremities is God's opportunities." In China, a new convert asked Hudson, "How long have you had the Glad Tidings in England?" Ashamed Hudson vaguely replied that it was several hundred years. "What exclaimed Nyi in astonishment, "Several hundreds of years! Is it possible that you have known about Jesus so long, and only now have come to tell us! My father sought the truth for more than twenty years," he continued sadly "and died without finding it. Oh why did you not come sooner?"

In 1889, J. Hudson Taylor issued a pamphlet entitled: *To Every Creature*, part of which read: 'The Masters words are 'to every creature,' how far are we fulfilling them.... How are we going to treat the Lord Jesus Christ in reference to this command? Shall we definitely drop the title Lord as applied to Him?'

J. Hudson Taylor founded the China Inland Mission (CIM) in June 1865 and before his death in June 1905, he had opened up every Province in China, with one thousand CIM missionaries!

In 1965, during the Cultural Revolution, the Protestant Cemetery where J. Hudson Taylor and many other missionaries had been buried was ploughed up, and industrial units, like warehouses were later built on the site. In June 2011, I visited the Zhenjiang Museum, Jiangsu Province, which was part of the former British Consulate in search of Hudson Taylor's tombstone, but it was not located there. However, I was able to overlook the site of the former cemetery where the warehouses had been built, and backing up to the museum on the main road was a church, where we found the elusive tombstone. It was located in a specially built room adjacent to the church. The large ten feet tall tombstone, topped with a spire and cross had been smashed into seven pieces by the Communists and was lovingly put back together by local Christians. Whilst I was taking photos of the tombstone, a 'neighbour' who overlooked the courtyard was taking photos of me, presumably to pass on to the local authorities. Inside the church a senior member showed me around and after communicating via the Bible, she showed me Psalm 83:2-4, from her Chinese Bible. It translates into English as: 'For behold, Your enemies make a tumult; and those who hate You have lifted up their head. They have taken crafty counsel against Your people, and consulted together against Your sheltered ones. They have said, "Come, and let us cut them off from being a nation, that the name of Israel may be remembered no more." ' This was a real account of persecution against our brothers and sisters in Christ, who are also in desperate need of Bibles. There are not enough Bibles for every Christian to own their own copy. 'Remember the prisoners as if chained with them – those who are mistreated – since you yourselves are in the body also' (Hebrews 13:3).

Northern Provinces of Shantung c.1843 – China

In 1807, Dr. Robert Morrison of the London Missionary Society (LMS), though employed by the East India Company became the first Protestant missionary to China and was based at Canton. By September 1813, assisted by fellow missionary, William Milne (who had arrived in July 1813) they finished translating the Chinese New Testament. The following year, Dr. Morrison saw his first convert, Tsae-Ako (one of his early teachers) and possibly the first Chinese *Protestant* Christian in China. By November 1819, the entire Chinese Bible was completed. In the same year, a Chinese printer called Leang Afa, who acted as tutor, professed faith in Christ and after probation was baptised and received into church membership. Afa noted that 'neither Marsham's [of Serampore, India] nor Morrison's Bible is fully intelligible, much less attractive' because 'sufficient time has not elapsed to make the books accurate, intelligible and idiomatic.' He was the first native ordained to the work of the LMS and laboured as an evangelist in several parts of China. He suffered loss of property, scourging and imprisonments but stayed faithful to the end.

Dr. Robert Morrison was viewed by suspicion by the Roman Catholics on one hand and the Chinese officials on the other that by the end of 1827 he was entirely unable to preach or teach the Gospel to anybody, except the few Chinese workers who he employed. Thus he was compelled to reach them through the printing press which had been active since 1814.[9]

Mr Hu was born in a large city near the mouth of the Peiho River. His father was a merchant, who owned several seagoing junks (flat-bottomed sailing vessels). One day, aboard his father's junk which was heading in a southerly direction he was hijacked by pirates who robbed him of everything and cast him ashore at Shanghai. He got a job as teacher of northern Mandarin to the consular service; one of his pupils was *the son of Dr. Robert Morrison who (upon the death of his father in 1834) *became the Chinese secretary and interpreter to the British embassy at just nineteen.

One day as Mr Hu was wandering along the main streets of Shanghai, he was compelled by curiosity on seeing a foreigner speaking to a group of people, to enter the mission chapel, which as per custom had its doors swung open onto the street. He repeated his visit and obtained a Bible which he carefully read, and upon conversion united himself to the church in which he first heard the Good News.

Soon after Mr Hu's conversion he felt compelled to return to the neighbourhood of his early days and duly left the treaty port of Shanghai, carrying with him letters of recommendation to the missionaries in the town of which he was going. The agents at that time were praying for a native worker and Mr Hu was welcomed into their midst.

Mr Hu had an excellent voice and style of speaking, and was courageous. W. J. Townsend wrote: '...As he became familiar with the truths of the Gospel he proved himself to be a preacher of extraordinary power. Soon after his ordination to the work of the ministry [in around 1843] a very wonderful revival of religion broke out in a number of towns and villages in the northern part of the province of Shantung, and Mr Hu was sent to inspect and take charge of the work. He went and for about twelve years he laboured with untiring zeal, going round the districts as an evangelist, superintending the building of chapels, keeping the accounts of the various churches and fulfilling the duties of a pastor with extraordinary diligence and success.'[10]

This revival I believe is the first Protestant Revival in China, though 1832 is known as the year of the resurgence of modern Christianity in China.

Christians and Jews in China
Christianity first arrived in China in AD 635 during the Tang Dynasty (618-906) and is described on the Nestorian Stone which was inscribed in AD 781. This stone is also referred to as a tablet and as a stele. In 2011, I saw this large stone tablet at the Xian Beilin Museum, China, where there is a 'forest' of stele; a museum of some four thousand stone tablets, some of which are 12 feet high. The Nestorian Stone is about 7 feet high, rectangular in shape and is on a tortoise base which is from 2 ½ to 3 feet high; about 10 feet high in total. It was discovered in AD 1625 and moved from its location in 1907. On the top you can see a very clear carving of a cross. It documents how Nestorian Christians (Syriac Christians) came to China in AD 635 and the message was accepted by the

Emperor who encouraged its good teachings. The first Nestorian Church was built in AD 638.

Matteo (Matthew) Ricci (1552-1610) was one of the founding figures of the Jesuit China Mission. Ricci first went to Goa, India, as a missionary in 1578 and then on to Macau, a Portuguese colony in China, in 1582. Macau was ceded to Portugal in 1557 for their help in ridding the area of pirates. In 1584, Ricci drew the first European-style map of the world in Chinese. Together with Michele Ruggieri, they compiled a Portuguese-Chinese dictionary during 1583-1588. It was the first European-Chinese dictionary. The manuscript was misplaced in the Jesuit Archives in Rome, Italy and not re-discovered until 1934, and first published in 2001!

Matteo Ricci arrived in Beijing in September 1598 and was one of the first Westerners to master the Chinese language and script. He was the first Western person to enter the Forbidden City in 1601 and was made an advisor to the Imperial Court, though he never met the Emperor. The grave of Matteo Ricci and other missionaries – sixty-three tombstones in total are in what was once the Zhulan Cemetery, which is now in the grounds of the Beijing Administrative College at #6 Chegongzung Street. A sign says Ricci was buried in 1611, but he died in May 1610. The tall gravestones are inscribed in Italian and are what I consider in a remarkable state of preservation when I saw them in July 2011.

Matteo Ricci was the first Westerner to learn about the Kaifeng Jews in Henan Province, of which only a handful now survive. Jews first came to China as traders via the Silk Road which began in Xian, five hundred miles inland from eastern China. A member of the Jewish community, who visited Peking (Beijing) in 1605, contacted Ricci. Ricci never visited the community but in 1608 he sent a junior missionary there. The elderly Chief Rabbi of the Jews was ready to cede his power to Ricci, as long as he gave up eating pork, but Ricci never accepted the position.

At the Kaifeng Museum in north-eastern China, which is free to visit; you can request (and pay) to view three stele and one Lotus cup all Jewish related artefacts which are located in a private room. One of the stele was from the Zhao family, and the other two (which were back to back) were very badly damaged, and documents the Jewish history of the Jews in Kaifeng. From photos which I have seen in Victorian era books, the steles which were in situ, have greatly deteriorated over the past 140 years.

At Torah Lane in Kaifeng, at house #21 is a small Jewish Memorial Centre – a home of a young Jewish woman (Esther from the Zhao family) with her grandmother's home next door. She showed me around her grandmother's home and hers – just three rooms in total. Esther wants to rebuild the synagogue which is now the #4 hospital at the end of Torah Lane. It has a well in the boiler room which was part of the original synagogue, and is the only original feature denoting where the synagogue once stood. Esther had never seen the steles from the Kaifeng Museum, one of which used to be located outside her family's home. In 2008, a stone tablet was erected outside the hospital by Chinese officials, commemorating the Jews of Kaifeng. On the reverse side was the history of the Jews.

Westgate Chapel Revival 1832 – England

On 27 July 1761, John Wesley preached in Mapplewell, later known as Staincross, near Barnsley, Yorkshire, England. Some time later, Elizabeth Shaw of Staincross was crippled by an attack of rheumatism and had been bedridden for many months, but having "trusted in the Lord," as the Methodists called it, she was healed instantly and the entire neighbourhood heard of it! This was around the year 1775. The home of Joseph and Elizabeth Shaw was opened as a Methodist meeting place, where John Wesley himself was entertained. Across the UK there are hundreds of such homes, chapels, market crosses, fields, or just a tree, often with a plaque or a marker denoting that John Wesley stayed here, preached here, or on this site stood a home where John Wesley stayed etc.

James H. Taylor, a stonemason, the great grandfather of J. Hudson Taylor, founder of the China Inland Mission (CIM), was converted on the day of his wedding (to Betty) in February 1776, during the Evangelical Revival (1739-1791). The word of the Methodist preacher which he heard in his home town of Barnsley some time before, and from his next-door neighbours, the Shaws, was brought home under the power of the Holy Spirit and he put his faith in the death and resurrection of Jesus Christ – the finished work of Jesus Christ through His shed blood.

James and Betty Taylor, alongside five other people were part of the first ever Methodist class meeting in Barnsley, but it was not until 1791 that the Wesleyans of Barnsley began to build themselves a chapel. It was built on Pinfold Hill and was completed in 1794.[11]

James H. Taylor's grandson was James Taylor, a chemist who was engaged to Amelia Hudson, whose father was a Methodist preacher. They married in April 1831, thus uniting the two names of Hudson and Taylor. Their son, J. Hudson Taylor was born in May 1832 and it was he who founded the CIM in June 1865. Like the two preceding generations, John Taylor aligned himself with the Methodists and like his grandfather was a preacher on the Methodist Circuit.

James and Amelia Taylor lived in Market Place, Barnsley, and attended Westgate Chapel where a localised revival broke out on the Watch Night service on 31 December 1832. In the twentieth century, Dr. and Mrs Howard Taylor wrote: 'His [John Taylor's Methodist] class of forty or fifty lads felt the influence of her [Amelia's] sympathy and prayers only less than the girls who became her special care, and one of the joys of the early married life was an old-time revival in the chapel that resulted in the conversion of many of these young people.'

One of the converts in James Taylor's class was his cousin John Bashforth whose mother was a daughter of John and Betty Taylor. The Bashforths became one of the leading families in Barnsley. John Bashforth from this time forward lived a consistent life and was for many years Superintendent of the Sunday school.[12]

Yorkshire District Revival 1839 – England

James Taylor was a Chemist by trade who made it his duty to pay every debt on the day it fell due. "If I let it stand over a week," he would say, "I defraud my creditor of interest, if only a fractional sum." He never sued for the payment of a bill and did not think it desirable for Christians even to press for the payment of an account. He even went so far as to return payment, in whole or part that his customers could ill afford. James Taylor was so upright, honest and skilled in financial ability that his fellow-townsmen appointed him the manager of their building society, the Barnsley Permanent Building Society which he served for twenty-two years from 1853-1875. His own business was very successful and he retired in either 1864 or 1865.

James Taylor was an anointed Methodist preacher – his obituary in the Barnsley Chronicle noted: 'James Taylor was a most able and effective preacher. His manner was at once pleasant and dignified. His sermons bore much evidence of thought and much study and as a literary composition bore evidence of much thought and study.'[13]

The year 1839 was the Centenary Jubilee of the Evangelical Revival (1739-1791) and was celebrated on both sides of the Atlantic in a spirit, worthy of the memories it recalled. Methodists everywhere exceeded themselves in their liberal giving for world missions. Thank-offerings filled their treasuries, whilst worldwide prayers resulted in a great increase of spiritual blessing and notable advances were made in evangelistic labourers both at home and abroad. Dr. and Mrs Howard Taylor wrote: 'The quickening impulse of the great Centenary was being felt in that Yorkshire district and James Taylor's ministry was in power and blessing. Even his little son [seven year old J. Hudson Taylor, who would found the China Inland Mission] entered into the spirit of the time.'

J. Hudson Taylor's mother wrote: 'When about seven years of age, Hudson frequently accompanied his father into the country when he was going to preach. It was a time of religious revival and an after-meeting was usually held at the conclusion of the service to pray for blessing upon the word and for conversion of sinners. On such occasions persons deeply convinced of sin and desiring to obtain peace with God were invited to come forward to be prayed with and pointed to 'the Lamb of God that taketh away the sin of the world.' In these meetings his devout and prayerful earnestness were often remarked and when, as was frequently the case, burdened souls found comfort by resting on Jesus and His atonement and believers sang "Praise God, from whom all blessing flow," he would join as heartily as nay, while his face glowed with delight.'[14]

Pitt Street Chapel Revival 1849 – England

James and Betty Taylor were converted in 1776; alongside five other people they were part of the first ever Methodist class meeting in Barnsley, England. They met in a room at Eastgate but it was not until 1791 that the Wesleyans of Barnsley began to build themselves a chapel. It was built on Pinfold Hill and was completed in 1794.

In 1846, the congregation at Pinfold Hill migrated to larger premises on Pitt Street and in late November 1849, a mission was held for four nights and Mr Greenbury preached. Dr. and Mrs Howard Taylor wrote: '...[It] resulted in so real a revival of spiritual blessing that within a few days more than a hundred converts were gathered in.'

J. Hudson Taylor was seventeen at the time and had given his life to Christ in June 1849. He was present at those meetings in the last week of November 1849. In a letter to his sister he wrote: 'When Mr Greenbury was here, in only four nights the names of more than one hundred persons were taken who had found peace. I went to the prayer meeting on Wednesday night after shutting up shop [a chemist]. I sat in the free seats as there was no room elsewhere and asked several to go to the penitent form. One went. He told it afterwards in the class Susan attends and said he found peace. I was very thankful to hear it. It shows the necessity for doing all the good we can. I went again on the Thursday night, after eight o'clock and got a place on the pulpit stairs. There was no standing room in either pews or aisles. I took down the names of those who found the Lord. On Friday John and I were both there. I got six names and addresses. Mr Keeling told me to go inside the communion rail to talk to the inquirers better. Oh we had a gracious time of it!'[15]

'Who may ascend into the hill of the Lord? Or who may stand in His holy place? He who has clean hands and a pure heart, who has not lifted up his soul to an idol, nor sworn deceitfully. He shall receive blessing from the Lord and righteousness from the God of his salvation. This is Jacob, the generation of those who seek Him, who seek Your face' (Psalm 24:3-6).

Chapter 12

The Parson is Converted!

'Bow down Your Heavens, O Lord, and come down; touch the mountains and they shall smoke' (Psalm 144:5).

Baldhu Church Revival 1851-1854 – Cornwall, England

In 1831, Billy Bray was walking over the barren Baldhu Hill which was less than one mile from Twelveheads, his home village in Cornwall, England, when God spoke to him, "I will give thee all that dwell on this mountain." Immediately he fell down on his knees and thanked the Lord. He then ran to the nearest cottage where he led the inhabitants to the Lord. The same happened in all three cottages. He then told 'Father' in his thick Cornish accent, that there were only three 'housen' in that place and asked for more to be built in what neighbours considered an 'ungain' place and what Rev. William Haslam called a 'desolate spot.' This he prayed for sixteen years.

In 1846, Billy Bray, who had moved away from the area, received a letter from his brother James, informing him that the 'croft' on the hill was being hacked up to plant trees and that a Church of England church and school-room would be built. Billy was almost beside himself with joy. The potato crop had failed and the Earl of Falmouth who owned the land employed hundreds of his distressed tenants to break up the barren croft and plant trees. He also gave Rev. William Haslam (who was born in 1818 and ordained in 1843) a central site for his church which Rev. Haslam had designed himself. The Baldhu parish was created in 1847 from parts of Kea and Kenuyn parishes. On 1 January 1847, Baldhu was formed as an ecclesiastical parish out of the parishes of Kea and consisted of 3,000 people. Rev. Haslam began using a school-room as a church for a few months and then after only five days work, workers had enlarged the school-room for use as a temporary church, which could hold 300! The Baldhu Church foundation stone was laid in July 1847. It was known as the Church of St. Michael and All Angels.

In the summer of 1848, Billy Bray, who was then living near Bodmin, nearly thirty miles away, visited the Baldhu Church, which had been recently completed and consecrated to the glory of God. After the service, he came away disappointed because the parson, Rev. William Haslam was an unconverted High Churchman as were many of the Church of England ministers of his day. In the afternoon,

God told Billy that he had no business there at present and that he had come too soon *and* without His permission.

Rev. William Haslam was very religious and pious and genuinely believed that the way of salvation was through the Church in obedience to its rituals and sacraments. Each Sunday communion was held and every week he would visit every home in his parish, between twelve and twenty houses each day. He always left tracts, yet was still unregenerate and completely baffled by the meaning of 'conversion.' In time, he realised that evangelical tracts from the Religious Tract Society were more ardently read than those on sacramental topics and wondered why his daily services (except Sundays) were often only accompanied by himself.

Gradually people from his parish became converted, three of them through reading tracts which he had given them. Rev. Williams Haslam was not amused as he now thought that they were Dissenters and schismatics. As Rev. Haslam attended to his pastoral duties, different people used to talk to him about their own conversion which he found quite baffling and challenging. A real turning point came when his gardener, John Gill, 'a good Churchman' became ill with consumption. The Church's teaching could not console him in the face of death. He never asked Rev. Haslam to visit him, but instead, asked a converted man; he told him that he was a sinner and duly pointed him to Christ. This news spread throughout the parish, 'the parson's servant is converted' which brought great disappointment to Rev. Haslam! John Gill sent for him many times and eventually he relented. Rev. Haslam, was surprised at the joy of the face of the dying man, but 'disappointed and disgusted' as his 'favourite and most promising Churchman had failed.'

Robert Aitken of Pendeen, a fellow minister (who had already seen revival in his own parish in around 1850) and a friend of Rev. William Haslam greatly helped him see the light when he stayed at his manse for a few days. Also, James B, 'a good and holy man' had often spoken to Rev. Haslam about his soul and had been praying for at least three years for his conversion. Mr Aitken frankly told Rev. Haslam that he was not converted and said that he needed to distinguish between the work of his conscience and the work of the Spirit. Mr Aitken then took him to John 4:10-14 (the woman of Samaria at the well) and told him that he needed the living waters within himself. They prayed for this 'living water,' Robert Aitken rejoiced out loud, while Rev. Haslam broke down in tears. After he left, he bought a tract by Robert Aitken, which he saw in a shop window. He began to read it and came across the statement of Jesus, "Then He say unto them, depart from Me I never knew you," which greatly disturbed him as conviction lay hold of him. Three days passed and he resolved, under the advice from Robert Aitken never to preach again until he was converted.

On Sunday, 19 October 1851, Rev. William Haslam, 'was so ill' that he 'was quite unfit to take the service.' Before he knew it, the bells had been rung for service. His clerk took most of the service and then Rev. Haslam stood up and read Matthew 22:42, 'What think ye of Christ?' and then thought that he had better give a few words of explanation before dismissing the congregation. During his explanation of the passage, he realised that Jesus Christ had come to save him. He later wrote: 'I felt a wonderful light and joy come into my soul...' and was brought to saving faith in Christ Jesus, under his own preaching! A local preacher stood up, outstretched his arms and shouted, "The parson is converted! The parson is converted! Hallelujah." The congregation of three to four hundred went wild in jubilation and praised the Lord. Rev. Haslam wrote: 'Instead of rebuking this extraordinary "brawling," as I should have done in a former time, I joined in the outburst of praise; and to make it more orderly, I gave out the Doxology – "Praise God from whom all blessing flows" – and the people sang it with heart and voice, over and over again. My Churchmen were dismayed, and many of them fled precipitately from the place. Still the voice of praise went on, and was swelled by numbers of passers-by, who came into the church, greatly surprised to hear and see what was going on.

'When this subsided, I found at least twenty people crying for mercy, whose voices had not been heard in the excitement and noise of the thanksgiving. They all professed to find peace and joy in believing' and three were from Rev. Haslam's own household; this was the beginning of the Baldhu Church Revival (1851-1854). Billy Bray's prayers of twenty years were answered! The church for six hundred persons 'could not hold the crowds who came in the evening' to see the minister who was converted in his own pulpit under his own preaching! Rev. William Haslam plainly told them that if he had died last week he would have been lost forever and for many this was a wake-up call. From that moment on, Rev. Haslam began to preach the Gospel and did not shun to preach on the subject of Hell. He wrote: 'Gospel preaching...is to first awaken them to see their danger, and to bring them from death into life, which is manifestly the Lord's chief desire. This was the definite object of my work; I preached for and aimed at it; and nothing short of this could or would satisfy my longing. In the church, in the school-room, or in the cottages, we prayed that the Holy Spirit would bring conviction upon sinners, and then we sought to lead them to conversion with the clear ringing testimony, "You must be born again, or die to all eternity." '

The 1851 Census reveals that only 360 persons lived in the Baldhu parish whilst a decade later, the 1861 Census reported 2,070 persons and yet the church which only had seating for 600 was sometimes swelled to 1,500! So many people from far and near came to visit the church, but even more so when the local papers (and those in Plymouth, sixty miles away) reported of the work of God. These papers were sent to friends, some of whom lived in London, who in turn visited Baldhu Church.

Rev. William Haslam wrote: 'In the providence of God, my conversion was the beginning of a great revival in my parish, which continued without much interruption for nearly three years. At some periods during that time there was a greater power of the Divine presence, and consequently more manifest results, than at others; but all along there were conversions of sinners or restoration of backsliders every week – indeed, almost everyday!'

'During the revival, the outpouring of the Spirit of God was manifest and unmistakeable, and was seen in various ways.' 'Every week, almost every day, we heard of some remarkable dream or striking vision.'

On one occasion, Rev. William Haslam was rebuked by the Lord when a woman told him her dream – of the Devil preaching in the pulpit and being delighted in it. The day before, Rev. Haslam 'was getting a little impatient with the people' and taking a leaf from his Scripture-reader, 'preached a furious sermon about "damnation" representing God as pursuing the sinner to cut him down, if he did not repent there and then...' Rev. Haslam 'went home rather satisfied' and after hearing this old woman's dream, 'a sudden fear fell upon him' and returning to the church, he 'begged God's forgiveness, and thanked Him for His warning.'

There were many physical phenomena, bodily manifestations; people being 'stricken down' under the power of the Holy Spirit; cries for God's mercy, shrieking, weeping, tears, and much open repentance etc., whilst others shouted for joy and praised the Lord. Rev. William Haslam wrote: 'We could not help people being stricken down, neither could they help it themselves; often the most unlikely persons were overcome and became excited, and persons naturally quiet and retiring proved the most noisy and demonstrative. However, it was our joy to see permanent results afterwards, which more than reconciled us to any amount of inconvenience we had felt at the time.'

'In the school-room, evening by evening, the Lord wrought a great work, and showed forth His power in saving many souls. I have seldom read of any remarkable manifestations in revivals the counterpart of which I did not witness in that room; and I saw some things there which I have never heard of as taking place anywhere else.'

Rev. William Haslam knew that his clerk was unconverted and so one morning forbade him to partake of communion until he had given his heart to God. In the evening, 'the poor broken-hearted man sobbed and cried aloud for mercy;' and it was not long before he found peace with God.

One of the bell-ringers, called James was also unconverted and Rev. Haslam spoke to him and he resolved to give his heart to God. He knelt down and began to say, "Lord have mercy upon me!" "Lord have mercy upon me!" This he repeated with every returning breath and continued for two hours, working himself into a frenzy and then stopped in an exhausted state. Rev. Haslam pointed him to the cross and reminded him of what Jesus had done for him, though it appeared that he took no notice. After a little while he commenced praying as before and 'got into a terrible distress. What with the noise, and energy he put forth, it was frightful to see his struggle. He cried and beat the form till I thought his arms would be black and blue [bruised]; then he took the form [a long bench without a back / a back-less pew] and beat the floor with it, till I expected every moment it would come to pieces. The noise he made brought some of the neighbours out of their beds in a fright to see what was the matter.

'At two o'clock in the morning, four hours after he began, [James] laid himself across the form and begged with tears that the Lord would not cast him off. I told him that the Lord was actually waiting for him. At last he found peace...springing up, he began to shout and praise God; and we all joined with him.... From this time he became a changed man and steadfast believer.'

Many fellow clergymen criticised the work, whilst others embraced it and Rev. William Haslam was the means to pointing a good number of clergy to Christ! On many occasions Robert Aitken was invited to preach and other fellow clergymen who came to visit.

Rev. William Haslam concluded that Mr Aitken was 'the most effective' preacher that he had ever seen. When he came to Baldhu Church, 'as many as fifteen hundred packed into it. Not only were the wide passages crowded, and the chancel filled, even up to the communion table, but there were two rows of occupants in every pew. The great man was king over their souls, for at times he seemed as if he was endued with power whereby he could make them shout for joy, or howl for misery.... Souls were awakened by scores whenever he preached, and sometimes the meetings continued into the night, and occasionally even to daylight of the next morning.'

After each service, seekers were invited over to the school-room for personal or group counselling, depending on the numbers. At one time at the school-room at Baldhu there was a continual meeting without cessation for three days and three nights with people constantly coming and going!

'The first Christmas Day, during the revival [1851], was a wonderful time' as the people realised what Christmas was truly about. At the New Year's Eve service, those gathered dedicated themselves afresh to God's service. 'It was a blessed season, and several hundreds were there, who together with myself, were the fruits of the revival during the previous two months. The new year opened upon us with fresh manifestations of Divine power and large blessings.'

After the Christmas holidays, the Baldhu schoolmaster returned with his wife, but both were indignant and prejudiced about the work. They went from house to house speaking against Rev. William Haslam's preaching and the revival, though he still attended the services and took notes. In one of the after meetings in the school-room, Rev. Haslam found the schoolmaster on his knees, crying out, "Oh, I fear there is no mercy – the sentence is surely gone forth against me..." and then he 'howled aloud in his distress.' Others 'prayed for him with shouts of thanksgiving, while he threw himself about in agony of mind, and made a great noise, which only drew louder acclamations from the people. In the midst of this tremendous din he found peace, and rejoiced with the others in unmistakable accents, and as loud as the loudest.' The next Sunday, during the service the schoolmaster ran out of the church, leapt over a wall and then over a hedge, and ran into a field, shouting all the time – it was discovered afterwards that the *Prayer Book* (Thomas Cranmer's *Book of Common Prayer*) was now full of meaning!

'The schoolmaster became a very earnest Christian, and took much pains and interest in the religious instruction of the children [there was around one hundred pupils]. There were several revivals in the school while he was there, and many of the children were converted' as was his wife and her sister.

In January 1852, Rev. William Haslam was invited by Billy Bray to preach at Three Eyes Chapel at Kerley Downs, less than two miles from Baldhu Church, and saw revival. Afterwards, Billy Bray assisted Rev. Haslam at Baldhu Church, the Church of St. Michael and All Angels. Three Eyes Chapel c.1835, so named because of its three windows is the only surviving chapel built by Billy Bray and has been extended in size. It is now maintained as a Methodist memorial to Billy Bray and several services are held throughout the year. The chapel is unusual because the majority of the pews are on a gradient like an auditorium (part of the extension) so that the back pew, nearest the front door is the highest whilst the front rows are on level ground. Just four miles away is Gwennap Pit, which consisted of two halves of an "amphitheatre," a depression in the ground, where John Wesley preached on eighteen occasions from 1762 to 1789. In 1806 it was remodelled into a full amphitheatre with terraces for seating. Billy Bray preached there as have many other Methodists over the years. It adjoins Busveal Chapel (1836).

Rev. William Haslam wrote: 'Our friend Billy [Bray] remained with us at Baldhu, and was very useful. He spoke in the school-room with much acceptance and power in the simplicity of his faith, and souls were added to the Lord continually.'

In 1852, Rev. William Haslam inaugurated cottage meetings at the home of Frank, a former drunkard who was saved during the revival 'and became very zealous for Christ, and for many years preached the Gospel.' Soon the cottage was uncomfortably full, so a miller in the neighbourhood begged Rev. Haslam to come and preach in his home. He did, but found there was no power there and so reverted back to Frank's cottage 'and there again the manifest presence of God was discernable; and every time we did so, souls were saved.'

It was also in the summer of 1852 that Rev. William Haslam began open-air preaching outside of his own parish. Sometimes he preached outside of a church building, because it could not hold the crowds, but more often than not it was because the vicar would not permit him the use of it. Rev. Haslam, as he was often invited away for days or weeks at a time, saw revival in several places: Perran Beach Revival (1852), Mount Hawke Revival (1852), Veryan and Fish-Cellar Revival (1853), Golant Revival (1854) – all in Cornwall, and St. James Revival (1854) in Staffordshire, England. It was on Rev. Haslam's return to his church in mid November, after the Golant Revival (1854) that the Baldhu Church Revival (1851-1854) began to flag as there were no longer the ardent and eager attendances at the services and meetings.

Rev. William Haslam left Baldhu parish in the summer of 1855 for Plymouth. After a promised incumbency fell through when the Bishop went back on his word; he felt at liberty to preach wherever he was led and saw three revivals: G — Revival (1855), an unnamed location beginning with G in the North of England, Tregoney Revival (1855) in Cornwall, and the Hayle Revival (1860) in Cornwall, with his dear friend Robert Aitken.[1]

Rev. William Haslam was the clergyman in several additional parishes, on and off, though from 1878-1893 he continued his evangelistic ministry with the Church Parochial Mission Society. Rev. Haslam passed into glory on 26 January 1905 and is buried at Reigate Cemetery, Surrey, England.

'Sing praises to the Lord, who dwells in Zion! Declare His deeds among the people...He does not forget the cry of the humble' (Psalm 9:11-12).

Chapter 13

The Church Ablaze

'Out of Zion, the perfection of beauty, God will shine forth. Our God shall come...a fire shall devour before Him and it shall be very tempestuous all around Him' (Psalm 50:2-3).

Prayer Meeting Revival 1857-1860 – America

This revival is also known as the Fulton Street Revival or the Laymen's Revival, though at the time it was known as the Great Revival because is swept across America, igniting 'at least 2,000' revivals which were in 'active progress' at the time of William C. Conant's collation in 1858! Within the space of just over two years, one million people had become "born again" and another one million church members were set ablaze!

William Arthur on the last page of *The Tongue of Fire* (1856), wrote: 'And now, adorable Spirit, proceeding from the Father and the Son, descend upon all the Churches, renew the Pentecost in this our age, and baptise Thy people generally – O baptise them yet again with tongues of fire! Crown this nineteenth century with a revival of "pure and undefiled religion" greater than the last century, greater than that of the first, greater than any "demonstration of the Spirit" ever yet vouchsafed to men!'[1]

William C. Conant in his book, *Narrative of Remarkable Conversion and Revival Incidents* (1858), noted that on the first day of October 1856, the Holy Spirit began to 'especially manifest' at the Stanton Street Baptist Church, New York City; there was not a week when less than five or six persons presented themselves as inquirers to the Christian faith. During December 1856 to January 1857 'the interest increased' and by February, meetings were held every night. In March and April, sixty persons were baptised. During the summer there was a plateau and when 'the autumn and winter months came, the revival began anew, with increased fervour. In the space of eighteen months, about two hundred were baptised.'

The Prayer Meeting Movement in New York started when Mr Jeremiah C. Lanphier, a lay missionary was greatly burdened for souls. Most days he would be found in the lecture room of an old Dutch church on Fulton Street, New York City. He decided to invite others to join him in prayer and announced a weekly meeting to be held at noon, beginning on 23 September 1857. Lanphier distributed leaflets announcing the date, time and place of the prayer meeting, informing the reader that it was for workers during their lunch break who could spare, five or ten minutes or the full hour, to 'call upon God amid the perplexities incident to their respective vocations.' The leaflet asked: 'How Often Should we Pray?' The answer was: 'As often as the language of prayer is in my heart, as often as I see my need of help, as often as I feel the power of temptation, as often as I am made sensible of any spiritual declension or feel the aggression of a worldly spirit. In prayer we leave the business of time for that of eternity, and intercourse with men, for intercourse with God.'

The prayer meetings were to be informal, but Jeremiah Lanphier wisely wrote out a basic set of rules. These were later modified by different churches; for example at some prayer meetings you were not permitted to pray for more than three minutes, as opposed to Lanphier's five minute rule.

1. Be prompt. Commence precisely at 12 noon.

2. The leader of the meeting to open with the singing of 3-5 verses of a hymn, followed by a prayer and a Scripture reading, and the announcing that the meeting is open for prayer and exhortations.

3. Read one or two prayer requests at a time, requiring a prayer to follow with specific reference to the same.

4. If any person speaks out of turn, say simply that this is a prayer meeting and they are out of order and call someone to pray.

5. Give out the closing hymn five minutes before one o'clock.

6. Request the benediction from a clergyman if one is present.[2]

On the first public prayer meeting, after 30 minutes the first person turned up, followed by another and in total six people attended. The following week around twenty people arrived to pray and the numbers began to grow. In the second week of October, after the tenth, the prayer meeting was held daily.

The autumn of 1857 was signalised by a sudden and fearful convulsion in the commercial world, as sources of prosperity dried up. Thousands lost their jobs, masses of people tramped the streets with banners demanding bread. People started to attend the established prayer meetings, many searching for salvation, others killing time. The Fulton Street hall grew too small so the meeting was moved to the largest hall in the city with seating capacity for four thousand.

Other prayer meetings were birthed in New York, Philadelphia and beyond, and many businessmen and workers would take their lunch hour and go to these prayer meetings which lasted exactly an hour. In other places daily prayer meetings were held in the evenings. In New York, a hymn would be sung and then prayer began, along with prayer requests and testimony of answered prayer. No person was permitted to openly pray for more than five minutes, so that others present would have an opportunity. Prayer was for conversions, for their city, for help in honest dealing in business, for healing etc. Many merchants and businessmen got right with God and started to deal honestly, even debts of more than two decades old were repaid in full and those who had overcharged made restitution. One merchant within New York told the people that fifty thousand professed to be Christians within this city and the way to reach the one million residents was to take an individual or family under one's special supervision and to lead them to Christ.

Gordon Pettie in his book, *Do It Again Lord* (2017), wrote: 'The prayer meetings in themselves were not different to many thousand of prayer meetings that have been held around the world. But historians see four distinct characteristics of the prayer meetings of the [mid to late] 1850s.'

1. Spontaneity. With the exception of a patterned beginning, the meetings generally conducted themselves. Almost everyone participated.

2. Their interdenominational nature. Leaders came from every evangelical faith: Baptists, Brethren, Congregational, Episcopalians, Friends [Quakers], Lutheran, Methodist, Presbyterian and Reformed. Issues and items which distinguished them were not discussed.

3. Promptness. The meetings started promptly at noon and closed promptly at one. Pray-ers [those that prayed] were held accountable to the five minute rule.

4. Their focus on prayer. The agenda was prayer for salvation and for the Holy Spirit's empowerment. No business was conducted. The prayer groups prioritised prayer for the lost, for the presence of God and for the empowerment of the Holy Spirit.[3]

Even the crime rate during the winter of 1857-1858 dropped, and under the circumstances of mass unemployment it could have been expected to rise. The wealthy looked upon the under classes as their brothers and sisters in Christ, and their physical needs were met, but their spiritual needs were deemed more important.

On 20 March 1858, the editor of the *New York Times* wrote: 'The great waves of religious excitement which is sweeping over this nation, is one of the most remarkable movements since the Reformation.... This matter is an absorbing topic. Churches are crowded...converts are numbered by the scores of thousands... churches of all sects are open and crowded by day and night. It is most impressive to think that over this great land, tens and fifties of thousands of men and women are asking themselves at this time in a simple, serious way, the greatest question that can ever come before the human mind, "What shall we do to be saved from sin?" '[4]

In 1859, on the second anniversary of the first noon prayer meeting, a convention was assembled in Cooper Institute, New York City, to consider the means to sustain and enlarge the influence of the meetings. Representatives came from as far away as San Francisco. In Boston, a man stood up in one of the meetings and said, "I am from Omaha, Nebraska. On my journey east I have found a continuous prayer meeting. We call it about two thousand miles from Boston to Omaha, and here was a prayer meeting about two thousand miles in length."[5]

The New York dailies (newspapers) published several extras filled with accounts of the progress of the work in various parts of the land. Charles Finney stated of this revival that the winter of 1857-1858, will be remembered as a time when a great revival prevailed. It swept over the land with such power, that for a time it was estimated that no less than 50,000 conversions occurred weekly. The lay influence predominated to such an extent that ministers were overshadowed. This awakening was not a remote piety in little corners of churches, but to the fore of everyday business life, college life and home life. It was right there in the nitty-gritty of everyday work, not just a Sunday affair. The awakening became known as the Prayer Meeting Revival, as from its beginning it was marked far and wide with fervent prayer.

After long and careful research, revival historian, J. Edwin Orr endorsed the estimate that one million people were fully converted out of a population of less than thirty million in the period of 1858-1859. These converts were solid, lasting, genuine converts.[6]

During the revival that swept America, the *Methodist Advocate* for January 1858 reported ten noteworthy features of the revival:
1. Few sermons were preached.
2. Lay brethren were eager to witness.
3. Seekers flocked to the altar.
4. Nearly every seeker had been blessed.
5. Experiences enjoyed remained clear.
6. Converts were filled with holy boldness.
7. Religion became a day-time social topic.
8. Family altars were strengthened.
9. Testimonies given nightly were abundant.
10. Conversation was marked by a pervading seriousness.[7]

There is much information that is not known about the ministry of Jeremiah C. Lanphier from when the revival ended until his death in 1898. However he is buried at Green-Wood Cemetery, Brooklyn, Kings County (Brooklyn), New York, USA. The inscription on his large tombstone in capital letters is as follows:

Jeremiah Calvin Lanphier
Sept. 3, 1809 – Dec. 26, 1898
Missionary of the Reformed
Dutch Church in New York City
And founder of the Fulton St.
Noon Day Prayer Meeting
Jesus only
Lanphier

For the 150th anniversary of the Prayer Meeting Revival, in 2007, a life-size bronze statue of Jeremiah C. Lanphier sitting on a bench, 'Invitation to Pray' was unveiled outside of the American Bible Society, in New York City, America. In May 2015, the statue was relocated to King's campus on Broadway in lower Manhattan.

Worldwide Influence

In early October 1857, a revival broke out in Hamilton, Ontario, Canada, which is known as Canada West. It began when Holiness Methodist preachers, Dr. Walter C. Palmer and his wife, Phoebe, began holding evangelistic campaigns. The American revival affected different men across Great Britain to see the same blessing in their community. This led to revival in Wales, Ireland, Scotland and England as they prayed and believed for the revival blessing which in turn went around the world, touching many countries and people groups. resulting in a Great Awakening on a global scale.

In Chicago, America, D. L. Moody was greatly affected by the revival. He left his very successful shoe business and went into full-time Christian ministry. Over the next few decades, he went on to see phenomenal success on both sides of the Atlantic with his singing assistant, Ira Sankey. When Moody passed into glory in 1899, he left behind a legacy, his Bible Institute in Chicago, a girl's school in Northfield, a boy's school at Mount Hermon and an estimated one million souls won through his ministry!

The 1857 revival also launched a great American missionary movement, with missionaries going to India, China and Korea. Horace Underwood was a seminary student at the time. He went to Korea in 1885 (the year in which the Korean Church was founded) and was a key leader in the Pyongyang Great Revival (1907-1910).

In late 1859, revival broke out across India in what became known as the India Awakening, though the broadest work was seen in the South of India.

The year 1859 was the beginning of the evangelisation of Japan and Brazil. However, a colony of Protestants was founded in Rio in 1555, they saw their first native converts, though just a handful, in 1556. In 1841, David Livingstone en-route to Africa as a missionary met the first modern Protestant missionary to Brazil, an American Episcopal Methodist, whilst the ship docked in Rio de Janeiro.

In 1860, revival also broke out in Jamaica, in various towns and in areas across the Cape Colony of South Africa, (especially among the Dutch Reformed Church) and in Shanghai, China.

J. Hudson Taylor a newly qualified medical missionary arrived in China in March 1854. Six years later he was back in England on furlough in broken health. In June 1865 he founded the China Inland Mission (CIM) and in May the following year, aged just thirty-four, he sailed back to China as the mission leader of a group of twenty CIM missionaries and four children.

J. Hudson Taylor's son and daughter-in-law jointly chronicled his life and work of the CIM in two large volumes. They wrote: 'To understand aright the fruitfulness of this period it should be borne in mind that Mr Taylor, among others was reaping the aftermath of the great Revival of 1859. That wonderful awakening had not only swept thousands into the Church of Christ; it had prepared the way for a new order of things, an up-springing of individual faith and effort, characterised by love for souls and new resourcefulness in seeking their salvation. It was a day in new departures in the development of lay agency and a striking fulfilment might be seen in many directions of the prophecy of Joel: 'Also upon the servants and the handmaids in those days will I pour out my Spirit.'

'To mention a few only of the evangelical movements that had their beginnings in that formative time: Mrs Ranyard was pioneering a way for the work of Bible-women [those who teach women and sell Bibles] and Mrs Bayley for that of Mothers' Meetings; Miss Macpherson had just commenced Gospel services in Birds Fair, and the rescue of little waifs from the lowest slums of London; Miss Robarts, Mr (afterwards Sir George) Williams and others were laying the foundations of the Young Men's and Young Women's Christian Associations; Mrs Daniel and her helpers were developing work for soldiers, with their special needs; and Mr and Mrs Pennefather, at Mildmay, were launching out in the training of deaconesses for all manner of home missions. All these were making use of the consecrated energies of young converts in their first love, many of them comparatively 'unlearned and ignorant men,' but no opening had as yet been found for a similar employment of lay agency on the foreign field.'

'...Into this prepared soil the seed-thought of the China Inland Mission was providentially cast. It could not come at a better time. Christian hearts were kindled to fresh devotion, drawn together in a new sense of oneness, and awakened to the fact that God by His Holy Spirit was using a class of workers hitherto largely excluded from the spiritual ministries of the Church.'[8]

Revival in Wales 1858-1860

Rev. Humphrey R. Jones, a Wesleyan and Rev. Dafydd (David) Morgan, a Calvinistic Methodist, were the main instigators of this revival in Wales which began in October 1858, though the year 1859 is a prominent year. It was estimated that 300,000 people were saved and at least 50,000, who could prove a confession of faith became a member of an established church. By 1859, revival broke out in Ireland, which later spread to parts of Scotland and England, as the blessing of the manifold presence of the Holy Spirit came and convicted sinners of their need for the Saviour.

In 1858, William Jenkins was a minister in a church in one of the Welsh valleys. He wrote: 'Ever since the news of the outpouring of the Spirit upon the American churches [1857] reached our country I longed and prayed that the Lord would, in His infinite mercy, visit poor Wales. I immediately brought the subject before the church and earnestly exhorted them to 'seek the Lord.' I related every fact and incident I could glean...in order to produce in the minds of my people the desire for a similar visitation. Some of our members prayed and continued to pray as I have never heard them pray before. A new burden seemed to press upon their hearts. They became persistent almost to the point of being obsessed. Even before revival came there was no less than eighty-five added to the church in about six months.'[9]

Rev. Humphrey R. Jones had been touched by revival in America in 1858 and wanted to see the fire fall in Wales. As reports filtered through from America, many Welsh churches held a day of prayer for revival on the first Sunday in August 1858. Rev. Jones returned in September with glowing reports to tell. The two ministers, Humphrey R. Jones and Dafydd Morgan and their churches came together for prayer, to hold joint services and to arouse the country in prayer. Rev. Morgan received a remarkable endowment of power from on high and became the main leader (amongst many) and thousands were converted. As other churches heard these good reports, they sent for these men and revival broke out around the country and by August 1859, most of the chapels and churches in the southern counties of Wales were crowded everyday. Prayer meetings, morning and evening were held everywhere.[10]

Some of the young converts from a local church near Morlais Castle decided to invade the Devil's territory, where every Sunday men from the local ironworks used to congregate to get drunk and fight. As they made their intentions known to pray and praise, the intoxicated men jeered and laughed them to scorn. But the faithful believers knew who had the victory and began to sing a Welsh hymn, which was rich and melodious. The men were so overcome by the Spirit of God that tears rolled down many a hardened face and the beer was thrown away. Within one month hundreds were holding revival meetings on the highest summit of Morlais Castle.[11]

The Wesleyan Methodist Magazine in an article for January 1860 had the title: The revival in North Wales – Movement at Festiniog slate-quarries, Merionethshire. A correspondent of the *Record* says, 'The revival that attracts so much attention in different parts of the world has broken out in this neighbourhood within the last fortnight, and has quite convulsed the whole population. For some weeks previous a greater degree of solemnity was manifested throughout the community, all places of worship were unusually well attended, drunkenness and disorder were decidedly on the wane, and numbers were added weekly to the church.

'On Monday evening, October 10th [1859] , a prayer meeting was held at St. David's, the district church, at which many of the audience became very much excited, some breaking into lamentations, and others groaning audibly, and shedding tears profusely. And, strange to say, on the same evening, and at the same hour, similar scenes were witnessed at the different Dissenting chapels in the locality.

'On the following Tuesday, the workmen of several of the slate-quarries in the neighbourhood were observed to leave their work and congregate in small knots on the surrounding mountains. They gradually however, followed the main stream, converging from different directions towards the middle glen midway between the slate-works. There on the banks of a small lake several hundred men were assembled by eleven o'clock AM, and a prayer meeting was held on the spot, which lasted until five PM, the attendance continually increased until most of the works were deserted. The proceedings were entirely conducted by laymen, singing and praying alternately. The scene was quite affecting in the extreme, and few could restrain their tears; but there were not many cases of violent and uncontrolled agitation. Two young men were so far excited as to require the assistance of their friends to help them home. Both of them are young men of unimpeachable moral character, and have been religiously brought up.

'A similar prayer meeting was held on the same spot on the following day, and was conducted much in the same manner. No one in the assemblage could account for the strange attractions that brought them together. They felt some mysterious undefined feeling quite overcoming them, and absorbing all their thoughts, and left their work almost mechanically. There is less agitation and excitant [an active physiological or behavioural response] exhibited now than at first; but the deep undercurrent of religious feeling continues unabated and is rapidly radiating in all directions. Prayer meetings are still held every evening at St. David's Church, and also at

Dissenting places of worship; and it is but due to the Incumbent of the district, as well as to the Ministers of two other denominations, to mention that they endeavour, as far as in them lie, to turn the current feeling to the proper channels, and direct the people aright. It is not for the writer to make any comment upon the movement, but merely add that great improvement has taken place in the morality of the people and that all places of worship are crowded, when all join in prayer with greater fervency of spirit than was ever before witnessed in this place.'[12]

In October 1859, Thomas Jones gave a typical statement of the nature of the work accomplished during the Welsh Revival of 1859.

1. The additions to the churches amount to many thousands, far greater than has ever been known in Wales within the same period of time,

2. I have gathered from inquiry that not one person in every fifty of those who have assumed a profession of religion within the last four to six months, has relapsed into the world.

3. The people generally have been solemnised and brought to think of religious things. I asked an individual near Machynlleth whether the morals of the people had improved, he replied, "Oh, dear, yes, entirely," and then turned to his wife for a confirmation of his statement, "Yes," she said, "They are; every day is a Sunday now."

4. A missionary spirit has taken possession of the churches. There is no limit to their desire to save the whole world.

5. The ministers and preachers are anointed with fresh zeal, and are animated with a new spirit. The churches and their office-bearers are filled with ardour of their 'first love.'

6. There is a great increase of brotherly love amongst professing Christians, and more cordial co-operation amongst the various denominations in their efforts to do good, and to oppose the common enemy. These are undoubted facts; and I am sure they have not been produced by Satan; nor could they be effected by men without aid from above.[13]

The year 1909 was the Jubilee year of the 1859 Revival. J. J. Morgan, son of Rev. Dafydd (David) Morgan noted how it was celebrated in England in the summer and in winter in Wales. He wrote: 'The General Assembly of the Calvinistic Methodists, which met at Rhosllanerchrugog in June, instructed all the churches in the denomination to observe the first Sunday in November as a '59 Revival Commemoration Sunday.

'In 1859, it was the Irish Revival that attracted the attention of Christians in England. Thousands of them journeyed through North Wales, taking the Irish packet [ship] at Holyhead, that they might witness the power of the Holy Spirit in Ireland, little realising that they were steaming through towns and villages [on the trains] where a far intenser, and certainly a far more permanent, work of grace was in full swing.' Whilst J. J. Morgan confined his research within the boundaries of his Connexion, the Calvinistic Methodists, he noted: 'It is well known that the '59 movement was almost, if not quite as powerful among the Congregationalists. The Baptists and the Wesleyans also received large accession to their numbers at this time. There was an increase of 37,724 communicants to the C. M. [Calvinistic Methodists] denomination during the revival period. It may be safely accepted that the whole harvest of the revival in Wales did not fall far short of a hundred thousand souls. Neither were the results ephemeral.'[14]

On 9 May 2009, a 150th commemoration service of the 1859 Welsh Revival was held at Ysbyty Ystwyth village hall which was organised by Netta Rowlands, the great granddaughter of the 1859 revivalist, Rev. Dafydd (David) Morgan.

On 20 June 2009, there was a commemoration service, 'Redigging the Wells of Revival' in Siloam Chapel, Cwmystwyth. Dudley Griffiths wrote: 'In the afternoon we gathered in the vestry to worship, pray and to prepare for the evening service. After about an hour we made our way down to the older chapel where the local revivalist Dafydd Morgan [of the Welsh Revival of 1859] was converted in 1836. The ruin of that chapel, now without windows or roof, has been converted into a garden....' In the evening service which was mostly bilingual, in English and Welsh, the Aberystwyth Male Voice Choir participated whilst Rev. Meirion Morris preached from Joshua chapter four, on the memorial stones.[15]

The third commemoration service was held at Llanegitho, on 9 August 2009. Netta Rowlands wrote: 'The prayer gathering in Llanegitho was uplifting but as far as numbers went well that's another story! It was another one of those amazing coincidence days! The vestry must have been the school-room in the olden days and after hearing stories of the spiritual goings on in the village and praying we went down the road into the square and prayed upon the places and people there then we went to the parish church.... On the way we crossed over a beautiful stream and it reminded me of all the other Heavenly places there are in Wales, and we burst into song on the bridge as they did in the olden days. We shared communion in the middle of the field opposite the chapel, amazing prayers were spoken.... It was a really awesome feeling to be there where all those thousands had been all those years before.[16]

Revivals in Norway and Sweden 1858-1859

In 1858, Sweden saw 200,000 conversions as revival touched them for two years. In August 1860, *The Wesleyan Methodist*

Magazine recorded the revivals in Norway and Sweden, and the results from the previous year. Dr. Robert Baird wrote: 'During the last twelve months a most extensive and glorious work of grace – a work of reviving and quickening, as the Swedish brethren call it – has been going on in that country. It is said to reach almost every parish. Norway too has shared in the blessings. Some of the professors and nearly a fourth part of the students; about four hundred in number, in the University of Christiana are reported to be pious men. The gracious work has reached very many of the villages and hamlets at the head of the fiords or bays along the isle-grit coast of that long and narrow country. Even the Laplanders, both the nomadic and stationary, far up to the north have shared in its influence.

'Probably in no other part of the Protestant world has true Christianity, as a vital religion, made more progress within the last few years than it has done in these hyperborean [the extreme north] kingdoms. And the inquiry is natural and pertinent, "What has been the means by which this great change, under the Divine blessing has been wrought, and is still being wrought?" I answer it has been greatly brought about by distribution of the Bible and religious tracts. In this good work a considerable number of colporteurs [a person who sells or distributes religious materials] have been employed; there are more than a hundred at work in these days.'

Dr. Robert Baird noted that in both Norway and Sweden a 'most important means of keeping alive and extending the truth…has been the holding of little meetings for prayer, praise and reading of the Bible,' alongside the reading of tracts and books in the home, in the villages and hamlets. Whilst in the summer time people could often be seen reading Christian literature in the forests, on the hill or on a mountainside.

The meetings did not go without opposition. 'In many places at first, and for a long time the unconverted pastors of the National Church, as well as the openly wicked, greatly opposed these meetings,' so wrote Dr. Robert Baird. 'Fines, imprisonments and other modes of punishment were resorted to, but in vain. Several thousands indeed emigrated to America and are now to be found in Illinois and Wisconsin; but the good work has gone forward. Within the last eight or ten months, such has been its extension and power, that almost all parts of the kingdom have felt its influence. It is believed that nearly, if not quite a quarter of a million in a population of at the very utmost 3,500,000 have embraced religion.' Relating to Sweden: 'There is now a great demand for good books. Nor are the high classes in all cases unaffected by this great movement. A member of the royal family, the Princess Eugenie, the sister of the King has been occupying herself with the task of translating….'[17]

Chapter 14

The Fire of the Lord

"God is not a man, that He should lie, nor a son of man that He should repent. Has He not said, and will He not do it? Or has He spoken, and will He not make it good?" (Numbers 23:19).

Revival in Ireland 1859-1860

The revival in Ireland is known as the Ulster Revival, Ulster Awakening, '59 Revival or affectionately known as Eighteen Fifty-Nine. Rev. J. Reid Dill of Dromore, Co. Tyronne was licensed to preach in 1834. In his *Autobiography*, he wrote: 'The Synod of Ulster was in a very deplorable state as regarded ministerial unfaithfulness and as a consequence, the low state of morals and religion in many congregations.'

In the *Centenary Brochure* (1959), John T. Carson wrote: 'For some years before 1859, there were signs of quickening in the religious life of Ulster.... The names of Chalmers and McCheyne were household words in the homes of the godly. The stories of the "awakenings" under W. C. Burns and McCheyne at Kilsyth and Dundee and in other parts of Scotland gave ministers and people an eagerness to see the same thing happening at home. "Wilt Thou not revive us" became their prayer. Another very powerful influence was that of the famine in 1846. Although it was not as severe in Ulster as in the other provinces where it brought death and great distress to many a household, it was nevertheless used by God to arouse many to think of eternal things and to turn the hearts of many to seek the Lord.'[1]

The revival had its beginning when four young men who lived in different villages became so encouraged by the work of faith in the life of George Müller with his orphanages in Bristol, England, that they began to meet together for secret prayer and fellowship. These men were already attending the Tannybrake Sabbath-School weekly prayer meetings, which had begun in 1857, and as a result, they soon noticed a marked increase of attention amongst the children which encouraged them to step out deeper.

In September 1857, the men began meeting together, in a central location, in the neighbourhood of Kells, in the same month and year as the Fulton Street, New York City prayer meeting began, though unknown to each other. They prayed that, "Their labours and that of others might be eminently owned by God." From this prayer meeting many were birthed, but it took nearly two years before large numbers of sinners came under deep conviction.

Rev. J. H. Moore of Conner, inspired by the revival in America encouraged his flock to pray for revival. He preached and taught his congregation on the subject of revival and read accounts of past revivals; the idea of God coming down and touching the people finally gripped his congregation and it became a subject for serious prayer. Rev. Moore later reported: 'That there was no human leader in this movement; the Holy Spirit was the leader.'

From Ulster, the revival spread to Cavan County. In Corglass, a church was crowded inside and outside. As the preacher preached, people fell to the floor slain under conviction of sin. The entire graveyard was full of prostrate people in deep weeping and anguish of soul, and that at ten o'clock at night!

In Coleraine, upon seeing the fire fall in Ballymena, both churchmen and dissenters forgot their differences and joined in united prayer for the blessing of God.

An Ulster minister wrote: 'After examining the facts, as far as I could gather them, I judge that not less than 100,000 persons in Ulster were brought under gracious influence during that time. The revival had the help of almost the entire secular press. It was not confined to any one denomination, but embraced all evangelical churches; and up till the present time, all those have maintained unprecedented unity. I consider it the most glorious work of God ever known in this country in so short a time.'[2]

Charles H. Spurgeon in July 1859, speaking in London, England, about the Ulster Revival (1859-1860) said, "In the small town of Ballymena, [in Ireland], on market day, the publicans have always taken one hundred pounds for whisky and now they cannot take a sovereign [nominal value of £1] all day long in the public houses."

It was noted that 'at the Quarter-Sessions for Londonderry, in April 1860 held before Wm. Armstrong, Esq., Assistant-Barrister, there was no criminal business, and his worship was presented with a pair of white gloves.'[3]

Some ministers during the revival died due to the neglect of the human body, deprivation of food and sleep, coupled with exhaustion or burn-out. They were so caught up in the revival that they neglected the essential needs of the body and mind. I believe that most of them were elderly ministers so their bodies would have been frailer than if they were younger men.

At county Antrim, Ireland, an old Roman Catholic woman was in her garden in the afternoon when 'a perfect flood of light as she imagined bathed her dwelling.' She rushed inside, cried out in mercy and 'fainted away.' She woke up saved!

On a few occasions during times of revival, as the preacher was speaking on the Judgment Day, lightning flashed across the sky. This happened at Rasharkin Presbyterian Church on 7 June 1859, when lightning filled the church, five hundred people prostrated themselves on the floor and one hundred came under deep conviction of sin!

At Lurgan, county Armagh, some people were so caught up in revival that the harvest of grain had been left uncut! (Whilst work productivity increases amongst the saved during revival it decreases amongst those under conviction of sin).

During the revival there are several recorded instances of God giving remarkable stimulus to people's mental powers and spiritual graces, which can last longer than the duration of a revival. The Holy Spirit gives them boldness to pray publicly or to evangelise whereas before they were afraid to. In a sense it is like Jesus on the road to Emmaus with the two disciples when He opened their understanding and expounded the Scriptures to them (Luke 24:25).

In many localised towns and communities where Roman Catholicism was strong, it was the Catholics who largely opposed the revival, this 'Protestant' move of God.

Dr. James C. L. Carson, a prominent medical practitioner in Coleraine during revival, speaking about the physical phenomena said, "Without doubt, there is a great physical agent, as well as a spiritual one, abroad. The one is, as it were, the hand-maid to the other. They are both specially from God, and are most admirably calculated to work out His great design.... It would be well for those parties who look on physical manifestations as an evil, which should be avoided and repressed, to reconsider their ways. It is an awful thing to be found fighting against God. How dreadful is this presumption which will dare to dictate to the Almighty the way in which He should save sinners!"[4]

There were many people claiming the work to be from the evil one. One country boy who had been affected by the revival stood on a stone and addressed the people in a street in Coleraine, saying, "Some people call it the work of the Devil. All I can say to this is, that up to last week I have been serving the Devil as well as I could, and I am sure he was well pleased with my service; but if he is employing me now, he is so far changed that I would not know him to be the same man!"[5]

When new converts applied to become members of a church they were asked three questions:
1. Do you know yourself to be a lost sinner?
2. Do you know Christ to be an Almighty Saviour?
3. Have you accepted Him as such?

There was also a Decision Card for new converts that had to be signed and dated. It stated:

- I take God the Father to be my God (1 Thessalonians 1:19).
- I take God the Son to be my Saviour (Acts 5:31).
- I take God the Holy Spirit to be my Sanctifier (1 Peter 1:2).
- I take the Word of God to be my rule (2 Timothy 3:16-17).
- I take the people of God to be my people (Ruth 1:16-17).
- I likewise dedicate myself wholly to the Lord (Romans 14:7-8).
- And I do this prayerfully (Psalm 119:94).
- Deliberately (Joshua 24:15).
- Sincerely (2 Corinthians 1:12).
- Freely (Psalm 110:3).
- And forever (Romans 8:35-39).[6]

Towards the end of the revival in Ireland, in 1860, the effects of the revival were renewed and summarised as follows:

1. The preaching services were thronged.
2. Numbers of communicants were unprecedented.
3. Prayer meetings were abundant.
4. Family prayers were increased.
5. Scripture reading was unmatched.
6. Sunday schools were prosperous.
7. Converts remained generally steadfast.
8. Liberality seemed greatly increased.
9. Vice was abated.
10. Crime was much reduced.[7]

From January to April 2009, for the 150th anniversary of the 1859 Ulster Revival, three different churches in Northern Ireland held special services. In addition, for seven consecutive evenings in October, Rev. Tom Shaw spoke on 'Biblical Teaching on Revival' at five different churches.

Revival in Scotland 1859-1860

The west of Scotland is closely related to the north of Ireland, and from Ireland, the fires flowed to Scotland. As visitors told of the stories from Ireland, the Scots started prayer meetings and prayed like never before.

On 10 August 1859, the General Assembly of the Free Church of Scotland sent out a call to prayer. It said, "The Commission also feels the deep solemnity of our position as a Church in such circumstances. These events which have recently taken place in America, in Wales, in Ireland and to a small extent in Scotland, strikingly illustrate the Sovereign Power of the Holy Spirit and the efficacy of believing prayer, and ought to encourage us to attempt great things for God and to expect great things from God, and they call upon all ministers and people of this Church earnestly, to pray that God may be graciously pleased to pour out His Holy Spirit abundantly upon our land that His work may be revived everywhere." People began to pray in churches, at home, in shops and even in the University of Edinburgh.

In Scotland, it was estimated that ten percent of the population were converted! That was 300,000 conversions out of a population of three million Scots![8]

The Wesleyan Methodist Magazine in their Religious Intelligence for January 1860 noted what was happening in Kirkintilloch, Scotland. Citing the *Scottish Guardian* newspaper: 'The Wesleyan daily prayer meeting conducted regularly by Mr Forsyth continues to be accompanied with gracious influence, refreshing seasons and revival-fruits. Night after night as the meeting is dismissed at ten o'clock, persons present themselves for counsel and prayer in concern for their souls. These comprise of persons of all ages and both sexes. The little striplings and the hoary-haired [old person], the child and the parent, the brother and the sister, the careless and the professor [of being a Christian], the scoffer and the communicant [a person entitled to receive Communion], the learned and the illiterate – alike under the teaching and influence of God's truth and Holy Spirit, come to the feet of Jesus, and alike under deep conviction of sin, ask, "What must I do to be saved?" During the two months this meeting has been held [presumably October to November 1859], more than a hundred have thus presented themselves; and with them have the people of God rejoiced in their joy of believing in Jesus unto forgiveness and peace.

'A few of these have been "prostration cases" but they are the exception. One young man who tarried on his knees in prayer after all had left, on being raised [lifted to his feet] for conversation, soon after dropped down on the floor as if shot. Another, a young woman, dropped three times off the seat and had to be assisted home. Both seemed under very keen conviction and deeply anxious.

'A very considerable number of the cases were persons connected with the various churches in town who had been in the communion of the same. One young woman on obtaining peace, exclaimed, "What a sinner I have been – sitting down at the Lord's Table and not His child; eating and drinking damnation to myself! O, the goodness of God in bearing with me so!" Another, an old communicant said, "My religion till now has been nothing but a form."

'In October [1859] Mr Haltridge from Coleraine, [in Ireland], addressed the meeting which was crowded to excess and large numbers could not be admitted. While he narrated his remarkable history and career of wickedness, and conversion to God, a deep solemnity rested on the people and many were in tears. After the address a very considerable number were in deep concern of soul who experienced the blessing of peace [conversion, reconciled back to God]. Repeatedly had the meeting to be concluded before the audience would depart. Mr Haltridge's visit was one of great blessing and will long be remembered. So great was the interest excited that a meeting was held the next morning (Thursday) at ten o'clock that he might be further heard. This meeting was also of a most interesting nature.

'On the evening of the half-yearly fair, when full license is generally taken to indulge in vice, the chapel was filled at the meeting with an anxious audience. A gracious influence rested on the service and seven professed to enter into the liberty of God's dear children [John 1:12]. One young person in deep conviction seemed almost convulsed, she lay back as pale as death, but fully absorbed in the interest of her state; for while the hymn was sung, "My God is reconciled, His pardoning voice I hear," she started up with a countenance now radiant with joy, exclaiming, "My God is reconciled! My Jesus!" Amid this rapturous deliverance, other penitents laid hold of the hope set before them in the Gospel and rejoiced together.

'Thus is the Lord showing His goings forth among us, exhibiting His glory, and displaying His saving power in refreshing His people, and adding to the number of the faithful. Surely it may be said in the language of the prophet, 'Thou shalt no more be termed Forsaken, neither shall thy land any more be termed Desolate, but thou shalt be called Hephzibah and thy land Beulah, for the Lord delighteth in thee' (Isaiah LXII.4).'[9]

In late 1859, the East Gorbals Free Church in Glasgow held a mission. A correspondent of the *Scottish Guardian* wrote: 'Having heard that the Lord was pouring out His blessing in connection with this station, I paid a visit to the place of meeting in Commercial Road.' The reporter relayed how the large school-room was filled mostly with boys: 'I was somewhat prepared for the sight, as I was informed that the awakening had been very marked among the boys; but I did not expect to see such earnest and devout attention, nor to look upon so many happy faces, lighted up with a smile of Heavenly joy, listening to the "story of grace." '

The service which was one and a half hours consisted of praise, prayer and an exposition of a portion of Scripture. After this was the children's prayer meeting which was held in an adjoining room; 'upwards of one hundred children retired, accompanied by the missionary and one or two friends.' The meeting was conducted by three boys, from eleven to thirteen and lasted for about thirty minutes. 'The exercises were simple praise and prayer, and more earnest or appropriate supplications I never heard presented to the throne of grace. They seemed the very outgushings of the renewed heart, just delivered from the bondage of sin, and rejoicing in Jesus, and the liberty whereby He makes us free. I felt that these boys had not only offered up the petition, "Lord teach us to pray," but were rejoicing in the blessed experience of the answer to it. Then the songs of praise – O how joyous! They seemed to come welling up from the very depths of the heart.'

There was no meeting on a Saturday in the school-room, so the boys 'meet in each other's houses;' so noted the missionary, 'and he believes that numerous cases of conviction and conversion are the result.'[10]

In November 1860, *The Wesleyan Methodist Magazine* published an account of the work of grace at Skene in north Scotland. The unnamed person wrote: 'About eight months ago [March 1860] an evident work of God appeared in this parish. Since then it has gone on steadily, but after the meetings at Huntly, at which people from Skene were present, a fresh impetus has been given it. Such was the state of feeling that open-air meetings were proposed and were held on 14th and 15th of August [1860], on the edge of the loch, which reposed in calm beauty, rendering the place of meeting lonely and picturesque.

'Throughout the forenoon parties from the parishes around might be seen wending their way to the spot, till at length not fewer than sixteen hundred had assembled. A temporary platform had been erected and the chair was occupied by Captain Shephard of Kirkville, who opened with an impressive and singularly appropriate prayer, followed by a short statement of the object of the meeting. The first hour was occupied exclusively with prayer for the special outpouring of the Holy Spirit, after which a succession of short Gospel addresses were delivered by a number of ministers and others from various parts. The whole proceedings were of the most solemn and impressive kind. At an early stage of the meeting it was evident that the Spirit of God was at work awakening many and deepening impressions in others.

'A tent which had been pitched in a quiet spot at some distance was resorted to for private conversation by many in deep anxiety of soul, while in the adjacent wood, groups might be seen praying and conversing together. At seven o'clock pm the large assemblage was dispersed; but many still lingered around the spot, as if unwilling to go without the blessing.

'At eight o'clock a meeting was held in the church and the stillness which pervaded the assembly, with the number of anxious souls asking what they must do to be saved, betokened [a sign of] the presence and power of the Lord. Many went home rejoicing making the woods resound with the voice of melody. On Wednesday, the following day, many of those who had taken part in the work of the preceding day, dispersed themselves over the parish, two by two and held open-air services at different places. At three o'clock pm, on the lawn of Kirkville, a second large meeting, though not as large as the first was held with similar results. All was wound up by a large meeting in the church and seldom has it been our privilege to see so many young men seeking salvation, or to feel more of the gracious presence of Jesus as the Healer of souls.'[11]

William E. Allen of Revival Publishing Co. wrote: 'The revival in Scotland was as definite and striking as the movement in Ulster.' In May 1860, the Moderator of the Free Church of Scotland said, "Two years ago our Assembly was deeply stirred by the intelligence of what God was doing in the United States of America. One year ago the impression was deepened.... The pregnant cloud had swept onwards and was sending down upon Ireland a plenteous rain. This year, the same precious showers have been and are even now falling within the limits of our own beloved land.

"We as a church accept the revival as a great and blessed fact. Numerous and explicit testimonies from ministers and members alike bespeak the gracious influence on the people. Whole congregations have been seen bending before it like a mighty rushing wind."

In 1861 a new Moderator said, "Fathers and brethren, I congratulate you on your meeting again in the midst of an outpouring of the Spirit of God, and a remarkable work of grace pervading the whole church and the whole land."[12]

'There is a river whose streams shall make glad the city of God, the holy place of the tabernacle of the Most High. God is in the midst of her, she shall not be moved; God shall help her, just at the break of dawn' (Psalm 46:4-5).

Chapter 15

Mighty to Save

'Surely His salvation is near those who fear Him, that glory may dwell in the land' (Psalm 85:10).

Revival in England 1859-1860

England was the last place in the Anglo-Saxon world to experience the 1859 Revival, which swept the world, though in parts of London it continued until 1864 under many evangelists. Reports from America and other parts of Great Britain stirred the hearts of the English. The revivals were reported in many of the religious periodicals in England. Early in June 1858, a prayer meeting of forty people soon grew to four hundred in Exeter as the faithful sought God to pour out His Spirit from on high.

On 29 November 1858, the Lodiani Mission in north India held its twenty-third annual conference. The theme was revival and how could they receive the same blessing like America. This led them to issue a worldwide proclamation for a week of prayer for revival for the second week of 1860.

In November 1859, a circular letter was issued containing the Lodiani invitation and the endorsement of forty-one ministers of England. In London during the week of prayer, January 1860, there were at least two hundred prayer meetings in the capital alone. After the week of prayer many continued to seek God and beseech Him for His mercy to rain down from on high.

In Newcastle-on-Tyne, a united prayer meeting was held for over a year before any great results were seen. In Leeds, within a month one church had received one hundred new members after the union prayer meetings had begun and were still going strong by February 1860.

In Staffordshire, prayer meetings and Bible studies were held in the mines as hundreds of colliers were converted, along with drunkards and a multitude of vices were stopped. Daily meetings for prayer and Bible readings were held in the bowels of the earth, in the pits and mine shafts! In one locality 500 people professed conversion.

An eye-witness from Bicester said, "It is not asserting too much to say that a greater number of sinners have been converted to God in Bicester, and within eight miles of it, during the last ten months than have made an open profession of religion during the last two hundred years."[1]

England did not see a sweeping revival as did parts of Ireland and America because of a lack of prevailing prayer. In 1881, Mrs Catherine Booth of The Salvation Army wrote: 'Some years ago, when the wave of revival was sweeping over Ireland and America, you know the churches in this country held united prayer meetings to pray that it might come to England; but it did not come and the infidels wagged their heads and wrote in their newspapers: 'See the Christians' God is either deaf or gone a-hunting, for they have prayer meetings all over the land for revival, and it has not come.' Oh! My cheeks burned with shame as I thought of it; how I mourned over it. I knew it was not because God was asleep; not because His arm was shortened; not because His bowels of compassion did not yearn over sinners; not because He could not have poured out His Spirit and given us the same glorious times of refreshing they had in other places. That was not the reason. There was only one reason, and that was that His people asked amiss. They did not understand the conditions of prevailing prayer. They did not fulfil them [abiding, John 15:7; believe, Mark 11:24; ask in faith, James 1:5-7; and the Spirit makes intercession, Romans 8:26-27]...there are conditions to these promises...these are only a tithe of the glorious promises with respect to prayer.... 'The effectual fervent prayer of a righteous man availeth much' [James 5:16].'[2]

William E. Allen wrote: 'In England prayer meetings multiplied in towns and villages, and there was a great awakening among the Christians. Local revivals were experienced in different places, and a great deal of evangelistic work was carried on. Bolton was the scene of a powerful movement under the ministry of Charles G. Finney.' Finney who was sixty-eight years old began his ministry in Bolton, northern England, at the latter end of April 1860 and continued in that city for three months. Mrs Finney also preached exclusively to women and held special meetings for married and unmarried women.[3]

In Charles Finney's *Autobiography* he wrote: 'Our first meeting was in the chapel occupied by Mr Davison, who had sent for me to come to Bolton. I tried to press upon them as a fact, that prayer would be immediately answered, if they took the stumbling-blocks out of the way, and offered the prayer of faith. The word seemed to thrill through the hearts of Christians.

'Through the whole of that week the spirit of prayer seemed to be increasing, and our meetings had greater and greater power. About the third or fourth day of our meeting, I called for enquirers, and his vestry was thronged with them. We had an impressive meeting with them. There was a hall in the city, which could accommodate more people than any of the chapels. The brethren secured the hall for preaching. Soon the interest became very general. The Spirit of God was poured out copiously.

'All classes of persons, high and low, rich and poor, male and female became interested. I was in the habit of calling enquirers to come forward. Great numbers would come forward, crowding as best as they could through the dense masses that filled every nook and corner of the house. The work went on and spread in Bolton, until one of the ministers said publicly, that they found that the revival had reached every family in the city, and that every family had been visited.'

In the second Preface to *The Tongue of Fire* (1856, 1859), eighteenth edition, William Arthur of London, England, wrote: 'The last two years have been eventful ones in the churches of Christ. Both in America and in the United Kingdom, the Lord has been pleased to pour His Spirit, in such a manner as sensibly to affect the public mind. Such a change has been made by these visitations that much contained in this volume appears more fitted to the present moment than to that in which it was written. When it appeared three years and a half ago [April 1856], many things in it would have been regarded as extravagant by some who today would gladly declare that they have beheld such things with their own eyes. Not a few share with us the firm hope that we shall witness greater things than have yet come to pass. The great revival of the nineteenth century has fairly begun [December 1859], but only begun: the world lieth in the wicked one, the bulk of the nominal Church is still cold and powerless; and among the most favoured populations lively Christians are the minority.

'This new and cheap edition is issued with the fervent prayer that some of the servants of God labouring for the general revival and spread of true religion, may find in it an [sic] humble auxiliary.'[4]

Charles H. Spurgeon (1834-1892), London, England

Charles H. Spurgeon, the 'Prince of Preachers,' saw hundreds, if not thousands come to Christ in his 6,000-seat Metropolitan Tabernacle during the English Revival (1859-1860) and in the years either side of it. During his ministry in London, it has been estimated that 14,000 new members joined his congregation which resulted in many churches being planted around the city.[5]

Evangelist and revivalist, James A. Stewart wrote: 'In Newport, Wales, there was a prayer circle of praying men who met together every Saturday night for over thirty years to pray for blessing. Not one death occurred in the circle during that time. They began to pray, in the first place, because they felt burdened that Charles Spurgeon needed a mighty anointing as he was beginning his ministry in London [in 1854]. It is very remarkable to notice that on the very

Lord's Day following the first prayer meeting, Spurgeon began to preach with such unction that it was noticeable to all.'[6]

Charles H. Spurgeon made his first visit to Wales in July 1859, to a place called Castleton, between Newport and Cardiff in South Wales. About 6,000 people assembled for the 11am service on Wednesday, 20 July 1859, at Castleton Baptist Church. Many of those present were miners/colliers who had been brought from the valleys by special trains. Nigel Faithful wrote: 'They sat in a semi-circle facing the speaker, who began by entreating their prayers that he 'may be enabled to preach the Gospel with power. You may have men to preach the Gospel in Wales in a better manner than I can, but you have no one who can preach a better Gospel.'[7]

Charles H. Spurgeon in his *Autobiography* reveals the secret of his ministry. He said, "When I came to New Park Street Chapel [London, England in 1854], it was but a mere handful of people to whom I first preached; yet I can never forget how earnestly they prayed. Sometimes they seemed to plead as though they could really see the Angel of the covenant present with them, and as if they must have a blessing from Him. More than once, we were all so struck with the solemnity of the meeting, that we sat silent for some moments while the Lord's power appeared to overshadow us; and all I could do was to pronounce the benediction, and say, 'Dear friends, we have had the Spirit of God here very manifestly tonight; let us go home and take care not to lose His gracious influence.'

"Then came down the blessing; the house was filled with hearers, and many souls were saved. I always give the glory to God, but do not forget that He gave me the privilege of ministering first to a praying people. We had prayer meetings that moved every soul...each one appeared determined to storm the Celestial City by the might of intercession; and soon the blessing came upon us in such abundance that we had not room enough to receive it."[8]

On 17 July 1859, Charles H. Spurgeon was at the Surrey Music Hall, London, England. He preached on the text, 'We have heard with our ears O God, our fathers have told us, what deeds You did in their days, in days of old' (Psalm 44:1). Spurgeon was recalling various revivals from Church history, such as the British Great Awakening under John and Charles Wesley, George Whitefield and William Grimshaw, the 1857 Prayer Meeting Revival in America and the 1859 Revival at Belfast, Ireland, and said, "Has God changed? Is He not an immutable God, the same yesterday, today and forever? Does not that furnish an argument to prove that what God has done at one time He can do at another? Nay, I think I may push it a little further and say what He has done once, is a prophecy of what He intends to do again – that the mighty works which have been accomplished in the olden time shall all be repeated and the Lord's song shall be sung again in Zion, and He shall again be glorified. Others among you say, "...We are not to expect them every day." That is the very reason why we do not get them. If we had learnt to expect them, we should no doubt obtain them, but we put them up on the shelf, as being out of the common order of our moderate religion, as being the curiosities of Scripture history. We imagine such things, however true, to be prodigies of providence; we cannot imagine them to be according to the ordinary working of His mighty power. I beseech you my friends, abjure that idea [and] put it out of your mind. Whatever God has done in converting sinners is looked upon as a precedent, for 'His arm is not shortened that He cannot save, nor is His ear heavy that He cannot hear.' Let us...with earnestness seek that God would restore to us the faith of men of old, that we may richly enjoy His grace as in the days of old."[9]

Charles H. Spurgeon's 6,000-seat Tabernacle in London, England, had a 5,000 strong membership for more than thirty years! In October 1857, he preached at the Crystal Palace to a crowd of 24,000. His sermons were sold across Britain and as far away as America and Canada at an average of 25,000 per week and read even further afield. His sermon on 'Baptismal Regeneration' sold 200,000 copies. In 1867, when his Tabernacle was being renovated, he preached in the Agricultural Hall for five consecutive Sundays with no less than 20,000 present each Sabbath day to hear the greatest preacher of his time. In the same year, Stockwell Orphanage (now Spurgeons Children's Charity) was founded for "fatherless boys."

On 9 February 1892, 60,000 people filed past his coffin. The *Christian World* in 1892 wrote: 'Including the weekly sermon, and his many articles in the *Sword and the Trowel*, Mr Spurgeon's printed works have probably been more voluminous than the productions of any modern author. The weekly sermon, beginning with the first week of 1855, has completed 36 yearly volumes. The average circulation has been maintained at 25,000 weekly. The monthly magazine has also completed 26 yearly volumes. Of the *Treasury of David*, in seven large volumes, something like 130,000 volumes have been sold. Of *Lectures to My Students,* and *Commenting on Commentaries*, between sixty and seventy thousand volumes have been disposed of [distributed or sold]. Then *John Ploughman's Talk* and *Pictures* together show a circulation of half a million volumes. The other works are very numerous, all being more or less popular.'

Much of the royalties from Charles H. Spurgeon's works went to supporting his Pastor's College, founded in 1856; the Stockwell Orphanage which cost £12,000 per annum, and other Christian enterprises. From 1856-1892, about 845 students passed through the Pastor's College in London. In addition, Mrs Spurgeon was able to distribute 130,000 volumes among poor ministers of all denominations.[10]

In May 1892, Charles H. Spurgeon became ill, and later A. T. Pierson was asked to fill-in as preacher of the Tabernacle in London, and stayed on after Spurgeon's death for two years. In a discourse, Pierson noted how the congregation for twenty-one weeks had daily prayed for Spurgeon's recovery, in the morning and evening at the Tabernacle, and had prayed 'without ceasing,' and highly commended them for it. He said. "And now in the name of God I challenge this great Church of Jesus Christ to a spectacle more sublime than which has greeted the eyes of angels of men. I want to challenge you – and this is the solemn conclusion of this solemn appeal – to an unceasing and united prayer for a new coming of the Holy Ghost on the Church and the world. If this spectacle was sublime of all disciples of every name, uniting for the rescue of one beloved pastor from the jaws of death, how think you the Heavenly host would thrill with delight, and even the heart of our Saviour, itself, if disciples of Jesus Christ of every name could be found represented in morning and evening for prayer during six months to come, in this consecrated place, in an importunate, believing and anointed supplication that the greatest manifestation of the Holy Ghost since the days of Pentecost might come upon the Church of God in this apostate age. And that this, that the world might soon hear the tiding of the Gospel. That they might flash like electric lights from pole to pole, till every creature shall have learned the message of salvation, and that the Gospel shall have been preached as a witness to all nations, that the end might come, when the King in His glory shall once more descend to take His throne and wield His sceptre over the world."[11]

> Jesus said, "...I will build My Church, and the gates of Hades shall not prevail against it" (Matthew 16:18).

Revival at Trichinopoly 1860 – India

In a letter dated 10 April 1860, from Trichinopoly, India, Rev. William O. Simpson wrote: 'The news of the home-revival is to us in this heathen land, "as cold water to a thirsty soul." We returned from the district meeting expecting to hear much and to see much of the "works of the right hand of the Lord most high." The delightful communion with our brethren in the district meeting, the marked spiritual profit attending the meetings for united prayer, held whilst we were in Madras, and the lively, expectant tone of piety diffused, were all sources of strength and hope for us.

'I think we have the promise of great things from the Lord in our English congregation. There were signs of a movement before we left for district meeting; but we were not prepared for the success which greeted our return. The chapel is filled every Sunday to the doors. A plan has been drawn up for doubling the number of sittings and for putting the chapel in thorough repair.... A meting for united prayer and for reading the holy Scriptures is held under our direction every Thursday evening at the house of the Brigade-Major; and this has been, and continues to be, a great blessing to Christians of every name [denomination]. A Sunday school has been commenced in a large room near the European barracks. Seventy children are in attendance and it is a great pleasure to us to be the means, in conjunction with many earnest Christian men, of bringing home Divine truth to the minds and conscience of the children of our fellow countrymen. We also have a prayer meeting every Saturday evening.

'Mr White has taken charge of the soldiers' class and two or three men have presented themselves for membership; the first-fruits we trust of a large ingathering from the 2d European Regiment. Several Christian officers, men of the stamp of the Hedley Vicars are the life of the movement. After five years of mission-life spent more or less in educational work, I am at length entirely free to do the work of an evangelist. Mr Gloria and I are out in the streets almost every morning in the week. Our congregations are generally large and attentive, but we want the "power from on high," to break the heart of apathy and worldly-mindedness, to create a conscience and endue poor cowards hearts with courage.'[12]

'Righteousness exalts a nation, but sin is a reproach to any people' (Proverbs 14:34).

North Tinnevelly Itinerancy Revival 1860 – India

On 5 July 1860, Rev. John Pinkney from Bangalore, India, wrote: 'We have lately heard strange things respecting God's doings amongst some of the natives in Tinnevelly [south India]. "We learn from the *Church Missionary Record*," says the *Madras Times,* "that during the past month accounts have been received at the Presidency of a deeply interesting revival of spiritual religion amongst some of the schools and congregations of the district, known at the North Tinnevelly Itinerancy. There is reason to believe that many professed Christians have been brought to earnest spiritual life, and a few of the neighbouring Heathen seem also to have been roused. The movement is said to have attended with the same physical emotion which marked the movement known as the Ulster Revival [1859-1860], but through the judicious treatment of the missionaries, these physical manifestations were kept in check."

'We trust that the churches in Britain and in America will wake up and perform that great and glorious work to which the Almighty is calling them in India.'[13]

An Awakening Among Some Aboriginals 1860 – Australia

In October 1860, *The Wesleyan Methodist Magazine* recorded an 'Awakening among the Aboriginals of Australia.' A gentleman near Melbourne, in a letter dated 19 April 1860, wrote: 'You may have heard of the awakening begun among the aborigines of this colony through the instrumentality of two Moravian missionaries. Some months ago they commenced a station, but as it was found to be one of their most expensive and difficult settlements, it was resolved that these two missionaries be recalled and sent to some other country, and this settlement be abandoned. In the meanwhile however, the work had commenced.'

One Sunday morning in January 1860, one of the missionaries called the Aboriginals to assemble for worship as they did each week. However, none of them came. 'Such a decided refusal had never once been given before and the poor missionary returned to his place quite disconsolate [very unhappy and unable to be comforted]. That same evening after he had spent the day in prayer by himself the work was begun. For while he was mourning over the thing before God he heard to his great surprise, the sound of devotion near him. Going out he found that a settler, a pious man, five miles off had it strongly impressed upon his mind to go and pay a visit to that encampment. On arriving he was able after much persuasion to prevail upon four young men to come out with him for devotional exercise [prayer, Bible reading and worship] and it was the sound of this which the missionary heard. From that evening, first the youths, and then the others became awakened till the thing had gone on and increased.'

The different denominations were so impressed with the move of God, that in Melbourne they began to defray the entire cost of sustaining the mission, without any expense to the Moravians. 'The whole story is so wonderful,' wrote the gentleman in his letter, 'and so different from what one would be led, humanly speaking to expect that one cannot help exclaiming, "What has God wrought!" '[14]

'Help us, O God of our salvation, for the glory of Your name; and deliver us, and provide atonement for our sins, for Your name's sake!' (Psalm 79:9).

Chapter 16

Expect Great things from God

Jesus spoke of the Great Commission just before His ascension into Heaven. He said, "All authority has been given to Me in Heaven and on earth. Go therefore and make disciples of all the nations, baptising them in the name of the Father and of the Son and of the Holy Spirit, teaching them to observe all things that I have commanded you; and lo, I am with you always, even to the end of the age." Amen (Matthew 28:18-20).

Cornish Revivals 1861-1862 – William and Catherine Booth

William Booth's love for God and his fellow man led him into the Methodist Church, but the Methodist's asked him to leave (or told him to go) and withdrew his membership as they found it hard to accept his fiery open-air preaching at Kennington Common, London, England.

In 1855, aged twenty-six, William Booth was sent out as a travelling evangelist under more spiritual Methodists. As a circuit preacher, God's hand was very evident upon him as he saw on average, twenty-three new converts a day! Three years later in 1858, he was ordained as Rev. William Booth, and became the Methodist pastor of Bethesda Chapel in Gateshead which could seat 1,300.

In December 1859, Catherine Booth heard about Dr. and Mrs Palmer who were holding evangelistic services in Newcastle, England. The principle speaker was the wife, Phoebe Palmer and there was remarkable success in their labours for the Lord. In 1860, Catherine Booth began to preach as she felt compelled by the Spirit of God and could not stay silent any longer. Rev. William Booth was so impressed by her anointing that his views on women preachers radically changed.

A turning point for Rev. William Booth was when he had a vision of the lost perishing amidst a black, dark, stormy sea. In the vision he saw and heard the screams and shrieks of those bobbing and struggling for air, as the waves crashed over them, and the lightning and the wind struck and howled overhead. Out of the sea arose a great rock where survivors had clambered but stayed in leisurely pursuits and pastimes, not caring for those who were struggling around the base. Some even argued about how best to save the drowning but still did nothing. But there was the Wonderful Being, who came to aid those who were drowning and He beckoned to the other survivors to assist Him but they wanted to be comforted, and wanted Him to come to them to give them more reassurance.

In 1861, Rev. William Booth, whilst at the Methodist New Connexion's Annual Conference, asked to be released from his duties so as to be able to evangelise more, but the committee wanted to promote him to the Superintendent of the whole Newcastle District. Within two months Rev. Booth resigned his position due to the burden of administration, which was not as important as the burden he had for souls. In August 1861, Rev. Booth headed for Hayle, Cornwall, and his wife Catherine joined him later, where 7,000 Cornishmen were converted in just eighteen months during the Cornish Revivals at Hayle, Redruth, Camborne, Penzance, St. Ives, and St. Just 'where the local police inspector reported a dramatic drop in crime,' and other locations.[1]

No longer being part of the Methodist New Connexion meant that the Booths were free to preach in any churches of any denomination, in any town that would permit them. F. De L. Booth-Tucker in *The Short Life of Catherine Booth* (1892), wrote: 'However great in some instances might be the secret antagonism of the pastors, it would be compelled, they thought, to succumb to the influences of the revival [of 1859-1860], and to the clamour of the people for a share in the blessing that were being reaped by so many around.' The Booths had planned to stay six or seven weeks, but ended up staying for eighteen months because the anointing of the Holy Spirit was upon them!

Revival at Hayle, Cornwall 1861 – England

The Booths received a letter from Rev. J. Shone of the New Connexion in Hayle, Cornwall, England. He had been converted during the revival at Chester and had been a colleague with Rev. William Booth in Gateshead, where he lived under the same roof as Rev. Booth. The letter was written in an apologetic tone, 'the smallness of the chapel...the scantiness of the population...[and that] nothing could be guaranteed in the way of remuneration.'

Mrs Catherine Booth wrote: 'Hayle we found was but a small straggling place with a port, at which some little coasting trade was carried on, and a large foundry employing six or seven hundred people. The chapel was a barn-like affair, holding perhaps six hundred people. The numbers were crowded into it night after night was quite a different matter. The Cornish system of packing a congregation was certainly somewhat singular. The first comers occupied the seats, and then another row of people would stand in front of them. The aisles would then be filled, beginning at the pulpit stairs, till the whole place was literally gorged. Then the window sills would be besieged, and through the open windows another crowd outside would listen to the echoes of the songs and to such stray sentences as might reach their ears.'

Throughout the Cornish Campaign, Rev. William Booth preached on Sunday morning and evening, plus the first four evenings of the week, whilst Catherine Booth preached on Sunday afternoons, the Friday night meetings, and on the afternoons of several of the week days. They also 'visited the sick and conducted other accessory gatherings.' Saturday was a day of rest and preparation for the Sunday services.

The first meeting was held on Sunday, 11 August 1861; Rev. William Booth spoke in the morning 'to a good congregation' and left many knowing that they were sinners. 'In the afternoon the place was jammed,' so wrote Catherine Booth and the Lord gave 'great liberty. At night there was another crowd and a powerful impression was made. Indeed, I have always reckoned that God in an especial manner put His seal upon the services of that day, giving us as it were, a Divine commission for our subsequent lifework, though we little dreamed at the time how much was involved in it.'

There was 'no immediate break,' so wrote Catherine Booth, 'the people listened with the utmost earnestness and assented to the truth, but they would not respond to our invitation to come forward to the communion rail [an altar call]. The next night the result was much the same. In spite of the strongest appeals, not a single person came forward. Knowing that there were many present who were deeply convinced of their sin, the invitation was repeated again and again, without eliciting the slightest response, when suddenly the silence was broken by the loud cried of a woman who left her seat, pushed her way through the crowd, fell upon her knees at the penitent form, and thus became the first-fruits of what proved to be a glorious harvest of souls.' F. De L. Booth-Tucker noted that over the eighteen months it 'proved to be one long continuous revival.'[2]

Rev. William Booth in his own report, noted the woman who came forward. He wrote: 'She was quickly followed by others, when a scene ensued beyond description. The cries and groans were piercing in the extreme; and when the stricken spirits [the people] apprehended Jesus as their Saviour, the shouts of praise and thanksgiving were in proportion to the previous sorrow.'

In another report Rev. William Booth wrote: 'The work of the Lord here goes on gloriously. The services have progressed with increasing power and success, and now the whole neighbourhood is moved. Conversion is the topic of conversation in all sorts of society. Every night, crowds are unable to gain admission to the sanctuary. The oldest men in the church cannot remember any religious movement of equal power. During the second week, the Wesleyans opened a large room for united prayer meetings at noon; since then, by their invitation we have on several occasions spoken in their chapels to densely crowded audiences; services being simultaneously conducted in the chapel where the movement originally commenced. One remarkable and gratifying feature of the work is the large number of men who are found every night amongst those who are anxious. Never have I seen so many men at the same time smiting their breasts, and crying, "God be merciful to me a sinner." Strong men, old men, young men, weeping like children, broken-hearted on account of their sins. A number of these are sailors and scarcely a ship has gone out of this port the last few days without taking among its crew one or more souls newly-born for Heaven.'

George S. Railton, the First Commissioner of General Booth, in his book, *General Booth* (1912), wrote: 'Can it be believed that just such victories as these led to the closing of almost all the Christian Churches against him?' Looking back, General Booth wrote: 'In these days [1901] it has almost become the fashion for the churches to hold yearly "revival" or "special" services, but forty years ago they were unanimously opposed to anything of the kind, and compelled me to gain outside every church organization the one liberty I desired – to seek and save the lost ones, who never enter any place of worship whatever.' Booth continued, stating that he held no resentment: 'But I want to make it clear to readers in lands far away from Christendom why I was driven into the formation of an Organization [The Salvation Army] entirely outside every Christian church in order to accomplish my object....'[3]

In the first week of September 1861, Mrs Catherine Booth in a letter to her parents wrote: 'On Wednesday night William preached in the largest Wesleyan chapel, about half a mile from the other. It was crammed out into the street. I should think there were 1,800 people inside, and I never witnessed such a scene in my life as the prayer meeting presented. The [penitent] rail was filled in a few minutes with great strong men who cried aloud for mercy, some of them as though the pains of Hell had actually got hold of them! Oh it was a scene! No one could be heard praying and the cries and shouts of the penitents almost overpowered the singing.'

Referring afterward to this meeting, Mrs Catherine Booth said, "This unusual noise and confusion was somewhat foreign to our notions and practices. William believed strongly in everything being done 'decently and in order.' Indeed, I think he somewhat mistook the application of this direction [inferred that he tried to bring order and calm to the meeting]. How much more acceptable must be this *apparent* disorder in the eyes of God and angels and all the holy beings, who are alive to the importance of salvation and damnation, than the stoic indifference and pharisaic propriety so common in places of worship! How much better to have twenty people smiting their breast and crying, 'God be merciful to me a sinner,' with its necessary consequent commotion, than a congregation of equally guilty sinners sitting with stiff propriety and in their own estimation 'needing no repentance!' I must say that even then I thought the one far more philosophical and Scriptural than the other."

Mrs Catherine Booth addressed the congregation about the noise and stated that if a person is 'so overpowered by their feelings' whilst the sermon is in progress, 'or by a sense of their danger, [fear of Hell] as to be unable to contain themselves, let them be taken into the vestry, and let two or three praying men or women, as the case may be, show them the way of salvation, and pray with them there until after the meeting commences, while we go on with the preaching. It is the truth that makes people free [John 8:31-32], and if we are to go on spreading the work of salvation, we must go on with the proclamation of the message of God."

F. De L. Booth-Tucker in relation to the revival at Hayle wrote: 'Each succeeding meeting appeared to surpass in power and results all that had gone before. The whole neighbourhood was moved. Salvation was the universal theme of conversation in the mines, on board the ships, on the wharves, in the factory, in the public houses [drinking salons / bars], by the wayside, and in almost every home. Not only was this the case in the town itself, but from the surrounding villages and hamlets it was usual for both the saved and the unsaved to walk eight, ten or fifteen, and twenty miles to the meetings.' The Booths received many invites to conduct meetings in neighbouring towns.

'Thirty years have elapsed and yet it is common to meet with the fruits of that revival in all quarters of the globe, and to receive letters from those who date their spiritual birth from these meetings.'

The services in Hayle were brought to a close with a festival picnic for one thousand people on a large common, The Towans, on the cliff overhanging the sea. However, no less than two thousand people turned up! The congregation then adjourned to the large Wesleyan Chapel which was crowded out. The final sermon was on the following night when sixty people sought the Lord for salvation![4]

Revival at St. Ives and St. Just, Cornwall 1861-1862
The Methodist New Connexion invited Rev. William and Catherine Booth to hold meetings at St. Ives. Their children joined them having been in London with the Booths faithful servant, Mary Kirton. The population of St. Ives was 7,000 and was chiefly known for its pilchard fishery. Meetings began on Monday, 30 September 1861 and ended on Saturday, 18 January 1862, and saw 1,028 adults profess conversion. The converts included twenty-eight captains of

vessels, three mine agents and two members of the Corporation (council). Some weeks after the meetings commenced shoals of herring arrived and within thirty minutes, some 30-40 million fish were caught in nets to be landed at leisure. Two thirds of the population were employed in landing the fish, putting them into pickle, draining the oil from them and packing them into barrels for export to the Mediterranean.

In a letter to her mother Mrs Sarah Mumford, Mrs Catherine Booth wrote: 'At my meeting last Sunday we had the chapel packed while hundreds were unable to get in.... I have held morning meetings throughout the week. They have been well attended and much blessed. This morning there was a very gracious influence.' Mrs Booth spoke at the morning meetings; children's meetings on another day and the services at night, 'I was never so busy in all my life.'

F. De L. Booth-Tucker wrote: 'Meetings were held in all the principal places of worship in the town, with the sole exception of the Established Church, the members of which, however joined with the rest of the people in attending the services....'

Rev. William Booth wrote: 'We commenced our services here in the Bible Christian chapel [at St. Just on Sunday, 26 January 1861]. At night the place was literally besieged with people and it was calculated that some 2,000 were turned away, unable to gain admission. I never witnessed anything like the crowd.... On Thursday much prayer had been offered, and at half past nine that night the answer came. The windows of Heaven were open and a shower of blessed influence descended upon us. The effect was electrical. It was sudden and overpowering. The sinners could restrain themselves no longer. Hearts were breaking, or broken in every direction. The chapel was filled with the glory. The meeting was continued until midnight and numbers found peace. The tidings spread with astonishing rapidity throughout the neighbourhood and the people rejoiced in all directions to hear that revival had begun in real earnest.'

In a letter Mrs Catherine Booth wrote: 'I can scarcely believe that three weeks have elapsed since I last wrote to you.... It has been reported in Penzance that all the sinners in this town [St. Just] have been converted save sixty! Although this is far from true, yet events and influences seem to be rapidly shaping in that direction and the signs of the times indicate the possible realisation of such a happy result. When I say the whole place is moved, I mean that nearly every individual of the neighbourhood is more or less interested in religion. Little else is talked about, and in many instances little else besides soul-saving work is done. A gentleman informed me yesterday that a great number of the miners are too absorbed either with their own salvation or with that of others to do much work. Many of the agents of the mines had expressed their willingness to allow the men to leave their work, only too glad that they should be converted. Whether saved or not themselves, they knew that Christianity will bring about a reformation of character only too desirable in many instances.

'The Inspector of Police says that last Saturday night was the best night he has had since he came into the place, the Saturday night prior to the commencement being the worst. Indeed, some of the vilest characters in the town are being saved. One poor fellow, who has been in the hands of the police, times without number, cried out in the school-room on Wednesday afternoon, "He has saved me, the very worst of sinners. In that corner I found the blessing. I shall never forget that corner." '

Mrs Catherine Booth continued: 'Conviction is spreading in every direction and it must be so. Everywhere the newly saved, their hearts glowing with the love of Christ are publishing His praises. The public houses are deserted. A friend said last night that during the day he had been to three of them, the entire customers of them all consisting of two travelling chimney-sweeps. One parlour is the most frequented of these houses, usually too well furnished with guests, was on this occasion tenanted by its solitary landlord.'

On Sunday, 23 February 1862, the meetings moved from the Bible Christians to the Wesleyan Chapel which could seat about 2,000 people. Rev. William Booth wrote: 'After preaching on holiness we invited those who would make the entire consecration of all to Jesus and take Him as a complete Saviour to come forward. Many of the principal Christians led the way and within a few minutes more than a hundred persons were bowed in tears and prayer, waiting for the baptism of the Holy Ghost. And the Holy Spirit descended, cleansing the polluted, and signifying the acceptance of the many whole-hearted sacrifices here laid on the altar. Never shall I forget that scene. All who witnessed it were well-nigh overwhelmed with a sense of the Divine presence. It was the nearest approach to the descent of the mighty rushing wind on the day of Pentecost to anything in my experience, or in that of those present. The Sabbath morning will be hallowed in the recollections of St. Just for many years to come.

'The work now assumed more formidable proportion. It widened as well as deepened. Afternoon and Evening, similar outpourings of the Spirit were realised and during the succeeding week as many as forty, fifty and sixty sought the Saviour day-by-day. The revival is everywhere the engrossing theme [being talked about].

'Last Wednesday *The Cornish Telegraph* [newspaper] announced that the drill of the rifle corps had been suspended and that business generally was at a standstill in consequence of the revival. The motto of the county arms is 'One and All,' and this is a true characteristic of the people. A friend told me the other day that in passing one evening he was accosted by a man who told him that all the adult population were gone to a distant chapel to a revival service, leaving him the sole guard and protector of their children and property, so that he was going from house to house looking after all. I was also informed three weeks ago [early February] that at Truthwells, a village half a mile away, out of fifty-eight adults; fifty-two were already saved. By this time I trust that the Devil has been deprived of the remaining six.'[5]

It was at St. Just on Good Friday, 18 April 1862, when Mrs Catherine Booth held her first meeting for women only. It was calculated that in the spacious Wesleyan Chapel some 2,500 were present. F. De L. Booth-Tucker wrote: 'These services subsequently became a special feature in her life work, invariably attracting large and select gatherings, and by their practical and convincing character revolutionising the homes and lives of multitudes.'[6]

Rev. William Booth and Mrs Catherine Booth also held meetings at Buryan, and Pendeen in the immediate neighbourhood of St. Just; as well as at Lelant. By the end of July 1862, the Booths went to Penzance where they ministered for two months. They had received invites from a number of the leading Wesleyans, and Mr Hobson, the superintendent, who 'had been at the onset greatly impressed by the services.... It is possible that he would have favoured them to the end, but for the powerful pressure brought to bear upon him by some of his ministerial brethren.' Because of this the Wesleyan Conference adopted a resolution forbidding the use of their chapels to Rev. William and Catherine Booth! While the opposition continued they ministered in Mousehole before returning to Penzance where they held meetings in a small chapel; 'many sought salvation in both places,' so wrote Catherine Booth, but it was not like Hayle, St. Ives or St. Just due to the opposition and disunity; therefore there could be no fullness of blessing (Psalm 133).[7]

Revival at Redruth and Camborne, Cornwall 1862

On 28 September 1862, revival broke out in the Free Methodist chapel in the prosperous town of Redruth. The population was about 10,000 and the chapel could accommodate about 1,000 people and was a much larger building than those used at Mousehole and Penzance. F. De L. Booth-Tucker wrote: '[It] was the scene of an awakening, the influence of which extended through all the surrounding countryside.'

F. De L. Booth-Tucker continued: 'So great was the penitents that Mr Booth had the usual communion rails extended across the entire breadth of the chapel, besides erecting barriers to keep off the crowds of onlookers, who pressed so closely to the front that it was found almost impossible to deal effectually with those who were seeking salvation.' This was Rev. Booth's practice, to complete these arrangements *before* a service began, such was his faith! 'At the conclusion of the services, in the course of which 1,000 persons professed conversion, Mr and Mrs Booth commenced similar meetings in the neighbouring town of Camborne.' The chapel could seat 1,000 but 1,300 or 1,400 usually crowded into it! 'On a somewhat smaller scale the revival here was a repetition of the glorious work in Redruth, the tokens of God's presence and favour being with them to the last.' Over eighteen months 'no less than 7,000 persons had professed conversion. Not only had the majority of these joined the religious bodies of their respective towns, but a considerable number had developed into active works, and not a few became preachers of the Gospel.'[8]

The *Wesleyan Times* surveyed the Booths Cornish Campaign of 1861-1862 and after stressing the remarkable conversion of sinners and the awakening of slumbering churches noted: 'All the friends in every place unite in the delightful testimony that the results of the movement abide more generally than those of any other similar work in past experience.'[9]

In 1865, Rev. William Booth was in the East End of London, England, preaching to crowds in the streets when some Christian workers invited him to hold an evangelistic campaign on an old Quaker burial ground in Whitechapel. Rev. Booth later known as General Booth founded The East London Christian Mission which was renamed in May 1878, The Salvation Army. This denomination went on to do incredible things for God, across Britain and abroad, and many of its soldiers (as they were known) saw revival in their own field of labour.

> The psalmist declared: 'You visit the earth and water it, You greatly enrich it; the river of God is full of water; You provide their grain, for so You have prepared it. You water its ridges abundantly, You settle its furrows; You make it soft with showers, You bless its growth. You crown the year with Your goodness, and Your paths drip with abundance' (Psalm 65:9-11).

Chapter 17

The Presence of God

'Restore us, O God of our salvation, and cause Your anger towards us to cease. Will You not revive us again that Your people may rejoice in You? Show us Your mercy, O Lord and grant us Your salvation' (Psalm 85:4, 6-7).

Gold Coast Revival 1875-1878 – Ghana and Beyond

English born Thomas Birch Freeman (1809-1886) was the free son of a slave, (hence the surname), of supposed West Indian origin. In January 1838, he began his pioneering work along the Gold Coast of West Africa (modern day Ghana, Togo, Benin and Nigeria) and laboured there as part of the Wesleyan Missionary Society until he resigned due to differences, but was reinstated many years later. His pioneering work lasted nearly fifty years of service amongst fierce tribes, fetish priests, native kings and their customs, and the cruel, inhuman rituals of human sacrifice and slavery for profit. Thomas Freeman, first saw revival on the Gold Coast (Ghana) from 1851-1852.

In October 1875, Bishop Thomas Birch Freeman visited Kuntu, an outstation of Anamabu, where he found the Christians greatly quickened and in great spiritual expectancy. During his preaching the people were moved and cried aloud. As they knelt penitently at the communion rail, many trembled exceedingly, and clutched the rail to prevent them from falling. A few days later communion was conducted at Anamabu, where three hundred partook. In the same month Freeman visited Cape Coast, and alongside the native minister Andrew W. Parker, a special meeting was conducted for penitents. Cries of mercy resounded around the school-room. Many found the peace of God (reconciled to God / converted) and the others moved to a house and continued all night in prayer. At Salt Pond and Accra, the same happened as the churches burst at the seams, metaphorically speaking and spilled into the streets.

At Elmina, the chapel was full, as people stood outside by the doors and windows. Freeman wrote: 'There was a gracious influence resting on the congregation. We invited the penitents to the communion rail, to which they came in crowds. The Blessed Spirit brooded over us, and we had a fine revival meeting. Scores of the congregation were in tears and crying for mercy and many found peace and joy in believing. At Kormantine, the people 'cried mightily to the Lord for salvation.' Leaving the chapel, Freeman preached to the fishermen in the open-air, 'who were greatly moved by the truths declared.'

One woman had to have her wedding delayed by a few hours, as in the morning prayer meeting she was prostrate on the floor 'under the hallowed fervour.' Such were the number now attending church at Cape Coast, discussion commenced about enlarging the Wesleyan Church. Freeman also warned his leaders about excesses and advised them how to act during the revival. 'Less the people come to think that loud cries and trembling as a necessary part, or as adjuncts to conversion.'

In Anamabu, Freeman's wife wrote for him to return as the chapel was overflowing into the streets. She wrote: 'While one girl was praying and crying all that were in the chapel trembled.' In another letter she wrote: 'One of our sisters, as she was passing along the street, met a group of about twelve heathen people, men and women, from the fishing quarters of town, who were saying, "We will go to chapel to be Christians; we will go and give ourselves to God omnipotent." '

In early December 1875, Freeman revisited Salt Pond, where the candidates for baptism, occupied a line of benches forty-seven paces long. On the same day he returned to Anamabu where two hundred and twelve people were baptised in the presence of hundreds. J. Milum in *Thomas Birch Freeman – Missionary Pioneer* (1894) noted that there were many extraordinary cases of people trembling violently, loud cries, which might rank with some recorded in John Wesley's *Journal*.

One day in January, Freeman baptised two hundred and sixty adults and children, one of whom was the head of a pagan family. He was a former extravagant drinker of rum, which was part of a ritual connected with the burial of the dead.

On 9 April 1876, one thousand Christians flocked to the Gold Coast, at Great Kormantine village camp meeting. Fifteen hundred people partook of the love feast later that day. Freeman remarked, "It may be deemed important to notice that the extraordinary meetings in *feeding the revival* has been their suitableness to the national genius of the people. In their pagan life they are accustomed to frequent and extensive gatherings in their occasional and annual customs. Thus the national habits have been utilised to promote the spread of the Gospel, and to uplift the Church of Christ into a higher atmosphere of Christian life."

In 1876, four thousand five hundred natives were baptised. Whole villages forsook their pagan ways and idols to serve the Living God. By the end of 1877, no less than three thousand more people had been added to the church and fifteen hundred had been baptised by Freeman himself and still the revival continued.[1]

Movements in China and Japan 1885

In February 1885, missionaries of the China Inland Mission, the Cambridge Seven departed London, England, and arrived in Shanghai, China, after a six week voyage. Rev. W. W. Cassels, one of the Seven wrote: 'There was an almost overwhelming thought of the enormous work which has to be done here. Even in a place like Shanghai, which I suppose to be the centre of missionary activity, how many thousands there are entirely untouched by the efforts at present put forth! If this is of Shanghai what shall we say of the rest of the country. We felt more than ever that nothing but a mighty outpouring of the Spirit of God can be of any use...how one longs to be able to speak the language and talk to these dear people!'[2]

Mr Montagu Beauchamp, another of the Seven in a letter from Shanghai, dated 25 April 1885, wrote: 'We had meetings twice and sometimes three times a day. We were quite a large gathering; no less than sixteen of us...we took as our subject "In Christ." One Sunday evening we had the Lord's Supper, which was a very precious time together...we were abundantly rewarded by a special manifestation of the presence of the MASTER Himself. At this meeting we may attribute special blessing to the fact that everyone present contributed something to the edifying of the Body; though in some cases it was only a Scripture....'

A circular letter from missionaries in Peking (Beijing), dated 22 June 1885: 'Dear brothers...in the afternoon meetings [two hours each] they dwelt largely on the theme that the baptism of the Holy Ghost was promised to all believers...our object in these has been, first, the baptism of the Holy Spirit on our hearts, giving power for our work, and second, the outpouring of the Spirit on China. The present revival in Japan began with a daily prayer meeting. If we would all unite, have we not faith to believe that God would shake China with His power? Yours in the Gospel.' The letter was signed by twenty-five missionaries of five different mission organisations, and the Inspector-General of I.M. Customs, Peking.[3]

Prayer for World Revival 1885

In August 1885, D. L. Moody, with several hundred delegates attended a ten day convention in Northfield, America, where they discussed and prayed for world revival. On 10 August, the sixth day, Dr. Pierson warmly contended that the promise of supernatural power with the preaching of the Gospel, accompanied by supernatural signs, is as binding today as when it was made by the departing Saviour. A circular letter was soon prepared, made by resolution and carried by acclamation in the name of the convention to all believers throughout the world. The letter went as follows: 'To fellow believers of every name scattered through the world, greetings: Assembled in the name of our Lord JESUS CHRIST, with one accord in one place, we have continued for ten days in prayer and supplication, communing with one another about the common salvation, the blessed hope, and the duty of witnessing to a lost world.

'It was near our place of meeting that in 1747, at Northampton, Mass., Jonathan Edwards sent forth his trumpet peal calling upon all disciples everywhere to unite in prayer for an infusion of the Spirit upon the whole habitable globe. That summons to prayer marked a new epoch in the Church of God. Praying bands began to gather in this and other lands. Mighty revivals of religion followed; immorality and infidelity were wonderfully checked [came under control]; and after 1,500 years of apathy and lethargy, the spirit of mission was reawakened. In 1792, the monthly concert was begun, and the first missionary society was formed in England. In 1793, William Carey, the pioneer missionary sailed for India. Since then over 100 missionary boards [societies] have been organised, and probably no less than 100,000 missionaries including women have gone out into the mission field...results of missionary labour in the Hawaiian and Fiji Islands, Madagascar, in Japan, probably have no parallel even in apostolic days, while even Pentecost is surpassed by the ingathering of 10,000 converts in one station in India within sixty days in the year 1868...God has thus in answer to prayer opened the door of access to the nations.... The first Pentecost covered ten days of united, continued supplication. Every subsequent advance may be divinely traced to believing prayer, and upon this must depend a new Pentecost. We therefore earnestly appeal to all disciples to join us in importunate and daily supplications for a new and mighty infusion of the Holy Spirit on all ministers, missionaries, pastors, teachers, and Christian workers and upon the whole earth, that God would impart to all Christ's witnesses the tongues of fire, and melt hard hearts before the burning message. It is not by might, but by the Spirit of the Lord that all true success must be secured; let us call upon God till He answereth by fire! What we are to do for the salvation of the lost must be done quickly, for the generation is passing away, and we with it.... 'Thy Kingdom come.' '[4]

The Welsh Revival 1904-1905 – Wales

Wales has long been known as the 'Land of Revivals,' though there have actually been more revivals in Scotland than in Wales! See *Land of Many Revivals* and *Glory in the Glen*, both by Tom Lennie, an expert of revivals in Scotland. In Wales between 1762 and 1862 there were at least sixteen outstanding revivals. Some were localised, while others were far reaching in their effect. 'Many of the famous preachers of Wales attributed their spiritual birth and their ministerial power to movings of the Spirit felt at such times,'[5] whilst for others it was a vitalization, a recharging, a fresh impetus for their already successful ministry.

Evans Roberts was converted at age thirteen and swiftly became a member of Moriah Chapel in 1893-4; his local Calvinistic Methodists Chapel. He attended church meetings six days a week, having once been challenged by an elder, "What if the Spirit came and you were absent?" Evan Roberts carried a deep burden for revival for thirteen years before he saw it, and God had given him a vision of 100,000 souls. During the revival many thought of Evans as a mystic because of his visions and prayers, though he suffered from depression for many periods of his life. Some said he was an eccentric at best and a lunatic at worst! Perhaps this was his thorn in the flesh as it was with Rev. Duncan Campbell and others, to keep them humble.

In early 1904, Rev. Joseph Jenkins of New Quay, Cardiganshire was praying that change would come over the churches in his neighbourhood, including his own. On Sunday, 14 February, Valentines Day, at a young peoples meeting, Rev. Jenkins asked those present to stand up and tell everyone what has happened to them concerning their Christian faith. Different ones stood up and shared with difficulty, and then Florrie Evans, a young teenager rose to her feet and said, "I love Jesus Christ with all my heart." A work of the Holy Spirit began which touched other places, including the village of Blaenannerch, sixteen miles away, where its minister, Rev. M. P. Morgan threw himself heart and soul into the movement. It was arranged to hold a conference there in September 1904.

In the spring of 1904 for three months Evan Roberts was woken up at 1am every morning and had Divine communion with God for about three hours. In the summer of 1904, age twenty-six, Evan Roberts began studying at Newcastle Emlyn School in preparation for his training for the ministry at Trevecca College – which never happened. In late September 1904, Evan Roberts whilst a student attended a series of meetings under Seth Joshua, a Forward Movement minister, at New Quay, in Ceredigion. At Blaenannerch on Thursday, 29 September 1904, Evan Roberts had a momentous encounter with God. He was perspiring, hanging over the pew in front of him and cried out in his native welsh, "Plyg fi O Arglwydd," which translates as, "Bend me, oh Lord!" But can also be translated as: "Fold me, oh Lord," bearing in mind he was a tall man and was hanging over the pew. In an instant his nervousness and speech impediment was removed. A small brass plaque screwed onto the back of the pew which he hung over, barely three inches in height and engraved in Welsh, marks the seat that Evan Roberts sat in.

In October 1904, Evan Roberts received a vision of Hell; a fiery bottomless pit surrounded by impenetrable walls with countless numbers of people surging towards it, and pleaded that Hell's door be closed for one year so that they might have opportunity to repent. He also had a vision of 100,000 souls and a vision of himself preaching at Moriah Chapel in front of people who he recognised. He sought the Principal for advice and Rev. Evan Phillips of Newcastle Emlyn School gave him leave for one week, stating that the Holy Spirit wished him to return to Loughor. Evan Roberts' family were startled when they saw him on 31 October 1904 and wanted to know if he was unwell. He told them he was well and was going to hold meetings and tell them about what happened at Blaenannerch.

Revival broke out in Moriah Chapel, Loughor, South Wales, UK, on 31 October 1904, the same day that Martin Luther nailed his 95 theses to the church door at Wittenberg in 1517. Evan Roberts' call went forth to the Lord in the presence of the youth meeting, "Send the Spirit now for Jesus Christ's sake," and the youthful congregation of seventeen people followed suit. When the adults heard what had happened they to wanted to attend the meetings. Within a week, the local and national papers got a hold of the move of God and free advertisement through its reporting began to spread, which drew people who were hungry for God from across the globe.

At around the same time, as the revival that began at Loughor, spread south, revival broke out in Rhos, South Wales, and spread north. The *Wrexham Advertiser* (newspaper) reported: 'The prayer meetings are so crowded that the places of worship are inadequate to contain them. Some last eight hours, with no cessation in prayer or singing! From the lips of the humblest and lowliest put forth petitions which thrill the whole being – the spell of earthly things seem to be broken. In the streets, in the train, in the car, even in public houses, all this is, in hushed and reverential tones, the theme of conversation.'[6]

A circular issued by the Free Church Council of Carmarthen, about the time of the great outburst in 1904 stated: 'We cannot justly expect sinners to be saved, and our places of worship be filled by those from outside, until we ourselves get right with God; and this can only be done by an absolute surrender of our whole lives to Jesus Christ as King, and a faith acceptance of the Holy Spirit.' An awakened church creates the atmosphere in which decisions by the lost to accept the Saviour will be made easier.[7]

Daniel Powell Williams of Penygroes, in Carmarthen, South Wales, UK, was converted on Christmas Day 1904 in Loughor. In reference to the revival he wrote: 'The manifestation of the power was beyond human management. Men and women were mowed down by the axe of God like a forest. The glory was resting for over two years in some localities.'[8]

Evan Roberts received invitations from numerous churches and chapels around South Wales and beyond. Within six weeks, 100,000 souls were swept into the Kingdom of God (some authors incorrectly state that 100,000 souls were converted in total), at the time, the population of Wales was only around one million and within eight months 150,000 had made application for church membership. Revival historian, J. Edwin Orr stated that as many as 250,000 people could have been converted during this revival. Those who emigrated, moved away to other towns outside of Wales or who attended or even built a non-established church, chapel or mission hall would not have been recorded on official church membership roles. Sadly many churches and Christians rejected the revival and doors were bolted shut to Evan Roberts. As the Holy Spirit flowed through the valleys, some villages were entirely bypassed. Rees Howells was converted in America and came back to Wales during the revival. He founded a local mission in 1907 and was involved in evangelism and intercession. He was challenged by the Holy Spirit to see revival in a village nicknamed Hell-Fire Row which had not been touched during the Welsh Revival (1904-1905)![9]

Leonard Ravenhill stated that when Evan Roberts visited Anglesey in North Wales, there were open manifestations of the Spirit of God in at least five places. Roberts knew that God was there and (in one place) told the people, "Obey God" and left them to it.[10]

A few months after the revival broke out Evan Roberts was invited to speak at a very successful Congregational Chapel in Dowlais, South Wales. Within thirty minutes of his arrival, he announced that someone in that service was blocking the way of revival [for the chapel] by criticism of the revival and, more especially criticism of the revivalist. He declared that unless the spirit was expunged he would be compelled to leave. He would not remain or take part in mock worship where the Holy Spirit was grieved. He soon departed, leaving the service to the opposition.[11]

Unless a leader in the midst of revival is wise and delegates responsibility to others he or she will soon become worn out, or encounter burnout and have a breakdown or suffer collapse due to exhaustion. Sometimes you have to say, "No" for the greater good. You cannot be at every meeting or accept every invite. Some leaders have died prematurely for neglect of the human body, deprivation of food and sleep. Evan Roberts had four breakdowns during the revival where he was not seen for days or for a week. On the other hand, he would often be in the pulpit, laughing and smiling and some thought that this was irreverent. '...Whom having not seen [Jesus] you love. Though now you do not see Him, yet believing, you rejoice with joy inexpressible and full of glory' (1 Peter 1:8). Spiritual adrenaline will only take you so far before something gives. We must look after our bodies as well as our minds.

A friend once asked Evan Roberts for a message to the churches that were praying for revival. Closing his eyes for a moment, he prayed for guidance and then said, "They have the Word and they know the promise. Let them keep God to His promise, 'ask and ye shall receive.' "

The daily shifts at the coal mines soon started with a word of prayer. Miners would become aware of the presence of God while deep in the mines and fall on their knees in repentance. The mineshafts resonated with the hymns of the converted miners who were so taken up into glory, and this was whilst doing their hard labour and intensive work. Some of the miners were so changed by God that the pit ponies which were used to being commanded by the unconverted foul mouths refused to work as they could not recognise the sanctified tongues! Many of the workers' drinking songs had their lyrics changed and sanctified to suit the well known and popular tunes. In church services people would cry out, "What must I do to be saved?" others would cry out, "O God forgive me," as the weight of their sins came upon them in deep reality.

In the Rhondda Valley and beyond, the magistrates were given white gloves, a symbol of purity, as there were so few cases to hear; God's Spirit that brought conviction of sin, which eventually led to salvation as people called upon God, brought about changed lives, sobriety and restraint. White gloves were also handed out in Swansea County Court and Aberdare; whilst Aberdare on Christmas Eve was almost entirely free from drunkenness, and on Christmas Day there were no prisoners at all in the cells. At Abercarn Police Court, responsible for a population of 21,000 there was not a single summons on a Thursday before the New Year – a thing unknown since the Court was formed fourteen years previously, and the ceremony of the white gloves was observed. In Cardiff, the Mayor handed the chief constable a pair of white gloves in memory of there being no cases at all on the charge sheet on the last day of 1904.[12]

The Christian Herald newspaper, dated 16 February 1905, consisted of twenty-four pages, much of which was dedicated to the revival; with illustrations. One of the illustrations in the *Christian Herald Archive* (Welsh Revival Issue) showed Father Christmas holding a Christmas tree over his shoulder whilst a husband, wife and three children sat around the meal table. The article stated: 'The revival in Wales brought many a family a far happier Christmas than they ever had before. The aforementioned drunken husband and father, now made a new man in Christ Jesus, spent the money which had hitherto gone to the public house and in betting, in clothes and feeding his family, and provided such a Christmas treat as they had only before seen in dreamland. No wonder the artist has shown Old Father Christmas looking on with approval.'

In 1905, Dr. Handley Carr-Glyn Moule, the Bishop of Durham, near Sunderland, England, in the *Record* wrote: 'The revival in Wales is attracting attention in a degree altogether unusual and in quarters not always likely. One of the notices of it which met my eye was in the *Times*, an extended and most respectful communiqué [an official report]. Today the *Yorkshire Post* prints a noteworthy letter from a special correspondent, also entirely respectful. A dear friend of mine and former Cambridge student writes to me from his vicarage near Wales, confirming to the full the published accounts of profound and widespread spiritual movement, and of the splendid moral results which have already resulted in countless cases. Those of us who remember the great revival of 1859 feel as if again one of those times of mysterious but manifest blessing might be at our doors, not in Wales only, but over England, when by a power secret and Divine, the cry of the soul for a true salvation is met by the eternal answer, the Lord Jesus Christ. I appeal to my brethren in the ministry, and not least to those of us who call ourselves evangelicals, to observe this movement with a reverent welcome and a sacred hope.'

The Bishop of St. David's in Pembrokeshire, Wales, made reference to the revival at the reopening of Brawdy Church in Pembrokeshire. His text was from Revelation 2:29: 'He that hath an ear, let him hear what the Spirit saith unto the churches.' "It was a significant thing," he said, "that this movement, which so strongly stirred the hearts of men and women, and had stopped more drunkenness in two months than Parliament had in two years, began not with the ministers, but with the young laymen. The deepest lesson of the movement was that the spiritual power did not come from men, but from the Spirit of God Himself." The Bishop also 'urged his bearers to pray for the Spirit [to come].'[13]

Whole football and rugby teams were converted, and praying became more important than playing! Games were either cancelled or put off until a more convenient time, whilst other teams disbanded. Theatre attendance dropped, dance halls were deserted and pubs (drinking establishments) were emptied and closed; the proprietors were furious! Talented actors and actresses failed to draw the crowds, and those foolish enough to jest about the revival, indulged in by comedians, not only fell flat, but aroused indignation.

In many of the revivals from Church history, groups of evangelists, lay workers or prayer bands, have travelled from one spiritual hotspot to a spiritually dead location to help ignite the flames of revival, to stir the Christians to pray or to encourage those who already are, and to hold meetings or campaigns. During the Welsh Revival (1904-1905) there were a number of teams ranging in size from three to eight people, often with a male leader with teenage or young women singing evangelists / preachers. However, the first team consisted of only five young women and no men!

The prominent male leaders were Evan Roberts, Dan Roberts (brother) and Sidney Evans (future brother-in-law to Evan and Dan Roberts), whilst Sam Jenkins was a singer who on occasions teamed up with Sidney Evans. Mr E. Lloyd Jones was also prominent but not as much as the first three men. Some of the young women, all unmarried and known as evangelists were: Mary and Ann Davies (sisters from Maesteg), a Mary Davies (from Gorseinon), Maggie Davis (from Maesteg), S. A. Jones (from Nantymoel), Annie M. Rees (from Gorseinon), Livinia Hooker (from Gorseinon), Priscilla Watkins (from Gorseinon), May John, and Nellie Borthwick-Clarke.

Under the inspiration of the Holy Spirit, many chapel soloists became inspired worship leaders, carrying the heart of the nation in song, one in particular was Anne Davies, from Maesteg, who often sung, 'Dyma Gariad' – 'Here is love, vast as the ocean.' This love song from the revival has been said to be the most popular, and like most of the revival hymns was best sung in the native Welsh language.

Choruses began to break through which were sung in English, especially Moody and Sankey's, which before the revival had been taboo in many Welsh speaking congregations. As the singer and minister, David Matthews in *I Saw the Welsh Revival* wrote: 'I had never heard a single English chorus sung in our orthodox assemblies. To make such an attempt would have been rated almost "a sin against the Holy Ghost." Such a statement may seem strange, but it is nevertheless, strictly true (the exception being during singing competitions)... the singing of Gospel choruses in another language was unthinkable....'

If the revival had anything that might be called a slogan, it was this, 'Bend the church, and save the people.' The word 'bend' in Welsh conveys the meaning of submission to God, and the taking away of resistance to His will.

In spring 1905, E. Morgan Humphreys wrote an eyewitness account of a revival meeting at Anfield Road Chapel, Liverpool: 'The crowds were pressing against the chapel doors, trying to push their way in, and elderly ladies were climbing over the railings to get to the door and, falling on the others were being thrown inside by the police like sacks of flour.'[14] A visual account of the Welsh Revival can be found on the DVD *Great Christian Revivals* by ByFaith Media.

In 1905, Evan Roberts prayed in a packed meeting where thirteen hundred new converts were rejoicing in their new-found faith. He said, "Lord Jesus, help us now, through the Holy Spirit to come face to face with the cross. Whatever the hindrances may be, we commit the service to Thee. Put us all under the blood, Oh Lord, place the blood on all our past up to this moment. We thank Thee for the blood. In the name of Jesus Christ, bind the Devil this moment. We point to the cross of Christ. Oh, open the Heavens. Descend upon us now. We shall give all the glory to Thy name. No one else has the right to the glory but Thee. Take it Lord, glorify Thy Son in this meeting. Oh, Holy Spirit, do Thy work through us and in us now. Speak Thy Word in power for Thy name's sake. Amen and Amen."[15]

Jessie Penn-Lewis in *The Awakening in Wales* (1906) wrote: 'We find all sections of the church affected by it, for the Holy Ghost is no respecter of denomination any more than persons, and He freely wrought in every place where He was welcomed when He began to work, and was given room.'

A visitor to Blaengarw in the county of Bridgend, thirty miles by car from Swansea, wrote: 'I had keen recollections of the Bank Holiday loafers I had seen there many times before. The crowds of aimless wanderers, wandering from public house to public house [for a drink], banding fearful language with one another on the road! But what a change I found as I walked from Blaengarw to Pant-y-gog without hearing or seeing one drunken man! There was hardly a sound to be heard in the public houses. None of the bustle of a holiday, notwithstanding the day was fine. As I passed down Oxford Street, Pontycymmer, I met groups of men who sang quietly as they walked such hymns as 'Dim ond Calvary' [Only Calvary], their voices raising and falling in harmony as they strolled along. They were rough fellows enough, but there was a new light in their eyes and a new song in their mouths. Further on I met a long procession of men, women and children singing in English, 'Oh Where Is My Wandering Boy?' They passed on down the road, the haunting melody of the simple hymn growing fainter till it died away. Wales is the land of song, but two days in the Garw Valley makes me think it will be before long what it was in the long [sic] ago, 'The Land of Saints.'

In 1905, a reporter noted: 'During the months of November and December, orders for Bibles for Wales were over three times the amount for the corresponding months of 1903, and this demand shows no signs of falling off.' A bookseller said, "No trouble now to sell Bibles, the trouble is to get them!" Another bookseller wrote: 'Please send these at once. Great demand for Bibles now the revival is in our midst.' A third bookseller said, "I find an increased demand for Bibles and religious literature since the great revival wave burst over Cymra [Wales]."[16]

Miss Minnie F. Abrams in her book, *The Baptism of the Holy Ghost and Fire* (1906), wrote: 'Prayer is ascending for a worldwide revival. The Spirit was first poured out upon Wales. There, in places they all prayed at once, or sung the same chorus a hundred times over, or quietly; listened to the Word and exhortation as the Spirit led. Eyewitnesses have described the scene at Keswick [in England] last year (1905), when people were weeping, making confession, and praying in apparent confusion. Yet there was no confusion in the mind of the infinite God.'[17]

In Anglesey, Caernarfon and Bala, Evan Roberts repeated the challenge *to witness in every possible form*. He said, "It will not do for us to go to Heaven by ourselves. We must be on fire, friends, for saving others. To be workers, will draw Heaven down and will draw others to Heaven. Without readiness to work, the spirit of prayer will not come."[18]

In the spring of 1938, a teenage Arthur Wallis was at Moriah Chapel, Loughor; the birthplace of the Welsh Revival (1904-1905). He thought to himself: 'If God can achieve such mighty things in times of revival, and if the spiritual labourers of fifty years can be surpassed in so many days when the Spirit is poured out, why…is the Church today so satisfied with the results of normal evangelism? Why are we not more concerned that there should be another great revival? Why do we not pray for it day and night?'[19]

Count Zinzendorf of the Moravian Church said, "I am destined by the Lord to proclaim the message of the death and blood of Jesus, not with human wisdom, but with Divine power, unmindful of consequences to myself." The declaration of The Salvation Army is "Blood and Fire." Rev. John Greenfield noted how it was a 'favourite phrase of Evan Roberts, the youthful leader of the Welsh Revival: "Remember the blood! Catch the flame." '[20]

During the revival some of the chapels, especially the Congregationalists had not associated themselves with the preaching of the great revival. They had missed out on the blessing and had multitudes of unregenerate members – church goers with the nickname Christian. During the revival many mission halls were founded and there was estrangement between those who had been blessed and the chapels. John Howells of Brynamman, (the eldest brother of Rees Howells who founded the Bible College of Wales in 1924) was an elder in the Congregational chapel, yet he alongside with some friends was responsible for building the Gospel Hall in their village. But where the Congregationalist ministers were blessed in the revival, the converts remained in the chapels.

After the revival, Rees Howells also founded a mission hall in Garnet, two miles away from his home, when after three years, by the command of God; he handed the leadership over to a co-worker and was called into the hidden life. Around five years later when he began attending chapels again, many Christians in the locality thought he had backslidden. After this time, Rees for a period of two years was preaching the simple Gospel; the new birth, 'preaching to the multitudes in many chapels in the district' and was later ordained by the Congregationalists and saw revival across Southern Africa under the South Africa General Mission.[21]

The Legacy of the Revival

Sidney Evans of the Welsh Revival (1904-1905) wrote: 'The revivals of past history have often safeguarded the Christian ministry for a whole generation.' He was ordained in 1916 and went out to India in 1920 as a missionary with his wife, Mary, a sister of Evan Roberts, until his retirement in 1945. Dan Phillips was converted on Christmas Day 1904 during the revival and went on to found the Apostolic Church, a Pentecostal denomination with more than ten million members in 2017. In 1933, the Apostolic Church International Bible School was founded at Pen-y-groes; which was later renamed the Apostolic Church School of Ministry. Brothers, George and Stephen Jeffreys were converted in November 1904 during the revival. They would both go on to have healing and evangelism campaigns across Britain. Stephen first saw revival in Cwmtwrch, Wales in 1913, where he asked for his brother's assistance. George Jeffreys first saw revival in Ireland in 1916. He went on to found the Elim Foursquare Gospel Alliance, and was known as Principal George Jeffreys. The Jeffreys' brothers were Britain's greatest evangelists since the time of John Wesley and George Whitefield of the eighteenth century.

Rees Howells from Brynaman, Wales, was converted in America and was greatly touched during the Welsh Revival (1904-1905). He married in 1910 and with his wife Lizzie, joined the South Africa General Mission (SAGM), and was based in Rusutu, Gazaland. They were missionaries in Southern Africa from 1915-1920, and saw revival at Rusitu and across Southern Africa. For nearly three years they did deputation work on behalf of the SAGM, before founding the Bible College of Wales (BCW) in Swansea, Wales in 1924. Rheinard Bonnke was a student at BCW in the early 1960s and went on to found Christ For All Nations (CfaN) where in one meeting in Nigeria, Africa, he led over one million people to the Lord in a single meeting. Bonnke has seen 56 million decisions for Christ mostly in Africa, whilst his ministry, CfaN has seen a total of 76 million decisions for Christ by June 2017.

Norman Grubb first met Rees Howells in 1928 and learnt the life of faith through him. In 1931, upon the death of his father-in-law C. T. Studd, founder of the Worldwide Evangelization Crusade (WEC),

Norman Grubb became the leader of WEC, which was struggling financially and numerically, coupled with a power dispute over leadership. Rees Howells was able to advise Grubb how to proceed and under Grubb's leadership the mission grew from the Heart of Africa to a worldwide missionary movement. Grubb wrote *Rees Howells Intercessor* (1952) which went on to sell more than 11 million copies, which has touched the lives of tens of thousands! The history of Barry and Bryntirion Colleges in Wales also have their genesis with the Welsh Revival (1904-1905) under different Christian workers. R. B. Jones began the Porth Institute in 1925. The Barry School of Evangelism was opened in 1936 under B. S. Fidler who had worked at the Bible College of Wales and at the Porth Institute. The Porth Institute was renamed the South Wales Bible College in 1950, which merged with Barry School of Evangelism in 1985 to become Bryntirion College.

Last Decades of Evan Roberts' Life and Revival Celebrations
In 1928, Evan Roberts attend the funeral of his dad at Moriah Chapel. The preacher was quite dull and Evans stood up and exclaimed, "This is not a death but a resurrection. Let us bear witness to this truth." One person who was present testified, "Something like electricity went through us. One felt that if he had gone on there would have been another revival there and then." Shortly afterwards Evan Roberts was asked by Mary Davies, one of the women singers from the Welsh Revival (1904-1905), now in her early forties, to help her with some converts at Gorseinon, near Swansea, Wales. God's power once again flowed and a mini-revival broke out in Loughor and Gorseinon! For two years he was well known again and exercised a ministry in healing and exorcism; as well as training young disciples in his Bible School. He lived the remainder of his life in relative obscurity; much of it was spent in intercession for the nations as part of the hidden life, though on occasions he did preach.

In 1928, Evan Roberts attended the Moriah Chapel Centenary Celebration, but did not want to be involved in the 40th Anniversary Celebrations of the Welsh Revival in 1944. From 1931-1933 he avoided conferences as in 1930 or 1931 he was mobbed at the Ammondford Convention by those eager to see and hear him, though at other times, he could slip into a chapel and be unnoticed. In 1932, he retired from public ministry and became involved in the Eisteddfod Association (poetry festivals) for which many thought he had truly backslide![22]

In the late 1930 and possibly into the early 1940s, Evan Roberts who then lived in Cardiff went to Swansea once a month (or thereabouts), with Rees Howells, founder of the Bible College of

Wales (d.1950 in Sketty, Swansea) and Stephen Jeffreys, healing evangelist and revivalist (d.1943 in Mumbles, Swansea) for prayer. In December 1942, Evan Roberts' health began to decline and for some time he was under a specialist doctor's supervision because of a disease (unknown to us), and was admitted to hospital again in 1949. He used to annually visit a guesthouse in London for free, staying for up to a month where he attended theatres and concerts and had days out with his Christian host, Sam Jenkins a singer from the revival.

In 1951, age 72, Evan Roberts was promoted to glory and was buried on 29 January in the family grave at Moriah Chapel, Loughor. For the jubilee of the revival, 1954, the Presbyterian Church of Wales erected an 8 feet granite memorial column outside the chapel with an inscription in Welsh and English to the memory of Evan Roberts and the Welsh Revival (1904-1905), as a testimony for future generations. A book aimed at children, *Something Wonderful Happened* by Mabel Bickerstaff (1954) was also written and published for the jubilee.

In March 1969, the sixty-fifth anniversary of the revival was celebrated at a packed Moriah Chapel when Dr. Eifion Evans preached in English in the morning service and Dr. Martyn Lloyd-Jones preached in Welsh at the evening service. In 2004, the Centenary Celebration was held in the chapel and was packed to maximum capacity, which it had not seen since March 1969.

For the Centenary Celebrations of 2004, revival memorabilia had been collated and was on display in the school-room of Moriah Chapel in Loughor. Special porcelain plates were commissioned and on sale. On display were other revival related items: including books, revival hymnbooks, paper cuttings, photocopies, postcards and porcelain. Cotton handkerchiefs with the face of Evan Roberts were also manufactured during the revival, as was a Staffordshire figurine similar to the busts of other revivalists. There was also an antique white mug with Evan Roberts' face and shoulders emblazoned on it, whilst A. B. Jones and Sons, Grafton Works, Longton, Staffordshire, England, produced cups and saucers with the face of Evan Roberts on them.

The revival postcards at Moriah were of Evan Roberts, his brother and some of the women helpers, which had been printed during the revival by the *Western Mail* newspaper. On 4 November 1904, Evan Roberts wrote to the editor of the *Sunday Companion* asking for a quotation for a visible representation of his visions on printed postcards, which would give the message wider circulation. I am not aware of this "visible representation" postcard ever being printed, however, there are at least forty-one different types of 1904-1905 revival related postcards.

Worldwide Influence of the Welsh Revival

Because of the Holy Spirit being outpoured in Wales it encouraged people to pray for revival across the globe which ignited revivals in many places from 1905 onwards. Some of these revivals include:

- Some churches in London, England (1905).
- Wanganui and Waihi, New Zealand (1905).
- Orkneys, Scotland, in March (1905).
- Madagascar, Africa (1905).
- Patagonia, South Seas (1905).
- State of Assam, India (1905).
- Khasi Revival, India (1905-1906).
- Mukti Revival, West India (1905-1906) under Pandita Ramabai.
- Dohnavur, India (1905) under Amy Carmichael amongst the Tamils in the South West of India.
- North America (1905).
- Denmark (1905).
- Mexico City (1905) amongst English speaking communities.
- France (1905) sporadic places when revived French people returned home with evangelistic fervour.
- Sweden (1905).
- Villiersdorp, South Africa (1905).
- Rhur, Germany (1905) under Jakob Vetter, a tent evangelist.
- Hungary and Bulgaria among the evangelical minorities (1905).
- Algiers, Algeria (1905-1906) under Reuben Saillens, where he saw from 1,200-2,000 converts by 1906.
- Shanghai and Canton, China (1906) and in the north under the China Inland Mission.
- Azusa Street Revival (1906-1909).
- Telugu Revival, India (1906) under the Canadian Mission.
- Norway under T. B. Barrett (1907) of the Oslo City Mission.
- Pyongyang Great Revival, Korea (1907-1910).[23]

Revival in South Woodford, London 1905 – England

The following is from the *Baptist Times*, 3 February 1905: 'For the past months in South Woodford, following a week of united prayer held in connection with the Free Churches, the Holy Spirit has been working His glorious miracles of conviction and conversion. There has been no advertisement nor any organising, but a simple, though strongly expressed, demand on behalf of the people of God that evangelistic services should be held, and now the good work gone on night after night with blessing upon blessing. Bible readings have been held every afternoon conducted by Revs. A. A. Savage and F.

D. Robbins, and evening meetings presided over by the same two ministers. Midnight meetings have been held and a number of notorious drunkards have been brought to know the saving and keeping power of Christ. One man who had not been inside a place of worship for twenty years was brought nearly drunk into the midnight meeting and on Tuesday last gave himself up to the "keeping" Saviour. A man and his wife, who but a day or two before were fighting in their drunkenness outside one of the public houses, were brought to Christ; the wife came first, and then fetching her husband, had the joy of seeing him yield to the gracious influence of the Spirit.

'One meeting must be described. After parading the streets singing the old hymns of the Church, such as: "Rock of Ages" and "Jesus Lover of my Soul," the service inside the church having concluded with no apparent results, a hymn was sung, and the benediction pronounced. No sooner had Mr Savage said Amen, than some lady came and said, "May we sing 'Almost Persuaded'?" The first two verses were sung but as the third verse proceeded, "Almost persuaded, harvest is past," the leader arose and said, "That is not true with anyone here," recommencing the verse. The words died away and only the organ was left to finish the terrible last line or two. The congregation wept, broken prayers were offered, and five souls asked for help and were led to the "Lamb of God who taketh away the sins of the world." The end of the meeting was one of intense joy.

'On Friday night last a pause in the meetings came by way of a Baptismal service in the George Lane Baptist Church which will never be forgotten by any who were privileged to be present. After a sermon by the minister from John 2:5, the two ministers descended the baptistery together. The first to be baptised was the eldest daughter of Mr Savage and the second, the daughter of Mr Robbins. Both the ministers were deeply moved as were the congregation also. Then followed twenty-three others. Many more are waiting for baptism and it is impossible to see where it will end. The services are being continued this week at the Baptist Church, George Lane, and next week are to be held in the Wanstead Church. It is quite impossible to give numbers as so many have come to salvation outside the meetings and the workers have set their faces against counting of heads; but the numbers brought to Christ in the meetings is well on for a hundred and many pledges have been taken."

'...I will remember the years of the right hand of the Most High. I will remember the works of the Lord; surely I will remember Your wonders of old. I will also meditate on all Your works, and talk of Your deeds' (Psalm 77:10b-12).

Chapter 18

From the West to the East

The Lord of hosts says, "For from the rising of the sun, even to its going down, My name shall be great among the Gentiles; in every place incense shall be offered to My name, and a pure offering; for My name shall be great among the nations" (Malachi 1:11).

Mukti Revival 1905-1906 – India

In 1897 a localised revival broke out in the Sharada Sadan, Poona, a school for child widows and the Mukti Mission, Kedgaon, India, which is forty miles south of Poona. Both these sites had been founded by the esteemed Pandita Ramabai. This former Hindu prior to the revival of 1897 was the most prominent woman Christian social pioneer of India. Helen S. Dyer in *Pandita Ramabai, The Story of Her Life* (1901) wrote: 'Pandita Ramabai is a spiritually minded Christian, one whose testimony by life and lip, has no uncertain sound, a woman who believes the Bible to be the inspired Word of God and whose teaching is untouched by the fatal poison of higher criticism [where the Bible is questioned and challenged as untrue]. One who believes unreservedly in the efficacy of the atoning blood of Christ for the guilt of sin, and who reckons upon the power of the Holy Ghost for service; a woman equipped by God to lead and to organise, and under God's grace to educate and train India's sons and daughters for lives of service along Holy Ghost lines.'[1]

Pandita Ramabai hearing of the revival in Australia (1902) under evangelist Reuben Archer Torrey and inspired by the 2,000 prayer circles that had been formed requested that prayer circles, or prayer bands be formed throughout the world, which was communicated through her magazine *The Mukti Prayer Bell*. In 1903, Ramabai sent her daughter, Manoramabai and her assistant Miss Minnie F. Abrams, who had worked at Mukti since 1897, to Australia and New Zealand, with the message: "Brethren, pray for us!"

The prayer circles were implemented at Mukti Mission station, Kedgaon, India, in early 1905 and each circle was given the names of ten girls or women to pray for. The Welsh Revival (1904-1905) 'encouraged Ramabai to ask God to duplicate such experiences in India, and the Welsh Revival also overflowed through the Welsh missions in the hills of Assam, India.' In January 1905, she told her pupils about the Welsh Revival and called for volunteers to meet with her in prayer. Each morning Pandita Ramabai and seventy other people met for special specific prayer at the one hundred acre Mukti Mission station, where nearly two thousand girls and women lived, 'for true conversions of all Indian Christians,' and for revival across India and the nations. Ramabai then asked for volunteers from her Bible School who would give up their secular studies and go into the villages to preach. Thirty young women volunteered and met daily for an enduement of power from on high. Within six months there were 550 prayer circle people, praying twice daily and their prayers were answered in June 1905 when the revival began.

Helen Dyer wrote: 'Miss [Minnie F.] Abrams had been giving some definite teaching on the subject of the baptism of the Holy Spirit as power for service, and one morning she was awakened by one of the senior girls, saying, "Come over and rejoice with us. J. has received the Holy Spirit. [This happened at 3:30am, 29 June 1905]. I saw fire, ran across the room for a pail of water, and was about to pour it over her when I discovered she was not on fire!" '[2]

When Miss Minnie F. Abrams arrived she found all the girls in that compound on their knees, weeping, praying and confessing their sins, pleading with God to empower them with the Holy Spirit. One girl, J., was exhorting the others to 'repent' and 'yield supremely to God.' The next evening, 30 June 1905, Pandita Ramabai was teaching from John 8 in her usual quiet way when the Holy Spirit descended and the girls began to pray, 'many wept bitterly and confessed their sins.' Helen Dyer wrote: 'Some few saw visions and experienced the power of God and things too deep to be described.' Two girls had the spirit of prayer poured out on them and continued for hours. 'They were transformed with Heavenly lights shining on their faces,' prayer 'continued all night in various compounds on more than one occasion.'

Miss Minnie F. Abrams in *The Baptism of the Holy Ghost and Fire* (1906) wrote: 'From that time the two daily meetings of the Praying Band became great assemblies, morning and evening, and the Bible School was turned into an inquiry room. Girls stricken down under the power of conviction of sin while in school, in the industrial school, or at their work, were brought there. Regular Bible lessons were suspended and the Holy Spirit, Himself, gave to the leaders such messages as were needed by the seeking ones. Soon three large rooms were needed. After strong repentance, confession and assurance of salvation, many came back in a day or two saying, "We are saved, our sins our forgiven, now we want a baptism of fire."

One Sunday the text spoken from was, "He shall baptise you with the Holy Ghost and fire" (Matthew 3:11). Miss Minnie F. Abrams wrote: 'The usual explanation of the fire here spoken of is that it means the trials, losses, sickness and difficulties which God allows in order to bring us nearer to Him. But the Holy Spirit evidently had taught the girls through this passage and the one in Acts 2:1-4, as well as through the experience of the first Spirit baptised girl, to expect an actual experience of fire; and God met them in their expectations. They cried out with the burning that came into and upon them. Some fell as they saw a great light; and while the fire of God burned, the members of the body of sin, pride, love of the world, selfishness, uncleanness, etc. passed before them. Such sorrow for sin! Such suffering under the view of the self-life, while it was all being told out to God. The person being wholly occupied with God and her sinful state! This would have been too much for flesh and blood to bear save [except] that all these sufferings were intermingled with joy, wooing the stricken soul on, until the battle was won. Finally complete assurance and joy took the place of repentance. Some who had been shaken violently under the power of conviction, now sang, praised, danced for joy. Some had visions, others had dreams. The Word of God confirmed all of this. The Holy Ghost had been poured out according to the Scriptures. Such intense seeking could not have been endured save [except] that it had been done in the power of the Spirit. They neither ate nor slept until the victory was won. Then the joy was so great that for two or three days after receiving the baptism of the Holy Ghost they did not care for food.'[3]

The revival at the Mukti station brought a renewed interest in Bible study, evangelistic services and prayer meetings were held daily. Helen Dyer stated that the Bible School was filled with those crying for mercy and the work 'went on rapidly for three days. Satan was also busy, and tried to counterfeit all he saw,' when some tried to 'imitate what they had seen the others do.' Some of those 'stricken down with the spirit of repentance...cannot eat, sleep, or work till they get to the bottom of things.... They say that when the Holy Spirit comes upon them the burning within them is almost unbearable. Afterwards they are transformed; their faces light up with joy, their mouths are filled with praise.... One little girl of twelve is constantly laughing...she is occupied with Jesus...some claim to have seen the Lord.'

One of the Mukti workers wrote: 'Waves of prayer go over the meetings like the rolling thunder; hundreds pray audibly together. Sometimes after ten or twenty minutes it dies away and only a few voices are heard, then it will rise again and increase in intensity; on other occasions it goes on for hours. During these seasons there are usually some confessing their sins, often with bitter weeping which is painful to hear. The conflict seems so great they are almost beside themselves. It reminds one of the narratives in the Gospel about our Lord casting out evil spirits and truly evil spirits are being cast out.' See Matthew 8:16, Mark 5:1-15 and Luke 4:36.

A month into the revival a request came from Bombay for the mission to write about the revival. Mukti had their own printing presses where since 1904 sixty to seventy girls worked printing tracts, the Gospels, the *Mukti* magazine and later the Marathi Bible. Pandita Ramabai declined fearing it would hinder the work of God, but shortly after 'the Spirit of power decreased' and the revival began to wane. She realised she had made a grave mistake in not giving God the glory for what He was doing throughout India and the world. An article was written and published in the *Bombay Guardian* and elsewhere and the revival fires rekindled.

Two weeks later, Pandita Ramabai and a band of her Spirit-filled assistants visited Poona, forty miles away and began daily prayer meetings, as well as holding three services a day which were attended by Indian Christians and Europeans, which included British soldiers. She confessed that she had often neglected spiritual opportunities to preach Christ, but was now boldly 'resolved by God's mercy to rectify the past and openly and persistently magnify the Christ, the crucified.' Ramabai visited the learned Hindus in the city and preached Christ to them and was met with opposition, insult and scorn. The revival spread across Poona to the orphanages and schools and from there to the various missions of India.

For many years the first Tuesday in each month had been set aside for a special day of prayer and in November 1905 God revealed to Pandita Ramabai that she should close the school, suspend every type of work, and set apart ten days for waiting upon Him. The Mukti church could hold between four to five thousand people sat on the floor and held services four times a day. During the different services the Bible was discussed, there were Bible readings and silent prayer, testimony and praise and prayer requests etc., at other gatherings there was simultaneous and loud praying. Dr. Basil Miller wrote: 'As the Divine Word was opened, the girls were convicted powerfully of stealing, the great sin of India, and, as a consequence, "swept the house of their souls clean," as they expressed it, and turned from their iniquities to serve the true and living God.'

American missionary, Rev. Franklin wrote: 'We are now seeing the results of God's work in transformed lives marked by intercessory prayer, Bible study, and more preaching to the heathen. Bible study and prayer have characterised the work here from its beginning and were the preparation for the revival, yet both have been deepened by the revival.'

At the end of 1905, Pandita Ramabai wrote: 'You will rejoice to know that the revival is bearing fruit. Seven hundred girls and women of the Mukti Mission give themselves to prayer and the study of God's Word that they might go to the place where God sends them to take the Gospel. They are already visiting the villages around where they sing Gospel hymns and read the Word of God to the village people. About sixty go out daily by turns so that each one gets her turn every twelfth day. [An average of 55 girls x 12 days = 660 active girl evangelists]. They pray regularly for those they visit. The Lord put this plan in my heart and He is going before.'

By January 1906, the Mukti prayer bands, who had requested names to pray for, were praying for 29,000 people by name, which for former Hindus was easy. Ramabai wrote: 'When we were Hindus we used to daily repeat one or two thousand names of the gods and repeat several hundred verses from the so-called sacred book in order to gain merit…as Christians should we not pray for many hundreds of people by name? Now that the Lord has poured the spirit of prayer on us we may and can spend hours very profitably praying for others.'

News of this revival spread across India and beyond which encouraged others to pray for a spiritual awakening within their community, whilst many Indian Christians and missionaries visited Mukti and carried the fire back to their stations. Basil Miller wrote: 'Consequently, in numerous other missions revival fires sprang up, and there was a spiritual awakening in at least a dozen different orphanages. Many of these were under control of American missionaries. God was no respecter of denominational barriers' as the work 'spread to other mission stations irrespective of denomination. A great revival, for example, started in a school in Japan.'

One visitor said, "I spent twelve days at Mukti, and during that time I saw the glory of the Lord and came home in the renewed strength of body and soul.…"

Winkie Pratney in his book, *Revival* (1994) wrote: 'India in 1905-1906 saw awakening in every province, with meetings in many places five to ten hours long…the Christian population jumped 70%, sixteen times faster than the Hindu population.'

The Mukti prayer bands, led by Miss Minnie F. Abrams and Manoramabai were invited to hold Christian meetings in various places – and 'the glory of the Lord was manifested.' After one of these visits in the state of Kolhapur, a missionary wrote: 'Day and night in the meetings and without, these priests of God are fulfilling the ministry to which all are called, pleading, praying, often with strong crying of tears for the salvation of souls, for the absolute cleansing of lives [from bondage to sin], and the outpouring of the mighty Spirit. In answer to these prayers a deep spirit of conviction and confession and a seeking after God and His richest blessings was poured out as I have never before this revival, seen or heard of in this land, and seldom at home.'

Mr Handley Bird, a seasoned missionary of sixteen years, working at Coimbatore in South India, spent seventeen days at Mukti in May 1906. He wrote about the intense intercessory prayer and worship: 'Days of blessing that, please God, will leave their mark on all his future life...there was hunger, real pain of hunger, for a share in this visitation of God...travailing in prayer.... Day after day it was meat and drink to gather to pray and praise. In one meeting we were seventeen hours together; the following day more than fifteen hours passed before the meeting broke up with great joy, and such songs of praise as hoarse and broken voices could utter. The work goes on...we daily saw souls seeking and finding, coming out into blessing so full and definite as often to be almost more than could be borne, filling the mouth with laughter and the life with gladness.... When some hundreds are carried away and can only sing, "Hallelujah, Hallelujah to the Lamb," until unable to sing anymore, God is surely getting his own, and His heart is refreshed.'

Looking back, Pandita Ramabai wrote: 'The Lord graciously sent us a glorious Holy Ghost revival amongst us and also in many schools and churches in this country...many hundreds of our boys and girls have been gloriously saved, and many of them are serving God and witnessing for Christ at home and in other places.'[4]

Writing in September 1906, Miss Minnie F. Abrams wrote: 'It is now fifteen months since this revival began. Lives are truly transformed and those fully saved are walking with God in daily victory, while those who have received this mighty baptism for service are growing in power. The Word of God confirmed by the example of these holy lives filled with power for service, convinced us that this baptism of the Holy Ghost and fire [Matthew 3:11] is for all who are willing to put themselves wholly at God's disposal for His work and His glory. A goodly number of the foreign missionaries and workers at Mukti, as well as in other places have sought and found....'[5]

Jonathan Goforth (1859-1936), Missionary to China

In 1840, John Goforth a widower with three sons emigrated from Yorkshire, England, to western Ontario, Canada, as one of the early pioneers. He married Jane Bates who came from the north of Ireland and they settled on a farm in London, Ontario. Together they had seven sons and one daughter. Jonathan Goforth was born in February 1859 and was converted in 1877. Goforth was very good at memorising Scripture and had his heart set on politics as a career. Coming from a farming background he was not able to attend school for all of the year and when he returned in autumn he was always behind. He was influenced by reading *The Memoirs of Robert*

Murray M'Cheyne of Scotland, and resolved to give himself to Christian ministry. The local minister arranged to help Goforth study in Latin and Greek in preparation for attending Knox College. For those two years of preparation he studied the Bible for two hours each morning before school or work.

Jonathan Goforth had intended to be a Christian worker in Canada, until he heard Dr. G. L. Mackay of Formosa, speak at Knox Church, Ingersoll. Dr. Mackay spoke about the claims of that country and that for two years he had travelled up and down Canada appealing for a young man to carry on the work which he had begun, but to no avail. Goforth said, "As I listened to these words I was overwhelmed with shame.... There was I, bought with the precious blood of Jesus Christ, daring to dispose of my life as I pleased. I heard the Lord's voice saying, 'Who will go for us and who shall we send?' And I answered, 'Here am I, send me.' From that hour I became a foreign missionary. I eagerly read everything I could find on foreign missions and set to work to get others to catch the vision I had caught of the claims of the unreached, unevangelised millions on earth."

In 1880, Jonathan Goforth was at Knox College, Toronto, a Christian college of training, but coming from the countryside to the city was quite different than what he was used to. For two years he worked with the William Street Mission, followed by the Toronto Mission Union for four years. He specialised in working among the slums of St. John's Ward, doing door-to-door work, as well as itinerate preaching, and looked to God for his support at college, as well as his ministry needs. He visited Don Jail every Sunday morning whilst a student and over the years was able to lead prisoners to the Lord.

In 1885, Dr. Randal of the China Inland Mission (CIM) was passing through Canada and gave Jonathan Goforth a copy of *China's Spiritual Need and Claims* by J. Hudson Taylor, the founder of CIM. Goforth had intended to join the CIM as the Presbyterian Church of Canada did not work in China, but his application letter to the CIM in London, England, was mislaid by the providence of God. The student body on hearing that his own church could not send him raised the funds to start a mission in China! Goforth became the first Canadian missionary to be supported by his class and was an advocate of the evangelisation of the world, and the claims of China's unreached millions.

In the spring of 1887, Knox College sent a deputation to the Synod at Hamilton and London, which was meeting in Chatham. Jonathan Goforth spoke while the students prayed and the 'missionary vision captured the Presbyterian Church of Canada as it never had before,' so wrote Rosalind Goforth. At the General Assembly in June 1887,

Goforth and Dr. J. Fraser Smith of Queen's College were appointed to China. In October 1887, Goforth was ordained and on 25 October 1887, he married Florence Rosalind Bell-Smith who was known as Rosalind, but her husband called her Rose. In early February 1888, they sailed from Vancouver, Canada and arrived after two weeks in Shanghai, China, Goforth met with the leading missionaries and a triangular section of country, north of the Yellow River, known as North Honan was given to the Canadian Presbyterian Church as their field of labour.

The Goforths moved to Chefoo, of the northern coast of China and began language study, a task that Jonathan struggled in. Within two weeks there was a fire in the home and the Goforth's lost most of their belongings. In August 1888, the first recruits arrived and on 13 September 1888, the first tour of North Honan began. Dr. J. Hudson Taylor wrote to Jonathan Goforth the following letter: 'We as a mission [the CIM] have sought for ten years to enter the Province of Honan from the south and have only just succeeded.... Brother, if you would enter that Province, you must go forward on your knees.' These latter words became the slogan of the North Honan Mission, so noted Rosalind Goforth.[6]

Within a few months of arriving in China, Jonathan Goforth said to his wife, "...the Gospel which saved the down and outs in the slums of Toronto is the same Gospel which must save Chinese sinners." When Goforth stood before a Chinese audience he always had an open Bible in his hand which he constantly referred to as, "The written Word of the One True God." In his latter years he was once asked the secret to his success by a group of young missionaries. He replied, "Because I just give God a chance to speak to souls through His own Word. My only secret in getting at the heart of a big sinner is to show them their need and to tell of a Saviour abundantly able to save. Once a sinner is shown that no flesh can be justified in God's sight by the deeds of the law and that he can only attain unto the righteousness of God through faith in the Lord Jesus Christ he readily yields. That was [Martin] Luther's secret [from the Reformation], it was John Wesley's and never did man make more of that secret than D. L. Moody."

More recruits arrived in December 1889 and two extended tours were accomplished in 1890. On 20 February 1890, the Presbytery of Honan was formed. The missionaries were known as "Foreign Devils" by the Chinese and often vile placards and anti-foreign posters were put up. It was not unknown for mobs to shout at the foreigners and to pelt them with whatever came to hand. The Chinese knew that the foreigner's medicine was powerful and rumours went round that they used children's eyes and hearts – thus implicating that they were child kidnappers and killers!

Eventually the British minister at Peking (now Beijing) had to intervene otherwise missionaries would have been killed. In 1894, the Goforth's went on a short furlough back to Canada for a few months and returned in autumn. Whilst they were away, a flood covered the mission compound at Chuwang, from six to eight feet deep and destroyed most of their possessions.

In a letter dated 12 April 1896, Jonathan Goforth wrote: 'Since coming to Changte five months ago, we have been cheered almost daily by the manifest tokens of the Holy Spirit's power. He has been making the people willing to hear beyond all our expectations. During this time upwards of 25,000 men and women have come to see us and all have had the Gospel preached to them. Preaching is kept up an average of eight hours a day. Sometimes fifty or more women in our yard at one time. The signs of blessing among women were even more cheering than among the men.... Almost every time we held up Christ as Redeemer and Saviour, the Holy Spirit moved one or more. It has been our privilege to see at one time from ten to twenty of these heathen women deeply moved and earnestly enquiring the way of salvation for a couple hours at a time.' Usually Rosalind Goforth or one of the native female Chinese workers would be preaching to the women whilst Jonathan Goforth or a Chinese evangelist would be preaching to the men. On occasions Jonathan would preach to the women whilst stood next to his wife, to give her voice a rest.

From when the Goforths first arrived in China, their eighth home was the first purpose-built home and was completed in the autumn of 1897. It was Chinese from the outside but Canadian in style from the inside and was a great curiosity. It was an "open house" and multitudes of Chinese people in groups toured the house and grounds, and they were permitted to open anything and to look anywhere. The Chinese were relieved that there were no jars of human flesh in the cellar; such were the rumours about the foreigners. This open house policy made it much easier to share the Gospel when the Goforths went into the surrounding villages and towns, they were known as friends, and it did much to dispel the negative rumours that had been spread abroad. One day in the autumn of 1899, 1,835 men passed through the house and Rosalind Goforth received 500 women![7]

Jonathan Goforth wrote: 'Right here at our doors is the city of Changte with a population of about 100,000.... Taking Christians with me, we will go from street to street preaching and singing the Gospel in true Salvation Army style, although without the aid of flag and drum. It ruffles the temper of some of the "upper ten" [members of the highest social class] Chinese residents on those streets, but we can't help that. We must awake them from the sleep of death. It is hard for some of these Christians to testify for Christ on the street. Some of them have had no education and when they stand up to speak they are afraid and tremble, yet a little practice gives confidence and power. In this way we have trained about a dozen men, besides the helpers who may be called upon in an emergency. We dread "dummy" Christians and strive to have all enabled to give a reason for the faith that is in them.'

Some of the listeners had forgotten about their dinner whilst hearing the Good News proclaimed, and Jonathan Goforth had known them 'to stand listening for hours...night after night,' and when he 'ceased preaching to go home,' he noted, 'I have heard one hundred to two hundred men cry out, "Stay and tell us more!" ' Sometimes as many as five thousand students from the five counties would turn up for their annual examinations at Changte city and Jonathan Goforth had a good ministry among them. A door was opened in his second year at Changte when in his study he showed them several maps, astronomical charts and a large globe of the world. Astronomy was Goforth's one hobby. After talking about the earth and the stars, the students realised that the foreigner knew far more than they did and had something worth listening to. The Chinese believed that the earth was flat and that China was the centre of the world. Then Goforth was able to share the Good News.

The winter of 1899-1900 became daily more threatening because of the political situation, but most believed it would pass, as had other anti-foreign sentiments and movements. By May 1900, the mission had fifty Christian communities and a great work had been accomplished. On 28 June 1900, the Goforths, their four children (two had already died in China), fellow missionaries and Chinese immediate helpers had to flee for their lives. The Empress Dowager of Peking (now Beijing), China, had ordered the death of all foreigners across her realm, this also included engineers who were building and laying railroads. The mission property was destroyed and their possessions were looted. This was the Boxer Revolution, also known as the Boxer Rebellion or Uprising. Across China, around two hundred missionaries were martyred and 32,000 Chinese Christians had been killed for their faith in Christ, whilst even more had suffered persecution, injury and lived to tell the tale. Jonathan Goforth was sliced to the bone on his arm with a machete as he tried to deflect the blows, whilst his pith helmet was nearly spilt in two and he received a blow to the head and neck. Other members of the party were injured and they fled with the clothes on their back, bleeding, bloodied and bruised. Many times they were harassed by mobs and clods of mud were thrown at them. Ten days they were on foot or cart with a further fourteen days on a houseboat before arriving at the safety of Shanghai, China. They were ordered on the first steamer back to Canada for recuperation, rest and recovery. They had been through a harrowing experience.[8]

Preparation, Inspiration and Evangelisation

In the autumn of 1901, Jonathan Goforth returned to China, whilst his wife and children returned the following year. Goforth began to be restless and dissatisfied by the results of his work. From a human perspective his ministry in the city of Changte, in the province of Honan, as part of the North Honan Mission was very successful, but Goforth called it, "just touching the fringes" of the multitudes without Christ, as he longed to see in his ministry the "greater works" which Jesus had promised (John 14:12-15).

Jonathan Goforth received a master plan from the Lord of how to reach the multitudes, which he told his wife Rosalind in May 1902. Every month they were to move to a new location, rent a native compound, preach the Gospel in extensive evangelism, plant a church and move on. At first the Honan Presbytery who he was in submission to hampered and held back this plan until he told them they should allow him a three-year trial of this plan which he would be self-supporting, which they eventually agreed to. Rosalind Goforth was also not happy with the situation because of the safety of the children and because they needed a fixed home. Changte was their base, but things had changed since the Boxer Revolution and new missionaries had arrived and the dynamics were different. Jonathan Goforth told his wife that he feared for the children, if she refused to join him as he believed it to be the will of God. The touring season was from February to June and September to December. Jonathan left without his wife and to shorten a long story, one child died and another was near death until Rosalind accepted it as the will of God, to go and evangelise from one month to the next. Jonathan always said, "The safest place is in the path of duty."

Rosalind Goforth in *Goforth of China* (1937) wrote: 'As time passed, at every centre opened, Christians multiplied. A statement made by Mr Goforth which to some seemed incredible, but nevertheless was true was that "every new place without one exception where we lived as a family for at most one month and carried on this aggressive evangelism we left behind what later became a growing church." This statement was not made in a spirit of pride or boastfulness, but humbly as a witness to what the glorious Gospel of the grace of God would do if given a chance.'

Jonathan Goforth, his family and other labourers, especially Chinese evangelists, began this ministry and were living in an out-centre when he received some pamphlets about the Welsh Revival (1904-1905), from an unknown source in England, which for a time arrived weekly. Then from India he received a little booklet called *A*

Great Awakening which contained selections of Finney's *Lectures on Revival.* Finney emphasised that any company of Christians can have a revival if they will fulfil the necessary laws; 250,000 people were saved under Finney's ministry. Finney wrote: 'I fully believe that could facts be known, it would be that when the appointed means have been rightly used, spiritual blessing have been obtained with greater uniformity than temporal ones.' Goforth said, "If Finney is right, and I believe he is then I am going to find out what these laws are and obey them, no matter what the cost may be." He requested from Canada various books and spent so much time in intensive Scripture study of the Holy Spirit and His ways, and prayer for revival that his wife was concerned for his mind. After all his study Jonathan Goforth said, "Slowly the realisation began to dawn on me that I had tapped a mine of infinite possibility." As part of this study he made notes in his two-inch wide margined Chinese Bible. Soon he began to preach on these notes to the locals and Christians alike. After eight or ten sermons, the Christians came under deep conviction of sin and were broken down; confessing their sins, while among the local heathen there was an increase in conversions.[9]

Revival at Hsunhsien 1906 – China

Early in February 1906, Jonathan Goforth was preaching at a great idolatrous fair in Hsunhsien (Hsun Hsien) in North Honan. Usually there would be more than one million pilgrims who over ten days of the fair would climb the hill outside the city and venerate the image of Lao Nainai (Old Grandmother). Rosalind Goforth in *Goforth of China* (1937) wrote: 'This fair was by far the greatest opportunity of the year for reaching numbers with the Gospel and all missionaries and native evangelists possible gathered there for intensive evangelism.' However, snow had blocked many of the roads and few pilgrims had arrived.

One day Jonathan Goforth was preaching on 2 Timothy 2:1-7, a good soldier of Christ Jesus, and 'many seemed deeply touched,' he wrote in *By My Spirit* (1929). An evangelist was heard to say in an awed whisper, "Why these people are being moved just as they were by Peter's sermon at Pentecost." That same evening whilst speaking to a heathen audience that filled the "street chapel," which was a rented a hall, there was 'a stirring of the people's hearts.' Jonathan Goforth was preaching from 1 Peter 2:25: 'He bore our sins in His own body on the tree....' He said, "It was at this fair I began to see evidences of the first stirrings in the people's heart of the greater power. Convictions seemed to be written on every face. Finally, when I called for decisions, the whole audience stood up as one man crying, 'We want to follow this Jesus who died for us.' " As he turned, he saw ten Chinese evangelists with awed looks. One whispered, "Brother, He for who we have prayed so long, was here in very deed tonight." This was the beginning of Goforth's revival ministry, and at every centre in Changte city, and to the north, which was his designated field of labour, for more than a year, until the spring of 1907, where the Gospel was preached, men came forward seeking salvation. It was customary within Chinese meetings for men to preach to men and women to preach to women.

Jonathan Goforth returned to his mission station at Changte and in the autumn of 1906 he came into conflict with another missionary. Other missionaries told them to settle it on their knees before the Lord, which they did. However, on the eve of leaving for a communion tour, it was revealed to Goforth that he had hidden resentment and was convicted of being a hypocrite. Goforth humbled himself before the Lord and was able to go on his tour and see the blessing of God. As Jonathan Goforth later wrote: 'We cannot emphasise too strongly our conviction that all hindrance in the Church is due to sin…. Indeed the appalling fact is that every sin which is found outside the Church is also found, although perhaps to a lesser degree within the Church…. We would point out that many of the Chinese churches of which mention is made are not even one generation removed from heathenism. At the same time, let us not think that all is well with our old established churches at home. It is sin in individual Church members, whether at home or on the mission field which grieves and quenches the Holy Spirit.'[10]

Jonathan Goforth went on lots of preaching tours over the years and subsequent decades, and met many missionaries and heard Christian testimonies from across China. He wrote: 'A modest tombstone in Nechchwang [also spelt Newchang and is present-day Yingkou] marks the resting place of William C. Burns of the revival in Kilsyth (1839) and St. Peter's Church, Dundee (1839-1841) in Scotland]. It was here [Nechchwang] that he last laboured for his Lord. It seems everywhere this great evangelist went; both in the homeland and in China, all with whom he came into contact were brought to a saving knowledge of Christ. Even the heathen carpenter who made his coffin [in April 1868] was no exception, and was an elder in the church when I arrived there' in the year 1907.[11]

'And I said, "This is my anguish; but I will remember the years of the right hand of the Most High." I will remember the works of the Lord; Surely I will remember Your wonders of old" ' (Psalm 77:10-11).

Chapter 19

Jerusalem of the East

'Let us lay aside every weight, and the sin which so easily ensnares us, and let us run with endurance the race that is set before us, looking unto Jesus the author and finisher of our faith, who for the joy that was set before Him endured the cross, despising the shame, and has sat down at the right hand of the throne of God. For consider Him who endured such hostility from sinners against Himself, lest you become weary and discouraged in your souls' (Hebrews 12.1-3).

Pyongyang Great Revival 1907-1910 – Korea

In September 1866, Welshman, Rev. Robert Jermain Thomas soaked the land in his own blood and became known as the first Protestant missionary and martyr to Korea when he was stabbed, beaten and finally beheaded at Pyongyang, the present capital of North Korea. The Korean Church was founded in 1885 and the following year the first Korean was baptised.

Korea saw its first revival in 1903; known as the Wonsan Revival Movement (1903-1906), but by the middle of 1906, after 30,000 new converts in that year alone, it had waned and died out. At the beginning of the Japanese Russian War of 1904, American missionaries were initially confined to Pyongyang by government order. In the autumn of 1906, the threat of Russian invasion had passed, but the Japanese did not withdraw. This caused anxiety amongst Korea's oppressed people who were constantly being fought over by Japan or China. William Newton Blair, a missionary at Pyongyang wrote: 'With the Japanese occupation accomplished, patriotism was born in Korea.' At the same time a number of young Korean Christian 'big heads' returned from America and caused problems with their personal ambition and true stories of American corruption. Also, America, following Britain's example 'hastened to recognise Japan's control' which caused an anti-American sentiment to sweep over the land.

In August 1906, the Pyongyang missionaries met for a week of Bible study and prayer. They invited Dr. R. A. Hardie, (William Newton Blair spells his name Hardy) of Gensan, on the east coast, to lead them, whose public confession and repentance in Wonsan in 1903 was the beginning of the Wonsan Revival Movement (1903-1906). In September 1906, Dr. Howard Agnew Johnston, of New

York, America, whilst in Seoul, Korea, informed a group of missionaries and Korean Christians about the Khasi Hills Revival (1905-1906) in India, where 8,200 had been baptised when two women missionaries from the Khassia Mission were influenced by the Welsh Revival (1904-1905) and called for prayer. Jonathan Goforth, missionary to China, wrote that because of this more than twenty missionaries from Pyongyang Presbyterian and Methodist missions resolved to meet together to pray daily for 'greater blessings.' Over the Christmas period the Pyongyang Christians instead of their usual social celebrations met each evening for prayer. The evening prayer ceased at the start of the Pyongyang General Class but continued at noon for those who could attend.

The text book for the missionaries over the summer period was the First Epistle of John. William Newton Blair wrote that the message became personal and living: 'We had reached a place where we dared not go forward without God's presence.' The missionaries poured out their hearts before Him, and searched their own hearts whilst seeking to meet the conditions. Before the meeting had ended the Holy Spirit showed those present that 'the way of victory' is the way of, 'confession, of broken hearts and bitter tears.' They decided to pray for 'a great blessing' a revival amongst their Korean Brethren and especially amongst the Pyongyang Bible-study classes for men which would take place in January 1907. They left those August meetings 'realising as never before that nothing but the baptism of God's Spirit in mighty power could fit us and our Korean brethren for the trying days ahead.' They knew that the Korean Church needed to repent of hating the Japanese and needed 'a clearer vision of all sin against God' because many had professed Christ as their Saviour 'without great sorrow for sin because of its familiarity.'[1]

Pyongyang in 1907 was known as a city of wine, women and song. It was a dark city in the early twentieth century with sin abounding and it even had its own Gisaeng (Korean geisha) training school.

In 1907, the Korean Church (Presbyterian) was to become independent of its American Board of Foreign Mission, which had been 'practically self-supporting for several years' but things did not look good. The Pyongyang General Class of one thousand began on 2 January 1907, it would last for two weeks and representatives came from as far away as one hundred miles. The evening meetings began on Saturday the sixth and 1,500 attended. William Newton Blair preached on 1 Corinthians 12:27, members of the body of Christ, and exhorted those present to get right with one another, 'as discord in the Church was like sickness in the body.' After the sermon 'a number with sorrow confessed their lack of love for others, especially for the Japanese' and 'many testified to a new realisation of what sin was.'

The Sunday evening meeting had no life in it and they were 'conscious that the Devil had been present, apparently victorious.' The next day the missionaries met 'and cried out to God in earnest,' they were 'bound in spirit and refused to let go till He blessed' them. As the people (and only some of the missionaries) entered the church at 7pm, God's presence was felt. After a short sermon, missionary Graham Lee led the meeting in prayer and soon, 'the whole audience began to pray out loud together.' It was 'a vast harmony of sound and spirit, a mingling together of souls moved by an irresistible impulse to prayer.'[2]

In the first year of the Korean Revival 50,000 people were converted. Dr. R. P. MacKay the foreign mission secretary of the Canadian Presbyterian Church who was in China at the time, along with Jonathan Goforth were invited to visit Korea in the summer of 1907. Goforth said, "The Korean movement was of incalculable significance in my life, because it showed me at first hand the boundless possibilities of the revival method. Korea made me feel, as it did many others, that this was God's plan for setting the world aflame."

Jonathan Goforth spent three weeks in Korea, visiting eight of the chief mission centres and documented what he saw in *When the Spirit's Fire Swept Korea* (1943). He noted that Elder Keel, (also spelt Kil and later known as Rev. Sun Joo Kil) of the Central Presbyterian Church, confessed his sin of 'Achan' (see Joshua 7:1, 20-21) in front of 1,500 people and thus the revival began. He had promised a dying man to look after his estate because his wife was unable to, but in the process he had taken one hundred dollars for himself. The next day he gave the money back.[3]

Soon the prayer turned to weeping. Graham Lee wrote: 'Man after man would rise, confess his sins, break down and weep, and then throw himself to the floor and beat the floor with his fists in perfect agony of conviction.' The meeting went on till 2am. Jonathan Goforth wrote: 'Day after day the people assembled now and always it was manifest that the Refiner was in His temple.' Writing about Elder Keel's confession he wrote: 'It hindered the Almighty God while it remained covered, and it glorified Him as soon as it was uncovered; and so with rare exceptions did all the confessions in Korea that year.'

On Tuesday afternoon, the whole community assembled to give thanks to God. The previous night, Elder Kang You-moon, of the Central Church confessed his hatred of Elder Kim, who was Blair's assistant in the Pyongyang Church. Kim sat silent. At the noon prayer meeting on Tuesday, they prayed for Elder Kim. In the evening meeting, Elder Kim stood behind the pulpit and confessed his hatred not only of Elder Kang, but also of William Newton Blair himself, and asked for Blair's forgiveness. Blair began to pray, "Father, Father" and got no further. Blair wrote: 'It seemed as if the roof was lifted from the building and the Spirit of God came down from Heaven in a mighty avalanche of power upon us.' Blair fell at Kim's side and wept and prayed as never before. Some prostrated themselves before the Lord whilst hundreds stood with arms outstretched towards Heaven. 'The cry went over the city until the heathen were in consternation [anxiety / dismay].' The missionaries had prayed for an outpouring of the Holy Spirit and He had come.

William Newton Blair in *The Korean Pentecost* (1977) wrote: 'Every sin a human being can commit was publicly confessed that night. Pale and trembling with emotion, in agony of mind and body, guilty souls, standing in the white light of that judgment, saw themselves as God saw them. Their sins rose up in all their vileness, till shame and grief and self-loathing took complete possession; pride was driven out, the face of men forgotten. Looking up to Heaven, to Jesus whom they had betrayed, they smote themselves and cried out with bitter wailing, "Lord, Lord, cast us not away for ever!" '[4]

Christians even confessed their sins to non-Christians for their past actions and attitudes which greatly affected the city. Even Japanese soldiers came under conviction! Soon Pyongyang became known as "Jerusalem of the East."

Mr Swallen who was one of more than twenty missionaries in Pyongyang said, "It paid well to have spent the several months in prayer, for when God the Holy Spirit came He accomplished more in half a day than all of us missionaries could have accomplished in half a year. In less than two months more than two thousand heathen were converted." By the middle of 1907 there were 30,000 converts connected with the Pyongyang Centre. Mr Swallen, Graham Lee (who was a good singer) and William Newton Blair were the main leaders prior to the revival, but it was Samuel Moffet and Kil Sun Mojo (this Korean rose before dawn to pray for revival) who brought them together from the missionary prayer meeting onward. During the revival, Elder Kil (who had confessed his sin of 'Achan' – coveting another person's property, which was accursed, see Joshua 7) was raised up as a Korean leader. He held meetings everywhere and got the people praying.

In 1907, the Pyongyang Theological School saw seven Koreans graduate and they became the first Korean Presbytery of Korea. Bible study groups increased and there was acceleration in missionary building growth. Illiterate people, especially women learnt the Hangeul script (Korean alphabet), and the understanding that God created all men equal in His eyes led to a greater status for women. The revival also crossed the border into Yeonbyeon and Manju, China.[5]

George McCune who personally witnessed the outpouring of the Spirit on the Korean Church reported that the movement greatly surpassed the ones in Wales and India, describing it as the most empowering presence of the Holy Spirit ever, and in 1909, the Movement of Saving One Million Souls began.[6]

The revival was still going strong in 1910 and the afterglow of revival continued for a least a few years after that date in various towns. Jonathan Goforth wrote: 'It was clear that the revival had not died down by 1910, for in October of that year 4,000 were baptised in one week and thousands besides sent in their names, saying they had decided to become Christians...' Korean Presbyterians receive a person publicly for Catechumen (catechism) after three months and then after a period of one year, examine them to see if they are ready for baptism. In Seoul, 13,000 'signed cards saying they wanted to become Christians, and in September...the Methodist churches...received 3,000 by baptism.'[7]

In 1910, William Newton Blair wrote: 'In all Korea today there are no less than 250,000 Christians worshipping God in more than 2,000 places.' In this year, the Old Testament was finally translated into Korean and The British and Foreign Bible Society through its Bible Colporteurs sold 666,000 books to the people of Korea, most of them single Gospels! In August 1910, Korea was annexed (add to one's own territory) by Japan which was the beginning of organised persecution, especially amongst the Christians.

Looking back, Jonathan Goforth in *By My Spirit* (1929) wrote: 'As I remember, those missionaries at Pingyang [Pyongyang] were just ordinary, everyday people. I did not notice any outstanding figure among them. They seemed to live and work and act like other missionaries. It was in prayer that they were different. Those missionaries seemed to carry us right up to the throne of God. One had the feeling that they were indeed communing with God, face to face.'[8]

Revival at Kikungshan 1907 – China

In July 1907, Jonathan Goforth and Dr. R. P. MacKay returned to China via the northern overland route through Manchuria and visited three mission stations, Mukden, Liaoyang and Peitaiho. Manchuria had been annexed by Russia from China and is situated in north east China. Impromptu meetings were held where Jonathan Goforth told of what they had witnessed in Korea and each station begged him to return for a ten day mission.

Jonathan Goforth returned to his base at Changteh, China in Honan, which in his writings he sometimes refers to as Changte – they are one and the same. He was asked to go to Kikungshan and to share of what he had seen and heard about the revival in Korea.

On Sunday evening he spoke at Kikungshan and went considerably over his generous time limit which he had set himself. He omitted the closing hymn and pronounced the benediction to allow those present to depart. Jonathan Goforth in *By My Spirit* (1929) wrote: 'To my surprise, for at least six minutes no one stirred. The stillness of death seemed to pervade the assembly. Then gradually suppressed sobs became audible here and there. In a little while, missionaries were rising to their feet and in tears confessing their faults one to another. It was late that night when we finally scattered to our homes.'

In Kikungshan a conference with a schedule had been prepared for the week, but on Monday the missionaries resolved to abandon the schedule and continue in prayer as led of the Lord. Jonathan Goforth wrote: 'Never have I passed more wonderful days among my missionary brethren in China.' At the end of the week before they went back to their respective mission stations across China, they resolved that they would 'pray every day wherever they were at four o'clock in the afternoon until the Divine blessing fell upon the Church in China.' In this way a prayer movement for revival was started, which prepared the way for Goforth's revival ministry in China and Manchuria.[9]

Revival in Manchuria 1908 – Russia

The Honan Presbytery gave consent to Jonathan Goforth for one months leave including travelling to and from Manchuria which had been annexed by Russia from (north east) China. In February 1908, Jonathan Goforth left for Manchuria 'with the conviction in my heart that I had a message from God to deliver to His people. But I had no method. I did not know how to conduct a revival. I could deliver an address and let the people pray, but that was all.' Goforth held around forty meetings and taught on the Holy Spirit from his wide margined Bible, and the Holy Spirit came and dealt with the people, Christians and non-Christians! Goforth had stipulated as the conditions of his acceptance to hold meetings in Manchuria, that both branches of Presbyterian Church in Manchuria, the Scotch and the Irish should unite, and that the ground should be softened and prepared by prayer. When in Mukten, Manchuria, Jonathan Goforth inquired and no extra prayer meetings for the campaign had been held and the two Presbyterian bodies had not united!

After the first evening meeting, dejected, Jonathan Goforth went back to his room and cried out to God, "What is my use of my coming here? These people are not seeking after Thee. They have no desire for blessing. What can I do?" God spoke, "Is it your work or Mine? Can I not do a sovereign work? Call upon Me and I will answer thee and will show thee great things, and difficult which thou knowest not" (Jeremiah 33:3), RV. Early next morning, an elder came into Goforth's room, sobbing his heart out and confessing his sin of embezzling the church funds during the Boxer Revolution (1900) which he spent on his business. The elder who had been the treasurer said, "After your message last night, I was searched as by fire. Last night I could not sleep a wink. It has been made plain to me that the only way I can find relief is to confess my sin before the church and make full restitution."

After Jonathan Goforth's address in the morning, the elder stood before the church and confessed his sin. Jonathan Goforth in *By My Spirit* (1929) wrote: 'The effect was instantaneous. Another member of the session, [an elder] gave vent to a piercing cry, but then something seemed to hold him back and he subsided without making a confession. Then many moved to tears followed one another in prayer and confession. All through the third day the movement increased in intensity.' The missionary at whose home Goforth was staying at said, "This amazes us. It is just like the Scottish Revival of 1859." The missionary suggested that Goforth drop his planned addresses and they continue with services of thanksgiving. Goforth told him that they were far from that, "There is still much hidden sin to be uncovered...."

After the address on the fourth morning, the floor was given over to prayer. A man left his seat, tears streaming down his face and confessed the sin of adultery and that he had tried to poison his wife three times! It was the elder from the second day who had given vent to that awful cry. He tore off the gold bracelets from his wrist and put them on the offering plate, and then tore up his elder's card and asked the congregation to tear his cards up as well which they had in their homes. For several minutes nobody stirred then the entire session tendered their resignations; followed by the deacons, and then the pastor! The pastor said, "If I had been what I ought to have been, this congregation would not be where it is today. I'm not fit to be your pastor any longer." From different parts of the congregation the cry was heard, "It's all right pastor. We appoint you to be our pastor." Then the elders were called to stand up, with heads bowed, the spontaneous vote of confidence went forth, "Elders, we appoint you to be our elders." The same happened with the deacons.[10]

Rev. James Webster who worked under the Scotch Presbyterian Mission in Manchuria, accompanied Jonathan Goforth. He wrote: 'The watchword of the Revival of 1859 [in Scotland] was, "Ye must be born again;" of 1870 [under D. L. Moody], "Believe on the Lord Jesus Christ," but of Mr Goforth's message [watchword] it was, "Not by might, not by power, but by My Spirit." This doctrine, presented in many aspects, iterated and reiterated, amply illustrated, emphasised and pressed home has been his one theme in Manchuria. He has not dealt in abstract theories about the work of the Holy Spirit. "We speak that we do know and testify that we have seen." ...The cross burns like a living fire in the heart of every address.'

Jonathan Goforth would condemn idolatry and superstition in no uncertain terms being not fruit of the Spirit and also denounced those who have 'been baptised in the faith of Christ, but are living under the influence of hatred, jealousy, falsehood and dishonesty, pride, hypocrisy, worldliness and avarice, are living in that which is in active opposition to the Spirit of God,' so noted Rev. James Webster. He continued: 'What oppresses the thought of the penitent...the thoughts of their unfaithfulness, of ingratitude to the Lord who had redeemed them, of their heinous sins of trampling on His love...this it is which pricked them to the heart, moved them to the very depths of their moral being, and caused multitudes, being no longer able to contain themselves, to break out into a lamentable cry, "God be merciful to me a sinner." '

Rosalind Goforth in *Goforth of China* (1937) wrote: 'Jonathan Goforth went up to Manchuria an unknown missionary, except to his own narrow circle. He returned a few weeks later with the limelight of the Christian world upon him.'[11]

Early in 1909, Jonathan Goforth 'at the close of some wonderful meetings in Tungchow, near Peking [Beijing],' so wrote Rosalind Goforth, 'left immediately for Canada via London [in England] where he was scheduled to give a series of addresses on "Prayer" under the auspices of the China Inland Mission. While in London he was taken to see a lady who he was told had been used in a remarkable way as an intercessor for others. During their conversation she told Mr Goforth that when she heard of his proposed meeting in Manchuria, she had felt a great burden laid upon her to pray for him. She then asked him to look at her notebook in which was recorded three dates when a sense of special power had come upon her for him. A feeling akin to awe came upon Goforth as he recalled those dates as being the very days when he had realised greatest power and had witnessed the mightiest movements in Manchuria.'[12]

Two and a half decades later after the revival in Manchuria, Jonathan Goforth in the foreword to *The Revival We Need*, wrote: 'In Manchuria and China, when we did nothing else than give the address and let the people pray, and kept out of sight as far as possible, we saw the mightiest manifestations of Divine power.'[13]

'Give ear, O my people...I will utter dark sayings of old...our fathers have told us. We will not hide them from their children, telling to the generation to come the praises of the Lord, and His strength and His wonderful works that He has done' (Psalm 78:1-4).

Chapter 20

Holy Spirit and Fire

Thus says the Lord, "And it shall come to pass afterward that I will pour out My Spirit on all flesh; your sons and your daughters shall prophesy, your old men shall dream dreams, your young men shall see visions; and also on My menservants and My maidservants I will pour out My Spirit in those days" (Joel 2:28-29).

Azusa Street Revival 1906-1909 – America

The Azusa Street Revival, also known as the Azusa Street Outpouring, in Los Angeles, California, America, was nurtured under the one-eyed African American William Seymour, with 'help' for a time from evangelist / journalist, Frank Bartleman. The Azusa Street Revival brought about a fresh touch of the Holy Spirit, bringing disciples into the new awareness of the old truth of the baptism in the Holy Spirit. This blessing ushered in the worldwide twentieth century Pentecostal renewal. At the centenary of the Azusa Street Revival, it was estimated that there were over 600 million Pentecostals worldwide! In 2017, Pentecostals worldwide are estimated at more than 800 million!

On 31 December 1900 at Topeka Bible School under Charles Parnham, eighteen-year-old Miss Agnes Ozman asked Parnham to lay his hands on her for the baptism of the Holy Spirit. It was 7pm and 'a glory fell upon her, a halo seemed to surround her head and face' and she burst forth into tongues. This was the beginning of the first-fruits of the Holy Spirit being poured out en masse at the very dawn of the twentieth century.[1]

In the second week of April 1905, Frank Bartleman heard F. B. Meyer of London, England, preaching about the Welsh Revival (1904-1905). Meyer had just come from Wales and had met Evan Roberts. In May 1905, Frank Bartleman was given the book *The Great Revival In Wales* by S. B. Shaw. After reading it, he resolved to give up his employment as a journalist and became a channel in which the burden for revival could come upon. He also distributed 5,000 pamphlets, *The Revival in Wales* by G. Campbell Morgan. Frank Bartleman wrote numerous articles on revival (exhorting the brethren to pray) which were published in various church and religious papers. He began selling S. B. Shaw's book amongst the churches that he spoke at, and 'God wonderfully used it to promote faith for a revival spirit.' Soon the spirit of revival consumed Frank

Bartleman and he was joined in prayer with Edward Boehmer, a convert of the Peniel Mission.

At the beginning of May 1905, a powerful revival broke out in the Lake Avenue M. E. Church, Pasadena. Most of the young male converts from the Peniel Mission were active in the church and had been praying for revival. Every night people were converted to the Lord Jesus Christ and on one night, 'nearly every unsaved soul in the house was converted.... Conviction was mightily upon the people.' Within two weeks, there were 200 new Christians and the church began to pray for revival not only for Pasadena, but for Los Angeles and the whole of Southern California.

In May 1905, Frank Bartleman wrote to Evan Roberts of the Welsh Revival (1904-1905), asking him and the Welsh people to pray for the brethren in California, and he received a reply stating that they were. In June, Frank Bartleman wrote again to Evan Roberts asking for continued prayer. Prior to the outbreak at Azusa Street, Frank Bartleman wrote to Evan Roberts three times and received four responses.

Frank Bartleman visited Joseph Smale's church, the First Baptist Church, Los Angeles, in mid June. Smale was on fire for the Lord and his church was praying for revival. He had just returned from Wales, where the revival fires were raging and had met Evan Roberts. Within a few weeks, Smale's church was filled with people who were 'anticipating wonderful things.' Soul travail (being burdened from God, often in prayer for others) and a fear of God began to come upon the people and some of the services would continue until the early hours. Frank Bartleman wrote: 'A wonderful work of the Spirit has broken out here...preceded by a deep and preparatory work of prayer and anticipation. Conviction is rapidly spreading among the people.' The revival lasted for fifteen weeks, until the leaders of the church wanted to return to the old order. Smale resigned and many followed him as he founded a new church in the area.[2]

Previous to the Azusa Street Revival breaking out in 1906, there were revivals in Houston, Texas, and Kansas City, where believers were being baptised in the Holy Spirit. Amongst the Christians, this led to a general excitement and hunger for the things of God. Prayer meetings were commenced for seeking the blessing in various quarters.

William Seymour was invited to be a pastor of a Holiness Church, on Santa Fe Street in Los Angeles, but as soon as he started to preach on the baptism of the Holy Spirit, he was locked out of his church and his lodgings upstairs! Some church members who agreed with his teaching on the baptism of the Holy Spirit and holiness, felt obligated to help him out, and took him in. In his prayer closet he pressed in after the things of God. A prayer meeting was held at his new lodgings and he became known as a man of prayer.

In late February 1906, William Seymour moved to new lodgings in North Bonnie Brae Street and was invited to hold meetings there, and with a small group they began to pray and fast. One man was healed instantly after being anointed with oil by Seymour, and after a second prayer, the man began to speak in tongues, and people flocked to this house church. As the spiritual fire from Heaven descended, many witnesses believed the house itself was literally on fire and the fire brigade (fire department) was called out! It was not until April 1906 that Seymour began to speak in tongues.

In April 1906, the house church found new premises on 312 Azusa Street as the crowds became too big! The building (formerly a Methodist church) was made of wood and had been previously used as a stable and storehouse for several years and was in quite a state of disrepair. People flocked to the building, where sawdust covered the floor.[3]

A Methodist layman wrote: 'Scenes transpiring here [at the Azusa Street Revival] are what Los Angeles churches have been praying for, for years. I have been a Methodist for twenty-five years. I was a leader of the praying band for the First Methodist Church. We prayed that Pentecost might come to the city of Los Angeles. We wanted it to start at First Methodist Church, but God did not start it in any church in this city, but in a barn, so that all might come and take part in it. If it had started in a fine church, the poor coloured people and Spanish people would not have got in, but praise God it started here' [on Azusa Street].[4]

On 18 April 1906, the San Francisco earthquake shook the ground for just under one minute; five hundred people were killed in San Francisco. The surrounding cities and country were devastated. The next day, a small earthquake hit Los Angeles, it was an earnest time and people were afraid. Frank Bartleman felt led to attend the Azusa Street Mission which had just moved from Bonnie Brae Street and he gave his first sermon there. The earthquake had opened many hearts to eternal issues. The vast majority of preachers were trying to calm the fears of the people, stating that the earthquake was from the Devil and not of God. Frank Bartleman's view was the complete opposite; he told the people that it was God's judgment and a wakeup call – 'the voice of God to the people on the Pacific Coast.' Frank Bartleman had a faith ministry in writing and distributing tracts and on 22 April 1906, 10,000 tracts, The Last Call were rapidly distributed around the city from workers of The New Testament Church (Burbank Hall) which had begun under Joseph Smale. In May, the Lord gave him a tract called the Earthquake and with the aid of helpers, 75,000 were given out in three weeks, and another

50,000 at Oakland, Bay Cities, under brother Manley in the same period of time.[5]

William Seymour sometimes preached behind a wooden box but as the move of God progressed, he was frequently found praying behind the box as the Holy Spirit did what He wanted. The meetings became spontaneous. Services lasted for hours, half a day, or continued all night. Eventually the meetings were held three times a day, morning, afternoon and night. Speaking in tongues was the central blessing which attracted multitudes of curious people, but healing of the sick soon followed, including creative miracles, and the walls were soon covered with the crutches and canes of those who had been miraculously healed. The gift of tongues was soon followed by the gift of interpretation.[6]

Trainloads of passengers from across the States came to experience this new move of God. People en-route to the meeting would be prostrated; some would rise and speak in tongues. By the summer, thousands were turning up and they saw the Shekinah glory (a Divine mist) in the meetings!

In the beginning in Azusa they had no musical instruments or hymn books, as they felt no need for them, all was spontaneous. Someone would give a testimony, sing or read some passages of Scripture and eventually someone would preach, regardless of age, colour or gender. All the well known hymns were sung from memory quickened by the Spirit of God and especially the song, 'The Comforter Has Come.'

On Friday, 15 June 1906, 'At Azusa, the Spirit dropped the "Heavenly chorus" into my soul,' wrote Frank Bartleman. 'No one could understand this "gift of song" but those who had it. It was indeed a "new song" in the Spirit…the Lord has sovereignly bestowed it, with the outpouring of the "residue of oil" the Latter Rain baptism of the Spirit. It was exercised as the Spirit moved the possessors, either in solo fashion, or by the company. It was sometimes without words, other times in "tongues"…it brought about a Heavenly atmosphere, as though the angels themselves were present and joining with us…this "new song" was altogether different, not of human composition. It cannot be successfully counterfeited. The crow cannot imitate the dove. But they finally began to despise this "gift" when the human spirit asserted itself again. They drove it out by hymn books, and selected songs by leaders. It was like murdering the Spirit, and most painful to some of us, but the tide was too strong against us.'[7]

On 16 November 1906, an article by Frank Bartleman was published in a holiness newspaper, *Way of Faith*. He stated: 'Los Angeles seems to be the place and this the time in the mind of God for the restoration of the Church.'[8]

In September 1906, a local newspaper reporter frowned on the events taking place and wrote that the Azusa Street mission was a 'disgraceful intermingling of the races...they cry and make howling noises all day and into the night. They run, jump, shake all over, shout to the top of their voice, spin around in circles, fall out on the sawdust blanketed floor jerking, kicking and rolling all over it. Some of them pass out and do not move for hours as though they were dead. These people appear to be mad, mentally deranged or under a spell. They claim to be filled with the Spirit. They have a one-eyed, illiterate, negro as their preacher who stays on his knees much of the time with his head hidden between the wooden milk crates. He doesn't talk very much but at times he can be heard shouting, 'Repent,' and he's supposed to be running the thing.... They repeatedly sing the same song, "The Comforter Has Come." '[9]

Eventually things turned bad at Azusa, people accused William Seymour of starting a new denomination. There were many misunderstandings and new ideas being thrown about which generally led to confusion and frustration, while others were working it up in the flesh. One of the misconceptions of tongues was that some who felt called to the mission field believed that they already had the ability to speak in another nation's language and were devastated on arrival at their mission field. Though at the meetings when some people spoke in tongues, other nationalities heard them speaking in their mother tongue and were converted because of this sign from Heaven!

Apostolic Faith Mission on Azusa Street 1911 – America

By 1909, Frank Bartleman's account of the Apostolic Faith Mission (Azusa Mission) was not good. At Azusa, everything was run in a set order and those present came into more and more bondage, it was a 'spirit of dictatorship.' The following year, Bartleman returned in late February 1911. One week before he arrived, William H. Durham, a former Baptist minister from the North Avenue Mission in Chicago, began to hold meetings at Azusa and revival broke out once again! It was known by many as the 'Second Shower of the Latter Rain' and on one Sunday, 500 people were turned away! However, on 2 May 1911, the doors to the Apostolic Faith Mission were locked with chain and padlock. William Seymour had been preaching in the east of America and the trustees of the Mission quickly summoned him back. They had decided to lock Durham out because they objected to his message. Durham then rented a large building and on a Sunday 1,000 people would attend, with 400 on a week night. He received much opposition and in the winter returned to Chicago where he was wonderfully used of God until he died of influenza the following year.[10]

Port of South Adelaide Congregational Church 1912 – Australia

In 1909, due to the death of his son, Rev. Lionel B. Fletcher accepted a call to a pastorate of the Port of South Adelaide Congregational Church in South Australia. For three years, Rev. Fletcher was the minister of the church before he 'did any distinctively evangelistic work amongst his people.' He was a firm believer in sowing, before he could expect a harvest, but as an evangelistic preacher he had always seen a steady flow of converts from among his people, but he was not satisfied. He knew other men that led thousands to Christ, why not him?

In 1912, Dr. Wilbur Chapman and Charles Alexander visited Adelaide for a month. The churches combined for a United Mission. Rev. Lionel B. Fletcher wrote: 'There were not many in my church who were influenced by that mission, because we were situated so far from the building in which the meetings were held' even though he attended regularly and had a prominent part in the work. After the Mission, many of the churches proceeded to settle down, but Rev. Fletcher believed that 'if a mission is vigorously followed up, and made the beginning of advance work, instead of the end of a special effort, then revival will follow.'

Rev. Lionel B. Fletcher informed his deacons that in June he intended to have a series of Sunday night evangelistic services. He also spoke to his Prayer and Fellowship Meeting, where two hundred and fifty people set themselves apraying. On the night of his first after-meeting, Rev. Fletcher was 'terribly nervous, and almost ill with strain,' after an appeal the people began to sing when three tall men marched to the front, and were soon followed by another three and a woman, and 'some who had expressed displeasure at the suggestion of an evangelistic service were deeply moved.' In all there were nineteen converted which was the beginning of a new anointing for Rev. Fletcher. In *Mighty Moments* (c.1931) Rev. Fletcher did not give specific dates or write chronologically. The reference to this revival was scattered across two chapters. It would appear that the big break came on the second Sunday evening or a subsequent week of June 1912.

In the following week, Rev. Lionel B. Fletcher began to become distressed and perplexed because he had a 'longing desire to see his people coming to Christ in full surrender.' In his study he threw himself onto his knees and poured out his soul to God which almost broke his heart, 'and literally wrestled with God.' He confessed his sin, laid bare his soul before God and pleaded for the souls of his people. Rev. Fletcher wrote: 'Was I to be content with a few ears of corn when the fields were white unto harvest? I pleaded the precious promises of God's Word [from the Holy Bible]; I pleaded the blessed sacrifice of Calvary; I felt that I must see revival or die, and I said so in my prayer that day. I reminded God that my people were praying and looking for revival, and were their prayers not to be answered?' As he prayed something within him broke, in a moment he was seized with fear and then an utterable peace filled his life, 'it was the lifting of an intolerable load.' At the prayer meeting that night he asked for volunteers who would covenant with him to pray from 7pm till 9pm on the following Saturday night. About two hundred made the promise.

Saturday night came, but Rev. Lionel B. Fletcher in his study was unable to pray, totally unable to pray, but had an assurance that God was going to work. He turned to Charles Finney's *Autobiography* where he described such an experience that he was now passing through, and Finney saw revival! He began to praise the Lord and knew that God had already answered his prayers.

The Sunday evening began. Rev. Lionel B. Fletcher later commented on that memorable service; 'I never conducted a service in which so many things went wrong!' In the middle of his sermon 'a lady fell on the floor uttering piercing cries, and it was nearly ten minutes before she could be carried out.' Rev. Fletcher was so upset by the episode and the tension which was present that he felt like closing the service, until he remembered the prayer and the expectation of those who had prayed. After the sermon, he invited those present for an after-meeting, where those that would surrender their lives to Christ would come forward and shake his hand, and stand before the congregation as a public declaration of their decision. 'The air was charged with a spirit of expectancy,' he wrote. For a moment there was complete silence, until a prominent businessman, an office-bearer in the church came forward and publicly confessed his sin of an inconsistent life, 'of unworthiness, and a lack of love to Christ and stated his determination to give Christ the first place in his heart from that time on.'

Rev. Lionel B. Fletcher wrote: 'The effect was instantaneous. His wife and then his daughters, and then other members of his family came and stood with him, and then from all parts of the building people came until forty men and women were standing with them in front of the communion table. No one wanted to go home that night. Few present had ever witnessed such a scene before, but it was followed by many just as remarkable during that and the following winters, and that wave of revival did not cease until it swept through dozens of other churches and nearly 2,000 people confessed Christ. I firmly believed that Australia would have been swept by revival in those days, but the Great War [World War I, 1914-1918] brought the conscriptions [drafts] issue to the people, and in the controversy and bitterness which followed, the spiritual blessing was stayed.... But my life and ministry were revolutionised in those days....'[11]

East Anglia Revival 1921-1922 – England

This revival by one author has been referred to as *The Forgotten Revival* as it has been widely overlooked within evangelical Church history. It is also known as the Lowestoft Revival as that is the town in which it began, whilst the revival which swept up into Scotland and is interconnected is known as the Fishermen's Revival (1921-1922). East Anglia is an area in the east of England and is bordered to the north and east by the North Sea.

In November 1920, Rev. A. Douglas Brown from Balham, London, England, UK, had been a minister for twenty-six years. Then God got a hold of him in the midst of a Sunday evening service and nearly broke his heart whilst preaching. He went back to the vestry, locked the door and threw himself on the floor. He had never known a Sunday at his church without conversions and was unsure of why he was heartbroken. His church was filled, he loved his people and he believed that they loved him. That night he went home and refused to take supper. God told him that he was a proud minister, that there were reservations in his surrender, and He wanted him to do a piece of work that he had been trying to evade. All November the struggle went on, but Rev. Brown would not give way, then the joy of Christmas seemed to mock him. Rev. Brown speaking at the Keswick Convention in 1922, retelling the incident, said, "I knew what Jesus wanted. He showed me pictures of congregations and Douglas Brown on his knees in the midst of them. I saw Douglas Brown praying with his own folk, to whom he had preached for over fifteen years, I saw it all in picture." The struggle went on and he told God, "You know that is not my work. I will pray for anyone else who does it, but please do not give it to me; it will kill me. I cannot get up into the pulpit and plead with people. It is against my temperament and You made me."

"All through January God wrestled with me," said Rev. A. Douglas Brown, "There is a Love that will not let go." It was in February 1921, "after four months of struggle that there came the crisis." On a Saturday night he wrote a letter of resignation to his church which was marked with his own tears. On the Sunday morning at 2am he tripped over his dog and fell to the floor. The dog licked his face, but he felt like an outcast. "Then something happened. I felt myself in the loving embrace of Christ for ever and ever; and all power and all joy rolled in and all blessedness rolled in like a deluge. How did it come? I cannot tell you. Perhaps I may when I get to Heaven." Rev. Brown had fully surrendered to the Master's will and said, "Lord Jesus, I know what You want; You want me to go into mission work. I love Thee more than I dislike that." For twenty-three years Rev. Brown had trouble with neuritis (inflammation of a peripheral nerve or nerves) in his arm and God healed him in an instant![12]

In the first week of March 1921, Rev. A. Douglas Brown was invited to hold a five-day evangelistic campaign in Lowestoft, East Anglia, England. There would be several meetings throughout the day, notably the prayer meeting in the morning in which prayer requests would be received, a Bible study in the afternoon and the evangelistic service in the evening. In the first week, more than a hundred people got converted – Rev. Brown stayed for one month (returning home to his parish at weekends) and more than five hundred people were saved.

For two years prior to Rev. A. Douglas Brown's visit, the weekly prayer meeting at the London Road Baptist Church, under Rev. Hugh Ferguson, was flourishing as the people prayed for revival, and the Bible classes for men and women were also very well attended. The seating capacity of the Baptist church in Lowestoft was seven hundred and fifty. During the service on Monday there was a spirit of expectancy. On Tuesday, the Holy Spirit's power was felt in the meeting. On Wednesday, Rev. Brown, after he had finished preaching told the people that he was going into the vestry and that those who wanted help or desired to surrender themselves to Jesus Christ should follow – and they did!

During the first week and subsequent weeks, Rev. A. Douglas Brown preached at different churches within Lowestoft, the ministers of various denominations working in unity, rejoicing together in the harvest. Christians got revived, drunks became sober, debts were paid and many saw their sin, and met the Saviour for the first time. The fourth week of the campaign saw the largest attendances. In St. John's, the eleven hundred-seat church was not big enough, people sat in the aisles, on the window sills and even on the pulpit steps!

Rev. A. Douglas Brown returned for another five day mission in the Whitsun week (Pentecost) in June 1921 and since his first visit, over a thousand people were converted in eleven weeks! He then held campaigns in other localities, Ipswich, Yarmouth, Norwich and Cambridge, the latter city with assistance from the evangelist and revivalist Gipsy Smith. God moved in all these localities and Rev. Brown returned to Lowestoft for a convention in the third week of September. Rev. Brown at the convention was able to state that during the past months they had known the 'felt presence of the Lord.' While the President of the Baptist union in 1921 wrote an article in which he dismissed the work in East Anglia as an 'emotional wave' produced by a 'hypnotic preacher' yet addressed Rev. Brown as his 'beloved friend.'[13]

At the Keswick Convention in the summer of 1922, Rev. A. Douglas Brown said, "The great need of England today is a revival of holiness in the Christian Church. I have had no time to prepare addresses for this Convention; this is my 1700th service since the beginning of last year [1,700 services in 18 months is an average of 3.1 meetings a day]. I come as a harvester in the field of Jesus Christ and I come as one who has given his life to the work, and when you have given Him all, He gives you a benediction for the little you have given."

On the subject of 'Defective Consecration,' Rev. A. Douglas Brown said, "You will forgive me, won't you, but for eighteen months I have been working in the midst of the men of this country, rough men who know nothing about theology, and they say, "Douglas Brown, we are going to believe the Christian Church when she is real." O God, make us real! We do love Thee; but whatever it costs us, we want to go back and face the great opportunity with a great anointing...." Nearing the end of his address he said, "Trust the Holy Ghost for power. I did eighteen months ago...."

Several decades before the revival in Lowestoft a nurse was converted in Luton, whilst at a meeting in the Corn Exchange under the preaching of Rev. A. Douglas Brown's dad. The nurse went home and told her mother who gave her a gold sovereign, saying, "Jesus Christ has given you tonight a heart of pure gold. Take this sovereign. Never spend it on yourself, whenever you look at it, remember the night that Jesus Christ gave my Dorothy a heart of pure gold. I shall soon be in glory." The mother died and Dorothy went wandering, compromised her Christian faith and broke all her vows. Whilst she was nursing someone at Boscombe, Dorset, she walked past St. John's Church, when God spoke to her, "Go into that church and you will hear words whereby you will be mended." Inside the church she was mended, and after retelling the story to Rev. Brown she said, "God has given me back my heart of pure gold tonight. It has been just wonderful. That coin was lost but the Holy Spirit has been sweeping, sweeping, sweeping, and He has not only found the coin, but Jesus came." She took out the gold sovereign and gave it to Rev. Brown which was forwarded onto Lowestoft to buy hymnbooks for the converts.[14]

Jock Troup, a well built man and former cooper (barrel maker), from Wick, turned evangelist was also used during the revival at Lowestoft (1921-1922) and the Fishermen's Revival (1921-1922) in the North-East of Scotland. Jock arrived in Yarmouth in October 1921, in the midst of economic downturn when the herring industry was long past its prime. He came under the auspices of the Baptists and The Salvation Army. Jock preached on the third Saturday night of October at the Plain Stone in the Market Place, where hundreds of people, notably fishermen and fisher-girls were milling around. His text was from Isaiah 63:1, speaking of the Messiah's judgment: 'Who is this that cometh from Edom, with dyed garments from Bozrah?' It was said that Jock's voice could carry 450 metres without amplification, and after this sermon, hundreds were slain to the ground under the sword of the Word of God – convicted of sin and fearful of the wrath to come. Further meetings were held in different churches and fishermen out at sea were also converted as God came down![15]

Rev. A. Douglas Brown 1921

In a report from an address by Rev. A. Douglas Brown from 1921, a reporter wrote: 'As a nation we have turned our back on God. As organised churches, we have put our programmes in the place of the Holy Spirit. We must get back to the primal message of the cross, to the simple evangelistic message of the Master Himself, and to the prayer of faith.'[16]

In 1921, Rev. A. Douglas Brown preached at Stowmarket on 'Divine Sovereignty and Human Responsibility in the Realm of Christian Witness.' He said, "When revival comes to England, the sermon-tasters will wither away and will become worshipers. When a man preaches in the power of the Holy Spirit, his message is a miracle of utterance.'[17]

In 1921, Rev. A. Douglas Brown was preaching at Norwich and said, "...I ask you to pray earnestly in your homes that there may be poured out upon this city a spirit of conviction of sin. Until men and women realise themselves to be sinners in God's sight, there will be no receiving of the Word of God unto salvation. Brothers and sisters, nothing will save our beloved land but a revival from Heaven...O God, this week send forth Thy Holy Spirit and purge the churches. Bring back backsliders, give a great sense of sin, answer mothers' prayers, fathers' prayers.... You cannot make a revival; but no multitude of people ever got on its knees before Calvary but what revival came. God bring us back to Calvary, back to the dear old Gospel in all its simplicity...."[18]

In 1921, Rev. A. Douglas Brown gave his appraisal of the spiritual climate of the nation as a whole and in East Anglia in particular. He said, "A momentous revival is within reach of the churches. In East Anglia it is commenced. Whether it becomes national depends upon the message and methods adopted by various churches during the coming winter. You cannot organise revival.... The army of organised religion is a great host. The possibilities are immense. But the great machine is hung up and powerless for want of water. When critics stop picking holes in Divine revelation, when cranks cease to prejudice others by religious squint, when preachers cease to be politicians, when churches put spiritual before social, when Calvary preaching replaces critical essays, when God's atmosphere impregnates man's activities, when pride, jealousy, gossip and worldliness wither and die in our churches under the blazing heat of

Calvary love, then the churches will strike the rock of salvation with Divine authority, and the waters will flow for the healing of the nations."[19]

Fishermen's Revival 1921-1922 – Scotland

The revival in Lowestoft, England, was exported by fishermen from East Anglia to Scotland (hence the Fishermen's Revival) and vice versa as they plied their trade in pickled herrings. The boats from Scotland followed the migratory fish southward, beginning in spring at Lerwick, Shetland, Scotland, moving down the east coast until they reached East Anglia, England, by October and returned. John Ferguson in *When God Came Down* wrote: '...In the course of time, all the fishing ports of the east coast of Scotland, including Dundee and Aberdeen and as far north as Wick and Thurso, were powerfully affected. He noted that it began in the fishing town of Yarmouth, England, where in October 1921, Jock Troup, a former cooper from Wick, was one of the preachers.

After Jock Troup left Yarmouth, England, for Scotland a few weeks later, the revival continued under Rev. A. Douglas Brown who continued his visits from his parish. 'News of the events at Yarmouth spread like wildfire back to the fishing communities in Scotland, and the fishing fleet had a home coming like never before,' so wrote George Mitchel in *Revival Man: The Jock Troup Story*.

Jock Troup received a vision from God, where he saw a man on his knees, praying to God to send Jock Troup to Fraserburgh in Scotland. Troup travelled to the Aberdeenshire town, arriving before the fishing fleet and preached in the square in the open-air until rain drove him and the people into a Baptist church. The deacons had been discussing about inviting Jock Troup to hold meetings there and the man in the vision on his knees was there! The church was made available for other meetings. Religious as well as secular newspapers reported this revival of religion.

The *Scottish Baptist Magazine* for December 1921 had the heading, Revival in the North. It stated: 'A revival is in process in Wick.' The reporter stated that The Salvation Army and Pilgrim Preachers of the Faith Mission had held campaigns in the previous year and 'the hunger and expectancy for revival, however, was aroused. Prayer was inspired.' Then the Baptist church had a deputation from the Highland Mission who began meetings on 20 August 1921, for four weeks. This was when 'the fishermen went to Yarmouth, and there one of the townsmen was instrumental especially in the open-air in reaching a number of our young fishermen, many of them the most unlikely fellows. The news of these "unlikelys" startled Wick from its sleep and when they came home and began to testify in the open-air in the Pulteney dialect, it had great power, and we believe hundreds have been converted since in The Salvation Army and the Baptist church....'

'The Salvation Army Headquarters have kept in close touch with the work and have sent a number of their ablest officers to superintend it. Taking the work among fisher-folk into account, some 300 people, mostly young people, have professed conversion. Such a result in a town of some 9,000 people must have a great and abounding influence. It almost means that a new generation has been won for Christ.' The reporter continued and noted the 'crowded Gospel services' at Peterhead, and at Hopeman, where 'remarkable scenes have been witnessed and the whole village is moved. Many [fishermen] were converted at Yarmouth and since their return, united meetings have been held each night in the United Free Church' and '140 have been converted, which adding to the 70 who professed at Yarmouth, means that the whole place is transformed, and praise of God is heard in the street far into the night. The people are crowding the churches.'

An article in *The People's Journal* dated, 17 December 1921 describes the movement: 'People thronging the streets are going to a church; nine out of ten can be counted on being bound for a place of worship.... Where the church should hold five hundred, a thousand or more have contrived to find entry and the doorway is blocked with others who would fain to get in. The story of the revival at Inverallochy and Cairnbulg...reads like a page from the ecclesiastical history of Scotland. Since the boats returned, the devotions have rose to fever heat. At Findochty, some miles from Buckie, a Divine spark has been fanned into flame. From six pm to midnight, prayer meetings, conventions and procession succeed each other.... Everywhere, in the homes and in the streets, there is joyous singing of hymns: At the cross, at the cross where I first saw the light. The revival is continuing....'

In the villages of Inverallochy and Cairnbulg, in December, six hundred people were converted in two weeks out of a population of fifteen hundred – that is forty percent of the population! Other towns, villages and cities were touched by the Holy Spirit in varying degrees including: Peterhead, Inverness, Wick, Burghhead, Aberdeen, Dundee, Anstruther, Pittenweem, Glasgow, Auchterarder and Buchan.

The Scotsman newspaper for Tuesday, 20 December 1921 reported on the Religious Revival at Eyemouth: 'At the little fishing ports of Eyemouth and Burnmouth the revival wave which is sweeping the ports in the North of Scotland has made itself felt, and nightly larger gatherings meet to listen to addresses by young fishermen who have become converted at the Lowestoft fishing where revival meetings are held.' The reporter went on to speak of the economic woes of the industry, many are near ruin, and 'the great October gale which robbed many a home in these ports of a breadwinner [death of fishermen at sea]...in that dark hour the people turned to the church.... Ministers and lay preachers are assisting the converted orators at the revival meetings being held and though the language and phrases of the later speakers may be innocent of oratorical merit, their testimony is given with the fierceness of a north-east gale, and it is this evidence which is bearing away hundreds on the revival flood.'

In many of the towns, cinemas and public houses became empty and dancing halls shut due to lack of interest in worldly amusement. The Salvation Army soon taught the new converts how to sing, whilst the leaders and lay members of the revival continued in earnest prayer for the Holy Spirit to come down. Jock Troup would constantly make appeals for people to embrace the Saviour.

The 1922 Assembly of the Church of Scotland Church and Nation Report contained a resolution from the Presbytery of Auchterarder: 'That the Presbytery gives thanks to Almighty God for the signs of revival and spiritual life in certain of the sea-coast communities and urges the Committee of Church and Nation to take the whole circumstances of the revival into earnest and prayerful consideration, with a view to determining whether any improvement in church life, work, or worship are suggested thereby. The Presbytery... recognises that this revival has brought to the front certain fundamental Christian truths of the first importance which are largely lost sight of in present-day Christian teaching. They further are concerned lest the Church not being fully alive to the possibilities of this movement, a great opportunity for deepening and enriching the spiritual life of the church may be lost.'

In 1922, Jock Troup was encouraged to study at Glasgow's Bible Training Institute, which he did for two years (on and off) in between preaching the Gospel, and went on to have a powerful evangelistic ministry.[20]

Speaking on 'Walking in the Spirit,' Rev. A. Douglas Brown noted that Scottish men who throw up their hats when a man kicks a piece of inflated leather between two sticks is known as a football enthusiast, but, "When North Sea fishermen sing in the streets of the Fountain, 'open for sin and uncleanness,' they call him a lunatic."[21]

'They shall lift up their voice, they shall sing; for the majesty of the Lord they shall cry aloud from the sea. Therefore glorify the Lord in the dawning light, the name of the Lord God of Israel in the coastlands of the sea. From the ends of the earth we have heard songs, "Glory to the righteous!"...' (Isaiah 24:14-16a).

Revival in Ruanda 1931 and 1936+

At the end of 1916, A. C. Stanley Smith, a missionary doctor in Uganda, went to spy out the land of Ruanda, alongside fellow labourer, Mr Leonard Sharp, his future brother-in-law. They were looking to open a mission station for the Church Missionary Society Ruanda Mission and by February 1921, work began at Kabale. Smith later documented the first thirty years of the Ruanda Mission in *Road to Revival* (1946). A. C. Stanley Smith was born on 14 February 1890 in China; he was the son of Stanley P. Smith, who had been converted under D. L. Moody and was one of the Cambridge Seven who sailed for China in 1885 with the China Inland Mission.

In June 1922, Stanley Smith wrote: 'A safari [overland journey] round the village churches always sends one to one's knees in prayer for revival. But if our teachers are to be revived we who lead them must be abiding in the place of power. Just recently, God has been giving us a time of spiritual reviving. A book which has greatly helped us has been *How to Live the Victorious Life* by an unknown Christian.... We took the opportunity of all our evangelists being in, of having a series of meetings in which we tried to pass on the thoughts and experiences which were blessing us.'

Five years prior to the Ruanda Revival of 1936 there had been pockets of localised revival. Stanley Smith wrote: 'Ever since 1931, the Holy Spirit had been at work in men and women here and there, lighting the fires of revival. They had one and all been brought through 'the valley of humiliation' to a deep and even agonizing sense of sin, they had been driven to painful and costly repentance, often with its exacting demands of open confession and restitution and they have found cleansing in the precious blood of Christ and victory over sin through His indwelling Spirit. They were marked men; joy shone in their faces and everywhere they went they had a testimony. But in the Church at large, the revival fires though smouldering had not yet burst into flame.

'Fired with zeal for Christ, they began to go about the country in little teams of twos and threes, witnessing everywhere. On one occasion an old grey-haired Mututsi went with a friend from Gahini to Buhiga. Their faces alone were sufficient to tell of changed hearts. On their own initiative they were touring the mission stations on foot, a walk of five hundred miles. They wanted to see the work of God, so as to pray for it better and to testify to what God had done for them.'[22]

In the last few days of 1933, which rolled into 1934, an African Keswick-type convention was held at Gahini in Ruanda which lasted for five days. Geoffrey Holmes, a missionary then extended the convention for a further day. On Saturday, 2 January 1934, while everyone was bowed in prayer, an African rose to his feet and began to confess his sins. A wave of conviction swept in and lasted for two and a half hours with as many as three on their feet at any given time trying to speak. Revival had come and teams of men and women from the mission stations of Gahini, Kabale, Shyira and Kigeme began visiting other out-churches and those who were unreached.[23]

The revival broke out at the Gahini mission station on 29 June 1936 in eastern Ruanda. Dr. Joe Church was in charge of this station, but was away in Mekono, Uganda, holding evangelistic meetings. The revival touched all aspects of mission work on the compound including the girls' and boys' school, the Hospital, the Church and the Evangelistic Training Centre. When Dr. Church returned he wrote: 'During that week men were gripped by uncontrollable forces, also spontaneously all over the district in the bush churches and some on the [mission] stations. In some cases there were signs and dreams, and outburst of hymn singing and prayer and remorse that often went on all night. In the Hospital servants' quarters, church, boys' school and in the houses of kraals of carpenters and headmen; even the government patients' Rest Camp was moved. The patients who were raw heathen and were lodging there behind the hospital were convicted.'

In early September 1936, Archdeacon of Kigezi (a district in southern Uganda) and Ruanda-Urundi, Arthur Pitt-Pitts wrote: 'I have been to all the stations where this revival is going on...the fire was alight in all of them before the middle of June, but during that week in June, it burst into a wild flame which, like the African grass fire before the wind, cannot be put out.'[24].

'Oh, do not deliver the life of Your turtledove to the wild beast! Do not forget the life of Your poor forever. Have respect to the covenant; for the dark places of the earth are full of the haunts of cruelty. Oh, do not let the oppressed return ashamed! Let the poor and needy praise Your name' (Psalm 74:19-21).

Dr. Joe Church's Testimony

In 1937, Dr. Joe Church, fresh from the Ruanda Revival told the students of the Missionary Training Colony in Croydon, England, his testimony. When he first arrived in Ruanda in 1927 as a medical missionary, he had high ideals, but was met with famine, rampant diseases and burials in mass graves. Two years later, in September 1929, sick in mind and body he was persuaded to take a holiday in Kenya. Passing through Uganda he met Simeon Nisbambi (whom he had met once before), a native civil servant and substantial land owner. They both yearned for holiness and righteousness and sought a deeper work of God. For three days they searched the Scriptures and based on 1 John 1: 'That the blood of Jesus Christ, God's Son cleanses us from all sin,' they claimed the cleansing of the blood of Christ and by faith received the fullness of the Spirit which they had discovered by searching the Word. Simeon Nisbambi gave most of his land to the Church, and though only a layman 'began a ministry of great effectiveness in the Church,' so wrote Bill Butler, and was instrumental in bringing revival to Ruanda.

Dr. Joe Church eventually returned to Ruanda and asked 'forgiveness from those Africans he had grieved or hindered by hastiness, anger or irritability – sins which missionaries had been slow to acknowledge as such at all.' Joe's senior hospital assistant, Yosiya Kinuka was one of the first to be affected and became an 'outstanding leader in the revival which gradually manifested itself throughout Ruanda, Burundi and Uganda and ultimately the whole of East Africa' in what became known as the East African Revival (1930s-1950s).

Dr. Joe Church told the students at the Colony in Croyden, England, the history of the Church in Uganda, its trials and persecutions and appealed for seven missionaries – the Uganda Seven. Bill Butler was one of them and was accepted by the Church Missionary Society and arrived in Africa in April 1939 and was ordained in November 1940.

Prior to the revival, the second generation of Christians were Christian in name and pagan in nature, where sins of witchcraft, drunkenness and adultery were rife. Some of the young African converts were so on fire for God that they were nicknamed the "Abaka" – the 'fiery ones' or 'those aflame' as A. C. Stanley Smith translated it.[25]

Because of the Ruanda Revival, Dr. Joe Church began compiling a discipleship booklet over several years, consisting of forty-four subjects, from Sin to the Second Coming, which was a reference book of the fundamental truth of the faith, preferable than the scraps of paper which had been used in the past by senior members of 'Bible Teams' who were initially sent to preach and teach at missions and conventions. Every Man a Bible Student was first published in May 1938 and up to 1961 went through fifteen editions (just under 50,000 copies), but was also translated into Swahili in 1940 (several reprints), Lugole, (Kenya) in 1941, Lunyaruanda, (Ruanda) in 1941, Luganda, (Uganda) in 1943, French in 1951 and other languages.[26]

Moses said to his assistant, Joshua, "Are you zealous for my sake? Oh, that all the Lord's people were prophets and that the Lord would put His Spirit upon them!" (Numbers 11:29).

Chapter 21

The Spirit of Revival

'For I will pour water on him who is thirsty, and floods on the dry ground; I will pour My Spirit on your descendants, and My blessing on your offspring; they will spring up among the grass like willows by the watercourses' (Isaiah 44:3-4).

Hebridean Revival 1949-1952

The Hebridean Revival is also known as the Lewis Revival or the Lewis Awakening. Rev. Duncan Campbell, due to unexpected circumstances had been asked to preach in the Outer Hebrides, Scotland, UK, for ten days, but he stayed for more than two years, on and off. There had been a revival on the island of Lewis in 1939 prior to the outbreak of World War II which was just as powerful as the 1949-1952 revival, but the war eclipsed its attention. However, "It was the people who were saved in the 1939 revival who spearheaded the 1949-1952 revival and who were the prayer warriors," said Donald MacPhail in *Sounds from Heaven* (2004) by Colin and Mary Peckham. "It was these people who followed Mr Campbell around the island and on whom he depended to pray through. They knew how to pray and to travail for souls."[1]

Before revival broke out, a declaration was read in every congregation of the Free Church on the Isle of Lewis, Outer Hebrides, exhorting its members to pray for God's awakening on their land. Some people took this declaration very seriously. However, the ironic thing was that during the revival the ministers of the Free Church opposed this move of God! Many Free Church communities were also warned to stay away from the meetings, though not all Free Church members heeded their denomination's or minister's warnings! It was not until August 1954, after the revival, that Rev. Duncan Campbell was invited to hold a mission in the Free Church, at Lemreway, Lochs, on the Isle of Lewis. This was largely because of the steadfastness of the converts from Gravir from August 1953. The small Free Presbyterian denomination was also vocal in its opposition, which found its way into the *Stornoway Gazette*, 22 June 1951, where they urged their people 'to have nothing to do with the so-called revival activities of the present day.'[2]

Two elderly sisters in their eighties, Peggy and Christine Smith, one being blind and the other being severely afflicted with arthritis, met at their home and travailed in prayer from 10pm into the early hours in their little cottage, often until three in the morning. Other members of the community were also praying people, they held cottage prayer meetings, and the native language was Gaelic, once a common language across northern Scotland. One night God gave one of the sisters a vision in which she saw their church crowded with young people and declared to her sister that she believed revival was coming. At this time not a single young person attended public worship in that community! The minister, Rev. James Murray MacKay of the Church of Scotland, Barvas was called for. He had been inducted at Barvas Church of Scotland in April 1949 and was promoted to glory in 1954. The sister explained to Rev. MacKay what she saw and believed. He took this word as from the Lord and asked what should be done. "What," she said, "Give yourself to prayer!" For two nights a week for at least three months many church deacons and elders met; they prayed for revival and waited upon God in a small thatched cottage, a traditional 'black house' (which Rev. Duncan Campbell referred to as a barn) at one end of the parish, pleading one promise, "I will pour water on him who is thirsty and floods upon the dry ground" (Isaiah 44:3), while the sisters prayed at the other end of the parish in their cottage (which has since been demolished). One night a young deacon, Kenneth MacDonald rose to his feet and in Gaelic read part of Psalm 24, 'Who may ascend into the hill of the Lord? He who has clean hands and a pure heart....' The deacon said, "It seems to me just so much humbug, to be waiting as we are waiting and to be praying as we are praying, if we ourselves are not rightly related to God." He lifted his hands to Heaven and cried, "Oh God tell me, are my hands clean? Is my heart pure?" He fell onto his knees as the others, and went into a trance. Something in the spirit realm broke and the awareness of God began to grip the community.[3]

Rev. James Murray MacKay noted that Rev. Duncan Campbell first held meetings in the district of Barvas, Isle of Lewis, on Wednesday, 7 December 1949. Three weeks of meetings began in the district of Barvas and Shadar and it was at those services that the awakening began. Rev. MacKay stated that 'the awakening broke out in Shadar on the night of Sunday, 11 December 1949' and then 'spread from Shadar to Barvas and Borve, and even young people from Ness and Kinlock came to know the saving grace of Christ in the meetings in Shadar and Barvas.'[4]

In the Church of Scotland at Barvas, on the Isle of Lewis, on Saturday, 16 December 1949, there was a great spirit of expectancy at Duncan Campbell's first meeting. At the end of the service, as the people dispersed, one of the church deacons declared, "God is hovering over; He is going to break-through. Do not be discouraged, He is coming. I hear already the rumbling of Heaven's chariots wheels." Then he suggested to the already travel weary Duncan, that they, and around thirty others go and seek God in prayer in a nearby cottage. Rev. Campbell later described what happened, "God was beginning to move, the Heavens were opening, and we were there on our faces before God. Three o'clock in the morning came, and God swept in. About a dozen men and women lay prostrate on the floor, speechless. Something had happened, we knew that the forces of darkness were going to be driven back, and men were going to be delivered. We left the cottage at 3am to discover men and women seeking God. I walked along a country road, and found three men on their faces, crying to God for mercy. There was a light in every home; no-one seemed to think of sleep." He arrived home at 5am. When Duncan and his friends gathered at the church late in the morning, it was crowded as fourteen buses had come from all-over the small island to fill the building, one bus even came from Harris. Revival was under way, some fell into trances, others swooned, and many wept and slumped to the floor.

Later in the day, Rev. Duncan Campbell pronounced the benediction (close of the service) and the people started to leave. "A young man began to pray and was so burdened for the soul of his friend that he continued for three-quarters of an hour. During this time, people flocked back to the church and by the end there were as many outside the building as inside. People gathered from Stornaway and Ness and other parishes. It was 4am the following day that Campbell pronounced the benediction for the second time! As he was leaving he was told of many people who were in deep distress of soul, under the starlit sky were people [prostrated] by the peat stacks, on the road, by the cottages crying for mercy; revival had truly come."[5]

Rev. Duncan Campbell sent weekly reports to the Faith Mission, some of which were published in the *Pilgrim News* letter. For the 21, December 1949, he wrote: 'We are in the midst of a glorious revival. God in His great mercy has been pleased to visit us with showers of blessing, and the desert is rejoicing and blossoming as the rose. Some of us will live to praise God for what our ears are hearing and our eyes are seeing these days in Lewis. Meetings are crowded, right up to the pulpit steps. On several nights the meeting continue until 3:00 and 4:00 o'clock in the morning in the homes. Already about seventy adults have professed [faith in Jesus Christ]; we are dealing with anxious souls in every meeting.'[6]

Rev. Duncan Campbell held missions in different villages, districts or communities often from two to three weeks in duration. The work would be left with the local minister. Rev. Campbell was assisted by the ministers of the Free Church of Scotland, fellow Pilgrims from the Faith Mission, or godly men from the area. Rev. Campbell left the Islands quite regularly to fulfil other engagements, to hold meetings, missions, campaigns or to attend conferences (often as a speaker) on the mainland of Scotland, in Wales, as far south as Oxford, England, or in Ireland. Rev. Campbell would often be away from two weeks but up to three months. His wife and five children lived in Edinburgh near the Faith Mission and each Christmas he went home to spend a week or more with them.

Rev. Duncan Campbell said, "Of the hundreds who found Jesus Christ at that time, seventy-five percent of them were gloriously saved before they came near a meeting, before they heard a single sermon from myself or from any other minister in the parish, the power of God was moving, the Spirit of God in operation, and the fear of God gripping the souls of men...." In Rev. Duncan Campbell's weekly reports to the Faith Mission there are often references to bad or severe weather and opposition and requests for prayer. He also mentioned that strong men had fainted whilst at work on their looms (making Harris Tweed), in some meetings people were crying for mercy, physical prostrations, swoonings and men in distress. Rev. Campbell often wrote about the multiple meetings each day, often four to six which ended in the early hours, frequently around 3am to 4am. On a number of occasions, Rev. Campbell assisted in communion, which was held twice a year in each Church of Scotland community and they were staggered across different districts so that more Christians could attend. Communion "weekends" or seasons, were held from Thursday morning to Monday morning and often two or three ministers, beside the minister of the church would assist. Mary Peckham noted that they were more like conventions (because of their duration and teaching).

Rev. Duncan Campbell said, "Revival is not churches filled with people, but people filled with God. Revival is God going among His people. In revival, the church, the roadside, the hillside – become places made sacred by the presence of God and the cry of the repentant."

God came down and met with the body of Christ and the unconverted, and a good number of converts later became ministers and missionaries. People were drawn to church by an unseen hand, woken out of bed and drawn to church, (or to fields) where too many people assembled to fit into any of the buildings, whilst many fell where they were in agony of soul as they were won through to Christ and delivered from past bondages. Two bagpipe players who were to play at a local dance in Carloway in January 1950 were converted, but the dance continued without them until the minister arrived at 3:30am and asked the people to sing a Psalm, the people broke down as God's Spirit swept in.

In these church buildings and during services there were no musical instruments as tradition said they were instruments of the Devil. They sang Psalms and paraphrases of the Bible and even today many Scottish and Highland churches still hold to this point of view. The Presenter would sing one line of a Psalm and the congregation would repeat what had been sung. God met with these people because their hearts were right before God. And that is the big lesson for all of us; "Is my heart right before God? Are my hands clean? Is my heart pure?" See Psalm 15 and Psalm 24:3-6.

Twice during the Hebridean Revival preceding a mighty movement, Heavenly music was heard. One night about twenty people were walking along a country road around midnight when suddenly, Heavenly music was heard above them; they fell on their faces in amongst the heather as some thought the end of the world had come!

Rev. Duncan Campbell's report for 14 November 1951: 'This has been another week of much blessing. Meetings have been much larger than ever and people have come from all over Lewis to witness the movings of God, some as far as about fifty miles.' This was before modern car ownership on poorly maintained single-track roads. Often people would walk across moorland in the bleakest of weather to attend a service, including driving rain, blizzard-like conditions, wild weather and deep snow. Rev. Campbell continued: 'Whole districts have been completely changed. Social evils have been swept away as by a flood, and a wonderful sense of God seems to pervade the whole district....'[7]

The revival on the Isle of Lewis spread to Harris (but did not sweep across the Hebrides as some reports at the time stated) and then was carried by Duncan Campbell who was drawn across the six mile body of water (as the crow flies) to the small island of Berneray (also known as Bernera) which had a population of just four hundred people. During the Easter of 1952, Duncan Campbell had been preaching at a conference in Bangor, and was booked to preach the following night, but felt constrained by the Spirit to leave. From the pulpit he turned to the chairman and stated that he had to leave immediately for Harris, apologised, and went to pack his case. From Harris he took the boat to Berneray and within a few days every home on the island was affected by the Spirit of God.[8]

The revival continued into early 1953, but most revival authors conclude the work in 1952. In 1953, several missionaries from the Fly River field of the Unevangelised Field Mission (UFM) in New Guinea, read about the Hebridean Revival. They were greatly challenged by Psalm 24 that Duncan Campbell quoted as being key to the outbreak of the revival. At a conference of missionaries and nationals a spirit of prayer came on those gathered as did intense conviction of sin, followed by confession, restitution and reconciliation and 'not a few professions of faith – a consummating revival.'[9]

P.S. Bristow wrote the introduction to *The Lewis Awakening 1949-1953* by Duncan Campbell (1954). He wrote: 'I have before me Mr. Campbell's own accounts of the work, received from him from week to week, and I can only say that *his much restricted accounts* [italics added for emphasis] in these pages gives but a glimpse of the great manifestations of Divine power witnessed throughout the island. For personal reasons *the vivid details of experience in the lives of individuals is withheld.* Could they be suitably narrated, they would be thrilling to read.' Could the reason be that it was too sacred? Rev. Gordon I. Thomas, in the foreword to the same booklet wrote: 'Story after story could be told of incidents that are in the realm of the miraculous and which indeed are positively breath-taking to hear. *Practically none of these has been mentioned in this booklet....*'

Rev. Hugh Black was Rev. Campbell's chauffeur during the latter end of the Hebridean Revival. They did not always see eye to eye, but Rev. Campbell did share things which no other author has put into print. In one prayer meeting which was full of godly people Rev. Campbell saw 'demons fleeing in all directions' and Rev. Black speaks of an angelic visitor in Barvas, and visible spiritual light in Stornoway![10]

Andrew A. Woolsey wrote the biography of Rev. Duncan Campbell, *Channel of Revival*. He noted the revivalist's view of physical phenomena, specifically visions and trances which occurred during revival. He wrote: 'This was an aspect of the work which Duncan did not attempt to encourage or explain, but he recognised it was of God and refused to interfere with it, warning those who would associate it with satanic activity, that they were coming perilously near to committing the unpardonable sin.'[11]

Rev. Duncan Campbell was preaching in one meeting when half the congregation put their hands in the air and the other half slumped to one side – both groups were stuck in this position. They stayed in the same position throughout one or two hours of preaching![12]

Rev. Duncan Campbell in *The Lewis Awakening 1949-1953*, wrote: 'I have seen this...in the Western Isles. Suddenly an awareness of God would take hold of a community and, under the pressure of this Divine presence, men and women would fall prostrate on the ground, while their cry of distress was made the means in God's hand, to awaken the indifferent who had sat unmoved for years under the preaching of the Gospel.'[13]

Rev. Duncan Campbell spoke to a gathering of ministers on the theme of revival and what he had witnessed years previous on the

Isle of Lewis during the Hebridean Revival. One minister stood up and said, "Brethren we want revival, but God save us from that!"[14]

One author wrote: 'In nearly every home of some districts one could find families regularly praying and reading the Scriptures together. Prayer meetings were better attended than the public meetings were before the revival! Converts came to be numbered by their attendance at the prayer meetings. Absence from the prayer meetings meant a "doubted conversion." Here is a standard, apart from revival, that very few churches would dare to adopt!'[15]

Rev. Duncan Campbell speaking about the time when he lay prostrate before God as 'wave after wave of Divine consciousness swept over' him, and the 'flood of the Saviour swept over' him, wrote: '...To me it was a baptism from on High, and if in any small measure God has been pleased to use me, it is all because of what He did for me that night, when two things became clear to me: *Christ's willingness to save the "whosoever,"* and *the awful state of the eternally lost in Hell.* That is what revival has meant to me.'[16]

During the revival, Rev. Gordon I. Thomas who spent ten days on the Isle of Lewis with Rev. Duncan Campbell, was disappointed as he preached at 'a very small meeting,' but then "God came down." For a moment he had to stop preaching and 'together we "felt" the silence' he wrote. 'Yes, how "dreadful" [fearful] was that place.' Rev. Thomas went on to say that just in case, 'any should think that the work in Lewis is due entirely to Mr Campbell or that it is exclusively linked with him' in 'some combination of personality and psychology'...Mr Campbell was not present on this particular occasion. GOD WAS THERE, and in revival there is an awareness of God.'[17]

Prayer Versus Persecution

During the revival, Rev. Duncan Campbell and fellow ministers came under persecution from sections of the Christian church in Arnol, on the Isle of Lewis. Arnol was just two miles south of Barvas where they had seen great blessing. Rev. Campbell wrote about this in his weekly report to the Faith Mission, dated, 26 April 1950, and stated that opposition meetings were being held just 200 yards away from where they were seeing revival!

After the revival Rev. Duncan Campbell recalled this in one of his meetings: They gave bitter opposition; accusing him of denying the Confession of Faith and saying that he was not sound in his theology, as he stressed the baptism of the Holy Ghost (Spirit) as a distinct and definite experience subsequent to conversion. Nonetheless the church was still filled by people coming from other parishes but very few, a mere handful attended from within the parish community at the church which he or the other ministers took part in. A prayer meeting was held in a house, #10A Arnol, the home of Donald and Bella Smith, where five ministers and others attended. The praying was heavy and the forces of Hell had been unleashed until an elder was asked to pray. John Smith the blacksmith rose to his feet and prayed for around thirty minutes, paused for a little while, lifted his right hand towards Heaven and prayed, "God, do you know that Your honour is at stake? You made a promise to pour water on the thirsty and floods upon the dry ground [Isaiah 44:3] and God You're not doing it! Your honour is at stake. There are five ministers in this meeting including Mr Campbell and I don't know where any one of them stands in Your presence, but if I know anything at all about my own heart, then I think I can say this, that I am thirsty for a manifestation of Your power and You promised to pour water on the thirsty and floods upon the dry ground, and You're not doing it." After a pause again he raised his hand and said, "God Your honour is at stake! And I now challenge You to fulfil Your covenant engagement, to pour water on the thirsty and floods upon the dry ground," and at that moment the granite built house shook like a leaf! Rev. Campbell pronounced the benediction and they went outside at two in the morning to find the people of this village ablaze with conviction of sin as the Spirit of Grace came down. The drinking house of that village was closed forever and fourteen of the regulars were soundly converted later on. During that weekend the road was black with people walking the two miles to church, prior to that movement only four people left the village for the church.[18]

Rev. Duncan Campbell, gave the following address at a meeting for ministers at Oxford and Manchester, England, in the early 1950s, 'There is a growing conviction everywhere, and especially among thoughtful people, that unless revival comes, other forces will take the field, that will sink us still deeper into the mire of humanism and materialism.

'...It has been said that "the Kingdom of God is not going to be advanced by our churches becoming filled with men, but by men in our churches becoming filled with God." Today, we have a Christianity made easy as an accommodation to an age that is unwilling to face the implications of Calvary, and the Gospel of "simply believism" has produced a harvest of professions which have done untold harm to the cause of Christ.'[19]

Snippets from the Sermons of Rev. Duncan Campbell
Rev. Duncan Campbell in *God's Standard: Challenging Sermons* (1964), said, " 'Walk before Me and be thou perfect' (Genesis 17:1) was the standard God asked of Abram, and no less demanding are the words of Christ: 'Be ye therefore perfect, even as your Father which is in Heaven is perfect' (Matthew 5:48). This is the New

Testament standard and we dare not put it lightly aside. It was the Master Himself who said, 'If any man will come after Me, let him deny himself and take up his cross daily, and follow Me' (Luke 9:23). From this we learn that the cross that called Jesus to a sacrificial death now calls His disciples to a sacrificial life."

Rev. Duncan Campbell said, "If we are to know the steadfastness of Christian character that is honouring to God and convincing as to the reality of Christian experience in the midst of men, we would do well to take to heart the testimony of Robert Murray McCheyne [who saw revival from late 1839 to 1841 at St. Peter's Free Church, Dundee, Scotland.]: 'I am persuaded that I shall obtain the highest amount of personal holiness, I shall do most for God's glory and the good of men, and I shall have the fullest reward in eternity by maintaining a conscience always washed in the blood of Christ by being filled with the Spirit at all times and attaining the most entire likeness to Christ in my will and heart that it is possible for a redeemed sinner to attain in this world.' "

Citing Dr. W. Graham Scroogie, Rev. Duncan Campbell said, "When we come to an end of ourselves, we have reached the beginning of God." Citing E. M. Bounds, he said, "The Church is looking for better methods; but God is looking for better men." Rev. Campbell said, "We do not have revivals to get men saved – men get saved because we have revivals."[20]

Lasting Fruit

Rev. Duncan Campbell after touring several places on the Isle of Lewis, in his weekly report, dated 28 May 1952, wrote: 'It was a great joy to find converts going on so well. Two-and-a-half years have now passed, and there has been practically no backsliding; only four of the hundreds who professed. For this we praise our God. From Leverburgh, at the end of October 1952, Rev. Campbell wrote: 'Several days have been spent visiting districts touched by the revival and in every place we saw much to encourage and praise God for; the converts are going on well and growing in grace.'

John Murdo Smith said, "So many of those who were converted were young, so many of them are still office-bearers in the churches of Lewis. From the revival there were at least eight ministers, many lay missionaries, many office-bearers and members."

On 26 August 1953, Rev. Duncan Campbell wrote: 'I along with several ministers from the south visit Uig [on Isle of Skye], Bernera [a small island], Barvas and Arnol [villages on the Isle of Lewis], and met with the converts of the movement. We were greatly cheered and encouraged to find them all going on and growing in grace, and to God's glory we can report that no-one in the districts mentioned has gone back.'[21] A visual account of this revival can be found on the DVD *Great Christian Revivals* by ByFaith Media.

In 1964, Rev. Duncan Campbell preached to groups of Christian workers in Canada and across north and South Africa. In one meeting he said, "During the Lewis Revival I well recall the mighty impact made as the powerful breath of the Spirit touched community after community. Everywhere, men and women of all ages became convicted and many came to a knowledge of the sovereign and saving grace of God. The past fifteen years of consistent Christian witness at home and abroad, whether in the everyday life of the community or as a Christian worker, goes to demonstrate how deep and real the work was."[22]

Sometime before Rev. Duncan Campbell passed into glory (1972), he spoke about the Hebridean Revival. "Ah, the steadfastness of the young people. I can say without fear or contradiction that I can count on my ten fingers all who dropped off from the prayer meetings. [If you were converted you attended the prayer meetings]. Of course they are all scattered all over the world. They are in the mission fields and different places today. They are standing true to the God of the Covenant, true to the Lord Jesus Christ.'[23]

The *Keswick Week* for 1952 noted that Rev. Duncan Campbell has said that eighty-three hymns were written during the revival; they were all on the love of God despite that Rev. Campbell's messages were of severity, and he was known as a fiery preacher who preached a full Gospel, the Law (God's judgment) and the grace of God (God's mercy), Hell and Heaven, damnation and salvation.[24]

In the spring of 2017 I was speaking on the subject of revival with Gordon Pettie, CEO of Revelation TV for a 6-episode TV series which was first aired across May and June 2017. I was asked about who had inspired me and went on to tell how my dad, (Michael) had introduced me (and my brother, Paul) to Rev. Duncan Campbell and his ministry through his books and teaching tapes. "He was man who was alive, a man who was on fire for God, a man for whom Christ was made, very, very real," I said.[25]

In June 2006, whilst on a mission in Scotland, I visited Duncan Campbell's grave, near Black Crofts at Ardchattan Church on the shore of Loch Etive, North Connel, near Oban in North Argyll. His tombstone reads: In loving memory of the Rev. Duncan Campbell who died 28th March 1972 aged 74 years and his wife Jessie Gray who died 10th June 1985 aged 87 years. John II, v 25-26.

Jesus said to the woman at the well, "I am the Resurrection and the Life. He who believes in Me, though he may die, he shall live. And whoever lives and believes in Me shall never die. Do you believe this?" (John 11:25-26).

Chapter 22

From Evangelism to Revival

'Seek the Lord and His strength; seek His face evermore. Remember His marvellous works which He has done, His wonders and the judgments of His mouth' (Psalm 105:4-5).

Buenos Aires Revival 1954 – Argentina

In 1954, evangelist Tommy Hicks from Lancaster, California, America, held a healing and evangelistic campaign in Argentina. This resulted in an eternal harvest of around twenty thousand souls with six million in attendance over sixty-two days, from 14 April until 13 June 1954. One of J. Edwin Orr's students researched the official church membership statistics, which revealed that more than eighteen thousand new members were taken into fellowship, which was the largest figure in the history of Argentina! J. Edwin Orr retelling the facts stated that Tommy Hicks naively concluded that three million people made a confession of Christ. 100,000 people attended each day for sixty-two days and half the people each night (50,000), put up their hand. Edwin Orr stated that Latin Americans will raise their hands for any invitation; "Do you want to love Jesus more?" Therefore, three million conversions was not a realistic figure. Hicks also stated that 100,000 took decision cards, but as Orr explained, "If you're piling out of a stadium and someone is holding out cards, you'll take one."[1]

In early April 1950, little known Tommy Hicks was called of the Lord to go to Argentina to see a man called Peron. Peron he found out in 1954 en-route to Argentina was the President of Argentina. Back in June 1951, students from City Bell Bible College just outside of Buenos Aires began praying and interceding for a move of God in their land, alongside Dr. R. Edward Miller, who soaked the land with tears. Dr. Miller arrived in Argentina in the late 1940s and would go on to witness 'seven great revivals' in his 'prolific ministry.'[2]

In 1953, Tommy Hicks received an invitation to Argentina to hold mass evangelistic meetings from some Pentecostal leaders, the Christian Missionary Alliance and the Assemblies of God. Hicks was not their first choice. Hicks agreed and told them to hire a football stadium, to which they disagreed. Initially the leaders had a hall that could hold five hundred, but Hicks believed 25,000 would turn up. Anyhow the President himself would have to authorise such a large gathering of people.

In 1954, Tommy Hicks asked the committee who had invited him to come over, to arrange a meeting with the President, to which they said it could not be done. Hicks walked to the 'Rose House' where the President lived and asked to see the President. Hicks explained to the guard on duty that he wanted to lead an evangelistic healing crusade. The guard laughed as he did not believe in God's healing ability. Hicks caught hold of the guards hand, who had told him he was sick and under a doctor's supervision. As Hicks prayed for the guard, the sickness disappeared. J. Edwin Orr states that Hicks got to see the Minister of Cults before he prayed for the guard (who was one of Peron's close bodyguards) and was healed of a swollen leg as Hicks kneeled, laid hands on him and prayed in Jesus' name. The guard (bodyguard) told him to return tomorrow for a meeting with the President! The next day, Hicks explained via his interpreter to President Juan Peron what he wanted to do and that he needed full media coverage. Peron asked if God could heal him, as he had an incurable and disfiguring skin condition. Hicks took him by the hand and prayed, and he was instantly healed! Peron gave Hicks everything he needed to organise such a crusade.

In Buenos Aires, on 14 April 1954 the crusade began in the 25,000-seat Atlantic football stadium, but this proved too small. They moved to the 180,000-seat Huracan bullfighting ring and upwards of 100,000 flocked in around the clock, with 200,000 on the final night. Around six million people attended and thousands were healed. Hicks for two months hardly slept or ate and the members of the local church who were ushers were rushed off their feet, working in twelve hour shifts.[3]

Louie W. Stokes, in the foreword to his booklet, *The Great Revival in Buenos Aires* (1954) wrote: 'It has been our privilege to initiate, and collaborate with other pastors, in the great revival of Salvation and Divine Healing that took place in Buenos Aires, Argentina during the two months period from April 14th until June 13th of 1954. Over thirty local churches lent their cooperation and the Lord used Brother Tommy Hicks as the evangelist. The revival continues and will have lasting effects upon the life, not only of the Evangelical groups in Argentina, but in all spheres of religious life. As it is our desire that our friends know about this great movement, we are printing this booklet in English. These notes were written during the rush of the Campaign, oftentimes after the night meetings, and claim no literary skill or value. However, it is a faithful and conservative record of what was happening, written by one whose heart was 100 percent in the work from the beginning....'

R. Edward Miller in *Thy God Reigneth* (1964) wrote: 'The Atlantic stadium with a seating capacity of 25 thousand was rented. God began to stretch out His hand, even though the beginning crowds were small. The news spread rapidly. God began to heal. Before long, larger crowds were coming out to see and hear this "miracle worker" as he was called. Ushers were soon working 12-hour-a-day shifts. Often the bleachers [cheap bench seats] were occupied several hours before the services were scheduled to begin. Because of the many people who had to remain on the outside, loud speakers were installed. Inside the stadium, the walk-ways were filled, then the crowd pushed down the fence surrounding the playing field and surged across, filling the field as well. They pushed down the doors of the stadium and shoved their way in.

'One night the workmen were unable to assemble the platform because of the pressing crowds. When Pastor Hicks arrived, escorted by a line of policemen, he went over to a corner of the field; the crowd surged towards him, giving the workmen room to put the platform up. As God began to move, some of the people shouted, others cheered, others wept, others pushed forward to touch the evangelist or to stand in his shadow as he passed. When the evangelist preached a simple sermon (for he was not a great orator) about Jesus, the Saviour and the Healer, the multitudes responded, "We want this Jesus as our Saviour and our Healer." Pastor Hicks turned to the ministers on the platform saying, "Do you see this beautiful scene? Argentina needs Christ. Don't your hearts burn?" When the prayer of faith was spoken, the evangelist cried, "Release your faith; do what you were unable to do before." There was a movement everywhere. Abandoned crutches were raised up in the air. Some cried, "I can see." Others abandoned their wheelchairs. People observed amazed, thrilled, hopeful and pensive.

'One night it was announced that the campaign would draw to a close. The multitude stood up, waved their handkerchiefs and shouted for about 15 minutes, "Let it go on. Let Hicks remain!"...After a hasty deliberation, it was decided to continue the campaign. The mushroom growth continued. People spent the night in the stadium to assure themselves of a better seat for the next service; the cold of early winter had already set in. Because of the overflow crowds, a much larger stadium was rented – the great Huracan stadium, the largest in the country with capacity for 180,000. It had never been filled; no sports event or political rally had ever filled it. And now the little, unknown Gospel preacher had dared to rent it.'[4]

'The power of God swept over that vast throng in wave after wave. Night after night the healing virtue of Jesus flowed out to the thousands who released their faith in God. Outstanding healings took place, too numerous to recount.... The thought and ordinary routine of the nation began to change as a new day dawned. Through press and radio the news flashed to all Argentina.

Magazines printed articles with photographs of what God was doing. Daily papers printed notices of meetings and miracles. All available copies of the Bible were sold, 55,000 of them. The people clamoured for a copy, nearly snatching them from the ushers' hands. Urgent request went out by airmail for more copies to be sent. Stolid cynicism gave way to hope. Proud Argentines became as emotional as any Pentecostal. Every night, a shouting, singing audience responded to the power of God as Pastor Hicks ministered to them the joy of deliverance.... Healing waters were flowing; the power of God was moving out to the people. Using busses, subways, trucks, trams, trains and any other available conveyance, they came. From as far away as Bolivia, Chile, Brazil, Uruguay and the farthest corners of Argentina, they converged to the place where God was meeting man's need. When chauffeurs were asked, "Where is the campaign being held?" There was a stock answer, "Where you see the people get off, you get off too. Follow them and they will take you to the stadium." For blocks around, the crowds all moved in the same direction, making a tremendous traffic snarl....'

'The president of the Huracan Football Club remarked publicly that he had never seen such an assemblage of persons in all his life, estimating that there must be at least 180,000 in the stadium. Wherever men met, there was one topic of conversation. In homes and on the streets people commented pro and con about the Gospel campaign in Huracan stadium; hymns and choruses were sung in public conveyances. On a bus a sceptic tried to convince another that the whole thing was nothing but a hoax. The other man argued that it wasn't. A third entered the conversation, affirming that everything was true, for God had healed his wife of paralysis. The sceptic offered no further arguments. In a factory, when comments were being made about the campaign, some tried to make fun. A man got up and obliged them to be silent; in the campaign his high-school age daughter had been healed. She had one leg shorter than the other and had been healed instantaneously, discarding her orthopaedic shoe. The lame were walking, the paralyzed set free. The blind were seeing and stretcher cases healed. Ambulances brought invalid patients and returned empty. Life and health flowed like a river, for God had come to Argentina.

'The hotel where Pastor Hicks stayed appeared more like a receiving ward in a great hospital. Ambulances brought people at any hour of the day or night; the lobby became crowded with needy people. Workers were recruited to help the ones who came to the hotel. Nightly the crowds increased until the stadium could seat no more. They filled the aisles and passage ways. Still on they came like a great surging tidal wave of humanity – people as a giant waving field of ready-to-be harvested grain. The stadium was filled to capacity; not even standing room remained. Still on they came, until for blocks around the stadium in every direction a great sea of humanity gathered. The doors had been closed an hour before the service began. Messages reached them through loudspeakers; the wave of healing power reached out to them as well.

'An English paper of Buenos Aires reported one of the services favourably, estimating the crowds as being 200,000. It spoke of the hundreds who waited from early morning for the stadium gates to open. A short time after the service had begun it was practically impossible to travel either by tram or bus in the direction of the stadium, for everyone appeared to be making his way there. Although a vast crowd filled the stadium, hundreds more milled around the entrances, swarming up the steps and blocking all gangways. Tommy Hicks, standing alone in the large expanse of green grass, looking around at the thousands of faces all looking in his direction, preached that Jesus Christ came to reveal God to the World. The multitudes said, "Hallelujah," clapped their hands, sang a hymn, raised their arms to God, stood, then bowed their heads in prayer. The silence was impressive. God was visiting Argentina in a sovereign way.'[5]

Revival in a Methodist Church, Eldora, c.1960 – America

In 1945, the Worldwide Fasting Crusade began under the direction of Rev. Franklin Hall. By 1961 they had printed and distributed more than 24 million pieces of free literature which were sent to many countries. In *Atomic Power With God Through Prayer and Fasting* (c.1946, c.1965) Hall printed the following letter from a Methodist minister, R. B. Krape of Woodhine, R.F.D. No. 1. Eldora, New Jersey, USA. The minister wrote: 'Dear Brother Hall: I am a Methodist minister who received your book two years ago. After fasting and praying ten days for a revival in three Methodist churches that I am in charge of, God stirred and sent revivals in our midst. The Lord richly blessed us in many ways. A Roman Catholic and his Protestant wife were among those gloriously saved.

'In one of my churches an Italian lady to whom I gave one of your books, went on a fast of twenty-three days for her old Catholic mother who came from the old country, was blind, and about to die. She was praying to beads and images. She became interested in Jesus and learned how to pray to the Lord. Finally she was gloriously saved. The lady who fasted twenty-three days was hopelessly afflicted with kidney stones. The doctor could do nothing for her, and said an operation would be necessary. Well praise the Lord, she has not had an attack since her fast two years ago. Before I became acquainted with fasting, my people said, "We have never heard of fasting." I said, "Bless your heart, have you never read your

Bible?" Pray for me as I work in these Methodist churches, and kindly send a good supply of pamphlets on fasting.'[6]

Indonesian Revival 1964-1974 – Indonesia

The Indonesian Revival is perhaps the most supernatural revival the world has ever seen – truly of biblical proportions with many personalities involved. During the revival, Muslims were affected as were nominal Christians and the animists or heathen. Indonesia has more than 13,400 islands; more than 8,800 are named, though there are many tidal islands and rocky reefs which appear at low tide. More than 920 of the 13,400 islands are inhabited, some are only inhabited at certain times of the year. In June 2017, the Indonesian government announced they were going to count all of their islands and submit them to the United Nations. This was due in part to prevent other nations claiming islands, reefs or land masses as theirs and building upon them, thus claiming territorial rights.

The vast majority of miracles took place on the Island of Timor, in the first five years of the revival, on the eastern extremity of the Indonesian archipelago. For this reason this revival though not confined to Timor, is sometimes referred to as the Timor Revival (1965-1974). It started a year later than in other places of Indonesia and continued for three years longer, though the afterglow in many places was still strong after these dates.

During the revival under the Indonesian 'umbrella,' multitudes were converted and set free from demonic oppression, and curses and sorcery were defeated, all in the mighty name of Jesus Christ through His shed blood, by the power of the Holy Spirit. The blind saw, the deaf heard, the lame walked, the lepers were healed, the dead were raised, the waters were calmed, the rain was commanded to stop; all in the name of Jesus Christ. People received visions and dreams, words of knowledge, prophecy and extraordinary discernment – knowing the secrets of men's hearts; whilst others received songs from God, a few were taught by angels (being illiterate), and Jesus even appeared Himself to others. Some of the missionary teams ate supernatural food (manna from Heaven), another team had flames of fire over the churches where they preached at, others saw supernatural light, which guided their footsteps by night, one mission team was transported in the Spirit, others witnessed food multiplying, and food not going-over in the tropical heat. In one place, the house shook as they prayed and two churches saw water turning into non-alcoholic communion wine. This happened on at least ten occasions at one church and sixty at the other!

A Holy Spirit sent movement began on the Island of Rote, also known as, Roti, south of Timor in 1964, as the word of the Lord was preached. Two men, Pak Elias and Pastor Gideon (who first met in 1966) were both figures at the forefront and natives of Rote. Prayer groups sprang up which became the backbone of the revival. As they preached the saving message of the cross, the locals became overwhelmed in their sins, and called on the Saviour, Jesus Christ, and within a year a thousand people had been converted.

On the island of Sumatra, a thousand miles away, God began a work amongst the Muslim 'poison mixers' on the southern tip. Their tribal leader, Abram, had finished attending a Communist educational course and heard the Nativity story through an open window of a church whilst a Christmas sermon was in progress. Abram decided to tell his people about the story of Jesus and sent a letter to some Christians asking for help as his people wanted to hear more about the Christ-child. The help duly arrived and within five years, 1,500 were converted.

From October to December 1964, a 'Healing Campaign' was held on the Island of Timor (on the eastern extremity of the Indonesian archipelago) where several thousand people were healed, but sadly the message of repentance was not prominent. 450,000 inhabitants out of more than one million belonged to the former Dutch Reformed Church, but there were only 103 pastors, so the Reformed Church was not in a healthy state. From 1963-1968 church communion attendance in Indonesia went up twenty-fold.

In July 1965, David Simeon arrived on Timor with an evangelistic team from the Bible School in East Java; they stayed for two months. The message was of repentance, rebirth and sanctification, and this became known as the official birthday of the revival. The Christians got cleaned up and on fire for God, and the natives piled their fetishes high and publicly burned them.

Out of the revival, as people got right with God, they desired to spread the Good News and missionary teams were formed, the first being in September 1965, under Pastor Joseph, the superintendent of the Presbytery in Soe. On 1 October 1965, the Communists tried to take over the country, but failed, this led to a bloody backlash by the Indonesian Muslims. In later years some of the converts became missionaries in other lands.

The evangelistic teams lived by faith and were guided by the Holy Spirit, and saw supernatural events and results. Drunks got sober, natives destroyed their fetishes, and some tore down their temples; Muslims saw Jesus as the Son of God, wrongs were righted and many illiterate people (especially women) received visions and were called to go and preach, under the leading of the Holy Spirit. Sermons of five hours were common and could be as long as fifteen hours as the people were hungry for the word of the Lord, and the sense of time was lost in the presence of God. Crowds flocked to hear these preachers. Within a year 80,000 people were converted to Jesus Christ, half had formerly been Communist and the other half heathen and 72 evangelistic teams were formed and sent out. Within three years, 200,000 had been converted.

The Bible School in East Java played a significant role in the revival, as converts were trained and then went forth with the Good News in the power of the Spirit. In 1967, the wind of the Spirit swept through the School bringing deep repentance and reconciliation between staff and students who had previously been at odds with each other.

Paul Hattaway in *Asia Harvest* Newsletter #141 (April 2017) wrote: 'The Lord Jesus has used political events in Indonesia for the benefit of His Kingdom. In 1967, the government of Indonesia decided they would rather live with religious people than with Communists, so laws were passed that every Indonesian citizen must identify with one of four accepted religions: Islam, Buddhism, Hinduism or Christianity. Before that time, Christians in Indonesia had been a small and persecuted minority, often struggling to survive in a sea of Muslims. All of a sudden it was legal to be a Christian, and over the next few years more than two million Indonesians joined Christian churches. Although it's true that some joined the churches out of political expediency, hundreds of thousands of people genuinely repented of their sins and placed their trust in Christ. In the five decades that have passed since the constitutional change guaranteeing freedom for Indonesian Christians, the Church has continued to grow steadily. The shining witness of their transformed lives has influenced many of the believers' friends and relatives. Millions of Indonesians have been blessed to discover that Christianity is based on the living Jesus, and is not a dead religion made up of oppressive rules.'

During an eighteen day missionary campaign in Irian Jaya (West Papua, island of New Guinea), nearly 3,000 people were converted and 250 young men dedicated themselves to full-time Gospel work. The evangelising and revival did not go without its opposition and God's judgment was poured out on many a person who stood in His way, some died whilst others were afflicted by the hand of God.[7]

Father Dennis Bennett, an Episcopalian Priest (American Anglican), who can be accredited as the father of the Charismatic Renewal that began in his church in 1960, had a missionary friend who was the head of a strong interdenominational missionary fellowship. He returned from Indonesia in the late 1960s and said, "I tramped seventy miles into the interior [probably Soe] – it was seventy miles to get a glimpse of Heaven as I heard these ex-Communists and ex-Mohammedans [Muslims] singing all day long, the praise of the true God for the joy He has brought them.

"I was a missionary in Indonesia many years ago. We would work for a year to get one convert from Mohammedanism to Christ, and then half the time he would recant. Now the Christians who used to be Mohammedans are organising evangelistic teams to go to Pakistan to win other Mohammedans to Christ! It is incredible!"[8]

In April 2017, Paul Hattaway of Asia Harvest wrote: 'While we should rejoice greatly over the awesome things God has already done in Indonesia, there remains 222 "most unreached" ethnic groups in the country today, totalling more than 150 million people. The linguistic, cultural, and spiritual barriers between Indonesian Christians and these unreached tribes means that few of those people have ever heard the Gospel in a clear way.'

Calvary Chapel Anaheim, California 1979 – America

On Mother's Day (Sunday, 13 May) 1979, a guest speaker gave a sermon at Calvary Chapel in Anaheim, California, America, which was the springboard for a localised church revival which in turn would affect others nationally. The church sprang out of John Wimber's home study group and was affiliated with the Calvary Chapels, a work that sprang out of the Jesus Movement under Chuck Smith. As John and Carol Wimber attended the Twin Peak Calvary Chapel, its pastor Don McClure suggested the affiliation in 1977. The Wimber's Church largely consisted of young people. They met in a school gymnasium and it was after the Mother's Day evening services that things would never be the same again.[9]

John Wimber was apprehensive of his young guest speaker who had come out of the Jesus People Movement (of the late 1960s and early 70s) but felt that it was the Lord's will for him to speak. The Jubilee of the Jesus People Movement was in 2017. The speaker gave his testimony of God's grace, much to Wimber's delight and proceeded to tell the congregation how the church throughout the world had been offending the Holy Spirit a long time and quenching Him (1 Thessalonians 5:9). The speaker then said, "Holy Spirit come" and He did!

The church was not Pentecostal, though some of the gifts of the Holy Spirit (1 Corinthians 12) had been used by members of the fellowship, largely behind closed doors in prayer sessions or home groups. What happened next greatly upset John Wimber, many of the young people, who had come to the front, fell on the floor and one man was flung forward, with his mouth over the microphone, speaking in tongues that sounded out around the gymnasium. The speaker began to shout, "More Lord. More!" . . . "Jesus is Lord" and went in amongst the people and prayed for them. Wimber, could not reach the guest speaker because of the people strewn all over the floor, but called to some young men to remove him. They could not obey his command. Several people got up and left, but eventually the commotion subsided.[10]

That night John Wimber could not sleep. Wimber spent the evening searching the Scriptures in vain for 'Holy Spirit come.' By 4:30am, he remembered reading in John Wesley's *Journal* about similar phenomena in his ministry. Looking through his books on revival and revivalists he found at least ten similar instances in church history by 6am. Wimber then asked God, if what had happened was from Him. At 6:30am, Tom Stipes, a pastor and friend phoned Wimber. Wimber explained what had happened and Stipes assured him that it was from God.

In *Power Evangelism* (1985) John Wimber wrote: 'In the aftermath, we lost church members and the staff were really upset.' Over the next few months, 'supernatural phenomena began to occur, frequently uninvited and without any encouragement, spontaneously. New life came into our church.' The experiences, regardless of whether people fell over, began to shake, speak in tongues, or without any phenomena, brought people closer to God, whilst the reading of the Bible, caring for others and the love of God increased. The young members of the church went out evangelising and praying for people. One man received prayer, he fell to the floor and came through converted.[11]

John Wimber once said, "In my experience all who have been overcome by the Holy Spirit – whether they fell over, started shaking, became very quiet and still, or spoke in tongues – thought the experience was wonderful and that it drew them closer to God. They found that prayer, Scripture reading, caring for others and the love of God all increased."[12]

John Wimber wrote: 'A revival began that May [1979] and by September we had baptised over seven hundred new converts. There may have been as many as seventeen hundred converts during a three-and-a-half-month period. I was an expert on church growth [in 1974, Wimber had joined the staff of the Charles E. Fuller Institute of Evangelism and Church Growth in Pasadena, California], but I had never seen evangelism like that.'[13]

John Wimber's Calvary Chapel would later become part of the Vineyard Christian Fellowship, Anaheim, California, whilst Wimber went on to become the Vineyard's unofficial leader. He was at the forefront of the Third Wave of the Holy Spirit, and an advocate of power evangelism – using the gifts of the Holy Spirit in effective evangelism so that non-Christians surrender their lives to Christ.[14]

Argentine Revival 1982-1997 – Argentina

Buenos Aires in Argentina had seen a revival in 1954, under Tommy Hicks' healing and evangelism campaign, which won to

Christ around twenty thousand souls. The pastors knew that what God did then, He could do again, as long as the conditions were met – prayer, holiness, reconciliation and preaching of the Gospel of the Lord Jesus Christ.

The years 1976-1983, were years of oppressive dictatorship under evil military rule. The Roman Catholic Church also had good sway over the people, and many had intertwined Christianity and native occult practice, which was rampant across the country. Daily, witches and warlocks etc. were on national television. The "Dirty War" in which people were detained in the middle of the night by the army or police for no apparent reason had claimed up to 80,000 lives. The economy was a disaster; inflation was over 1,000%! The loss of the Falklands War of 1982, between Argentina and Britain, shocked the proud nation who had been told by the military propaganda machine that they were winning. Argentina had invaded the Falkland Islands of Britain, in the South Atlantic Ocean, which are known as the Malvinas Islands in Argentina, and Britain sent an armada to take back her territory and to protect her citizens. All these situations gave the people a reason to look forward for answers, something new, which the old order could not give, and Jesus Christ became that answer to millions.

Carlos Annacondia, a nut and bolts businessman was converted in 1979. When he had fully consecrated his life to Christ, he had a powerful desire to be an evangelist and his evangelistic campaigns began in 1981. He held evangelistic campaigns in the provinces of Buenos Aires and hundreds started to come to Christ during different campaigns. He became the key figure of the revival, but others leaders were: Omar Caberera, Pablo Bottarai, Claudio Freidzon, Guillermo, Ed Silvoso, Carlos Mraida, Luis Palau and Duardo Lorenzo.

In the early days of the Argentine Revival, it was the poor and the destitute who filled the plots of land and later the stadiums which were brightly illuminated and pleasing to the eye, a crowd drawer. There were no seats which gave the people freedom to move around so that they did not become restless. As the years progressed, people from other social classes came to know the Lord in these mass evangelistic campaigns. Healings were common, signs and wonders the norm; creative miracles were not unknown, even raising the dead! Deliverance was essential for all new believers along with mass discipleship and being committed to a church of whatever denomination or style took the person's preference. Many people had to be trained to organise the crowds, others had food stalls to satisfy the natural appetites of man. Months before any campaign commenced, prayer would be going up to Heaven in which local churches participated.

In some areas, years prior to an event, spiritual mapping of an area would be done, various intercessions and obediences and prayers to help dislodge or disengage a principality / territorial stronghold (e.g. unbelief) over a geographical area. Once broken or dislodged this aided the people being able to respond to the Gospel as the veil had been taken away, and those who were blinded by the enemy were able to see the light of the truth. Old grievances were repented of between different leaders and denominations, which led to open confession and reconciliation, which aided rapid church growth.

By 1984, in La Plata, Ensenda and Tolosa, 50,000 people came to Christ and later that year 83,000 souls were won in Mar del Plata under Carlos Annacondia's ministry. In some of these campaigns he would preach for two months every night and behind the platform would be a 150-feet tent with yellow and white stripes, which was the "Spiritual intensive care unit" where mass deliverance sessions would be held. Trained workers, "stretcher bearers" would be on the lookout for people manifesting under the influences of evil spirits / demons and would carry them to the tent where they would pray for them to be delivered. As time went on mass deliverance sessions were commenced, as the strong man was bound, Jesus' name invoked and curses were broken in Jesus' mighty name.

After the revival, ten percent of the population were evangelical Christians and huge churches were birthed; Omar Cabrera, the 'dean of the revival,' Vision of the Future Church had over 150,000 members who met in various locations across the country.

Assembly of God Pastor Juan Zuccarelli and a prison warden in Olmos Prison, the largest and highest maximum security prison in Argentina saw revival, when three hundred prisoners came to a 'singing meeting' and were locked in! At the end of the preaching of evangelist Jose Luis Tessi (from Zuccarelli's church), the Holy Spirit swept in, guards and prisoners were slain on the floor and one hundred people gave their lives to Jesus Christ. Both prisoners and guards received deliverance, and a process of diligent discipleship begun. By the end of 1995, forty-five percent of the prisoners were converted (out of over three thousand prisoners) and began holding daily church services. Later the Christians had their own evangelical cell blocks, where formerly the various criminal elements were segregated, but are now one in Christ! The church at Olmos Prison loses members daily, not because they backslide, but because they are released or relocated to other prisons.[15]

'But You are a God ready to pardon, gracious and merciful, slow to anger, abundant in kindness, and did not forsake them' (Nehemiah 9:17).

Chapter 23

Fire Starters

'Through the Lord's mercies we are not consumed, because His compassions fail not. They are new every morning; great is Your faithfulness' (Lamentations 3:22-23).

Brownsville Revival 1995-2000 – America

The Brownsville Revival is also known as the Pensacola Revival, the Father's Day Outpouring or the Florida Revival. The vast majority of the information in this account relates to what I saw and heard when I visited this revival in July 1997. For over twenty years faithful members of the congregation had been praying for revival, but in the last two and a half years prior to the revival breaking out, the Sunday night meeting was given over entirely to prayer, praise and worship.

In 1961, Dr. David Yonggi Cho was ministering in the USA, and began praying for revival in America. As he prayed, he felt the Lord prompt him to get a map of America and to point his finger on the map. It landed on Pensacola, Florida. He sensed the Lord say, "I am going to send revival to the seaside city of Pensacola, and it will spread like fire until all of America has been consumed by it." By 2006, Dr. Cho had a church membership of over 800,000 in Korea, and retired as senior pastor of Yoido Full Gospel Church in 2008.

Pastor John Kilpatrick has pastored since 1970 in five different churches. At the large, successful Brownsville Assembly of God Church at Pensacola, Florida, America, he was fed up with his role and knew there was more. One night in the early hours, whilst alone, he went into the church, placed his keys on the platform and cried out to God in desperation for His glory, "God, I want to see You move. If You are not going to send revival here, please send me to a place where You are. I don't care if it's a small congregation in the middle of nowhere with just twenty-five people. Just take me where You're going to move." He walked out and left his keys there. Every Saturday night he returned to pray and the Sunday morning sermon was frequently on the theme of revival.

Dick Bernal is the senior pastor of Jubilee Christian Center in San Jose, California, a church of nearly 6,000 members. On the back cover of his book, *Storming Hell's Brazen Gates* (1997), it states: 'Originally printed in 1988, *Storming Hell's Brazen Gates* was a catalyst in sparking one of the greatest revivals in modern times –

the great Florida Revival at the Assembly of God. The principles of this book [spiritual warfare] helped open the skies over the Pensacola area...a tremendous outpouring.'

Evangelist Stephen "Steve" Hill, a former missionary to Argentina, came to preach on the Sunday morning Father's Day service in June 1995, and proclaimed that God was going to do something special. At the end of the service, Steve Hill started to pray for people and God turned up. Pastor Kilpatrick was touched by God and fell to the floor, and was in a wheelchair for the next few days, being unable to stand in the presence of God! When the people saw their pastor on the floor, then they knew that God was present as this was so out-of-character. Steve who came with only five sermons was asked to preach in the evening service and eventually stayed for five years!

Steve Hill in *The Pursuit of Revival* (1997), wrote: '...Many others at our revival services almost missed God because they listened to the opinions of others.... Remember, there will always be a wave of opposition against us when we begin to enter the deeper things of God. If we desire revival in our churches or in our personal lives, we must get ready to face the persecution.'[1]

Steve Hill never stepped into the pulpit without the intercessory team praying over him first. By July 1997, over 300,000 people had got right with God, of which 100,000 were first time converts and 1.7 million people from all sorts of social and economical backgrounds had visited from around the globe. The visitors came to witness, to be a part of, to see the presence of God manifest, and to get a fresh touch of holy fire. By the close of the millennium over 3.5 million people had visited Brownsville, and multitudes had taken fresh fire to their home churches and glowing reports of what had happened to them. I met a young man at a Christian camp in England who a year previously, as a backslider visited the Brownsville Church, got right with God and was still on fire (zealous) for God.

Thousands of people would turn up for the Tuesday night prayer meeting as the sanctuary was spiritually cleansed for the new week's meetings which started on the Wednesday. Some people queued at 4:30am (yes, am!) for the 7pm service! Hundreds upon hundreds of people queued on the streets in temperatures above 35 degrees centigrade in the summer months. I saw crowds hundreds of metres long, two to four people abreast in the mid afternoon summer heat. Security guards were employed: to check bags (because one Saturday night, a toxic gas bomb was ignited within the church, but no one suffered ill affects), and in people management, so as not to cause chaos in the rundown community and there was a big car park (parking lot) to look after and overflow parking. Night after night, as the doors were opened at 6pm (the service started at 7pm), people eager for God would cram into the two thousand-seat auditorium. Others would file into another building which could seat around seven hundred (a larger building was later built). People were also in the choir room, other overflow rooms, and even in the corridors as speakers were located throughout the complex of God's sanctuary, even in the toilets!

Lindell Cooley led the worship, which could last for two hours while Heaven and earth met as people and angels sung glorious tribute to the Lamb that was slain.

Preaching and the Fruit

Steve Hill, night after night (four nights a week) preached a hard core uncompromising message of holiness and repentance – get the sin out of your life, embrace the cross, look to Jesus and call upon Him. Hill would always use props in his sermons and it was different each night. Some of the more notable were: a coffin, a tombstone, shackles, a bed of affliction and enlarged playing cards. One night he preached on the blind leading the blind and wore dark glasses, held a white stick and was tapping his way around the stage. On another night the lights were dimmed as his wife Jeri, wearing a wedding dress marched to the front. One evening very late into the altar call, he felt prompted by God to ask one of the musicians to play the 'Last Post' (used in military funerals) where military persons came to the front at the last stages of the altar call.

Every night hundreds of people ran to the mercy seat (and I mean ran!) as teenage Charity James sang, "Run to the Mercy Seat." Hill called the people forth, to call upon God to repent; many cried, wailed and moaned in deep repentance, remorse and grief, tears flowed copiously as both child and adult alike called upon the risen Saviour. It was the most eerie sound I have ever heard and when people truly repent as I witnessed, then it was a truly born again experience (not just a prayer) as they passed from death to life (John 5:24), a new creation in Christ (2 Corinthians 5:17); and those who have been forgiven more, love more (Luke 7:47).

At the end of the service anybody could go forward for prayer. There were numerous helpers and some strong catchers as most people fell to the floor after being prayed for within a few seconds. Many people shook whilst under the power of God, and were covered with modesty blankets/sheets, to keep people decent, both men and women. Frequently the leadership would address the issue of ladies dressing like prostitutes and that it was not helpful for anybody. See Jude 23b – garments defiled by the flesh. They would also state that they were not talking to new Christians (as it does take time to buy a new wardrobe), but to those who should know better, being older in the faith. The scene was frequently like a close combat battle zone as hundreds and hundreds were touched by God, many appeared to be in a coma and lay on the floor motionless for hours, as issues were being dealt with by God, whilst others would twitch and their closed eyelids would move (repetitive eye movement), some had visions and revelations and some had to be carried out in the early hours and driven to their hotels! The hotel staff in and around the locality became used to these scenes and after a while realised where their guests had been.

Billionaires attended, as did prostitutes, the homeless, murderers, backsliders, homosexuals, witches and warlocks; burnt-out discouraged Christians and many left changed. Others mocked this revival and said God was not in it – it was of the flesh, or from below, of satanic origin they adamantly declared! On at least one night at which I was present, members from another church in the locality placed leaflets on those who had been slain in the Spirit, stating how foolish they looked. This was also addressed from the front the following evening, not to mock what God was doing.

Steve Hill often said, "Opinions are like trash cans [rubbish bins] everyone's got them and most of them stink!" But the results of the fruit of these individuals' lives speak for themselves, the drug addicts were set free, backsliders left their ways of sin for holiness, marriages and broken relationships were restored, restitutions were made, and several thousand adults enrolled into the Brownsville School of Ministry.

J. Lee Grady visited the Brownsville Revival in March 1996 and again in July 1996. In the foreword to *Time To Weep – Discover the Power of Repentance that Brings Revival* by Stephen Hill (1996), he wrote: 'I knew this was genuine revival not just because I felt the holiness of God in the room, or because people were literally convulsing as they fell to their knees in front of the podium. I knew because my own heart was laid bare by an invisible sword as Steve humbly shared from the Scriptures. His message was not hype; it wasn't manipulating people with his delivery. His words were simply bathed in God's power, and it melted all human resistance. Including mine.'

Derek and Ruth Prince visited the Brownsville Revival in February 1997. In the introduction to *The Pursuit of Revival – Igniting a Passionate Hunger for More of God* by Stephen Hill (1997), he wrote: 'I saw in the leadership there, a willingness to make room for the Holy Spirit. Even though some of the manifestations that came were very unexpected, unusual, and could be interpreted as somewhat undignified, nevertheless, they yielded to the Holy Spirit. Jesus was central, there was no focus on any human personality. He was the Alpha and the Omega [the Beginning and the End, Revelation 1:8 and 22:13] – it all revolved around Him.'

Before the revival only three out of the thirty-two schools in the area had Christian Unions, within two years, they all had them! Students in class would be touched by the Holy Spirit and collapse on the floor under the power of God, and many of the schools had separate rooms where these pupils could be placed. Countless testimonies of people poured in over the years and the healing power of God was very evident. One pastor in the area had lunch with two of the bar owners in the locality. They told him that business has never been worse and half of their former clients were sitting in his church on a Sunday morning!

The Brownsville School of Ministry (BSM) began in January 1997, for those who felt called into Christian ministry or for those who needed some practical biblical training. Within a few years, a few thousand have fanned throughout the world as witnesses for Jesus Christ, and been fire-starters in their own churches. The *Pensacola News Journal* for November 1997 stated that there were 507 students attending BSM, 120 of which lived on campus. By autumn of 2000, there were 1,000 students at BSM so reported *Charisma* magazine (June 2005). In July 1997, youth pastor Richard Crisco held Brownsville's first annual Youth Conference and in the same year, Pastor Kilpatrick held the first annual Pastor's Conference. In 1998, Lindell Cooley held Brownsville's first Worship Conference.

Beginning in 1997, senior members of Brownsville Church held Awake America rallies in different cities of America (Dallas, Toledo, Birmingham, Memphis etc.) which was their way of responding to the numerous invitations they had to decline. Steve Hill would preach, give an altar call and thousands of people would respond, if not tens of thousands during the near dozen rallies they held in 1997 and 1998.

The Brownsville Revival was also instrumental in the Smithton Outpouring (1996-2001), where 250,000 people from sixty nations visited a small farm town with a population of just 532, in Smithton, Missouri, America. This revival is documented in I Saw The Smithton Outpouring by Ron McGatlin (2002).

Several people over the years have shared their opinions and told me why the Brownsville Revival was not from God and never in a polite concerned manner, though they never visited the place or researched the facts for themselves. It was at my visit to the Brownsville Revival that I received my call to Bible College, which flowed into full-time ministry. If I had not been obedient to the Divine call then life would be quite different now and my series of revival books would not have been written. As Dr. Michael Brown said, "The Brownsville experience is not so that you have a story to tell in ten years from now. This is so you can be spiritually launched into orbit."[2] And that was true for me, glory to God.

John Kilpatrick speaking in March 2012 from Dallas, Texas, USA, stated that 4.5 million people in five years came through Brownsville doors during the revival from 1995-2000. Steve Hill was promoted to glory on 9 March 2014, after a six year battle with melanoma cancer. His Memorial Service was held at Brownsville AoG on Friday, 14 March 2014, whilst his body is interred in Texas.

For the twentieth anniversary of the revival, Dr. Michael Brown wrote *The Fire That Never Sleeps: Keys for Sustaining Personal Revival* (2015).

"For My thoughts are not your thoughts, nor are your ways My ways," says the Lord. "For as the Heavens are higher than the earth, so are My ways higher than your ways, and My thoughts than your thoughts" (Isaiah 55:8-9).

China's Christian Revival and Growth

During the Boxer Revolution (1900) many of the missionaries in China fled for their lives as anti-Western sentiment swept the nation, hundreds were martyred along with thousands of indigenous believers. Further persecution arose under the Cultural Revolution of Chairman Mao and his disastrous reforms from 1949 onwards. During 1959-1961 approximately forty million people died from malnutrition in the Great Famine of Communist China. In part, the famine was a direct result of unsuccessful new farming methods that were introduced by Chairman Mao after the formation of the People's Republic of China in 1949.[3] Since this time there has been severe persecution across China even though China itself claims: "Citizens of the Peoples Republic of China enjoy freedom of religious belief..." but as long as you register your church etc. and conform to the "administration organisation site autonomously." As a church / organisation you are accountable to the atheist Communist regime and they tell you what you can or cannot preach on (e.g. Second Coming of Christ) or do, and who you can and cannot employ. Yet from 1980-1984 there was 'explosive advances of Christianity' which concerned the government in Peking (Beijing).[4]

Since 1970, but especially in the latter part of the twentieth century the Church in China saw phenomenal growth, as the House Church movement was estimated to be growing by sixty thousand people each day at one stage and that in the midst of terrible persecution. China's pastors, evangelists, house leaders and ordinary Christians are frequently taken into captivity, imprisoned and tortured; breaking bones, ripping flesh and even killing their prisoners by over zealous sadistic provincial officials or guards. One evangelist was imprisoned for forty years and for at least three decades was routinely beaten for refusing to renounce the Lord Jesus Christ, another was released after forty-five years in a labour camp.[5] Other prisoners were incarcerated for ten, twenty or twenty-five years etc., but it appears that the maximum sentence is presently three years without a trial! Beijing hosting the Olympic Games in 2008 was conditional on many human rights issues.

One house church network had 400,000 believers by 1986! A Christian man began his ministry in Fujian Province and began preaching throughout the countryside.[6]

On Sunday, 20 November 2005, American President, George W. Bush during his visit to China attended a state-run "patriotic" church, one of only five Protestant churches permitted in Beijing. It was an appeal for China to grant greater religious and political freedom to its citizens. He said prayers and wrote in the guest book: 'May God bless the Christians of China.' Outside the church, President Bush said, "My hope is that the government of China will not fear Christians who gather to worship openly, a healthy society is a society that welcomes all faiths." Within a few days some of the leaders within the House Church movement were released from prison.

The city of Wenzhou is known as "China's Jerusalem" and has seen phenomenal growth. Out of a population of over seven million, there is believed to be nearly one million Christians (fourteen percent) and literally hundreds of churches in the city, some as tall as a five storey building. This amount of Christians in one area has led to a huge growth in private enterprise and a six hundred percent rise in Gross Domestic Produce (GDP) from 1980-1990. In this city the authorities generally turn a blind eye to the churches which though registered as "places of religious worship" are not associated with the government's legally registered Three Self Patriotic Movement (largely a puppet denomination of the Communist state). However, there have been crackdowns in the past, where churches and temples have been demolished by orders of the Religious Affairs Bureau.[7] This also reoccurred in late 2013 to 2016 in different provinces, where crosses have been forcibly removed from church buildings and many church buildings were demolished, even those of the Three Self Patriotic Movement! From late 2013 to July 2015, activists state that 'more than 1,200 crosses have been stripped from churches in Zhejiang Province since the government initiative began.'[8]

In 2006, the House Church in China, was estimated to be over 120 million strong out of a population of 1.3 billion and had permeated all social levels of society. But China Aid, in the same year, reported that Ye Xiaowen, Director of China State Administration for Religious Affairs, behind closed doors, claimed that the number of Christians is closer to 130 million.[9]

In late 1981, Henan Province had more than one million Christians. Yet, in three southern counties of Henan they only had 30 Bibles for between 120,000 and 140,000 believers! The Bibles fanned the flame of revival during the 1980s. Project Pearl happened on 18 June 1981, where one million Bibles were secretly delivered by sea in one night in a single vessel, with the cargo packed into a submerged barge! Whilst this was a big help, more help is still needed.[10] I spent two months in China in 2011 and stayed in sixteen different cities. What Christians in China greatly need and desire, is to own a Bible. There is a severe lack of them, but especially amongst House Churches.[11]

'For the Lord will not cast off His people, nor will He forsake His inheritance' (Psalm 94:14).

Bay of the Holy Spirit Revival 2010 – America

The Bay of the Holy Spirit Revival (2010), sometimes referred to as Bay Holy Spirit Revival, named because of its location, the Bay of the Holy Spirit in Mobile, Alabama, America. Historically, Mobile Bay was named on early Spanish maps Bahía del Espíritu Santo, (Bay of The Holy Spirit). In 2008, the Alabama Historical Association approved a memorial historical sign commemorating the name, Bay of the Holy Spirit and a commendation was signed by Governor Bob Riley.

The revival was fronted by English evangelist, Nathan Morris, of Shake the Nations Ministry who moves in the gifts of the Spirit, including words of knowledge and the gift of healing. Morris is the son of a pastor in northern England, UK, and was converted in 2002. Whilst he "grew up in church," before he was converted he "came out of the pit," to use his own words. However, he was at the Pensacola Revival in 1997 with his dad and Pastor John Kilpatrick hugged him. Little did he know that in 2010, he would be preaching in Kilpatrick's church and revival would break out! After he was saved, Morris went to Kenya with Chris and Sue Clay and as he began to preach it began to rain, and the people began to disperse! "Not a good start to my ministry," he later jokingly said. The team prayed for it to rain and it did.

The first miracle Nathan Morris witnessed was in Cambridge City centre, England, in 2006. After this he began Shake the Nations Ministry (from Haggai 2:7). He held crusades in Tamul Nadula, India, and in towns in Kenya and Sierra Leone, Africa, and saw 30,000 conversions by the end of 2006, alongside many healings and deliverances in Jesus' mighty name. By July 2010, Morris had seen 100,000 conversions.

The revival broke out in the evening on the last day of Open the Heavens Conference 2010, hosted by the Church of His Presence in Daphne, Alabama, on 23 July 2010. The senior pastor is John Kilpatrick who ministers in the Alabama Bay area, as the Church of His Presence rents buildings for their services. Morris and his ministry team, who only came for two days, ended up staying for four months!

On 23 July 2010, 'Nathan Morris, was ministering as God's Presence was ushered in. Notable healings took place and children began to be touched by the power of God. Pastor John Kilpatrick, former pastor and overseer of the Brownsville Revival (1995-2000) in Pensacola, Florida, stated it felt like Father's Day 1995 when that historic revival began.'[12]

The day revival broke out, the service was being filmed and Kilpatrick said, "It looks like Father's Day 1995, it feels like Father's Days 1995 – Oh God, DO IT AGAIN!" At the beginning of the revival, Pastor Kilpatrick was walking amongst the people and blind eyes began to see and deaf ears began to pop open!

'A spontaneous decision was made to extend the meetings at the Daphne Civic Center to see what God would do.' Nathan Morris and his team cancelled their flights to Hawaii, which were scheduled for that weekend. To accommodate the growing crowds, from America and other countries, the meetings were moved to the Mobile Convention Center in Mobile, Alabama, and held on Thursday, Friday and Saturday nights. 'Since that miraculous night of July 23, hundreds have given their lives to Christ and been delivered by the power of God. Extraordinary miracles and healings are continuing each night. We are seeing the lame walk, the blind see, deaf ears open and diverse terminal illnesses healed.'[13]

On Friday, 5 November 2010, God TV began airing the meetings in the United Kingdom for four hours per night, 9pm-1am GMT, four nights a week and repeated the evening programme on the following afternoon and beyond. The revival had been going for thirteen weeks before the world was able to tune in from the comfort of their living rooms and many viewers watched the revival online; from Thursday to Sunday. Broadcasts were a day behind actual events so the revival services took place from Wednesday to Saturday when possible; as the rented Mobile Convention Center in Mobile, Alabama is not always available and therefore there was not always services. Some nights and afternoons, God TV aired repeats from previous evenings.

My first impressions of the revival were refreshing, it was as if the leadership team had learnt many lessons from watching the controversial Lakeland Revival (2008), which had aired on God TV, of what not to do, how to improve the general management of such large gatherings, not to make wild boasts or claims etc., as they tried to squash all negative aspects before they sprouted, things that had sadly brought the previous move of God into disrepute. See *Understanding Revival* (2009) by the author, chapter 31.

The Bay of the Holy Spirit Revival had the mature spiritual oversight of Pastor John Kilpatrick from the Brownsville Revival (1995-2000). He would advise Nathan Morris and his team and keep a watch on the proceeding as he walked back and forth from the platform. To cite an example, on the first night of airing, Nathan Morris asked a person to come onto the stage and the man began to clamber up onto the platform. Pastor Kilpatrick advised Nathan to tell the people to use the stairs at the end.

Pastor John Kilpatrick stated that the offering was deliberately edited out of the TV broadcasts – as a sign of integrity. The official website of the revival also stated on its donation page, that tithes should go to your home church; very reminiscent of what was preached by Kilpatrick on Sunday mornings during the Brownsville Revival. However, within two weeks, the Friday night offering (aired on Saturday, 20 November – nearly three months into the revival) was briefly shown as people came to the front to put their offerings into large baskets, as the cameraman then focused on the worship leader, Lydia Stanley, for the next two or three minutes. Pastor Kilpatrick first met Lydia a few days before her twelfth birthday on 26 May 1996, at the Brownsville Revival when her parents came to visit (her dad is also a pastor), and it was there that Lydia received her call to the ministry of worship. She graduated from the Brownsville School of Ministry in 2004 and is the worship leader of Church of His Presence.

Healings and Miracles

Nathan Morris, whose focus during the revival was on Jesus Christ and giving God the glory, said, "Salvation and healing go hand in hand and we have seen hundreds of people give their lives to Christ as they experience the power of God at work. Miracles and healings are continuing each night. The lame walk, the blind see, deaf ears open and terminal illnesses are healed." For twelve months prior to the outbreak of revival, Morris had preached one message, wherever he was sent. It was, "Are you living for eternity? Now!" Morris is a firm believer in the Full Gospel of salvation, healing, deliverance from demons and the baptism of the Holy Spirit and fire (Matthew 3:11), and constantly emphasises the importance of preaching "the blood and the cross."

Nathan Morris had his sermon notes and quotes on his iPad which he left in the pulpit as he walked around the stage and up the aisles preaching the Gospel, and other messages that the Lord had put on his heart. Morris' right-hand man was Matthew Murray who used his iPad to recall testimonies and comments received by email. On stage, he introduced those giving testimonial to Morris and the congregation, and began by summing up the testimony in a 30-second synopsis. Morris frequently asked those on stage to tell in their own words what God has done, and repeatedly declared, "Give God the glory" – "Give Jesus a mighty hand [clap]" – "Give Jesus all the praise and glory" – "Give Jesus a mighty shout of praise," and other similar phrases. Most people who went onto the stage received prayer, and those who fell over under the power of the Spirit were covered by a bath-towel sized modesty blanket/sheet, whilst a folded cloth was placed under their neck for support.

Nathan Morris went on 'walkabouts' as he preached, and often placed his hands on people's heads without even looking at them, and they received some impartation, touch and/or blessing. At other times, in the midst of his 'walkabout sermons' he pointed to a person and told them to come to him; catchers and helpers were always on hand to assist, and Morris quickly prayed for them. On occasions, he would make a beeline to one side of the auditorium towards the very sick people and pray for them. There was reserved spaces for wheelchairs and those with terminal illnesses, whilst some people were so unwell that they were laid out across the chairs. The front of the centre row was reserved for pastors.

On 6 November 2010, Nathan Morris recalled the healing of the wife of Bishop Knox who had been paralysed from the waist down. This happened due to a car accident on Christmas Day night, nearly twenty-three years ago in 1987. Film footage of the miraculous event of 27 August 2010, was shown, followed by Delia Knox's testimony as she ran around the stage in high heels worshipping the Lord! Six weeks previously, Nathan Morris asked Bishop Knox if the woman in the wheelchair was his wife. It was. Morris felt led of the Lord to pray for Delia Knox and laid his hands on her legs, began praying and she soon felt his hands as feeling returned. After a few minutes, without anyone asking her to rise, she tried to stand and fell back into her wheelchair. After a second attempt, she stood on her feet and the congregation went wild. With her husband on one side and John Kilpatrick assisting her, she walked around the front of the meeting place, taking large clunky steps.

"Lady Delia" as Pastor John Kilpatrick always refers to Delia Knox, gave her honest testimony, how as the years and then decades passed, she gave up hope of being healed, but when she saw a baby on stage with her parents, how her heart went out to her in compassion and she fervently desired of the Lord to heal the baby. How her focus was on someone else. She also stated how the healing was not instantaneous and that she still needed to learn how to walk again and strengthen her leg muscles that had been inactive for nearly twenty-three years. This included being wheeled out in her wheelchair at the end of the meeting and being seen around town in her wheelchair. Pastor Kilpatrick explained that her muscles needed to be built-up and if the Son of God had to pray for a man twice, the blind man, who said, "I see men walking like trees" (Mark 8:24), then we should not be discouraged if we have to pray for people multiple times. The footage of Delia Knox's healing can be viewed on YouTube (and the revival website) and had received more than 180,000 hits by the second week of November 2010. Delia's testimony of when she came back to the revival, shared her life-story and worshipped across the stage in her high heels was the most requested video via the ministry's website during the revival.

Another woman gave her testimony of how God had given her bladder, which she did not have! That she could now use the bathroom normally, instead of her internal colostomy bag which the surgeons had made. On the screen inside the auditorium, they showed the doctor's letter stating her condition then, and now present condition. Not everybody was healed and sometimes, those who did not see an instant result (e.g. deafness), were told to wait in a particular area up the front where they received further prayer and ministry.

On Wednesday, 24 November 2010, a woman gave her testimony of healing in her neck, which happened in Daphne, a few months earlier as she worshipped the Lord during the revival. The healed woman had sixteen or eighteen pins in her neck during an operation in 2006, and previously was unable to look up or down except by the use of her eyes. She was the sister of Charity James. Charity first sang for the Brownsville Revival (1995-2000) when she was fourteen years old. Pastor John Kilpatrick introduced the congregation to Charity James (then 29) and invited her up on stage. Charity is married to a preacher and they travel across America.

One night, a lady who was healed of a black spot on her leg via a word of knowledge (she testified on Saturday, 4 December 2010) brought some prayer clothes as directed by the Lord and asked Pastor Kilpatrick and Nathan Morris to pray over them, which they did. As she was directed by the Lord she would use them on people who would receive their healing – reminiscent of the apostle Paul's anointed handkerchiefs and aprons that had healing virtue imparted into them (Acts 19:11-12).

The Meetings
Doors opened one hour before the service began and revival services ran each evening from Thursday to Saturday, with the Church of His Presence having their Sunday morning service which

was not aired. A three hour TV airing would generally consist of 1-1 ½ hours of worship, 1-1 ½ of praying for the sick, testimonies, some notices or an occasional guest speaker sharing for 5-20 minutes and/or around 30 minutes of evangelistic preaching from Nathan Morris, who looked smart in jeans and a jacket. Often Morris would have a word of knowledge, sometimes even stating the person's first name and problem, and it would be weeks or months later that people would email in, or come up on stage and state that that it was them, and how they had been healed. There was also documented evidence of healing from doctor's reports. One teenage boy had two tumours in his brain, inoperable and God healed him. C.T. scans of 'before' and 'after' were shown on the big screens and the golf ball size tumour had vanished! Some nights, during times of worship or testimony you could see people down the front taking pictures on digital cameras or their mobile/cell phones whilst others recorded sections of the meetings on their smartphones. This was something that was not permitted during the Brownsville Revival, but technology has advanced and people can be more discreet by turning off the flash and zooming in.

Some nights the Holy Spirit took over the meeting during times of extended worship or in ministering to peoples' needs, especially in relation to healings, that Nathan Morris did not preach, because the Holy Spirit was doing a work in peoples' lives. During Morris' preaching he would wander all over the stage, preaching his heart out, perspiring profusely and often jumped off the raised platform, which was waist high, and preached amongst the audience; every night sweating his t-shirt and jacket through. During the altar call, Lydia Stanley sang, "Nothing but the blood of Jesus" – what can wash away my shame; what can make me whole again; nothing but the blood of Jesus. Then Pastor Kilpatrick led those at the altar in a sinner's prayer, which they repeated out loud after him.

During the last three days of the revival 2-4 December 2010, a live worship CD was recorded by Lydia Stanley and the worship team. As Pastor John Kilpatrick said, "Every revival has its own sound." On Friday, 3 December 2010, Lindel Cooley, worship leader during the Brownsville Revival (1995-2000) was present that night and the following day, as a participant of the worship team, playing the keyboard, behind, and to the side of Lydia. An hour into worship, after a shofar (a long ram's horn) was blown from the stage, Lindel led the worship for a few songs, breaking into, "Blow the trumpet in Zion, Zion," which was a particular favourite at the Brownsville Revival. Bishop and Delia Knox also testified and shared for about fifteen minutes. The service ended with Nathan Morris, his team and Pastor John Kilpatrick, at either end of the space in front of the stage, anointing with oil all those who came to the front.

The last meeting of 2010 took place on Saturday, 4 December, a break of thirty-three days that resumed on 6 January 2011 in the Exhibition (Expo) Center / Exhibition Hall of I Ten. Pastor John Kilpatrick called it, "Rest equity." He had hoped to have a watch-night service on 31 December, but the building was unavailable. By March 2011, the building in which they met was no longer available and had been booked solid, as were all the other large auditoriums in the area until 2018. The team knew this back in autumn 2010 and waited for the Lord to show them what to do. Nearing the end of the third week of November 2010, Nathan Morris preached on "cities of refuge" – "canopies of God's glory" and how they were going to visit cities throughout America, for about five days until revival broke out. These would be cities of refuge where people could go to, to be blessed by God, saved and healed, under the canopy of His glory.

The last Bay of the Holy Spirit Revival meeting was on Saturday, 23 April 2011 (Easter). Nathan Morris and his team went on the road, a Revival Tour, resuming his ministry in different cities and States, and intended to be back once a month at Pastor John Kilpatrick's church. Nathan had to leave America over a visa issue in July 2011. Pastor John Kilpatrick continued speaking in different places and the blessing continued.

Nathan Morris

In 2006, Nathan Morris was baptised in the 'Holy Spirit and with fire' (see Matthew 3:11, Luke 3:16 and Acts 1:8).[14] Morris said, "The fire of God [the experience] is to go out into all the world and preach the Gospel." In relation to the experience of how God met with him, he said, "Hunger can drive you to a place where others will not go." "Hunger will drive you to a place where God can do a work in your life." It enables you to, "Weep the tears, pray the prayer and get on their knees." Morris explained that it was, "An encounter with God" and that we have to be, "A pursuer of the glory and presence of God." Morris stated how the fire of God, "Burns up the dross...and dead old religion;" that "you cannot skip the Pentecost, but have to go through the fire." The experience "Is not a one-off experience," and you have to "lay it all down" and say, "I'm not going to fight You any more." Morris went on to explain that God does what He wants to do and that you cannot say, "I want to be dignified. I want the fire of God, but *not* the shakes![15] I want to see healings, but *not* the drunkenness!" When the fire of God fell on Nathan Morris, he shook, rolled, cried, shouted and got up a changed man! Glory to God.[16]

'Through the Lord's mercies we are not consumed, because His compassions fail not' (Lamentations 3:22).

Chapter 24

The Need for Revival

'Who is this who comes from Edom, with dyed garments from Bozrah, this One who is glorious in His apparel, travelling in the greatness of His strength? – "I who speak in righteousness, mighty to save" ' (Isaiah 63:1).

Revival is needed because God said, "By those who come near Me, I must be regarded as holy; and before all the people I must be glorified" (Leviticus 10:3). Revival is therefore primarily for the glory of God and for the honour of His name. God sends revival to the body of Christ, "That all the people of the earth may know the hand of the Lord, that it is mighty, that you might fear the Lord your God forever" (Joshua 4:24). Revival is a vindication of Himself and asserting His own power and glory so that the people of the earth, "Shall know that the living God is among you..." (Joshua 3:10). Revival reminds us that God dwells in the Church (Ephesians 2:21-22) and that 'the Gospel of Christ is the power of God to salvation' (Romans 1:16). The Church is not a pure and spotless Bride, which Jesus is coming back for (Ephesians 5:27) and therefore needs to be purged of sin, revived and made holy. Each individual member must live a holy life, a God-glorifying lifestyle (1 Peter 1:16).

Revival is not an option; revival is a must. God will not stand to be mocked by worldly church members or by popular society without either sending His judgment or revival. "I must be glorified," are His words and only in times of Heaven-sent revival will nations turn and truly glorify the Lord. In addition, some godly laws have been repealed (Proverbs 22:28), and what God calls 'evil' is called 'good' by man (Isaiah 5:20) and often enshrined and protected under law!

Revival is needed when the name of Jesus Christ is spoken in a derogatory manner, a cuss word and blasphemy; when Christians are lukewarm and worldly; when materialist mindsets have become more important than reaching-out to the lost; when the Word of God has been diluted, or the Bible's veracity is questioned, and when popular culture transcends the Word of God – revival is needed! When church attendance and religion is down, yet binge drinking and crime is up; alongside vandalism, a lack of the fear of God, low morality, high promiscuity; where lawlessness abounds and where there is total disrespect for those in authority, then revival is needed. Jesus Christ needs to be lifted high as a banner across our land.

For those who do not put their trust in the Lord Jesus Christ for their eternal redemption, they will be doomed in Hell for all eternity. 'The wages of sin is death but the gift of God is eternal life in Christ Jesus our Lord' (Romans 6:23). 'God requires an account of what is past' (Ecclesiastes 3:15) and 'the Judge of all the earth will do that which is right' (Genesis 18:25).

Andrew Bonar, writing on revival said, "The rousing up and reviving of believers is not a small matter; it concerns the glory of God. If the lamps do not shine, it does not speak well for the oil, nor for the care of the keeper. And if the children of God do not testify for Him, it does not speak well for their High Priest in Heaven, nor for the Holy Spirit within them."[1]

Revival is a two-edged sword – a blessing for many and judgment for a minority. It is 'a sign that is spoken against' for 'the fall and rising of many' because God's presence will reveal the true state of people's hearts (Luke 2:35). The blessing of revival is to cut free and deliver, for the cleansing, purging, sifting, shaking and restoration of the Church, '...do not despise the chastening of the Almighty. For He bruises, but He binds up; He wounds, but His hands make whole' (Job 5:17-18). Be warned, the judgment of revival is for a minority of the body of Christ who are unrepentant and wilfully living in habitual sin, those who continually dishonour the name of the Lord, because judgment always begins at the house of the Lord (1 Peter 4:17), and it is the 'Lord [who] kills and makes alive; He brings down to the grave and brings up...He brings low and lifts up' (1 Samuel 2:6-7). 'Do not be deceived, God is not mocked; for whatever a man sows, that he will also reap' (Galatians 6:7).

'Righteousness exalts a nation, but sin is a reproach to any people' (Proverbs 14:34). As Christians, we are called to be holy (1 Peter 1:16), set apart for God, so let us get the sin out of our lives and the rubbish out of our homes. We are in the world, but not of the world. We are called to be set apart and different, a holy people, a royal priesthood. Let us walk worthy of our most holy calling in true assurance of our faith, being built up and grounded upon the Word of God, looking to the Author and Finisher of our faith; Jesus being our Rock of hope and Chief Cornerstone in whom we can depend.

When a Revival is Needed by Charles Finney

- When there is an absence of love, confidence, and unity among Christians. It is vain to call upon them to love one another while they are sunk in stupidity and coldness.
- When there are jealousies, dissensions, bitterness, and evil speaking among Christians [especially badmouthing or erroneous and negative comments relating to brothers and sisters in Christ on blogs, social media, email lists and on

websites], and when the Church becomes worldly in dress, parties, amusements, reading novels and worldly books.

- When professing Christians fall into gross and scandalous sins; when a spirit of controversy prevails among Christians and when the wicked triumph over, and mock and scoff at the Church.
- When sinners are careless and stupid (going down to Hell unconcerned). The duty of Christians is to awake them, like that of a fireman in the case of a fire. Their guilt is similar to that of firemen who will sleep-on when the city is ablaze.
- Without a revival sinners will grow harder and harder under preaching. There is no other way in which a Church (the body of believers) can be sanctified, grow in grace and be ready for Heaven. Hearing sermons week after week is not enough and every week it is more difficult to rouse the believer to do his duty.[2]

'Search me, O God, and know my heart; try me and know my anxieties; and see if there is any wicked way in me, and lead me in the way everlasting…' (Psalm 139:23-24).

Revival is needed because the Church needs to be revived and quickened. Revival is needed because there are vast sways of ripe harvest, which at any time could go over and be spoiled forever. Without Jesus Christ no man can get to Heaven and without holiness no man can see the Lord. When the Holy Spirit comes in revival power, He can move vast multitudes of people to see their unholy state before a holy God and cause them to cry unto God most high. This is not man's persuasion to compel them to come in, but God's arm of love drawing them to Himself in convicting power of sin; the goodness of God leads to repentance, enabling a realisation that forgiveness is only found at the cross of Christ in faith and repentance in the Lord Jesus Christ – whoever calls upon the name of the Lord will be saved.

There are many who give lip service to God, having wrong motives and those who have no substance. We must be on our guard against those who are preaching another Jesus and a different gospel with another spirit (2 Corinthians 11:4). The Word of God warns about the last days; false: prophets, apostles and teachers and warns of people who will set up teachers to teach them what they want to hear, they are sugar coated preachers with smooth talking tongues. God will tell them on the Judgment Day, "I never knew you," and they will reply, "But Lord, we did all this in Your name, we prophesied, cast out demons and did many wonders," and God will reply, "I never knew you, depart from Me, you who practice lawlessness." Why? Because they did not do the will of our Heavenly Father (Matthew 7:21-23 and Luke 6:46-49).

In 1936, J. Edwin Orr was preaching in Johannesburg as part of his South African Campaign. Orr was told by a friend that people were criticising the meeting that he had held at the University in which souls were saved. Orr said, "I did not expect my denunciation of sin to please impenitent sinners. And I did not expect my enunciation of the remedy – the cleansing of the blood of Christ to please those who prefer psychological reformation. It is a good sign that there has been criticism."[3]

In the nineteenth century, Rev. Dr. T. C. Cuyler wrote: 'Much depends on the kind of fire that is used if a church is to be warmed up. A Lucifer match of mere human effort may start a bonfire of pine shavings; but as in the case of Elijah at Mount Horeb, 'the Lord is not in the fire.' Don't send first for man; send for the Holy Spirit. Reliance on the best man or measure is fatal. Religious machinery ends in empty clatter unless the 'living Spirit is in the wheels.' Jesus Christ promises to His faithful followers the baptism of the Holy Ghost.... God answers honest prayers and hard work. Whenever the Spirit kindles a spark, cooperate with Him and fan it to a flame. Genuine revivals often have small beginnings.'[4]

Why is revival needed? So that: God can be glorified, His name can be vindicated amongst the people, Jesus will be exalted, the Church can get right with God and become revived, backsliders restored and sinners can be saved and drawn by the Spirit of God into a saving knowledge of Jesus Christ.

The Devil does not help us to love God, our fellowman or to crucify the flesh daily and he certainly does not encourage us to. Also, the Devil does not encourage us to read the Bible, to pray more, to obey the Holy Spirit or help us in evangelism and world missions – all of which grow stronger during times of revival, bearing fruit for Jesus Christ (John 15:1-11). [5]

'Sow for yourselves righteousness; reap in mercy; break up your fallow ground, for it is time to seek the Lord, till He comes and rains righteousness on you' (Hosea 10:12).

Repentance and Personal Revival

One minister said, "We cannot expect God to bless us on the Lord's Day, if the Devil has use of us on Saturday night!" Within many churches, there is a lack of the fear of God, a denial of the Holy Spirit and His gifts which He distributes at will. These precious gifts to the body of Christ are too frequently ignored, denied, abused or neglected and sometimes even despised, brethren this should not be! The Holy Spirit should not be grieved, resisted or quenched.

Multitudes of Christians daily deny Jesus when they hear Him being mocked, blasphemed or ridiculed and say nothing. Others deny Jesus by being participants to dirty jokes (by listening to them) with work colleagues or friends, or join in the gossip. Some will not even mention that they went to church at the weekend when asked what they did, thus being ashamed of the Lord Jesus Christ.

Far too many Christians have compromised their testimony, broken God's laws and have therefore publicly dishonoured Him which has led to His name being blasphemed amongst the world (Romans 2:23-24). Whilst we live in the world we are not of the world. It is one thing to go into godless places to evangelise, but quite another to socialise. Why do so many people who profess the name of Christ enjoy the company of God haters? What has light got to do with darkness? (2 Corinthians 6:14). Or do you think that the Scripture says in vain, the Spirit who dwells in us yearns jealously? (James 4:5). It is one thing to socialise with those who have not yet fully comprehended the truth, but quite another to habitually socialise with those who openly reject the truth. Jesus said, "He who is not with Me is against Me, and He who does not gather with Me scatters abroad" (Matthew 12:30). Are you scattering abroad because your lifestyle and social activities are in opposition to the things of God? Or are you salt and light so that those who see your good works glorify your Father in Heaven? (Matthew 5:13-16).

Many Christians have not crucified the flesh life, acted in self control, taken up their cross daily and have not become disciples of Jesus. Either we deal with our sin in private or when revival comes we will have to deal with it in public! Let us never forget that judgment begins at the house of the Lord, and if the righteous one is scarcely saved, what about the ungodly?! (1 Peter 4:17-18).

It has been stated on many occasions that individuals can always have their own personal revival, a reviving of oneself – by getting the sin out of their lives. The story is told of a man who stood on a beach and drew a circle around his feet and then prayed, "Lord send revival, but start the work in me." 'He who covers his sin will not prosper, but whoever confesses *and forsakes them* will have mercy' (Proverbs 28:13). Decide each day to live your life for God, pray, "Holy Spirit, whatever You are doing today, if I am a part of it, I ask that You will make it plain to me as I desire to glorify Jesus Christ." Unless we are prepared to have our own personal revival then praying for revival for our Church or nation is just a mockery.

'O Lord, though our iniquities testify against us, do it for Your name's sake; for our backslidings are many, we have sinned against You' (Jeremiah 14:7).

Chapter 25

The God who Answers by Fire

'...Waters shall burst forth in the wilderness, and streams in the desert. The parched ground shall become a pool, and the thirsty land springs of water...' (Isaiah 35:6-7).

To fully understand revivals, awakenings and Heaven-sent visitations of the Holy Spirit, we must understand the sovereignty of God, coupled with our responsibility to live up to the conditions that have been laid down in Scripture. The fact that He is in control of all things, and that all things are under His control. God can use whomever He wills as His instrument(s), wherever and whenever He wills – because He is sovereign. God is the God of revival, though man has his part to play, as long as we abide by God's conditions then He will abide by His. God said, "If My people who are called by My name will humble themselves, and pray and seek My face, and turn from their wicked ways, then I will hear from Heaven, and will forgive their sin and heal their land" (2 Chronicles 7:14). However, we must remember that God's ways are not our ways and His timing is very different than ours. God's sovereignty does not relieve us of our responsibility – we have our part and duties to perform.

Whilst disciples of the Lord Jesus Christ can prepare themselves as a holy bride, waiting for the Bridegroom, pleading the promises of God, abiding in Him, getting on with the Great Commission, loving our neighbours as ourselves and seeking God with all our strength, heart, mind and soul; we must never forget that 'the wind blows where it wishes' (John 3:8).

Steve Hill of the Brownsville Revival (1995-2000) said, "Nothing will happen in our nation or in our churches unless we get rid of the sin in our lives." Rev. Duncan Campbell of the Hebridean Revival (1949-1952) said, "A God-sent revival must be related to heart purity, a God-sent revival must be related to heart holiness...are my hands pure? Is my heart clean? If I'm not prepared for that, then my talk about revival, my praying for revival are just a laughing stock of Devils; sincerity, honesty; if our hearts condemn us not, then have we confidence towards God."

Jonas Oramel Peck in *The Revival and the Pastor* (1894) noted a spontaneous revival under Dr. Lyman Beecher 'which came suddenly and powerfully' and 'swept the town with mighty power.' After the revival had concluded Dr. Beecher was visiting a bedridden member of his church in a remote part of the town. This member told him that for days he had felt 'a great burden of prayer for the unsaved and that he began at one end of the town, and prayed for each household till he had included every family. Then, as if this were not enough he prayed for each family again. In an instant Dr. Beecher knew from whence the revival came. It was born in the heart of a bedridden mighty wrestler with God!'

One Sunday a stammering blacksmith approached his pastor and told him to appoint an inquiry meeting for the following Monday as there was going to be a revival. The pastor said there was no indication to justify such a step, but he begged the pastor to announce the meeting and it was done. Jonas Oramel Peck wrote: 'The night was stormy, but to the pastor's astonishment the room was full. Many were weeping and the majority stated that they were brought under conviction [of sin] on the Friday afternoon previous. That was the precise time when the old blacksmith had felt a great burden for souls and locking himself in the shop, had given the afternoon to prayer until he had won the victory.'[1]

Billy Sunday, an evangelist from the Mid-West in America was converted in 1887. He later saw 40,000 'hit the sawdust trail' who were truly converted during one month in Philadelphia. He often said, "The carpet in front of the mirrors of some of you people is worn threadbare, while at the side of your bed where you should kneel in prayer is as good as the day you put it down."[2]

Steps Towards Revival

Charles Finney stated that before revival can come, there needs to be a necessity of union (Matthew 18:19). Obstacles of disunity that hinder the coming of revival and other factors are:

- Rotten members of the church (so called 'mature members') need to be removed if they refuse to repent and change whilst in gross sin. Sometimes when an attempt is made to cast them from the church, a division will arise, causing a bad spirit, an uneasy atmosphere to prevail – away with all the dross! Deliberate wilful sinning needs to be punished as a little yeast will work through the whole batch of dough. Correct young converts and help train them, teach them and don't beat them, be tender and faithfully watch over them.
- Unforgiveness is a great obstruction to revival which can lead to a revengeful and unforgiving spirit towards those who have injured them.
- Whenever wrong has been done to any, there should be a full confession.
- What is your motive for revival? For the denomination, for the church, or for the glory of God? An increase in attendees and

more money for the church? Sometimes ministers want revival because their church is going through difficulties which the minister needs to deal with and address, but is afraid to face the issue. At other times another denomination is being blessed more than them and the minister or congregation members wants to even the score.

- Parents who pray for their child's conversion need to realise that their children are rebels against God, obstinate in their rebellion against Him; a sinner through and through, having a depraved heart who is deserving of the fires of Hell; but is in desperate need of the Holy Spirit's quickening. The same is true of believers who pray for non-believers who feel that the sinner is not to blame for his or her actions! The sinner is to blame for his or her actions and will stand before God on Judgment Day to give an account!

Sanctification and Holiness

- Oswald Chambers said, "Sanctification costs to the extent of an intense narrowing of all our interests on earth and an immense broadening of all our interests in God."
- Evangelist and revivalist James A. Stewart wrote: 'Justification gives us our title to Heaven; sanctification for our fitness for Heaven.... We do not live a holy life in order to be justified, but we are justified in order that we might live a holy life.'
- James A. Stewart wrote: 'For a Christian redeemed by Calvary's blood to live a worldly life is treason and spiritual suicide.'
- Pastor and revivalist Robert Murray McCheyne wrote: 'A holy man is an awesome weapon in the hands of Almighty God.'
- German Reformation leader Martin Luther said, "The truest repentance is to do it no more."

'God came from Teman, the Holy One from Mount Paran. Selah. His glory covered the Heavens, and the earth was full of His praise. His brightness was like the light; He had rays flashing from His hand...' (Habakkuk 3:3-4).

Questions to Answer

- Would Jesus watch what you watch?
- Would Jesus listen to what you listen to?
- Would Jesus read that magazine or book?
- Would Jesus wear what you wear? Are you dressing to flaunt your sexuality or trying to draw attention to yourself?
- Would Jesus be welcomed in that establishment or party, or would He have to wait outside, weeping for you? If He was

permitted, would He join in, tell them a parable to reveal a spiritual principle or to point out an error, rebuke them or tell them to repent? If Jesus would not be welcome, then why take the Holy Spirit in with you?

- Would Jesus join in that conversation – is it edifying?
- Do you dishonour Jesus by your words or lifestyle?
- Do you use some of your disposable income to help advance God's Kingdom or to indulge yourself?
- Should you be thinking about this or that – is it wholesome?
- If something is questionable, then wisdom says, "Err on the side of caution and avoid it," and can you ask God's blessing on…?

Challenging Scriptures

- 'Adulterers and adulteresses! Do you not know that friendship with the world is enmity with God? Whoever therefore wants to be a friend of the world makes himself an enemy of God. Or do you think that the Scripture says in vain, "The Spirit who dwells in us yearns jealously"?' (James 4:4-5).
- 'Submit to God. Resist the Devil and he will flee from you. Draw near to God and He will draw near to you. Cleanse your hands, you sinners; and purify your hearts, you double-minded. Lament and mourn and weep! Let your laughter be turned to mourning and your joy to gloom. Humble yourselves in the sight of the Lord and He will lift you up' (James 4:7-10).
- 'Confess your sins to each other and pray for each other so that you may be healed. The prayer of a righteous man is powerful and effective' (James 5:16), NIV.

Holiness Scriptures

- 'Who may ascend into the hill of the Lord? Or who may stand in His holy place? He who has clean hands and a pure heart, who has not lifted up his soul to an idol, nor sworn deceitfully. He shall receive blessing from the Lord and righteousness from the God of his salvation. This is Jacob, the generation of those who seek Him…' (Psalm 24:3-6).
- 'Search me, O God, and know my heart; try me, and know my anxieties; and see if there is any wicked way in me, and lead me in the way everlasting' (Psalm 139:23-24).
- 'I acknowledged my sin to You and my iniquity I have not hidden. I said, "I will confess my transgression to the Lord" and You forgave the iniquity of my sin. Selah. For this cause everyone who is godly will pray to You…' (Psalm 32:5-6).
- 'One who turns away his ear from hearing the law, even his prayer shall be an abomination' (Proverbs 28:9).

- 'Let the words of my mouth and the meditation of my heart be acceptable in Your sight, O Lord, my strength and my redeemer' (Psalm 19:14).

Confession, Repentance and Restoration

If we want to see revival, then each of us needs to be revived. But before we can be revived we need to repent of all known sin and deal with the past, because 'he who covers his sin will not prosper, but whoever confesses and forsakes will find mercy' (Proverbs 28:13). It is the job of the Holy Spirit to bring conviction of sin to our lives, but our confession is our response to it. Once we have repented of specific sins, then we can express outwardly what has been revealed inwardly – the forgiveness and cleansing in Christ Jesus (Isaiah 1:18 and 1 John 1:9).

As disciples of the Lord Jesus Christ we are not allowed to pick and choose the bits of Scripture we want to obey, because that is disobedience and compromise. They're the paths that lead to destruction, to the eternal fires of Hell, where there will be weeping and gnashing of teeth, where the worm dieth not. Jonathan Edwards of the Northampton Revival (1734-1735) in his most famous sermon, *Sinners in the Hands of an Angry God,* said, "He is angrier with many who are now in the congregations of our churches, many who seem to be at ease, than He is with many of those who are now in the flames of Hell."

We have all sinned against God by breaking His laws, and sinned against each other by personal sin or personal failure by our wrong actions, reactions, attitudes or decisions that we have made. We may have also sinned against our own body by being sexually immoral (1 Corinthians 6:18). Specific sins need to be specifically repented of and confessed by name, 'when he is guilty in any of these matters, that he shall confess that he has sinned *in that thing'* (Leviticus 5:5). We cannot generalise sin and pray, "Lord forgive me for all I have done wrong," or deny sin and pray, "Lord if I have done anything wrong, please forgive me," for all have sinned, and if we say we have no sin, we deceive ourselves (Romans 3:23 and 1 John 1:8). We must repent of specific sins and pray, "Lord, please forgive me for being lustful, for stealing, for lying, for being bitter, for being critical, for being angry" etc. If we are not sure about certain situations (or habits) whether we have sinned or not, then we can pray the prayer of the psalmist, "Search me, O God, and know my heart: try me, and know my thoughts: and see if there be any wicked way in me, and lead me in the way everlasting" (Psalm 139:23-24).

Within the Christian Church there is a place for private confession to another brother or sister whom we have wronged (Matthew 5:23-24 and 1 John 1:8-10) and at times, a place for public confession so that our brothers or sisters can pray for us to be healed and delivered (Mark 1:4-5 and James 5:16). If we have sincerely confessed our sin before God then we have received His forgiveness; therefore there is no reason to keep the confession alive because God has forgiven and forgotten (Psalm 103:12 and Micah 7:19). The apostle Paul was the chief of sinners but did not retell the events. Too often those who give testimony, glory more on the past than in God's saving grace. If we need to publicly confess sin, we must specify the sin, but not necessarily go into the details of it. The body of Christ does not need to hear the details of a lurid fantasy or how you cheated in an exam; thus introducing thoughts to the listeners, which have not previously been there, or disturbing those of a sensitive disposition. To say that we have struggled with lust or cheated is adequate. If we are married, we should also ask ourselves, "What will be the response of my wife/husband if I decided to publicly confess the sin of adultery without her/his prior knowledge?" With some sins and in certain situations it is not appropriate to confess publicly only to cause another to sin because of what we have confessed. You confess adultery, unbeknown to your spouse, who is now publicly broken-hearted, humiliated and grieved, and they may want to divorce or kill you there and then! However, during times of revival sins are frequently publicly confessed, especially adultery, theft and murder (of the heart and flesh) under the spotlight and convicting illumination of the Holy Spirit.

If we are truly sorry for spreading malicious rumours about another, upon repenting of the sin, then it is our responsibility to ask forgiveness to the one we have wronged. Then we have to counteract our previous statements or opinions to those we have gossiped to, by word, email or social media – often by whatever medium the offence was committed. As a general guide the circle of apology only needs to extend to those within the circle of offence. In dealing with an offended party, the longer we delay our responsibility and put it off, the harder it will be. As long as we fulfil our responsibility and try to be reconciled to our brother or sister, then we cannot be held responsible for their decision if they choose to respond in a negative manner.

> Peter preached, "Repent therefore and be converted, that your sins may be blotted out, so that times of refreshing may come from the presence of the Lord" (Acts 3:19).

Evan Roberts of the Welsh Revival (1904-1905) stated that there were four conditions for revival. As he travelled and spoke in numerous churches in Wales he would ask:

1. Is there any sin in your past with which you have not honestly dealt with, or not confessed to God? On your knees at once. Your past must be put away and cleansed.

2. Is there anything in your life that is doubtful – anything which you cannot decide is good or evil? Away with it. There must not be a trace of a cloud between you and God. Have you forgiven everybody, EVERYBODY? If not, don't expect forgiveness for your sins. Better to offend ten thousand friends than grieve the Spirit of God, or quench Him.

3. Do what the Holy Spirit prompts without hesitation or fear. Obedience: prompt, implicit, unquestioning obedience at whatever cost.

4. Make a public confession of Christ as personal Saviour. Profession and confession are vastly different. Multitudes are guilty of long and loud profession. Confession of Christ as Lord has to do with His workings in your life TODAY!

Leadership and the Holy Spirit

Revival Church history records that if the leadership within a church, mission compound or Bible College/Seminary etc. are not right with God or with other people, especially members from the congregation or community, then *they* are a big hindrance to revival.

Christian leaders are on the Devil's number one hit list. He knows that if he can take out the shepherd or the leader then the sheep are more easily scattered. It is the responsibility of every Christian to pray for their minister and to lift them up before the throne of grace on a regular basis. If you feel that the pastor, elder, deacon or evangelists etc. is not doing a good job, don't criticise them – pray for them and pray blessing upon their lives, family and ministry.

It is imperative that Christian leaders permit the Holy Spirit to work in their midst, to do what He wants to do. The work is of God and not of man – we may have good ideas, but is it God's blueprint? Is this what God has called you to do? Each work must be God ordained and must have His seal of approval on it; otherwise it comes from the flesh. Many people will say on the Judgment Day, "Lord, Lord, did not we do great things in Your name?" But He will reply, "Get away from Me, I never knew you" (Matthew 7:21-23). Whose kingdom are you building and maintaining? God's Kingdom, yours or another's? See *The Baptism of Fire* (2017) and *Glimpses of Glory* both by Paul Backholer (2016).

'Be exalted, O God, above the Heavens; let Your glory be above all the earth' (Psalm 57:5).

Chapter 26

Praying for Revival

Jesus said, "Abide in Me, and I in you. As the branch cannot bear fruit of itself, unless it abides in the vine, neither can you, unless you abide in Me. I am the Vine, you are the branches. He who abides in Me, and I in him, bears much fruit; for without Me you can do nothing" (John 15:4-5).

  Most Christians accept that prayer is vital for the life of the believer, and still acknowledge their inadequacy in prayer. Perhaps it's because we think that we have more important things to do. On the other hand, there are numerous distractions lurking around every corner – the pleasures of entertainment or socialising, which would consume our precious time and distract us from the more important issues in life. Jesus frequently got up before dawn, or went away into a solitary place to have communion with the Father. Jesus set the benchmark for prayer and we have to strive towards that goal. The Spirit is willing, but the flesh is weak (Mark 14:38). We all need to crucify the flesh and take up our cross daily and follow the Master. How much time do we spend doing 'things' which are of non-eternal value? The object therefore is to get our priorities in order and to glorify the Master.
  Those who profess to name the name of Jesus Christ and who refuse to pray for revival are in effect saying, "I do not care about the glory of God or the church and those outside of the church. I'm fine and saved, it's not my concern." Is there a Scriptural basis to disregard our neighbours in spite of our knowledge? I think not! Should we not be concerned about our great cities (Jonah 4:11), our towns, our villages, our streets, our neighbours, my neighbours, your neighbours? We are our brother's keeper! (Genesis 4:9). 'Deliver those who are stumbling towards death and hold back those stumbling to the slaughter. If you say, "Surely we did not know this," does not He who weighs the hearts consider it? He who keeps your soul does He not know it? And will He not render to each man according to his deeds?' (Proverbs 24:11-12).
  God is a covenant-keeping God, because Scripture declares: 'Know that the Lord your God, He is God, the faithful God who keeps covenant and mercy for a thousand generations with those who love Him and keep His commandments' (Deuteronomy 7:9), and 'God of Heaven, O great and awesome God, You who keep

your covenant and mercy with those who love You and observe Your commandments' (Nehemiah 1:5). Arthur Wallis in regards to Nehemiah's intercession for Jerusalem wrote: 'Nehemiah was able to prevail in prayer because he held God to be faithful and pleaded His promises. He reminded Him of what He had covenanted to do [Nehemiah 1:4-11] and pressed Him to fulfil it. This is a spiritual lever that never fails to move the Hand that moves the world.'[1]

Praying for revival is taking God's promises as revealed in the written Word, the Holy Bible and presenting His own Words to Him and seeking the fulfilment of those Scriptures because He has promised – but it is foolhardy to pray these Scriptures whilst neglecting those which need to be lived out daily. Rev. Duncan Campbell of the Hebridean Revival (1949-1952) at a conference for ministers said, "God is not obliged to send revival because we pray. But He's bound by covenant promise, to send revival when we humble ourselves and pray; when we humble ourselves [in] brokenness of spirit."

Evangelist and revivalist, D. L. Moody said, "Move the arm that moves the world" and "The Christian who kneels more, stands better." From 1982-1983, Paul Y. Cho saw 230,000 conversions within the Yoido Full Gospel Church, Seoul, South Korea. He wrote: 'I decided years ago that we could not take the revival that we are experiencing in Korea for granted. Having studied Church history, I realised that revivals must not only be prayed for to begin, but they must also be prayed for so that they may be maintained. Throughout the revivals the Western world has experienced, after several years, people begin to take the revival for granted. The way this happens is that they forget about the very thing that birthed the revival, prayer. Once fervent and continuous prayer is forgotten, the impetus of the revival is lost and all that is left is the momentum of the past.'[2]

The following are Scriptures to aid us in our prayers for revival; some of which are conditional, our obligations in the eyes of a covenant-keeping God.

God's Spirit and God's Glory

- Thus says the Lord, "And it shall come to pass afterward that I will pour out My Spirit on all flesh; your sons and your daughters shall prophesy, your old men shall dream dreams, your young men shall see visions; and also on My menservants and My maidservants I will pour out My Spirit in those days" (Joel 2:28-29).
- The Lord said, "But truly, as I live, all the earth shall be filled with the glory of the Lord" (Numbers 14:21).

- 'For the earth will be filled with the knowledge of the glory of the Lord, as the waters cover the sea' (Habakkuk 2:14).

God's Glory and Vindication
- God said, "By those who come near Me, I must be regarded as holy; and before all the people I must be glorified" (Leviticus 10:3).
- God said, "For My own sake, for My own sake, I will do it; for how should My name be profaned? And I will not give My glory to another" (Isaiah 48:11).
- 'O Lord, though our iniquities testify against us, do it for Your name's sake; for our backslidings are many, we have sinned against You' (Jeremiah 14:7).
- Jesus said, "Most assuredly, I say to you, he who believes in Me, the works that I do he will do also; and greater works than these he will do, because I go to My Father. And whatever you ask in My name, that I will do, that the Father may be glorified in the Son. If you ask anything in My name, I will do it" (John 14:12-14).
- '[The] Gentiles...glorify God in the day of visitation' (1 Peter 2:12).

The Holy Spirit and God Descending
- Thus says the Lord, "For I will pour water on him who is thirsty, and floods on the dry ground; I will pour out My Spirit on your descendants and My blessing on your offspring" (Isaiah 44:3).
- Thus says the Lord, "Rain down, you Heavens, from above, and let the skies pour down righteousness; let the earth open, let them bring forth salvation, and let righteousness spring up together. I the Lord have created it" (Isaiah 45:8).
- 'Oh, that You would rend the Heavens and come down! That the mountains might shake at Your presence...to make Your name known' (Isaiah 64:1).

God's Merciful Nature and Reviving
- 'If My people who are called by My name will humble themselves, and pray and seek My face, and turn from their wicked ways, then I will hear from Heaven, and will forgive their sin and heal their land' (2 Chronicles 7:14).
- '...But You are a God, ready to pardon, gracious and merciful, slow to anger, abundant in kindness...' (Nehemiah 9:17).
- For Your name's sake, O Lord, pardon my iniquity, for it is great' (Psalm 25:11).
- 'Will You not revive us again...?' (Psalm 85:6).

- 'The eyes of the Lord are on the righteous and His ears are open to their cry' (Psalm 34:15).

Andrew Murray wrote: 'Jesus Christ taught us that the answer to prayer depended on certain conditions. He spoke of faith, of perseverance, of praying in His name, of praying in the will of God. But all these conditions were summed up in the one central one: "If ye abide in Me, ask whatever ye will and it shall be done unto you" (John 15:7).

'It is only by a full surrender to the life of abiding, by the yielding to the fullness of the Spirit's leading and quickening, that the prayer-life can be restored to a truly healthy state. In intercession our King upon the throne finds His highest glory; in it we shall find our highest glory too. The faith in God's Word can nowhere be so exercised and perfected as in the intercession that asks and expects, and looks for an answer.'[3]

Rev. Dr. Colin N. Peckham of The Faith Mission, Edinburgh, married Mary Morrison who saw the North Uist Revival (1957-1958). In the foreword to *When God Came Down,* Dr. Peckham wrote: 'God uses those who are available and useable. He uses those who are cleansed and filled with His Holy Spirit. He uses those who are prepared to pay the price of soul-travail. Burdened, broken, bold praying is the nerve-centre of revival...intercession costs...true intercession is sacrifice. Because of the demands and price of intercessory prayer, many do not enter its portals and consequently do not gain its benefits....'[4]

Canadian-born Jonathan Goforth is known as 'China's greatest evangelist.' He saw revival in China and Manchuria during 1906-1909, and in 1915. He wrote: 'If we all had faith to wait upon God in intense believing prayer there would be genuine Holy Ghost revival, and the living God would get all the glory.'[5]

'...For You, Lord, have not forsaken those who seek You' (Psalm 9:10).

Pray for Revival with Right Motives and a Pure Heart
- Praying for revival is praying for God to be glorified in your church, community or nation (Leviticus 10:3). Asking God to do it for His great name's sake so that His name will no longer be profaned (Jeremiah 14:7, Lamentations 3:22-25 and Isaiah 48:11).
- Cry out to God, ask Him to pour out His Spirit, to rend the Heavens, praise Him and be sure there is no iniquity in your heart (Psalm 66:17-19, Isaiah 64:1 and Joel 2:28-29).

- Live godly with integrity and walk in holiness (1 Peter 1:16) whilst abiding in God's presence (John 15:1-11).
- God wants us to ask for the nations for His inheritance as He desires all men to be saved and has no pleasure in the death of the wicked (Psalm 2:8, Ezekiel 18:23 and 1 Timothy 1:4).
- Confessions of one's sins, the sins of our forefathers and our nation's sins are paramount to make sure that we are right before God (Exodus 20:5-6, Judges 2:6-19, Nehemiah 9:2, Daniel 9:3-20 and 1 John 1:9).

Scriptures on Prayer
- 'As for me, I will call upon God...' (Psalm 55:16).
- Jesus said, "You did not choose Me, but I chose you and appointed you that you should go and bear fruit, and that your fruit should remain, that whatever you ask the Father in My name, He may give you" (John 15:16).
- Jesus said, "I say to you, ask, and it will be given to you; seek and you will find; knock, and it will be opened to you" (Luke 11:9).
- Jesus said, "Whatever you ask in My name that will I do, that the Father may be glorified in the Son. If you ask anything in My name, I will do it" (John 14:13-14).
- Jesus said, "...Whatever you ask the Father in My name He will give you. Until now you have asked nothing in My name. Ask and you will receive that your joy may be full" (John 16:23-24).
- Jesus said, "If you abide in Me and My Words abide in you, you will ask what you desire and it shall be done for you" (John 15:7).
- Jesus said, "I say to you that if two or three of you on earth agree concerning anything that they ask it will be done for them by My Father in Heaven. For where two or three are gathered together in My name, I am there in the midst of them" (Matthew 18:19-20).

'I have set watchmen on your walls, O Jerusalem, who shall never hold their peace day or night. You who make mention of the Lord, do not keep silent, and give Him no rest till He establishes and till He makes Jerusalem a praise in the earth' (Isaiah 62:6-7).

Keys to Prayer
- What is our motive in praying for —? Is the Father glorified through your prayers? (John 16:23 and James 4:3).
- Is it a need or a want? (Matthew 6:9-13).
- Is it God's will? (1 John 5:14).
- Ask in Jesus' name (John 16:23).
- Be persistent in prayer (Luke 18:1).

Seven Conditions for Answered Prayer

1. God will not hear your prayers if you lead a sinful lifestyle. 'If I regard iniquity in my heart the Lord will not hear' (Psalm 66:18).

2. Unforgiveness hinders prayers. Jesus said, "If you forgive men their trespasses, your Heavenly Father will also forgive you. But if you do not forgive men their trespasses, neither will your Father forgive your trespasses" (Matthew 6:14-15).

3. Continue to seek God. 'Seek the Lord and His strength; seek His face evermore' (Psalm 105:4).

4. Live a God-glorifying life. 'As He who called you is holy, you also be holy in all your conduct, because it is written, "Be holy, for I am holy" ' (1 Peter 1:15-16). Psalm 15, Psalm 24:1-6 and Galatians 5:22-25 denotes the characteristics of the godly.

5. Believe and have faith. James wrote: 'Ask in faith, with no doubting, for he who doubts is like a wave of the sea driven and tossed by the wind' (James 1:6).

6. Living in unity is a key to God's blessing. We must all 'endeavour to keep the unity of the Spirit in the bond of peace' (Ephesians 4:3).

7. Abide in God and pray what is on His heart. Jesus said, "If you abide in Me and My Words abide in you, you will ask what you desire and it shall be done for you" (John 15:7).

'I acknowledged my sin to You, and my iniquity I have not hidden. I said, "I will confess my transgression to the Lord," and You forgave the iniquity of my sin. Selah. For this cause everyone who is godly will pray to You...' (Psalm 32:5-6).

Cry Out to God

Holiness is the foundation for revival building and prayer and fasting (humbling oneself) are the supporting walls. As a place of abiding, humility and humbling, God may lead you into a period of fasting. Fasting is a state of humbling oneself in which we are able to give more time in beseeching God for His mercy, and in the context of revival, repenting of the sins of our nation (and the sin that we have committed) and pleading for the outpouring of the Holy Spirit to come and heal our land. Fasting is not necessarily just abstaining from food, but to walk in the statutes of God and to uphold justice and mercy, see Isaiah 1:12-17, Isaiah chapters 58-59 and Matthew 23:23.

Daniel was a godly man, full of understanding and the Spirit of God was with him. He searched the Scriptures and found out what they said about Israel's seventy years banishment and the desolation of Jerusalem. Daniel then prayed and made requests through prayer and supplication, with fasting, acts of humility and repentance for the past; his personal sins and for the sins of his forefathers (Daniel 9:1-19). Daniel pleaded with God based on His great mercies (not because of his righteous living), and pleaded for His great name's sake (Daniel 9:18). Daniel was only doing what King Solomon had laid down at the dedication of the temple in Jerusalem. When a nation goes away from God and is attacked by her enemies or suffers famine and pestilence, then its citizens need to acknowledge and confess their sin (and the sin of the nation), return with all their heart and call upon God to intervene (2 Chronicles 6:24-40). The prophet Samuel speaking to the nation of Israel after King Saul's inauguration said, "As for me, far be it from me that I should sin against the Lord in ceasing to pray for you..." (1 Samuel 12:23).

It was said that John Knox the sixteenth century Scottish reformer, cried out in passionate prayer for his people, "Give me Scotland or I'll die!" Will you be prepared to cry out for the lost? Will you cry out to God day and night and ask Him to send showers of blessing on this dry and barren land; has He not promised to give water to him who thirsts? But the conditions of clean hands and a pure heart need to be applied. As long as we do our part, then God will not fail to do His.

'Those who sow in tears shall reap in joy. He who continually goes forth weeping, bearing seed for sowing, shall doubtless come again with rejoicing, bringing his sheaves with him' (Psalm 126:5-6).

God has no pleasure in the death of the wicked, but that they would turn from their wicked ways – for God so loved the world that He gave His only begotten Son. What will you give for this world? God gave His all. God desires mankind to be drawn unto Him that He allowed, He permitted His Son to be smitten, to be beaten, to be mocked, to be whipped, to be humiliated, to suffer and hung on a cross for our eternal redemption. That's how much God wants people to turn to Him and be saved from the wrath to come and the damnation of Hell. When Jesus is lifted up, He will draw all men to Himself. God paid the ultimate price for revival, for a vast ingathering of people, so that He would be glorified.

In the mid seventeenth century, George Fox, upon Pendle Hill in Lancashire, England, saw a vision of 'a great ingathering of people' and founded the Society for Friends, 'Quakers' (who used to be a Christian sect). Pendle Hill stands high above the surrounding area and the view of fields upon fields spreads out in all directions for tens of miles. Maybe George Fox was reminded of the words of Jesus, "The fields are white unto harvest..." (John 4:35), "The harvest is truly plentiful, but the labourers are few" (Matthew 9:37). Anyhow, he got on with the job of preaching Scriptural truths and more than fifty thousand people were converted back to the pure faith in forty years; 'Bid ye tremble at the word of the Lord' was their watchword. Today we have to ask, do we have the fear of God inside of us? The fear of the Lord is the beginning of wisdom, the beginning of understanding is the knowledge of God (Proverbs 9:10), and the fear of the Lord is to hate evil (Proverbs 8:10).

At the Brownsville Revival (1995-2000), as in every revival there were intercessors that identified with the pain that God feels over those who reject the forgiveness that is found in Jesus Christ. We need more intercessors and prayer warriors that will pay the price, and cry out for the lost, pleading for mercy and redemption upon the lost sheep. Evangelist Steve Hill would often be preaching and weeping at the same time (like the prophet Jeremiah), falling to his knees and pleading with the people to get right with God. He did not just give a sermon, he gave it his all. This was true of John Wesley, who would ride through knee-high snow and driving sleet to preach to one sinner or a great gathering. Both Moses and the apostle Paul were prepared to be damned for all eternity, if only their brethren might be saved! Whilst the Reformers proclaimed that we are, "Justified by faith," and that 'there is no other name under Heaven given among men by which we must be saved' (Acts 4:12).

If you want Jesus to be lifted high as a banner across the land then cry out to God, "In wrath remember mercy," pray that the bowl of mercy will outweigh judgment (Revelation 8:1-5). "O Lord, though our iniquities testify against us, do it for Your name's sake; for our backslidings are many, we have sinned against You" (Jeremiah 14:7). Leonard Ravenhill's epitaph: "Are the things you are living for worth Christ dying for?" – What about you? Are you standing in the gap praying and interceding for revival for your church, town or nation? Have you begun with a personal revival of your life?

'Those from among you shall build the old waste places; you shall raise up the foundations of many generations; and you shall be called the Repairer of the Breach, the Restorer of Streets to Dwell In' (Isaiah 58:12).

Thank you for reading this book, please write a short (or long) review on your favourite review site, and give a shout-out on social media – thank you.

www.ByFaith.org

www.RevivalNow.co.uk

Books by Mathew Backholer

Christian Revivals and Awakenings
- Global Revival, Worldwide Outpourings, Forty-Three Visitations of the Holy Spirit: The Great Commission.
- Revival Answers, True and False Revivals: Genuine or Counterfeit? Do not be Deceived.
- Revival Fire, 150 Years of Revivals: Spiritual Awakenings and Moves of the Holy Spirit.
- Understanding Revival and Addressing the Issues it Provokes.
- Revival Fires and Awakenings, Thirty-Six Visitations of the Holy Spirit: A Call to Holiness, Prayer and Intercession for the Nations.
- Reformation to Revival, 500 Years of God's Glory: Sixty Revivals, Awakenings and Heaven-Sent Visitations of the Holy Spirit.

Christian Discipleship and Spiritual Growth
- Extreme Faith, On Fire Christianity: Hearing from God and Moving in His Grace, Strength & Power – Living in Victory.
- Discipleship For Everyday Living, Christian Growth: Following Jesus Christ and Making Disciples of All Nations.
- Christianity Rediscovered, In Pursuit of God and the Path to Eternal Life. Book 1.
- Christianity Explored. Book 2.

Christian Missions
- How to Plan, Prepare and Successfully Complete Your Short-Term Mission: For Churches, Independent STM Teams and Mission Organizations.
- Short-Term Missions, A Christian Guide to STMs: For Leaders, Pastors, Churches, Students, STM Teams and Mission Organizations – Survive and Thrive!

World Travel
- Budget Travel, a Guide to Travelling on a Shoestring, Explore the World, a Discount Overseas Adventure Trip.
- Travel the World and Explore for Less than $50 a Day, the Essential Guide.

Historical
- God Challenges the Dictators, Doom of the Nazis Predicted: The Destruction of the Third Reich (Rees Howells & Mathew Backholer).
- Rees Howells' God Challenges the Dictators, Doom of Axis Powers Predicted: Victory for Christian England and Release of Europe.
- Rees Howells, Vision Hymns of Spiritual Warfare & Intercessory Declarations: World War II Songs of Victory, Intercession, Praise and Worship, Israel and the Every Creature Commission.

Sources and Notes

Chapter 1
1. From Dr. Martyn Lloyd-Jones in 1959, the centenary of the 1859 revival, when he preached a series of sermons on the subject of revival at Westminster Chapel.
2. *The Skye Revivals* by Steve Taylor, New Wine Press, 2003, page 142.
3. As quoted by Duncan Campbell in a sermon. Unless otherwise stated all Duncan Campbell quotes are from his recorded sermons which can be listened to online for free at various Christian websites.
4. *Great Revivals* by Colin Whittaker, Marshall, Morgan & Scott 1984, page 92.
5. Ibid., pages 105-106.
6. See *The Baptism of Fire: Personal Revival, Renewal and the Anointing for Supernatural Living* by Paul Backholer, ByFaith Media, 2017.

Chapter 3
1. *Martin Luther: Student, Monk, Reformer* by John Rae, Hodder & Stoughton, 1884, *The Homes and Haunts* of Martin Luther by John Stoughton, 1874 as found in *Sunday at Home Magazine 1874*, in serialised form, *The Reformation* by Owen Chadwick, Penguin Books Ltd, 1964, *The Homes and Haunts* of Martin Luther by John Stoughton, Religious Tract Society, 1903, *A History of the Reformation in Two Volumes*, Volume I by Thomas M. Lindsay, T&T Clark, 1906, and *Philip Melanethon: The Wittenberg Professor and Theologian of the Reformation* by David J. Deane, S. W. Partridge & Co, c.1900.

Chapter 4
1. Used by permission and based on a section of *English Bible History* as found on www.greatsite.com/timeline-english-bible-history/index.html. Accessed 2002.
2. Based on a section of an article *The History of England/Britain* by the author, and found at www.xfaith.co.uk, (2017), *A History of the Reformation in Two Volumes*, Volume II by Thomas M. Lindsay, T&T Clark, 1907, 1923, Book IV, chapter I.

Chapter 5
1. *The Life of John Knox* by Rev. Thomas McCrie, Thomas Nelson and Sons, 1889, The *History of the Reformation of Religion in Scotland* by John Knox, edited for popular use by C. J. Guthrie, Banner of Truth, 1898, 1982, *The Swordbearer: John Knox and the European Reformation* by Stewart Lamont, Hodder & Stoughton, 1991, John *Knox: In the Footsteps of Scotland's Great Reformer* by David Campbell, Day One, 2003, *Historical Collections of Accounts of Revival* by John Gillies, 1754, revised and enlarged in 1845 by Horatius Bonar, Banner of Truth Trust, 1981, pages 60-62 and *A History of the Reformation in Two Volumes*, Volume II by Thomas M. Lindsay, T&T Clark, 1907, 1923, Book III, chapter vi.

Chapter 6
1. *The Journal of George Fox* revised by Norman Penney, Everyman's Library, 1924, 1948, page 1, *George Fox* by H. G. Wood (Leaders of Revival series), National Council of Evangelical Free Churches, 1912, pages 14-16, and *George Fox and the Quakers* by Henry Van Etten, translated and revised by E. Kelvin Osborn, Harper Torchbooks, 1959, page 15.
2. *George Fox and the Quakers* by Henry Van Etten, translated and revised by E. Kelvin Osborn, Harper Torchbooks, 1959, pages 8-12.
3. www.xfaith.co.uk – History of England and *George Fox and the Quakers* by Henry Van Etten, translated and revised by E. Kelvin Osborn, Harper Torchbooks, 1959, chapter 1.
4. *The Journal of George Fox* revised by Norman Penney, Everyman's Library, 1924, 1948, chapter I, *George Fox* by H. G. Wood (Leaders of Revival series), National Council of Evangelical Free Churches, 1912, chapter II, *George Fox and the Quakers* by Henry Van Etten, translated and revised by E. Kelvin Osborn, Harper Torchbooks, 1959, pages 9 and 115.

5. *The Journal of George Fox* revised by Norman Penney, Everyman's Library, 1924, 1948, page 335 and *George Fox and the Quakers* by Henry Van Etten, translated and revised by E. Kelvin Osborn, Harper Torchbooks, 1959, page 16.

6. George Fox's *Book Of Miracles,* 1948 (1973 and 2000) was edited by Henry Cadbury (1883-1974). Incidentally, two years into his ministry, Fox seriously considered becoming a physic (doctor).

7. *Annals of The Early Friends* by Frances Anne Budge, Henry Longstreth, Philadelphia, 1900, pages vi-vii and *George Fox and the Quakers* by Henry Van Etten, translated and revised by E. Kelvin Osborn, Harper Torchbooks, 1959, page 185.

8. *George Fox and the Quakers* by Henry Van Etten, translated and revised by E. Kelvin Osborn, Harper Torchbooks, 1959, page 86, 143 and 193 and *Annals of The Early Friends* by Frances Anne Budge, Henry Longstreth, Philadelphia, 1900, page 210.

9. *George Fox and the Quakers* by Henry Van Etten, translated and revised by E. Kelvin Osborn, Harper Torchbooks, 1959, page 46 and *Annals of The Early Friends* by Frances Anne Budge, Henry Longstreth, Philadelphia, 1900, pages 186-192 and *George Fox and the Quakers* by Henry Van Etten, translated and revised by E. Kelvin Osborn, Harper Torchbooks, 1959, page 86.

10. *Annals of The Early Friends* by Frances Anne Budge, Henry Longstreth, Philadelphia, 1900, pages 4-22.

11. Ibid., pages 404 and 411-413.

12. *The Journal of George Fox* revised by Norman Penney, Everyman's Library, 1924, 1948, chapter XXI.

13. *Friends Ancient and Modern* by Lucy B. Roberts, Published for the Friends Tract Association, 1910, No.14 (William Penn), *George Fox and the Quakers* by Henry Van Etten, translated and revised by E. Kelvin Osborn, Harper Torchbooks, 1959, pages 89 and 99-101 and *Yarns on Social Pioneers* by Ernest H. Haynes, The Religious Education Press, 1924, 1940, chapter VII.

14. *George Fox and the Quakers* by Henry Van Etten, translated and revised by E. Kelvin Osborn, Harper Torchbooks, 1959, pages 37 and 147 and *Friends Ancient and Modern* by August Diamond, Published for the Friends Tract Association, 1909, No.13 (William Wilson), pages 4 and 37.

15. *Annals of The Early Friends* by Frances Anne Budge, Henry Longstreth, Philadelphia, 1900, pages 1, 15, 31, 33-34, 36-37, 53, 60, 119, 129, 136, 250, 254, 301, 426 and 434.

16. *George Fox* by H. G. Wood (Leaders of Revival series), National Council of Evangelical Free Churches, 1912, *The Journal of George Fox* revised by Norman Penney, Everyman's Library, 1924, 1948, *Land of Hope and Glory - British Revival Through The Ages* by Bruce Atkinson, Dovewell Publications, 2003, chapter 4, *The History of Revivals of Religion* by William E. Allen (revival series No. 7), Revival Publishing Co., 1951, pages 22-23, *Yarns on Christian Pioneers* by Ernest H. Haynes, The Religious Education Press, 1928, 1936, chapter VII, *Friends Ancient and Modern* (various authors – No. 1-18 – booklets collated into a book), Published for the Friends Tract Association, 1907-1912, and *Annals of The Early Friends* by Frances Anne Budge, Henry Longstreth, Philadelphia, 1900.

17. *Friends Ancient and Modern* by John H. Barlow, Published for the Friends Tract Association, 1908, No. 10. (George Whitehead) pages 6 and 40.

Chapter 7

1. *Power From On High or The Two Hundred Anniversary of the Great Moravian Revival 1727-1927* by Rev. John Greenfield, World Wide Revival Prayer Movement, 1927, 1931, page 26.

2. Ibid., page 27.

3. Ibid., pages 27-28.

4. Between various authors there is a difference between the day of the week and the date of the month during the second and third week of August, and therefore to avoid confusion I have left the day of the week out in some paragraphs. *Power From On High or The Two Hundred Anniversary of the Great Moravian Revival 1727-1927* by Rev. John Greenfield, World Wide Revival Prayer Movement, 1927, 1931, page 27.

5. *Vanguards Of The Christian Army: Sketches of Missionary Life* by Anonymous, The Religious Tract Society, 1896, pages 383-384 and 390.

6. *The Pilgrim Boy*, Religious Tract Society, c.1900, pages 39 and 46-47 and *Vanguards Of The Christian Army: Sketches of Missionary Life* by Anonymous, The Religious Tract Society, 1896, pages 403 and 406.

7. *The Awakening That Must Come* by Lewis A. Drummond, Broadman Press, 1978, page 83. *Missionary Points and Pictures* by James Johnston, The Religious Tract Society, 1892, pages 113-114, *The History of Revivals of Religion* by William E. Allen (revival series No. 7), Revival Publishing Co., 1951, pages 15-16, *By My Spirit* by Jonathan Goforth, Evangel Publishing House, c.1948, pages 9 and 132-133, *In the Day of Thy Power* by Arthur Wallis, Christian Literature Crusade, 1956, pages 88 and 94, and *A History of the Moravian Church* by J. E. Hutton, Moravian Publication Office, 1909.

8. *Power From On High or The Two Hundred Anniversary of the Great Moravian Revival 1727-1927* by Rev. John Greenfield, World Wide Revival Prayer Movement, 1927, 1931, page 92.

9. Ibid., pages 50-51.

10. Ibid., page 51.

11. Ibid., pages 62 and 64.

12. Ibid., page 15.

Chapter 8

1. *Historical Collections of Accounts of Revival* by John Gillies, 1754, revised and enlarged in 1845 by Horatius Bonar, Banner of Truth Trust, 1981, pages 282-283.

2. Ibid., page 288.

3. Ibid., pages 288-289.

4. Ibid., page 289.

5. *The History of Revivals of Religion* by William E. Allen (revival series No. 7), Revival Publishing Co., 1951, page 17 and *The Awesome Work of God* by Jonathan Edwards, Ambassador Publications, 2000.

6. J. Edwin Orr speaking of The Awakening of 1727, filmed in 1981, at Church on the Way, Van Nuys, California, America. From a CDR.

7. *The History of Revivals of Religion* by William E. Allen (revival series No. 7), Revival Publishing Co., 1951, pages 17-18.

8. From the *Works of Jonathan Edwards – Religious Affections – A Christian's Character Before God,* edited by Dr. James M. Houston, 1884, 1996, pages xxvi and 25.

9. *Religious Affections* by Jonathan Edwards, edited by Dr. James M. Houston, 1984, 1996, page 40.

10. *Vignettes of the Great Revival* by E. Paxton Hood, The Religious Tract Society, 1887, page 184.

11. *Great Revivals* by Colin Whittaker, Marshall, Morgan & Scott, 1984, pages 35-36.

12. *Wesley His Own Biography – Selections From The Journals*, Charles H. Kelly, 1890, page 109. One author states this meeting of Howell Harris with John Wesley on 5 June 1747.

13. Ibid., page 118.

14. *The History of Christianity,* Lion Publishing plc, 1996, page 448.

Chapter 9

1. *Vignettes of the Great Revival* by E. Paxton Hood, The Religious Tract Society, 1887, pages 12-14.

2. *John Wesley The Hero of the Second Reformation* by Edward Miller, The Sunday School Union, 1906, pages 8-10.

3. Ibid., page 62.

4. *The Life of John Wesley* by John Telford, The Epworth Press, 1886, 1929, pages 115-118 and 129.

5. *The Inextinguishable Blaze: Spiritual Renewal and Advance in the Eighteenth Century* by A. Skevington Wood, The Paternoster Press, 1960, pages 70-71 and 161.

6. *Wesley His Own Biography – Selections From The Journals* by Charles H. Kelly, 1890, pages 139 and 157.

7. *The Life of John Wesley* by John Telford, The Epworth Press, 1886, 1929, page 144.

8. *Wesley His Own Biography – Selections From The Journals* by Charles H. Kelly, 1890, page 238.

9. Ibid., page 374.
10. *The Life of John Wesley* by John Telford, The Epworth Press, 1886, 1929, pages 121-125.
11. *Wesley His Own Biography – Selections From The Journals* by Charles H. Kelly, 1890, page 108.
12. Ibid., page 111.
13. Ibid., page 124.
14. Ibid., pages 119-120.
15. *The Life of John Wesley* by John Telford, The Epworth Press, 1886, 1929, pages 122-123.

Chapter 10

1. *Fifty Missionary Heroes Every Boy and Girl Should Know* by Julia H. Johnson, 1913, Fleming H. Revell Company, 1913, pages 47-48.
2. *Evangelical Awakenings in Africa* by J. Edwin Orr, Bethany Fellowship Inc., 1970, 1975, pages 13-14.
3. *Old Time Revivals* by John Shearer, Pickering & Inglis, 1930, pages 55-60 and *The Ten Greatest Revivals Ever* by Elmer Towns and Douglas Porter, Servant Publications, 2000, pages 75 and 92.
4. *Times of Refreshing 10,000 Miles of Miracle Through Canada* by J. Edwin Orr, Marshall, Morgan & Scott Ltd, 1936, pages 43-44.
5. *Billy Bray* by F. W. Bourne, Bible Christian Book-Room, 1877, 1898, pages 7-10, 29, 44, 59, 62, 84, 87, 91-94, 114-115, 118, 123-124, 130 and 145, and *From Death Into Life* by Rev. William Haslam, Jarold & Sons, 1880, 1904, pages 105 and 106.
6. *Striking Stories from Real Life* by J. Manton Smith, Passmore and Alabaster, 1894, page 149.
7. Facts taken from a video – a sermon on revival by Peter Scothen (Voice of Deliverance Ministry) which was preached at the West Wales Convention 1988. Peter Scothen's source was an old Welsh book, which at the time had recently been rediscovered.

Chapter 11

1. *Revival and You* by James Alexander Stewart, Revival Literature, 1969, page 29.
2. *Andrew A. Bonar Diary and Life*, Banner Of Truth, 1893, 1960, pages x and 78, *Travel With Robert Murray McCheyne*, Day One, 2007, pages 87 and 101 and *Old Time Revivals* by John Shearer, Pickering & Inglis, 1930, page 72.
3. Ibid., pages 65-67.
4. Ibid., page 72.
5. *Vanguards of the Christian Army: Sketches of Missionary Life* by Anonymous, The Religious Tract Society, 1896, page 174.
6. *Old Time Revivals* by John Shearer, Pickering & Inglis, 1930, page 75.
7. *Vanguards of the Christian Army: Sketches of Missionary Life* by Anonymous, The Religious Tract Society, 1896, pages 174-175.
8. *Revival Sermons* by Williams C. Burns, Banner Of Truth, 1869, 1980, page 13 and *Biographical Dictionary of Christian Missions* edited by Gerald H. Anderson, Wm. B. Eerdmans Publishing Co., 1998, page 102.
9. *Robert Morrison – The Pioneer of Chinese Missions* by W. J. Townsend, S. W. Partridge and Co., 1892, pages 105, 109, 132 and 216, and *Incidents of Missionary Enterprise*, by Anonymous, Thomas Nelson, 1841, page 119.
10. *Robert Morrison* by W. J. Townsend, S. W. Partridge and Co., 1892, pages 261 and 263-264.
11. *Hudson Taylor in Early Years – The Growth of a Soul* by Dr. and Mrs Howard Taylor, China Inland Mission, 1911, 1940, pages 4-6, 13 and 21.
12. Ibid., pages 25, 27 and 29-31.
13. Ibid., page 32.
14. Ibid., pages 51-53.
15. Ibid., pages 6, 13, 21 and 75-77.

Chapter 12

1. *From Death Into Life* by Rev. William Haslam, Jarold & Sons, 1880, 1904, pages 35-36, 46, 49-51, 55-62, 64-73, 79-88, 106, 110, 114, 127, 200 and 232. Chapters 8 to 19.

Chapter 13

1. *The Tongue of Fire or The True Power of Christianity* by William Arthur, Wesleyan Methodist Book Room, 1856, 1902, page 349.
2. *Do It Again Lord: The Story of Some of the Greatest Revivals the World has Ever Known* by Gordon Pettie, Fines Creek Publishing, 2017, pages 28 and 30.
3. Ibid., pages 43-44.
4. Ibid., page 38.
5. *The Half Can Never Be Told* by anonymous, World Wide Revival Prayer Movement, 1927, page 55.
6. *When the Fire Fell* by George T.B. Davis, 1945, (modern reprint), Schmul Publishers, no date, page 29.
7. *Great Revivals* by Colin Whittaker, Marshall, Morgan & Scott, 1984, pages 73-74.
8. *Hudson Taylor and the China Inland Mission* – Dr. and Mrs. Howard Taylor, China Inland Mission, 1918, 1940, pages 48-49, 63 and 70.
9. *Every Day with Jesus: Revive Us Again*, (May/Jun 2014) by Selwyn Hughes, revised and updated by Mick Brooks, CWR, 2014, 27 May.
10. *The History of Revivals of Religion* by William E. Allen (revival series No. 7), Revival Publishing Co., 1951, page 37.
11. *Land of Hope and Glory – British Revival Through The Ages* by Bruce Atkinson, Dovewell Publications, 2003, pages 259-260.
12. *The Wesleyan Methodist Magazine* for 1860, (An Abridged Edition), pages 41-42.
13. *Revival Comes to Wales – The Story of the 1859 Revival in Wales* by Eifion Evans, Evangelical Press of Wales, 1995, pages 97-98.
14. *The 59 Revival in Wales, Some Incidents in the Life and Work of David Morgan, Ysbytty* by J. J. Morgan, Ballantyne, Hanson & Co., 1909, pages v-vi.
15. www.walesawake.net/gpage.html. Accessed July 2009.
16. In an email to the author.
17. *The Wesleyan Methodist Magazine* for 1860, (An Abridged Edition), pages 387-388.

Chapter 14

1. *The 1859 Revival in Ulster, A Centenary Brochure* by John T, Carson, The United Committee of Irish Churches, 1959, pages 1-2.
2. *When the Fire Fell* by George T.B. Davis, 1945, Schmul Publishers, pages 61-62.
3. *The Year of Grace* by William Gibson, Ambassador Productions Ltd, 1989, page 253.
4. *The 59 Revival* by Ian R. K. Paisley, Ravenhill Free Presbyterian Church, 1958, 1969, page 174.
5. Ibid., page 175.
6. *Do It Again Lord: The Story of Some of the Greatest Revivals the World has Ever Known* by Gordon Pettie, Fines Creek Publishing, 2017, page 76.
7. *Great Revivals* by Colin Whittaker, Marshall, Morgan & Scott, 1984, page 81.
8. *The '59 Revival In Ireland, the United States of America, England, Scotland and Wales* edited by William E. Allen, Revival Publishing Co., 1955, page 20.
9. *The Wesleyan Methodist Magazine* for 1860 (An Abridged Edition), page 42.
10. Ibid., pages 42-43.
11. Ibid., page 531.
12. *The Half Can Never Be Told* by anonymous, World Wide Revival Prayer Movement, 1927, pages 62-65, and *The History of Revivals of Religion* by William E. Allen (revival series No. 7), Revival Publishing Co., 1951, pages 38-39.

Chapter 15

1. *The Half Can Never Be Told* by anonymous, World Wide Revival Prayer Movement, 1927, pages 65-68.
2. *Papers of Godliness* by Mrs General Booth, The Salvation Army, 1881, 1890, pages 74-75.

3. *The '59 Revival In Ireland, the United States of America, England, Scotland and Wales* edited by William E. Allen, Revival Publishing Co., 1955, page 20.
4. *The Tongue of Fire or The True Power of Christianity* by William Arthur, Wesleyan Methodist Book Room, London, 1856, 1902, pages vi-vii.
5. *Spurgeon on Revival* edited by Robert Backhouse, Kingsway, 1996, page 7.
6. *Revival and You* by James Alexander Stewart, Revival Literature, 1969, page 27.
7.www.evangelical-times.org/archive/item/6879/Historical/Spurgeon-in-Wales--1-/ Accessed February 2017.
8. *The History of Revivals of Religion* by William E. Allen (revival series No. 7), Revival Publishing Co., 1951, pages 46-47.
9. *Revival Year Sermons – C. H. Spurgeon, Preached in the Surrey Music Hall 1859*, The Banner of Truth Trust, 1959, page 29.
10. *The Life Story of C. H. Spurgeon or the Man and His Wonderful Message* by James T. Allen, c.1892, pages 36-40, 50 and 55.
11. *Revival and You* by James Alexander Stewart, Revival Literature, 1969, pages 86-87.
12. *The Wesleyan Methodist Magazine* for 1860, (An Abridged Edition), pages 489-490.
13. Ibid., pages 489-490.
14. Ibid., pages 486-487.

Chapter 16
1. *Land of Hope and Glory – British Revival Through The Ages* by Bruce Atkinson, Dovewell Publications, 2003, pages 207-208 and *Travel With William Booth* by Jim Winter, Day One, 2003, pages 72-73 and *Blood and Fire* by William. H. Nelson, The Century Co., 1929, chapter XII.
2. *The Short Life of Catherine Booth, the Mother of The Salvation Army* by F. De L. Booth-Tucker, Butler & Tanner, London, 1892, 1893 abridged edition, pages 135-137, 142-154.
3. *General Booth* by George S. Railton, Hodder and Stoughton, 1912, pages 49-51.
4. *The Short Life of Catherine Booth, the Mother of The Salvation Army* by F. De L. Booth-Tucker, Butler & Tanner, London, 1892, 1893 abridged edition, pages 139-141.
5. Ibid., pages 141-148.
6. Ibid., page 147.
7. Ibid., pages 149-150.
8. Ibid., pages 153-154.
9. *The Second Evangelical Awakening* by J. Edwin Orr, Marshall, Morgan & Scott, 1949, 1955, page 71.

Chapter 17
1. *Thomas Birch Freeman, Missionary Pioneer to Ashanti, Dahomey & Egba* by J. Milum, London, S. W. Partridge & Co., 1894, pages 141-149.
2. In 1925 the Shanghai Revival in China began and in 1932 the Shantung Revival in China broke out.
3. *Missionary Band A Record And Appeal,* London: Morgan and Scott, 1887, pages 22 and 37.
4. Ibid., pages 71-72.
5. *Revival Comes to Wales – The Story of the 1859 Revival in Wales* by Eifion Evans, Evangelical Press of Wales, 1995, pages 10-11.
6. *Rent Heavens the Revival of 1904* by R. B. Jones, Schmul Publishers, page 40.
7. Ibid., page 56.
8. *The Prophetical Ministry* or (*The Voice Gifts*) *in the Church*, 1931, pages 98-99, as cited in *The Welsh Revival of 1904* by Eifion Evans, Evangelical Press of Wales, 1969, 1987, pages 193-194.
9. See www.ReesHowells.org for more about this great man of God.
10. *Revival Praying* by Leonard Ravenhill, Bethany House Publishers, 1962, page 146.
11. *I Saw the Welsh Revival* by David Matthews, 1904-Centenary Edition-2004, Ambassador Publications, pages 100-101.
12. *When the Fire Fell* by George T.B. Davis, 1945, Schmul Publishers, pages 70-71.
13. *Christian Herald Archive* (Welsh Revival Issue), 1905, 2006, CPO, page 4.

14. *Revival and Its Fruit* by Emyr Roberts, R. Geraint Gruffydd, Evangelical Library of Wales, 1981, pages 7-8.

15. *Great Revivals* by Colin Whittaker, Marshall, Morgan & Scott, 1984, page 97.

16. *Christian Herald Archive* (Welsh Revival Issue), 1905, 2006, CPO, page 13.

17. *The Baptism of the Holy Ghost and Fire* by Miss Minnie F. Abrahams, Ramabai Mukti Mission, 1906, 1989, page 77.

18. *An Instrument of Revival: The Complete Life of Evan Roberts 1878-1951* by Brynmor Pierce Jones, Bridge Publishing, 1995, page 145.

19. *In the Day of Thy Power* by Arthur Wallis, CLC, 1956, page 15.

20. *Power From On High or The Two Hundred Anniversary of the Great Moravian Revival 1727-1927* by Rev. John Greenfield, World Wide Revival Prayer Movement, 1927, 1931, page 92.

21. *The Intercessions of Rees Howells* by Doris M. Ruscoe, The Lutterworth Press, 1983, 1991, page 91 and *Rees Howells Intercessor* by Norman Grubb, 1952, 1986, Lutterworth Press, pages 150-151.

22. *An Instrument of Revival: Complete Life of Evan Roberts, 1878-1951* by Brynmor Pierce Jones, 1996.

23. *The Welsh Revival of 1904* by Eifion Evans, Evangelical Press of Wales, 1969, 1987, pages 147-159. I have added to this list from my own research.

Chapter 18

1. *Pandita Ramabai, The Story of Her Life* by Helen S. Dyer, Morgan & Scott, c.1901, page 91.

2. *Pandita Ramabai, A Great Life In Indian Lessons* by Helen S. Dyer, Pickering & Inglis, c.1922, pages 99-101.

3. *The Baptism of the Holy Ghost and Fire* by Miss Minnie F. Abrahams, Ramabai Mukti Mission, 1906, 1989, pages 6-9,

4. *Pandita Ramabai, India's Christian Pilgrim* by Basil Miller, World-Wide Missions, undated, (extracts) pages 85-92 and 118, and *Pandita Ramabai, A Great Life In Indian Lessons* by Helen S. Dyer, Pickering & Inglis, c.1922, pages 100-110.

5. *The Baptism of the Holy Ghost and Fire* by Miss Minnie F. Abrahams, Ramabai Mukti Mission, 1906, 1989, page 10.

6. *Goforth of China* by Rosalind Goforth, Marshall, Morgan and Scott Ltd, 1937, pages 19, 24, 27-29, 35-36, 54, 64, 70, 72, 75, 78 and 80-81.

7. Ibid., pages 83-84, 89, 92, 98-99, 103, 113, 115 and 117.

8. Ibid., pages 123-126, 146 and 164.

9. Ibid., pages 157, 164, 169 and 181.

10. *Goforth of China* by Rosalind Goforth, Marshall, Morgan and Scott Ltd, 1937, pages 181-182 and *By My* Spirit by Jonathan Goforth, Zondervan Publishing House, 1929, 1942, pages 13, and 21-22.

11. *By My* Spirit by Jonathan Goforth, Zondervan Publishing House, 1929, 1942, page 45.

Chapter 19

1. *The Korean Pentecost & The Sufferings Which Followed* by William Blair and Bruce Hunt, The Banner of Truth Trust, 1977, pages 52 and 61-66.

2. Ibid., pages 67-72.

3. *By My Spirit* by Jonathan Goforth, Zondervan Publishing House, 1929, 1942, pages 22-23 and *When the Spirit's Fire Swept Korea* by Jonathan Goforth, Zondervan Publishing House, 1943, Timothy Conjurske 1994, page 9.

4. *The Korean Pentecost & The Sufferings Which Followed* by William Blair and Bruce Hunt, The Banner of Truth Trust, 1977, pages 72-74.

5. www.sarang.org. Accessed 2007.

6. www.english.sarang.org/again_1907.asp. Accessed 2007.

7. *When the Spirit's Fire Swept Korea* by Jonathan Goforth, Zondervan Publishing House, 1943, Timothy Conjurske 1994, pages 12-13.

8. *By My Spirit* by Jonathan Goforth, Zondervan Publishing House, 1929, 1942, page 23.

9. Ibid., pages 24-26 and *Goforth of China* by Rosalind Goforth, Marshall, Morgan & Scott Ltd, 1937, page 183-185.

10. *By My* Spirit by Jonathan Goforth, Zondervan Publishing House, 1929, pages 27-29 and Goforth *of China* by Rosalind Goforth, Marshall, Morgan & Scott Ltd, 1937, pages 185-187.

11. *Goforth of China* by Rosalind Goforth, Marshall, Morgan & Scott Ltd, 1937, pages 185-188.

12. Ibid., page 204. For more information on intercession see *Revival Fires and Awakenings, Thirty-Six Visitations of the Holy Spirit* by Mathew Backholer, ByFaith Media, 2009, 2017, chapter 21 and *Samuel Rees Howells: A Life of Intercession* by Richard Maton, ByFaith Media, 2012, 2017.

13. *The Revival We Need* by Oswald J. Smith, Marshall, Morgan & Scott, 1940, page v.

Chapter 20

1. *As At The Beginning – The Twentieth Century Pentecostal Revival* by Michael Harper, Hodder and Stoughton, 1965, pages 26-27.

2. *Another Wave of Revival* by Frank Bartleman, 1962, (Voice Christians Publication – *Another Waves Rolls In*), 1982, Whitaker House, chapter 1.

3. *God's Generals* by Robert Liardon, Albury Publishing, 1996, pages 145-148.

4. *Do It Again Lord: The Story of Some of the Greatest Revivals the World has Ever Known* by Gordon Pettie, Fines Creek Publishing, 2017, page 226.

5. *Another Wave of Revival* by Frank Bartleman, 1962, (Voice Christians Publication – *Another Waves Rolls In*), 1982, Whitaker House, pages 47-48 and 51.

6. *Azusa Street The Roots of Modern-Day Pentecost* by Frank Bartleman, Bridge Publishing, 1980, page xviii, and *They Told Me Their Stories* by Tommy Welchel, Dare 2 Dream Books, 2006, 2010.

7. *Azusa Street The Roots of Modern-Day Pentecost* by Frank Bartleman, Bridge Publishing, 1980, pages 56-57.

8. *Do It Again Lord: The Story of Some of the Greatest Revivals the World has Ever Known* by Gordon Pettie, Fines Creek Publishing, 2017, page 226.

9. www.azusastreet100.net/history.htm#. Accessed 2006.

10. *Another Wave of Revival* by Frank Bartleman, 1962, (Voice Christians Publication – *Another Waves Rolls In*), 1982, Whitaker House, pages 121-122 and 130.

11. *Mighty Moments* by Lionel B. Fletcher, Religious Tract Society, c.1931, pages 19-21 and 43-47.

12. *Revival Addresses* by A. Douglas Brown, Morgan & Scott Ltd., 1922, pages 80-83.

13. *A Forgotten Revival, East Anglia and North-East Scotland – 1921* by Stanley C. Griffin, Day One Publication, 1995.

14. *Revival Addresses* by A. Douglas Brown, Morgan & Scott Ltd., 1922, pages 41, 50, 52, 78 and 81.

15. *Revival Man, The Jock Troup Story* by George Mitchel, Christian Focus, 2002, pages 55-56.

16. *The Christian* June 2nd 1921, as cited in *A Forgotten Revival, East Anglia and North-East Scotland – 1921* by Stanley C. Griffin, Day One Publication, 1995, page 42.

17. *The Christian* June 30th 1921, as cited in *A Forgotten Revival, East Anglia and North-East Scotland – 1921* by Stanley C. Griffin, Day One Publication, 1995, page 45.

18. *The Christian Herald* July 21st 1921, as cited in *A Forgotten Revival, East Anglia and North-East Scotland – 1921* by Stanley C. Griffin, Day One Publication, 1995, page 49.

19. *Norfolk News and Weekly* Press, September 10th 1921 as cited in *A Forgotten Revival, East Anglia and North-East Scotland – 1921* by Stanley C. Griffin, Day One Publication, 1995, page 54.

20. *Revival Man, The Jock Troup Story* by George Mitchel, Christian Focus, 2002, pages 55, 57-63, 77-78, and *When God Came Down an account of the North Uist Revival 1957-58* edited by John Ferguson, Lewis Recordings, 2000, pages 24-25.

21. *Revival Addresses* by A. Douglas Brown, Morgan & Scott Ltd., 1922, page 70.

22. *Road to Revival – The Story of the Ruanda Mission* by A. C. Stanley Smith, Church Missionary Society, 1946, pages 21, 23, 71-72 and 115.

23. *Fire in the Hills* by H. H. Osbourne, Highland Books, 1991, pages 71-72.

24. Ibid., pages 16, 18-19 and 21.

25. *Hill Ablaze* by Bill Butler, Hodder and Stoughton, 1976, pages 40-42 and *Rwanda – The Land God Forgot* by Meg Guillebaud, Monarch books, 2002, pages 55-56.

26. *Every Man a Bible Student* by Joe. E. Church, Scripture Union and C.S.S.M., 1938, 1961, preface and inside back cover.

Chapter 21

1. *Sounds from Heaven: The Revival on the Isle of Lewis 1949-1952* by Colin and Mary Peckham, Christian Focus, 2004, page 86.

2. Ibid., pages 35, 49, 58, 72 and 117. Rev. Norman Macleod in *Lewis Revivals of the 20th Century*, Hebridean Press Service, Stornoway, c.1990, a 17-page A5-size booklet, dismisses the revival under Duncan Campbell because of the poor communion roll statistics for the Free Church in Shawbost in the year 1953 (page 15). The author, Rev. Macleod was from the Free Church, a denomination that opposed the revival and did not permit Rev. Duncan Campbell to speak in their churches, whilst the ministers told their congregations to stay away! Is there any wonder that the fruit was so little? Rev. Macleod also cites the statistics from the year 1953 when the revival had generally ended in 1952. Some converts from the Free Church had to leave their denomination (See *Sounds from Heaven: The Revival on the Isle of Lewis 1949-1952* by Colin and Mary Peckham). Rev. Macleod heard Rev. Duncan Campbell speak of the revival in a friend's house in Edinburgh and wrote: 'Afterwards I came to know that his account of the revival was highly exaggerated' (page 15). This appears to be an example of denominational bias and lack of thorough research. See *Revival Answers: True and False Revival* by Mathew Backholer, ByFaith Media, 2013, 2017.

3. The basis of this account is from various tapes of Duncan Campbell recounting his experiences during the revival.

4. *Sounds from Heaven: The Revival on the Isle of Lewis 1949-1952* by Colin and Mary Peckham, Christian Focus, 2004, pages 76-77.

5. Note: In later age, Rev. Duncan Campbell when retelling of his experiences would sometimes get place names and the stories muddled up. This is easily done because he held so many missions across different islands and amongst different communities over a four year period, and visited many of the communities on a number of occasions.

6. *Sounds from Heaven: The Revival on the Isle of Lewis 1949-1952* by Colin and Mary Peckham, Christian Focus, 2004, pages 47-48.

7. Ibid., page 61.

8. Note: Rev. Duncan Campbell had never visited this island before and knew no one on the island, but an elder prayed him to the island and was expecting him! For more information, see *Channel of Revival, A Biography of Duncan Campbell* by Andrew A. Woolsey, The Faith Mission, 1982, chapter 16.

9. *Evangelical Awakenings in The South Seas* by J. Edwin Orr, Bethany Fellowship Inc., 1976, page 199.

10. *Revival Including the Prophetic Vision of Jean Darnall* by Hugh Black, 1993, New Dawn Books, pages 92-93, and *Revival Personal Encounters* by Hugh Black, 1993, New Dawn Books, pages 44-45.

11. *Channel of Revival, A Biography of Duncan Campbell* by Andrew A. Woolsey, The Faith Mission, 1982, page 136.

12. *Let No One Deceive You: Confronting the Critics of Revival* by Michael L. Brown, Revival Press, 1997, page 194.

13. *The Lewis Awakening 1949-1953* by Duncan Campbell, The Faith Mission, 1954, page 33.

14. *Channel of Revival, A Biography of Duncan Campbell* by Andrew A. Woolsey, The Faith Mission, 1982, page 163.

15. *The Fire of God's Presence – Powerful Lesson from the Hebrides Revival* by Owen Murphy and John Wesley Adams, Ambassador Press, 2003, page 43.

16. *The Lewis Awakening 1949-1953* by Duncan Campbell, The Faith Mission, 1954, page 36.

17. Ibid., page 9.

18. *The Lewis Revival,* tape 6, Rev. Duncan Campbell, The Faith Mission.

19. *The Lewis Awakening 1949-1953* by Duncan Campbell, The Faith Mission, 1954, page 31.

20. *God's Standard: Challenging Sermons* by Duncan Campbell, The Faith Mission, 1964, pages 10, 16, 33, 35 and 56.

21. *Sounds from Heaven: The Revival on the Isle of Lewis 1949-1952* by Colin and Mary Peckham, Christian Focus, 2004, pages 109-110.

22. *God's Standard: Challenging Sermons* by Duncan Campbell, The Faith Mission, 1964, page 25.

23. *Do It Again Lord: The Story of Some of the Greatest Revivals the World has Ever Known* by Gordon Pettie, Fines Creek Publishing, 2017, page 214.

24. *Sounds from Heaven: The Revival on the Isle of Lewis 1949-1952* by Colin and Mary Peckham, Christian Focus, 2004, pages 99-100 and 109.

25. This short clip can be viewed on Youtube.com under the title: What Motivates Revival Historian & Author Mathew Backholer?

Chapter 22

1. J. Edwin Orr preaching on a series presented in 1981, at Church on the Way, Van Nuys, California, America. From a CDR, *J. Edwin Orr Revival Library, The History of Revival,* Orr Latin America, 2005.

2. *Cross Pollination, The Miracle of Unity in Intercession, Revival & the Harvest* by Lila Terhune, Destiny Image Publishers, 1998, pages 5 and 10. Lila Terhune was the chief intercessor at Brownsville, AOG.

3. *Cross Pollination* by Lila Terhune, 1999, pages 15-19, and *Great Revivals* by Colin Whittaker, Marshall, Morgan & Scott, 1984, pages 102-104.

4. *Thy God Reigneth: The Story of Revival in Argentina* by R. Edward Miller, Argentine Bible Assemblies Inc., 1964, pages 35-36.

5. Ibid., pages 37-39.

6. *Atomic Power With God Through Prayer and Fasting* by Rev. Franklin Hall, c.1946, c.1965, PDF copy, pages 19-20.

7. *The Revival in Indonesia* by Kurt Koch, Evangelization Publishers, West Germany, c.1970. A detailed account of the Indonesian Revival (1964-1974) can be found in *Revival Fire: 150 Years of Revivals* by Mathew Backholer, ByFaith Media, 2010, 2017.

8. *Nine O'Clock in the Morning* by Dennis J. Bennett, Logos International, 1970, page 196.

9. *Power Evangelism – Revised and Updated with Study Guide* by John Wimber with Kevin Springer, Hodder and Stoughton, 1985, 1992, pages 61 and 64 and *When The Spirit Comes in Power* by John White, Hodder and Stoughton, 1988, 1992, page 166.

10. *Power Evangelism – Revised and Updated with Study Guide* by John Wimber with Kevin Springer, Hodder and Stoughton, 1985, 1992, pages 61-62 and *When The Spirit Comes in Power* by John White, Hodder and Stoughton, 1988, 1992, page 158.

11. *Power Evangelism – Revised and Updated with Study Guide* by John Wimber with Kevin Springer, Hodder and Stoughton, 1985, 1992, pages 62-64.

12. *Overcome By The Spirit* by Francis McNutt, Eagle, 1990, 1991 Great Britain edition, back cover.

13. *Power Evangelism – Revised and Updated with Study Guide* by John Wimber with Kevin Springer, Hodder and Stoughton, 1985, 1992, pages 9 and 64.

14. *Power Evangelism – Revised and Updated with Study Guide* by John Wimber with Kevin Springer, Hodder and Stoughton, 1985, 1992, pages 60 and 64 and *When The Spirit Comes in Power* by John White, Hodder and Stoughton, 1988, 1992, pages 166 and 178.

15. *The Rising Revival Firsthand Accounts of the Incredible Argentine Revival* edited by C. Peter Wagner & Pablo Deiros, Renew Books, 1998. A detailed account of the Argentine Revival (1982-1997) can be found in *Revival Fire: 150 Years of Revivals* by Mathew Backholer, ByFaith Media, 2010, 2017.

Chapter 23

1. *The Pursuit of Revival, Igniting a Passionate Hunger for More of God* by Stephen Hill, Creation House, 1997, page 133.

2. *Revival in Brownsville* by Steve Rabey, Thomas Nelson Publishers, 1998, page 160.

3. *Guinness World Records 2002,* Guinness World Records Limited, 2002, page 114.

4. *When the Spirit Comes With Power* by Dr. John White, Hodder & Stoughton, 1989, page 152.

5. Note: For more information on the House Church Movement read: *The Heavenly Man –* Brother Yun with Paul Hattaway, Monarch Books, 2002.

6. *Project Pearl* by Brother David and Paul Hattaway, Monarch Books, 2007, pages 263.

7. *Jesus in Beijing, How Christianity Is Transforming China and Changing Global Balance of Power* by David Aikman, Monarch Books, 2003, chapter 9.

8. www.msn.com/en-gb/news/world/chinas-christians-protest-evil-communist-campaign-to-tear-down-crosses/ar-AAdxBH9? Accessed 27 July 2015.

9. www.ChinaAid.org. Accessed Spring 2016.

10. *Project Pearl* by Brother David and Paul Hattaway, Monarch Books, 2007, pages 259, 262+ and 269-270.

11. A Bible costs just $1.80 (£1.20) to be printed and delivered inside of China! Whilst supporting a native evangelist costs $25 (£16) per month (2017) via www.AsiaHarvest.org. Also see *An Asian Harvest: An Autobiography* by Paul Hattaway, 2017, chapters 34-37.

12. www.bayoftheholyspiritrevival.com/about.php. Accessed March 2011.

13. Ibid.

14. For a greater understanding of the 'baptism of the Holy Spirit and fire' (Matthew 3:11), see *The Baptism of Fire: Personal Revival, Renewal and the Anointing for Supernatural Living* by Paul Backholer, ByFaith Media, 2017.

15. For a greater understanding of physical phenomena during times of revival (and the controversial Lakeland Revival (2008) under Todd Bentley) see *Understanding Revival and Addressing the Issues It Provokes* by Mathew Backholer, ByFaith Media, 2009, 2017.

16. Most of the facts of this revival are from TV and video footage. Some of the conversations were scribed from these sources across different services and placed together when it was on the same topic or subject, most notably those of Evangelist Nathan Morris.

Chapter 24

1. *Hot From the Preacher's Mound* by Stephen Hill, Together in the Harvest Publications, 1995, page 7.

2. *Finney on Revival* arranged by E. E. Shelhamer, Dimensions Books – Bethany Fellowship, no date, pages 11-13.

3. *If Ye Abide – 10,000 Miles of Miracle In South Africa* by J. Edwin Orr, Marshall, Morgan & Scott Ltd, 1936, page 78.

4. *The Revival and the Pastor* by Jonas Oramel Peck, Hunt and Eaton, 1894, pages 150-151.

5. See *Revival Answers, True and False Revivals* by Mathew Backholer, ByFaith Media, 2013, 2017, chapters 5, 14 and 21.

Chapter 25

1. *The Revival and the Pastor* by Jonas Oramel Peck, Hunt and Eaton 1894, pages 170-171.

2. *The History of Revivals of Religion* by William E. Allen (revival series No. 7), Revival Publishing Co., 1951, page 55.

Chapter 26

1. *In the Day of Thy Power* by Arthur Wallis, Christian Literature Crusade, 1956, page 118.

2. *Prayer: Key to Revival* by Paul Y. Cho with R. Witney Manzano, Word Publishing, 1984, pages 17-18.

3. *Prayer and the Coming Revival* (The Ministry of Intercession) by Andrew Murray, Ambassador Publications, 1999, pages 16-17 and 19.

4. *When God Came Down an account of the North Uist Revival 1957-58* edited by John Ferguson, Lewis Recordings, 2000, page 10.

5. *The Revival We Need* by Oswald J. Smith, Marshall, Morgan & Scott, 1940, page v.

ByFaith Media Books

The following ByFaith Media books are available as paperbacks and eBooks, whilst some are available as hardbacks.

Revivals and Spiritual Awakenings

9781907066-01-6. *Revival Fires and Awakenings, Thirty-Six Visitations of the Holy Spirit: A Call to Holiness, Prayer and Intercession for the Nations* by Mathew Backholer. With thirty-six fascinating accounts of revivals in nineteen countries from six continents, plus biblical teaching on revival, prayer and intercession. Hardback 9781907066-38-2.

9781907066-07-8. *Global Revival, Worldwide Outpourings, Forty-Three Visitations of the Holy Spirit: The Great Commission* by Mathew Backholer. How revivals are birthed and the fascinating links between pioneering missionaries and the revivals that they saw as they worked towards the Great Commission, with forty-three accounts of revivals.

9781907066-00-9. *Understanding Revival and Addressing the Issues it Provokes* by Mathew Backholer. Everything you need to know about revival and its phenomena. How to work with the Holy Spirit to see God rend the Heavens and pour out His Spirit on a dry and thirsty land and how not to be taken in by the enemy and his counterfeit tricks, delusions and imitations. Hardback 9781907066-99-3.

9781907066-06-1. *Revival Fire, 150 Years of Revivals, Spiritual Awakenings and Moves of the Holy Spirit* by Mathew Backholer. This book documents in detail, twelve revivals from ten countries on five continents. Be inspired, encouraged and challenged by the wonderful works of God. Hardback 978178822-002-6.

9781907066-15-3. *Revival Answers, True and False Revivals, Genuine or Counterfeit Do not be Deceived* by Mathew Backholer. What is genuine revival and how can we tell the true from the spurious? Drawing from Scripture with examples across Church history, this book will sharpen your senses and take you on a journey of discovery.

9781907066-60-3. *Reformation to Revival, 500 Years of God's Glory: Sixty Revivals Awakenings and Heaven-Sent visitations of the Holy Spirit* by Mathew Backholer. *Reformation to Revival* traces the Divine thread of God's power from Martin Luther of 1517, through to the Charismatic Movement and into the twenty-first century, with sixty great revivals. Hardback 9781907066-98-6.

Supernatural and Spiritual

9781907066-58-0. *Glimpses of Glory, Revelations in the Realms of God Beyond the Veil in the Heavenly Abode: The New Jerusalem and the Eternal Kingdom of God* by Paul Backholer. Find a world beyond earth which is real, vivid and eternal. A gripping read!

9781907066-18-4. *Prophecy Now, Prophetic Words and Divine Revelations for You, the Church and the Nations* by Michael Backholer. An enlightening end-time prophetic journal of visions, prophecies and words from the Holy Spirit to God's people, the Church and the nations. Read about the emptying of stadiums, which was witnessed during the Coronavirus pandemic of 2020!

9781907066-80-1. *Heaven, Paradise is Real, Hope Beyond Death: An Angelic Pilgrimage to Your Future Home* by Paul Backholer. Come on a journey to another world of eternal bliss, joy and light, in this enchanting narrative which pulls you in and shows you Heaven. Meet those who have gone before into paradise and found eternal peace. Enter into the Heavenly Jerusalem, with a man and an angelic guide to discover the truth about immortality, the afterlife and the joy of eternity.

Biography and Autobiography

9781907066-14-6. *Samuel, Son and Successor of Rees Howells: Director of the Bible College of Wales – A Biography* by Richard Maton. The life of Samuel and his ministry at the College and the support he received from numerous staff and students as the history of BCW unfolds. With 113 black and white photos. Hardback 9781907066-36-8.

9781907066-13-9. *Samuel Rees Howells A Life of Intercession: The Legacy of Prayer and Spiritual Warfare of an Intercessor* by Richard Maton, Paul Backholer and Mathew Backholer is an in-depth look at the intercessions of Samuel Rees Howells alongside the faith principles that he learnt from his father, Rees Howells, and under the leading and guidance of the Holy Spirit. With 39 black and white photographs. Hardback 9781907066-37-5.

9781907066-41-2. *The Holy Spirit in a Man: Spiritual Warfare, Intercession, Faith, Healings and Miracles* by R. B. Watchman. One man's compelling journey of faith and intercession, a remarkable modern day story of miracles and faith to inspire and encourage. (One chapter relates to the Bible College of Wales and Watchman's visit).

Christian Teaching and Inspirational

9781907066-35-1. *Jesus Today, Daily Devotional: 100 Days with Jesus Christ* by Paul Backholer. One hundred days of two minutes of Christian inspiration to draw you closer to God to encourage and inspire. Have you ever wished you could have sat at Jesus' feet and heard Him speak?

Jesus Today is a concise daily devotional defined by Jesus' teaching and how His life can change ours. See the world from God's perspective; learn who Jesus was, what He preached and what it means to live abundantly in Christ.

9781907066-33-7. *Holy Spirit Power: Knowing the Voice, Guidance and Person of the Holy Spirit* by Paul Backholer. Power for Christian living; drawing from the powerful influences of many Christian leaders, including: Rees Howells, Evan Roberts, D. L. Moody, Duncan Campbell and other channels of God's Divine fire. Jesus walked in the power of the Holy Spirit and declared His disciples would do even greater works. Today, God's power can still be released in and through Christians who will meet the Holy Spirit on His terms.

9781907066-43-6. *Tares and Weeds in Your Church: Trouble & Deception in God's House, the End Time Overcomers* by R. B. Watchman. Is there a battle taking place in your house, church or ministry, leading to division? Tares and weeds are counterfeit Christians used to sabotage Kingdom work; learn how to recognise them and neutralise them in the power of the Holy Spirit.

9781907066-56-6. *The Baptism of Fire, Personal Revival, Renewal and the Anointing for Supernatural Living* by Paul Backholer. Jesus will baptise you with the Holy Spirit and fire; that was the promise of John the Baptist. But what is the baptism of fire and how can you experience it? The author unveils the life and ministry of the Holy Spirit, shows how He can transform your life and what supernatural living in Christ means.

Historical
9781907066-76-4 Hardback. *God Challenges the Dictators, Doom of the Nazis Predicted: The Destruction of the Third Reich Foretold by the Director of Swansea Bible College, An Intercessor from Wales* by Rees Howells and Mathew Backholer. Available for the first time in 80 years – fully annotated and reformatted with twelve digitally enhanced black and white photos. Discover how Rees Howells built a large ministry by faith in times of economic chaos and learn from the predictions he made during times of national crisis, of the destruction of the Third Reich, the end of fascism and the liberation of Christian Europe during World War II. Paperback 9781907066-77-1.

9781907066-78-8 Hardback. *Rees Howells' God Challenges the Dictators, Doom of Axis Powers Predicted: Victory for Christian England and Release of Europe Through Intercession and Spiritual Warfare, Bible College of Wales* by Mathew Backholer. This is the story behind the story of *God Challenges the Dictators* (GCD), Rees Howells' only published book, before, during and after publication which is centred around World War II. Read how extracts of GCD were aired over occupied parts of Europe, and how Hitler and leading Nazi officials were sent copies in 1940! The book includes letters to Winston Churchill and Press Releases from Rees Howells and how he sent copies of his book to Prime Ministers N. Chamberlain and W. Churchill plus government officials, and what the newspapers had to say, at home and abroad, as afar away as Australia and the Oceanic Islands! With twenty-four black and white photos. Paperback 9781907066-78-8.

978-1-907066-95-5 Hardback. *Rees Howells, Vision Hymns of Spiritual Warfare & Intercessory Declarations: World War II Songs of Victory, Intercession, Praise and Worship, Israel and the Every Creature Commission* by Mathew Backholer. *Vision Hymns* gives a rare insight into the prophetic declarations, hymns and choruses used in spiritual warfare by Rees Howells and his team of intercessors at the Bible College of Wales (BCW). Spanning the pivotal years of 1939-1948 and brought to life for the first time in more than seventy years. Many of the songs of worship reveal the theology, spiritual battles and history during the dark days of World War II and the years surrounding it. From Emperor Haile Selassie of Ethiopia, Hitler's predicted downfall, to the Nation of Israel being born in a day and the glories beyond.

9781907066-45-0. *Britain, A Christian Country, A Nation Defined by Christianity and the Bible & the Social Changes that Challenge this Biblical Heritage* by Paul Backholer. For more than 1,000 years Britain was defined by Christianity, with monarch's dedicating the country to God and national days of prayer. Discover this continuing legacy, how faith defined its nationhood and the challenges from the 1960s till today.

9781907066-02-3. *How Christianity Made the Modern World* by Paul Backholer. Christianity is the greatest reforming force that the world has ever known, yet its legacy is seldom comprehended. But now, using personal observations and worldwide research the author brings this legacy alive by revealing how Christianity helped create the path that led to Western liberty and laid the foundations of the modern world.

9781907066-47-4. *Celtic Christianity & the First Christian Kings in Britain: From St. Patrick and St. Columba, to King Ethelbert and King Alfred* by Paul Backholer. Celtic Christians ignited a Celtic Golden Age of faith and light which spread into Europe. Discover this striking history and what we can learn from the heroes of Celtic Christianity.

Christian Discipleship
9781907066-16-0. *Extreme Faith, On Fire Christianity: Hearing from God and Moving in His Grace, Strength & Power – Living in Victory* by Mathew Backholer. Discover the powerful biblical foundations for on-fire faith in Christ! This book explores biblical truths and routines to shake your world.

9781907066-62-7. *Christianity Rediscovered, in Pursuit of God and the Path to Eternal Life: What you Need to Know to Grow, Living the Christian Life with Jesus Christ, Book 1* by Mathew Backholer. Since the beginning of time mankind has asked, "Why am I alive, does my life matter and is there an afterlife I can prepare for?" *Christianity Rediscovered* has the answers and will help you find meaning, focus, clarity and peace.

9781907066-12-2. *Discipleship For Everyday Living, Christian Growth: Following Jesus Christ and Making Disciples of All Nations* by Mathew Backholer. Engaging biblical teaching to aid Christian believers in maturity, to help make strong disciples with solid biblical foundations who reflect the image of Jesus Christ.

Short-Term Missions (Christian Travel with a Purpose)
9781907066-49-8. *Short-Term Missions, A Christian Guide to STMs: For Leaders, Pastors, Churches, Students, STM Teams and Mission Organizations – Survive and Thrive!* by Mathew Backholer. A concise guide to Short-Term Missions (STMs). What you need to know about planning a STM, or joining a STM team, and considering the options as part of the Great Commission, from the Good News to good works.

9781907066-05-4. *How to Plan, Prepare and Successfully Complete Your Short-Term Mission For Churches, Independent STM Teams and Mission Organizations* by Mathew Backholer. This book will guide you through all you need to know about STMs and includes: mission statistics, cultural issues, where and when to go, what to do and pack, food, accommodation, and more than 140 real-life STM testimonies.

Biblical Adventure and Archaeology
9781907066-52-8. *Lost Treasures of the Bible: Exploration and Pictorial Travel Adventure of Biblical Archaeology* by Paul Backholer. Unveil ancient mysteries as you discover the evidence for Israel's exodus from Egypt, and travel into lost civilisations in search of the Ark of the Covenant. Explore lost worlds with over 160 colour photos and pictures.

978178822-000-2. *The Exodus Evidence In Pictures – The Bible's Exodus: The Hunt for Ancient Israel in Egypt, the Red Sea, the Exodus Route and Mount Sinai* by Paul Backholer. Two brothers and explorers, Paul and Mathew Backholer search for archaeological data to validate the biblical account of Joseph, Moses and the Hebrew Exodus from ancient Egypt. With more than 100 full colour photos and graphics!

978178822-001-9. *The Ark of the Covenant – Investigating the Ten Leading Claims* by Paul Backholer. Join two explorers as they investigate the ten major theories concerning the location of antiquities greatest relic. Combining an on-site travel journal with 80+ colour photographs through Egypt, Ethiopia and beyond.

Budget Travel – Vacation/Holiday

9781907066-54-2. *Budget Travel, a Guide to Travelling on a Shoestring, Explore the World, a Discount Overseas Adventure Trip: Gap Year, Backpacking, Volunteer-Vacation and Overlander* by Mathew Backholer. *Budget Travel* is a practical and concise guide to travelling the world and exploring new destinations with fascinating opportunities and experiences. Full of anecdotes, traveller's advice, informative timelines and testimonies, with suggestions, guidance and ideas.

9781907066-74-0. *Travel the World and Explore for Less than $50 a Day, the Essential Guide: Your Budget Backpack Global Adventure, from Two Weeks to a Gap Year, Solo or with Friends* by Mathew Backholer. A practical guide for the solo backpacker or with friends that will save you time and money with ideas, and need-to-know information so you can have the adventure of a lifetime from two weeks to one year.

ByFaith Media DVDs

Revivals and Spiritual Awakenings

9781907066-03-0. *Great Christian Revivals* on 1 DVD is an inspirational and uplifting account of some of the greatest revivals in Church history. Filmed on location across Britain and beyond, and drawing upon archive information and rare images, the stories of the Welsh Revival (1904-1905), the Hebridean Revival (1949-1952) and the Evangelical Revival (1739-1791) are brought to life in this moving 72-minute documentary. Using computer animation, historic photos and depictions, the events of the past are weaved into the present, to bring these Heaven-sent revivals to life.

Christian Travel (Backpacking Short-Term Missions)

9781907066-04-7. *ByFaith – World Mission* on 1 DVD is a Christian reality TV show that reveals the real experience of backpacking short-term missions in Asia, Europe and North Africa. Two brothers, Paul and Mathew Backholer shoot through fourteen nations, in an 85-minute real-life documentary. Filmed over three years, *ByFaith – World Mission* is the best of ByFaith TV season one.

Historical and Adventure

9781907066-09-2. *Israel in Egypt – The Exodus Mystery* on 1 DVD. A four year quest searching for Joseph, Moses and the Hebrew slaves in Egypt. Join brothers Paul and Mathew Backholer as they hunt through ancient relics and explore the mystery of the biblical exodus, hunt for the Red Sea and climb Mount Sinai. Discover the first reference to Israel outside of the Bible, uncover depictions of people with multicoloured coats, encounter the Egyptian records of slaves making bricks and find lost cities. 110 minutes. The best of *ByFaith – In Search of the Exodus*.

9781907066-10-0. *ByFaith – Quest for the Ark of the Covenant* on 1 DVD. Join two adventurers on their quest for the Ark, beginning at Mount Sinai where it was made, to Pharaoh Tutankhamun's tomb, where Egyptian treasures evoke the majesty of the Ark. The quest proceeds onto the trail of Pharaoh Shishak, who raided Jerusalem. The mission continues up the River Nile to find a lost temple, with clues to a mysterious civilization. Crossing through the Sahara Desert, the investigators enter the underground rock churches of Ethiopia, find a forgotten civilization and examine the enigma of the final resting place of the Ark itself. 100+ minutes.

www.ByFaithDVDs.org

ByFaith Media Downloads and Streaming

The following ByFaith Media productions are based on the DVDs from the previous page and are available to download: to buy, rent or to stream via Amazon.

Revivals and Spiritual Awakenings
Glorious Christian Revival and Holy Spirit Awakenings: The Welsh, Hebridean and Evangelical Revivals, Evan Roberts, Duncan Campbell and John Wesley. 1 hour 12 minutes. Discover the Welsh Revival (1904-1905), the Hebridean Revival (1949-1952) and the Evangelical Revival (1739-1791), with Evan Roberts, Duncan Campbell, John and Charles Wesley, George Whitefield and others. Filmed on location across the UK and beyond. B07N2N762J (UK). B07P1TVY6W (USA).

Christian Travel (Backpacking Short-Term Missions)
Short-Term Mission Adventures, A Global Christian Missionary STM Expedition with brothers Mathew and Paul Backholer. 1 hour 15 minutes. The mission begins when two adventurers land in Asia, a continent of maximum extremes. After overcoming culture shock and difficult travel, the adventurous missionaries preach in the slums. From India they strike out into Nepal, Bangladesh, Thailand, Myanmar, Cambodia and Vietnam. The mission also touches down in the great cities of Europe: London, Paris, Rome, Dublin, Frankfurt & Amsterdam. B07N2PVZZK (UK). B07PNSWBKN (USA).

Historical and Adventure
The Bible's Lost Ark of the Covenant: Where Is It? Egypt, Ethiopia or Israel? With brothers Mathew and Paul Backholer. 1 hour 10 minutes. The Ark of the Covenant was the greatest treasure in Solomon's Temple, but when Jerusalem fell the Ark vanished from history. Now join two adventurers on their quest for the Ark of the Covenant, beginning at Mount Sinai where it was made, to Pharaoh Tutankhamun's tomb, crossing the Sahara Desert into the underground rock churches of Ethiopia and beyond in an epic adventure. B07MTTHHZ7 (UK). B07R3BMBW6 (USA).

The Exodus Evidence: Quest for Ancient Israel in Egypt, The Red Sea, The Exodus Route & Mount Sinai. Join two adventurers, brothers Mathew and Paul Backholer as they investigate a three-thousand year old mystery, entering the tombs of ancient Egypt seeking the exodus evidence. Discover the first reference to Israel outside of the Bible in hieroglyphics, uncover ancient depictions of people with multi-colored coats, encounter the Egyptian records of slaves making bricks and find lost cities mentioned in the Bible. 1 hour 15 minutes. B07P63BWZ2 (UK). B07Q3ST613 (USA).

Christian Revival & Holy Spirit Awakenings. Join revival historian and prolific author Mathew Backholer, as he joins CEO Gordon Pettie in the Revelation TV studios over 7 episodes to examine many powerful Christian revivals which shook the world. Including the: Layman's Prayer Revival of 1857, Ulster Revival 1859-60, Welsh Revival of 1904-05, Azusa Street Revival of 1906-09, Korean Revival of 1907-10, the Hebridean Revival of 1949-52 and more! B07R445S5W (UK). Coming to the USA soon!

Printed in the USA
CPSIA information can be obtained
at www.ICGtesting.com
LVHW021624061023
760215LV00002B/43